Gnostic Countercultures

# Gnostic Countercultures

*Terror and Intrigue*

*Edited by*

April D. DeConick
Lautaro Roig Lanzillotta

BRILL

LEIDEN | BOSTON

Originally published as Volume 1, No. 1–2 (2016) of Brill's journal *Gnosis: Journal of Gnostic Studies*.

The Library of Congress Cataloging-in-Publication Data is available online at http://catalog.loc.gov
LC record available at http://lccn.loc.gov/2020025961

Typeface for the Latin, Greek, and Cyrillic scripts: "Brill". See and download: brill.com/brill-typeface.

ISBN 978-90-04-43698-5 (Paperback)

Copyright 2020 by Koninklijke Brill NV, The Netherlands.
Koninklijke Brill NV incorporates the imprints Brill, Brill Hes & De Graaf, Brill Nijhoff, Brill Rodopi, Brill Sense, Hotei Publishing, mentis Verlag, Verlag Ferdinand Schöningh and Wilhelm Fink Verlag.
All rights reserved. No part of this publication may be reproduced, translated, stored in a retrieval system, or transmitted in any form or by any means, electronic, mechanical, photocopying, recording or otherwise, without prior written permission from the publisher.
Authorization to photocopy items for internal or personal use is granted by Koninklijke Brill NV provided that the appropriate fees are paid directly to The Copyright Clearance Center, 222 Rosewood Drive, Suite 910, Danvers, MA 01923, USA. Fees are subject to change.

This book is printed on acid-free paper and produced in a sustainable manner.

# Contents

Introduction   VII

### PART 1
*Antiquity*

The Countercultural Gnostic: Turning the World Upside Down and Inside Out   3
   *April D. DeConick*

"I Turned away from the Temple": Sethian Counterculture in the Apocryphon of John   32
   *Grant Adamson*

Transgressing Boundaries: Plotinus and the Gnostics   52
   *John D. Turner*

Forbidden Knowledge: Cognitive Transgression and "Ascent Above Intellect" in the Debate Between Plotinus and the Gnostics   81
   *Zeke Mazur*

The Apocalypse of Paul (NHC V,2): Cosmology, Anthropology, and Ethics   104
   *Lautaro Roig Lanzillotta*

Gnosis Undomesticated: Archon-Seduction, Demon Sex, and Sodomites in the Paraphrase of Shem (NHC VII,1)   125
   *Dylan M. Burns*

Gnostic Self-Deification: The Case of Simon of Samaria   149
   *M. David Litwa*

*Demon est Deus Inversus*: Honoring the Daemonic in Iamblichean Theurgy   168
   *Gregory Shaw*

## PART 2
## *Modernity*

The Coming of the Star-Child: The Reception of the Revelation of the Magi in New Age Religious Thought and Ufology    189
    *Brent Landau*

The Great God Pan    210
    *Sarah Iles Johnston*

Alan Moore's *Promethea*: Countercultural Gnosis and the End of the World    225
    *Wouter J. Hanegraaff*

Children of the Light: Gnostic Fiction and Gnostic Practice in Vladimir Sorokin's *Ice Trilogy*    249
    *Victoria Nelson*

Symbolic Loss, Memory, and Modernization in the Reception of Gnosticism    266
    *Matthew J. Dillon*

Gnostic and Countercultural Elements in Zora Neale Hurston's "Hoodoo in America"    299
    *Margarita Simon Guillory*

Index of Modern Authors    317
Index of Subjects    324

# Introduction

The gnostic is an elusive figure, escaping our borders, pushing our limits, reshaping us, with every act of transgression. Why does the gnostic at once intrigue and terrify? What is it about the gnostic that opens us up to a deviance so subversive that it reverses and redefines whatever it contacts? What is it about the gnostic that constructs new worlds whose brilliance exposes the pallor of our existence? What is it about the gnostic that fuels the courage to create something better than what tradition has left us?

These were the questions posed to twenty scholars who attended the international congress *Gnostic Countercultures: Terror and Intrigue*, convened at Rice University on March 26–28, 2015. This event was made possible by the financial support of the Rockwell Fund and the Department of Religion at Rice University. It was hosted by the GEM Collective, a group of faculty and students at Rice who study together gnosticism, esotericism and mysticism.

The twenty scholars present explored the concept of the gnostic in Western culture from the ancient world to the modern New Age. The gnostic was broadly conceived with reference to the claim to have special direct knowledge of the divine, which either transcends or transgresses conventional religious knowledge. Our goal was to trace the emergence, persistence and disappearance of gnostic religious currents that are perceived to be countercultural, inverted, transgressive and/or subversive in their relationship to conventional religions and their claims to knowledge.

With this conceptualization of the gnostic, the fellows of this congress acted to unlock the gnostic from its cage in the ancient world and to challenge the now popular academic opinion that the gnostic is a useless or highly problematic category because it reifies as heretics ancient people who simply were "alternative" devout Christians. The fourteen essays in this volume represent a selection of the papers delivered by congress members who sought to investigate countercultural aspects associated with the gnostic.

In the first part of the volume, several papers address various countercultural aspects found in ancient gnostic literature. April D. DeConick's contribution, "The Countercultural Gnostic: Turning the World Upside Down and Inside Out," works to examine more deeply the theory that the gnostic heresy is a social construction imposed by the early Catholics on religious people whom they identified as transgressors of Christianity. While most scholars conclude from this that gnostics were actually alternative Christians, this does not address the fact that gnostics were operating in the margins of the conventional religions with a countercultural perspective that upset and overturned everything from traditional theology, cosmogony, cosmology, anthropology, hermeneutics, scripture, religious practices, and lifestyle choices. Making the gnostic into a Christian only imposes another grand narrative on the early Christians, one which domesticates gnostic movements. Granted, the textual evidence for the interface of the gnostic and the Christian is present, but so is the interface of the gnostic and the Greek, the gnostic and the Jew, the gnostic and the Persian, the gnostic and the Egyptian. And the interface looks to have all the signs of transgression, not conformity. Understanding the gnostic as a spiritual orientation toward a transcendent God beyond the biblical God helps us handle this kind of diversity and transgression. As such, it survives in the artifacts that gnostics and their opponents left behind, artifacts that help orient religious seekers to make sense of their own moments of ecstasy and revelation.

Grant Adamson, in his contribution, "'I turned away from the Temple': Sethian Counterculture in the Apocryphon of John," examines how Sethian conflict with others is narrativized in the myth and the frame story of the Apocryphon of John. For instance, Adam and Eve withdraw from the biblical creator just as John turns away from the temple in Jerusalem after an altercation with a Jewish antagonist. The gnostic authors of the text portrayed the creator so negatively that he is incomparable with most demiurgic figures in Platonism, Judaism, and Christianity. Their ignorant, boastful, jealous and apostate Ialdabaoth was shocking to their ancient opponents. And for modern scholars, this countercultural vilification of the creator makes it difficult to categorize the authors of the Apocryphon in Platonic, Jewish, or Christian terms. Adamson concludes that, while lumping the Apocryphon and its gnostic authors in with fellow Jews, Christians, and Platonists might excuse us from having to define Gnosticism as something different from them, it misses the Sethians' main point. Their gnostic perspective was not just rhetorical or discursive. It set them apart from those who foolishly worshipped an apostate God who raped Eve and had Jesus killed.

John D. Turner, in his paper, "Transgressing Boundaries: Plotinus and the Gnostics," also focuses on Sethianism, in this case, the instances of Plotinus' critique in the first ten chapters of *Enneades* II.9. Turner studies the doctrines reflected in the Sethian Platonizing treatises and the Valentinian Tripartite Tractate insofar as they may be appropriately considered as transgressions of Platonic metaphysics and of traditional principles of philosophical hermeneutics and etiquette. Turner questions whether these transgressions merit the designation "countercultural" when the gnostics are compared to Plotinus and their mutual hermeneutical innovations. However, against the broader educated Greco-Roman stratum of society, the gnostics may be more counterculturally positioned with their preference for assertion rather than deliberation, their use of non-Hellenic, Judaeo-Christian terminology to describe the contents of the sub-Pleromatic world, their reliance on revelation rather than reasoned argument, and their violations of the dominant social and ethical norms of Plotinus' time: possible licentious or antinomian conduct, arrogant claims to a privileged status and extraordinary contemplative abilities exclusive to themselves alone, and excessive discontent with perceived defects and inequalities in the sub-intelligible world and human society. All this suggests their resistance to accept the natural hierarchical ordering of the entire universe by the divine necessity. Turner concludes, that perhaps against the backdrop of the broader society, we may speak of genuine counterculturalism.

In "Forbidden Knowledge: Cognitive Transgression and 'Ascent Above Intellect' in the Debate Between Plotinus and the Gnostics," Zeke Mazur argues that the Platonizing Sethian treatise, Zostrianos, maintains a rather more willfully eristic and even countercultural attitude towards Greek philosophy than is usually assumed. The Sethians' claim to ascent to a supercelestial God beyond the heaven of the Jews simultaneously elevates the gnostic visionary and denigrates both Jew and Christian alike. So too they elevated themselves at the expense of more traditional Platonists. To this end, Mazur examines Plotinus' complaint in *Enneads* 11.9.33, that the gnostics claim to possess an extraordinary capability to undertake a visionary ascent *beyond the divine Intellect itself* so as to attain the transcendent (and hyper-noetic) deity: a claim which he considers the height of arrogance. Plotinus further implies that this gnostic claim was in some way connected with the disparagement of Plato and the Greek philosophical tradition. Mazur compares this complaint with the tractate Zostrianos (NHC VIII,1) which envisions a complex hierarchy of types of souls, each correlated with both a different potential for visionary ascent and a corresponding position in the postmortem cycle of transmigration. He shows that Zostrianos suggests that the non-Sethian academic Platonists are those condemned to exile in the intermediary strata due to their cognitive overreach for the Good in the absence of Sethian revelation, and that this reflects a gnostic deployment—*against the Platonists themselves*—of the supposedly Platonic injunction that the soul's attempt to comprehend the supreme principle, with which the soul has no kinship, inevitably leads to a fall into evil.

Lautaro Roig Lanzillotta's contribution, "The Apocalypse of Paul (NHC V,2): Cosmology, Anthropology, and Ethics," is an astute study of the ramifications of this text's peculiar gnostic cosmology, which has a ten-heaven structure instead of eight heavens as one might normally expect in a Gnostic text. The cosmos is structured into three clear, separate regions. No reference to the first two heavens is made. The cosmology is especially fascinating because it is closely connected with the text's anthropology, and describes Paul's ascension through the heavens in terms of ethical progress and his ultimate fusion with the divine. Most interesting, however, are its transgressive elements, such as the presentation of the Biblical god as the Demiurge and a polemical view of the apostles. The latter are not only said to be stationed in the archontic region together with the Demiurge, but also to be surpassed by Paul, who is the only individual entitled to enter the divine region. Roig Lanzillotta concludes that the countercultural message is obvious. While conventional Christians follow the apostles and remain trapped in the purgatory of the archontic region, gnostics go far beyond this, knowing how to dispose of the accretions of both body and soul and how to supersede the cosmic realms related to them.

In "Gnosis Undomesticated: Archon-Seduction, Demon Sex, and Sodomites in the Paraphrase of Shem (NHC VII,1)," Dylan Burns pushes back against scholarship that seeks to domesticate Gnostic literature, situating Nag Hammadi texts in late antique Egyptian asceticism. Evidence about libertine Gnosticism is now regarded by many to be sheer fiction, entirely without parallel in the Nag Hammadi corpus. Yet not all Gnostic texts are so easy to tame. The Paraphrase of Shem, for instance, is a work replete with seemingly shocking material—ranging from the seduction of an archontic womb to a demonic sex scene and valorization of the Sodomites. Burns addresses these sexually explicit passages and demonstrates that they derive from mythic strata associated with libertine Gnostic practices, particularly amongst the Manichaeans and the Borborites known to Epiphanius of Salamis.

David Litwa, in his contribution, "Gnostic Self-Deification: The Case of Simon of Samaria," studies the gnostic practice of deification of the self as a step beyond the typical philosophical discourse about the divinity (*daimon*) within, a step that involved reflexivity of one's own divinity and resulted in integration into a higher self or unity with the mediate deity. Litwa uses the Simonian *Great Declaration* to demonstrate these ideas, showing that human deification within gnostic traditions is a kind of reverse spiral of divine reflexivity. God knows himself and the universe unfolds. In turn, the human being knows himself as divine and refolds back into God. Litwa summarizes that while gnostics are rebels and transgressors against the demiurge and his minions, there is nothing in this mythology that suggests rebellion against the true God. The myth of cosmic rebellion does not constitute the core story of gnostic deification. The dominant desire of the gnostic is not to do battle with the demiurge, but to bypass him and return to her true realm. In Litwa's opinion, gnostic self-deification is a form of self-construction and self-beautification, a process that gnostics engaged long before Michel Foucault made vogue the idea of the construction of the self.

Gregory Shaw contributes a study on Iamblichus, "*Demon est Deus Inversus*: Honoring the Daemonic in Iamblichean Theurgy." He reexamines Iamblichus's doctrine that the immortal soul becomes mortal, a doctrine that is puzzling for Platonic scholars. According to Iamblichus, the embodied soul not only becomes mortal. As human, it also becomes "alienated" (*allotriōthen*) from divinity. Iamblichus maintains that the alienation and mortality of the soul are effected by daemons that channel the soul's universal and immortal identity into a singular and mortal self. Yet, while daemons alienate the soul from divinity they also outline the path to recover it. Iamblichus maintains that daemons unfold the will of the Demiurge into material manifestation and thus reveal its divine signatures (*sunthēmata*) in nature. According to Iamblichus's theurgical itinerary, the human soul—materialized, alienated, and mortal—must learn to embrace its alienated and mortal condition as a form of demiurgic activity. By ritually entering this demiurgy, the soul transforms its alienation and mortality into *theurgy*. The embodied soul becomes an icon of divinity.

The apocryphal text, the Revelation of the Magi, taken up in the second part of this volume. It is the subject of Brent Landau's reflection, "The Coming of the Star-Child: The Reception of the Revelation of the Magi in New Age Religious Thought and Ufology." Landau, the world's expert on this text, explores the text's popular reception of the Revelation of the Magi after his premier publication of it (2010). He observes that the popular reception of the Revelation of the Magi has been dominated by New Age and ufological (that is, the theorizing of unidentified flying objects) interpretative perspectives. Rather than viewing these interpretations as anachronistic, Landau argues that they may have far more in common with the circumstances that gave rise to the Revelation of the Magi than might initially be supposed. Ultimately, the Revelation of the Magi can be profitably characterized as a "gnostic" text—despite its lack of a demiurge—because of its strongly countercultural religious outlook, an outlook it shares with much New Age religious thought.

Several papers focus on the persistent countercultural traces of the gnostic in modernity. Sarah Iles Johnston, a classicist, in her paper "The Great God Pan," takes on gnostic narratives found in late 19th and 20th century ghost stories. Johnston starts from the premise these ghost stories often engaged the same issues as older 'gnostic' treatises did, but had the advantage of being able to describe encounters between humans and higher entities far more vividly than the gnostic treatises. She focuses on how such stories explore the possibility that, through encounters with higher entities who emerge as negative, protagonists discover that the divine world is either corrupt and ill-intended or worse completely meaningless. She contextualizes Arthur Machen's *The Great God Pan* (1890) within contemporary reactions to Darwin's theories of evolution as well as contemporary conceptualizations of the debt that modern civilization owed to ancient Greece and Rome. She also examines how H.P. Lovecraft developed Machen's ideas in 'The Dunwich Horror' (1929), where mastery of ancient languages unleashes horror. Finally, she shows how Peter Straub's *Ghost Story* (1979) delivers an even darker 'gnostic' message that entities whom we assume to have purposes (even if dark purposes) have none at all. She concludes that these writers suggest that the most important gnostic revelation is that there is nothing beneficial to reveal because the Others play by no rules. We are left with the resources of our own corporeal existence and what we can learn from stories about the road out of the pit of darkness.

The comic strip *Promethea* is the subject of Wouter Hanegraaff's contribution, "Alan Moore's *Promethea*: Countercultural Gnosis and the End of the World." According to Hanegraaff, Alan Moore's *Promethea* (1999 to 2005) is among the most explicitly "gnostic," "esoteric," and "occultist" comic strips ever published. Hailed as a virtuoso performance in the art of comics writing, its intellectual content and the nature of its spiritual message have been neglected by scholars. While the attainment of *gnosis* is clearly central to Moore's message, the underlying metaphysics is more congenial to the panentheist perspective of ancient Hermetism than to Gnosticism in its classic typological sense defined by dualism and anti-cosmic pessimism. According to Hanegraaff, it presents a Hermetic alternative to Hans Jonas' classic reading of Gnosticism as both a product of and a revolt against alienation and nihilist despair. Most importantly, *Promethea* is among the most explicit and intellectually sophisticated manifestoes of a significant new religious trend in contemporary popular culture. Its basic assumption is that there is ultimately no difference between imagination and reality, so that the question of whether gods, demons, or other spiritual entities are "real" or just "imaginary" becomes pointless. It provides its readers with some serious food for thought concerning the nature and the role of the imagination in shaping our culture, our society, and our everyday life. Moore's personal vision of the end of time is a contemporary form of millenarianism. As such, it is a direct reflection of a radical countercultural critique directed against a society dominated by technology, mass media, corporations, and global Capitalist consumerism. Hanegraaff concludes that the comic strip exemplifies the subversive potential of popular comics. Its ultimate objective is to break the spell of corporate control and capitalist consumerism.

INTRODUCTION                                                                                                          XIII

In "Children of the Light: Gnostic Fiction and Gnostic Practice in Vladimir Sorokin's *Ice Trilogy*," the literary critic and author Victoria Nelson offers a close reading of the contemporary Russian writer Vladimir Sorokin's *Ice* trilogy and explores its deep roots in early gnostic spiritual movements of late antiquity, Russian esoteric philosophy and literature, and Western popular culture. Reflecting sources as varied as the Apocryphon of John, the Disney movie *Escape to Witch Mountain*, Russian New Age paganism, and esoteric Soviet science, these three interconnected novellas are based on the real-life "Tunguska event," the great fireball that appeared over the Tunguska region of Siberia in 1908, flattening more than 800 square miles of forest. Famous in UFO circles as the "Russian Roswell" and long a magnet for esoteric speculation, in Sorokin's hands this probable meteor strike becomes the springboard for a contemporary gnostic fantasy in which a giant chunk of ice carries the spirits of 23,000 gnostic demiurges to earth, where they inhabit human bodies that they despise and seek only to reunite and return to their source. More than a simple postmodern parable of the seventy-year Soviet regime and post-Soviet societal excesses, Sorokin's damning portrait of his "children of the Light" illuminates the deeper and darker currents of human nature, ethics, and spirituality.

Matthew J. Dillon in his paper, "Symbolic Loss, Memory, and Modernization in the Reception of Gnosticism," analyzes how the category Gnosticism opened up an imaginative possibility for individuals to reinterpret the cultural memory of the Christian past and achieve rapprochement with the tradition. Using the theoretical lens of the social scientist of religion Peter Homans who demonstrated that symbolic loss, cultural memory, and modernization are tightly intertwined, Dillon examines the repertoires of psychologist Carl Jung, visionary artist Laurence Caruana, and public speaker Jonathan Talat Phillips and their interactions with ancient gnostic texts. Each case exhibits how symbolic loss of the Christian tradition throws the individual into a period of inner turmoil. When Jung, Caruana, and Phillips read ancient gnostic texts and traditions, they do so to reinterpret the symbols of Christianity, specifically Christ, in ways that respond to forces of modernization. Dillon concludes that popular and religious interpretations of the ancient gnostics should be recognized as attempts by those who lost Christianity in the West to re-envision its cultural memory and reimagine Christianity in the present.

"Gnostic and Countercultural Elements in Zora Neale Hurston's 'Hoodoo in America'" written by Margarita Simon Guillory considers the important role of gnosis in Hoodoo. Guillory observes that over the last decade, religious studies scholars have given attention to Zora Neale Hurston's "Hoodoo in America," but these analyses have not considered the important role of gnosis in hoodoo. Guillory rectifies this by examining how Hurston employs secret knowledge to advance a particular understanding of hoodoo. Guillory argues that Hurston's ethnographic study of New Orleans hoodoo captures a system of African-derived magical practices that is characterized by *both* gnostic and countercultural elements. These elements in turn reveal an intricate relationship between gnosis, human agency, and material culture that finds expression in the complex ritual system of New Orleans hoodoo. She concludes that New Orleans hoodoo provides a space in which scholars of gnostic studies can have rich cross-cultural conversations about the significant role that gnosis plays in African American religion.

These articles represent a first attempt to investigate through rich case studies the countercultures that surround claims to special direct knowledge of the divine from antiquity to modernity. While the case studies vary widely, there are some common resonances including the inversion of traditional knowledge to critique aspects of culture and society, particularly conventional views of the body, constructions of the self, human agency, governance, materiality, reason, conventional wisdom and authorities (religious and philosophical), science, social hierarchies, sex, and media. Conventional religions are remodeled, undermined, and/or supplanted.

Four years after this conference, Jonathan Cahana-Blum published his book, *Wrestling with Archons*, in which he theorizes ancient Gnosticism as a form of cultural criticism.[1] This book is an outgrowth of work that he had published earlier in journals.[2] In his opinion, Gnosticism is less a philosophical and more a cultural phenomenon. It is precisely an ancient form of a critical theory of culture "transcribed in a religious alphabet" and the "vehicle of myth." He suggests that ancient Gnosticism deconstructed mainstream discourses of domination in the ancient world just as modern critical theorists do, such as Theodore Adorno, Stuart Hall, Jean Baudrillard, and Judith Butler. He thinks that Gnosticism presents as a form of cultural criticism, which has no real parallel until the twentieth century.

Cahana-Blum's work is a welcome contribution to the problem of Gnosticism's relationship to culture. The only chapter from the *Gnostic Countercultures* collection that Cahana-Blum interacts with is April DeConick's contribution, which Cahana-Blum says came to his attention as he was finalizing his book.[3] It appears, in fact, that both DeConick and Cahana-Blum had been working independently from different perspectives on Gnosticism's

---

[1] Cahana-Blum 2019.
[2] Cf. Cahana 2011, 2012, 2014a, 2014b, 2016.
[3] Her name is misspelled repeatedly: "Deconick"; which is better than "Moron Smith" fared on page 6.

relationship to culture, which DeConick theorizes through sociological approaches and the lens of historian Theodore Roszak's concept of counter culture and Cahana-Blum theorizes with reference to post-modern literary and philosophical critics, who critique hegemony and dominant culture.[4]

While Cahana-Blum's work provides a separate way to parse the problem of Gnosticism's relationship to culture, it runs the risk of reducing Gnosticism to a form of cultural criticism. The same problem occurs with Michael William's reduction of Gnosticism to biblical demiurgy, Karen King's reduction of Gnosticism to identity politics and rhetoric, and David Brakke's reduction of Gnosticism to Sethianism.[5] Gnosticism may effect or result in cultural criticism, biblical demiurgy (at least for groups that use the Bible), political slander, and the development of Sethian groups, but these things do not distinguish it.

What distinguishes it is the fact that the word Gnostic was used by ancient people to identify real religious people who created a wide variety of religious groups to worship a God Beyond All Gods (including the biblical God) whom they claimed to "know" through direct experience (*gnosis*) and be immanently related to. Once we understand that Gnosticism is a distinctive ancient spirituality that generates new religious movements to worship this transcendent God, we are then better situated to theorize its impact on ancient society, culture, conventional religions, and politics (including the turn of the phrase deployed by Irenaeus and his friends). We are also better situated to theorize how these different transcendental groups emerged, were related to each other (or not), and positioned themselves in relationship to conventional religious knowledge and authorities. Because the literature that many of these Gnostic groups produced has re-emerged in modernity, we are also better positioned to examine how Gnostic spirituality is read out of the old Gnostic texts, repurposed as religious knowledge by modern people, and becomes entangled in modern cultures and their religious, literary, artistic, and cinematic productions.

## Bibliography

Brakke, David. 2010. *The Gnostics: Myth, Ritual, and Diversity in Early Christianity*. Cambridge: Harvard University Press.

---

[4] For Cahana's work, see n. 1 and 2. Cf. DeConick 2013a, 2013b, 2016a, 2016b, 2018, 2019.
[5] Williams 1996; King 2003; Brakke 2010.

Cahana, Jonathan. 2011. "Gnostically Queer: Gender Trouble in Gnosticism." *Biblical Theology Bulletin* 41: 24–35.

Cahana, Jonathan. 2012. "Dismanteling Gender: Between Ancient Gnostic Ritual and Modern Queer BDSM." *Theology & Sexuality* 18: 60–75.

Cahana, Jonathan. 2014a. "None of Them Knew Me or My Brothers: Gnostic Antitraditionalism and Gnosticism as a Cultural Phenomenon." *Journal of Religion* 94: 49–73.

Cahana, Jonathan. 2014b. "Androgyne or Undrogyne?: Queering the Gnostic Myth." *Numen* 61: 509–24.

Cahana, Jonathan. 2016. "Gnosticism and Radical Feminism: From Pathologizing Submersion to Salvaging Re-Emergence." Pages 183–200 in *Submerged Literature in Ancient Greek Culture: The Comparative Perspective*. Edited by Andrea Ercolani and Manuela Giordano. Berlin: De Gruyter.

Cahana-Blum, Jonathan. 2019. *Wrestling With Archons: Gnosticism as a Critical Theory of Culture*. Lanham: Lexington Books.

DeConick, April D. 2013a. "Crafting Gnosis: Gnostic Spirituality in the Ancient New Age." Pages 285–308 in *Gnosticism, Platonism and the Late Antique World: Essays in Honour of John D. Turner*. Edited by Kevin Corrigan and Tuomas Rasimus. Nag Hammadi and Manichaean Studies 82. Leiden: Brill.

DeConick, April D. 2013b. "Gnostic Spirituality at the Crossroads of Christianity: Transgressing Boundaries and Creating Orthodoxy." Pages 148–184 in *Beyond the Gnostic Gospels: Studies Building on the Work of Elaine Pages*. Edited by Eduard Iricinschi, Lance Jenott, Nicola Denzey Lewis and Philippa Townsend. Tübingen: Mohr Siebeck.

DeConick, April D. 2016a. *The Gnostic New Age: How a Countercultural Spirituality Revolutionized Religion*. New York: Columbia University Press.

DeConick, April D. 2016b. "The Countercultural Gnostic: Turning the World Upside Down and Inside Out." *Gnosis: Journal of Gnostic Studies* 1: 7–35.

DeConick, April D. 2018. "Deviant Christians: Romanization and Esoterization as Social Strategies for Survival Among Early Christians." *Gnosis: Journal of Gnostic Studies* 3.2: 135–76.

DeConick, April D. 2019. "The Sociology of Gnostic Spirituality." *Gnosis: Journal of Gnostic Studies* 4.1: 9–66.

King, Karen L. 2003. *What is Gnosticism?* Cambridge: Harvard University Press.

Williams, Michael A. 1996. *Rethinking "Gnosticism": An Argument for Dismantling a Dubious Category*. Princeton: Princeton University Press.

# PART 1

*Antiquity*

# The Countercultural Gnostic: Turning the World Upside Down and Inside Out

*April D. DeConick*
Rice University, Houston, Texas
*adeconick@rice.edu*

## 1   Making the Heretic

For two thousand years, the gnostic has been defined as the heretic, as the impious sinner, as the dangerous transgressor. This construction of the gnostic as heretic has developed in relationship to emergent Catholic Christianity, indicating those people who belong to a *hairesis* or *scholê* that deviates from nascent Catholicism, the heir to the teaching of the twelve apostles.[1] This pejorative keying of *gnostikoi* with *hairesis* in a deviant sense is a strategic way that heresiologists marked the gnostics negatively as outsiders and transgressors of Apostolic Catholic Christianity as they understood it.[2]

Irenaeus, Bishop of Lyons (ca. early second century–202 CE), is certain that the knowledge the gnostic possesses is knowledge from the devil, making gnostics apostates and blasphemers against the biblical God. This is the god who is called in the Bible YHWH.[3] In his five-volume work *On the Refutation and Reversal of Falsely Called "Gnosis"* ("Ἔλεγχος καὶ ἀνατροπὴ τῆς ψευδωνύμου γνώσεως), he says that they are possessed by the devil and agents of Satan because, like Satan, they refuse to submit to the biblical God, who created the heavens and the earth according to scripture. Like Satan and his horde of rebellious angels, the gnostics will be confined to the fires of everlasting punishment.[4] He thinks that they use the name *Christian* in order to try to conceal their impiety.[5] They are wolves in sheep's clothing, drawing the unsuspecting

---

1   Cf. Irenaeus, *Haer.* 1.11.1; 1.29.1; 1.30.15; cf. Tertullian, *Val.* 11.2.
2   There are emerging many superb studies on the meaning of *hairesis* and its pejorative use in the battle for Christian identity. Cf. Boulluec 1985, 2000; Pietersen 1997; Henderson 1998; King 2003, 20–54; Cameron 2005; the collection of papers in Iricinschi and Zellentin 2008; Royalty 2012; DeConick 2013b; Lehtipuu 2014; G. Smith 2015. The classic piece on the subject is Wisse 1971.
3   Irenaeus, *Haer.* 4.pref.4 (Rousseau et al. 1965, 386–390).
4   Irenaeus, *Haer.* 1.10.1; 1.13.1, 3; 1.15.6; 1.16.3; 1.25.3 (Rousseau and-Doutreleau 1979, 154–159, 188–197, 250–253, 260–265, 284–289; 2.28.7 (Rousseau and -Doutreleau 1982, 336–339); 5.26.2 (Rousseau et al. 1969, 330–338).
5   Irenaeus, *Haer.* 1.25.3 (Rousseau-Doutreleau 1979, 336–339).

Christian into their perverted fantasies.[6] Like hyenas, they must be hunted and slain.[7] Given their absurd insolence and arrogance, Irenaeus thinks the gnostics are insane.[8]

Ps.-Hippolytus in his anthology of heretical writings, *Refutation of All Heresies* (Κατὰ πασῶν αἱρέσεων ἔλεγχος), considers them sexual offenders, certain that their nocturnal rites include orgies.[9] This accusation is an old one, already present in the writing of Justin Martyr (ca. 100–165 CE).[10] They keep their teachings and practices secret, Ps.-Hippolytus thinks, because who among them would want to admit publicly that they participated in such shameful deeds.[11] Like Hydra, they are monsters that must be exterminated.[12]

Tertullian of Carthage (ca. 160–220 CE) considers them threatening outsiders who lie when they call themselves Christians.[13] Really their teachings are poisonous. They produce a dangerous fever that weakens the body and makes it susceptible to sickness.[14]

Epiphanius of Salamis (ca. 320–403 CE) writes an entire treatise, *Medicine Chest* (Πανάριον), which he considers the medicinal antidote to the deadly poison of bites of heretics.[15] He characterizes the gnostics as biting insects and scorpions that live in manure and swarm around the unsuspecting in order to infect them with their rubbish, perversities, and obscenities.[16]

This portrayal of the gnostic as deviant heretic has also formed the basis of modern studies of gnosticism.[17] In fact, one of the earliest uses of the word *gnosticism* was by Henry More (1614–1687), a famous Cambridge Platonist.[18] He used it to designate the range of views the heresiologists wrote about. For him gnosticism was "the primal Christian heresy."

More was himself influenced by Henry Hammond (1605–1660) whose work on the New Testament showed some knowledge of the heresiological

---

6 Irenaeus, *Haer.* 1.pref.2 (Rousseau-Doutreleau 1979, 20–25); 3.16.8 (Rousseau-Doutreleau 1974, 318–320).
7 Irenaeus, *Haer.* 1.31.4 (Rousseau-Doutreleau 1979, 388–391).
8 Irenaeus, *Haer.* 1.25.4 (Rousseau-Doutreleau 1979, 338–341).
9 Ps.-Hippolytus, *Haer.* 1.pre f.5 (Marcovich 1986, 55). Cf. Roig Lanzillotta 2007.
10 Justin Martyr, *1 Apology* 1.26.7.
11 Ps.-Hippolytus, *Haer.* 1.pref.3–4 (Marcovich 1986, 54).
12 Ps.-Hippolytus, *Haer.* 5.11.1 (Marcovich 1986, 173); cf. Roig Lanzillotta 2007.
13 Tertullian, *Presc.* 30.1–2. For a more lengthy discussion of Tertullian's strategies, see Lehtipuu 2014.
14 Tertullian, *Presc.* 2.1–3.
15 Epiphanius, *Pan.* 4.pref.2.3.
16 Epiphanius, *Pan.* 2.26.1.1, 2.26.3.5.
17 Cf. King 2003.
18 Cf. Markschies 2003, 14.

literature.[19] He took the view that the *gnosticks* was a common name for "all the Heresies then abroad" among the Christians. According to Hammond, the *gnosticke-heresie* was morally depraved and corrupt. This is how the modern word *gnosticism* came to designate the reinscription of the position of the heresiologists, who demonized the gnostics.

From this perspective, gnosticism is viewed as a religious movement that is an ancillary development to real Christianity. Many scholars who perceive gnosticism in this way have argued strongly that gnosticism represents "the acute secularization and Hellenization of Christianity" or "Platonism run wild," and that this is an adverse or corrupting force that degraded original Christianity.[20] Over the last century, it was standard for gnostic writings to be characterized by scholars as "the underworld of Platonism" or as witnesses to the early perversion of Christianity.[21] Robert Grant and David Noel Freedman wrote in 1960 that gnostic literature stands, "like Lot's wife, as a new but permanently valuable witness to men's desire to make God's revelation serve them. Ultimately, it testifies not to what Jesus said but to what men wished he had said."[22] It was generally assumed that the gnostics who referred to Christian scripture did so by falsifying it and interpreting it violently in order to force fictitious meaning on it, creating "heretical theology" in the process.[23]

Gnosticism then has been characterized by scholars as a perversion of pristine Christianity (which is identified with emergent Catholicism or *normative* Christianity) and a dangerous heresy to boot. This understanding of gnosticism is still popular today because it reinforces the triumphant story of conventional Christianity that many Christians prefer. For instance, Darrell Bock, writing in 2006, argues that the diversity of gnosticism proves its "parasitic" quality.[24] It is not a "legitimate" development of the Christian faith.[25] According to Philip Jenkins in his 2001 publication, gnostic texts are "heretical texts" with "an odd slant" unconcerned with "historical realities." Because of this aberrant perspective, "they arouse widespread excitement among feminists and

---

19  Layton, 1995.
20  Harnack 1885 (1961, 227); Nock 1964, 256.
21  Dillon 1977, 384–396.
22  See Grant and Freedman 1960, 20.
23  For instance, see Gärtner 1961, 11–12, 78–80, who aligns his own academic interpretation with Irenaeus' rhetoric of falsification and violence.
24  Bock 2006, 24.
25  Bock 2006, 212, quoting and agreeing with Witherington 2004, 114–115.

esoteric believers, and aspiring radical reformers of Christianity."[26] They represent "a vital weapon in the liberal arsenal."[27]

However, another perspective has been argued forcibly by Elaine Pagels. Her reflection on the Nag Hammadi literature in her 1979 book *The Gnostic Gospels* was the first to seriously consider whether it is a misnomer to see the gnostic as a heretic. She follows the lead of Walter Bauer who suggested that, from the start, Christianity was made up of a diverse number of different groups, many of them not Catholic.[28] Pagels goes on to demonstrate from inside the gnostic literature that the gnostics were not really heretics, but religious competitors who challenged the Catholics. She notes that "ideas which bear implications contrary to that development come to be labeled as 'heresy'; ideas which implicitly support it become 'orthodox'."[29] While there was nothing theologically amiss with the ideas and practices of the gnostics, they lost the battle of faith because of extenuating social and political circumstances.[30] In the process of losing the battle, they were made into heretics by their Catholic opponents.

This position has been further substantiated primarily with the work of Karen King. She has argued that the characterization of the gnostic as a heretic is a fabrication of powerful Catholic leaders who constructed the gnostic heresy largely to suppress alternative forms of Christianity in the second century.[31] Influenced by New Historicism and literary and post-modern critics like Michel Foucault and Pierre Bourdieu, King's work deconstructs the gnostic and gnosticism.[32] Her main argument is that the rhetorical term gnosticism has been confused with an historical entity. Or to put it another way, because the words *gnostic* and *gnosticism* reflect the polemics and grand narrative of triumphant Christianity, we should not continue to reify them as historical facts. The gnostics were Christians, so we should discuss them under the Christian rubric, not the gnostic one.[33]

---

26   Jenkins 2001, 37.
27   Jenkins 2001, 39.
28   Bauer 1934.
29   Pagels 1979, xxxvi.
30   Pagels 1979, xxxv.
31   King 2008. Her essay fits nicely in this edited volume, where many of the papers also push away from the "objectification" of heresy.
32   King 2008.
33   King 2003.

## 2  Identity Work

While this deconstruction of the gnostic and gnosticism has been popular among many scholars, it has left me uneasy. Although it is true that the heresiologists framed the gnostic as the demonic and created a grand narrative that connected a variety of unrelated groups to the arch-heretic Simon Magus, this does not mean that gnostics did not exist historically, nor that gnostics were innocuous *alternative* Christians. Or to put it another way, while gnostics may have been made into heretics by the early Catholics, this does not erase the fact that gnostics were operating in the margins of the conventional religions with a countercultural perspective that upset and overturned everything from traditional theology, cosmogony, cosmology, anthropology, hermeneutics, scripture, religious practices, and lifestyle choices.[34] When we insist on gnostics as *alternative* Christians, we run the risk of taming the shrew. The word *alternative* points to equivalent acceptable routes to the same destination. The gnostic road, however, is countercultural, concerned with journeying on a road to a different destination, perhaps even along a road in the opposite direction.[35]

Making the gnostic into a Christian does not resolve the problem either. Rather it imposes another grand narrative on the early Christians, one which domesticates gnostic movements and presents them as no-nonsense alternative forms of Christianity. Granted, the textual evidence for the interface of the gnostic and the Christian is present, but so is the interface of the gnostic and the Greek, the gnostic and the Jew, the gnostic and the Persian, and the gnostic and the Egyptian. And the interface looks to have all the signs of transgression, not conformity.

It is not debatable that the *gnostic* was an identity that was known in antiquity. Bentley Layton has laid this out quite eloquently, demonstrating that the word identified a type of religious believer more than a specific group.[36] I too have reviewed the primary evidence, noting that the ancients' concept of the word *gnostic* associated it with religious people who claimed to know (gnosis) through direct experience the God who transcends the gods of all the religions, and to be substantially connected to him. Furthermore, they employed rituals to reunite themselves with this true transcendent God.[37] Ancient writers applied the word broadly to individuals including Basilides, Valentinus, Saturnilus, Colorbasus, Justin, Ptolemy, Secundus, and Carpocrates, and also

---

34  For more on this, see DeConick 2016b; also Kaler 2009.
35  For this wonderful image, see Yinger 1982, 42.
36  Layton 1995. See also M. Smith 1981.
37  DeConick 2013a. See also DeConick 2016.

groups including Sethians, Ophians, Barbeloites, Carpocratians, Prodicians, Justinians, Naassenes, Nicolaitans, and Valentinians.[38]

As different people and groups claimed to possess knowledge of this supreme God and linked themselves to him, competition in the religious marketplace intensified. In some camps represented by heresiologists like Irenaeus of Lyons, Tertullian of Carthage, and Ps.-Hippolytus, this led to the demonizing of the gnostic as a way to delegitimize competitors' claims to superior knowledge and contact with a supreme God beyond the biblical God YHWH. The heresiologists consider the knowledge that gnostics claim to possess to be false knowledge. For others, like Clement of Alexandria, it meant refashioning the gnostic to refer to the perfected Christian who followed the biblical God's law, rallied around the creator God, and engaged in self-restraint and the contemplative life.[39] According to Clement, the gnostic lifestyle was an extreme one, where Christians trained daily as contemplatives and mystics, to draw the biblical God toward themselves and to bring themselves toward him.[40]

Although Michael Williams has demonstrated for us that the diversity among the gnostics calls into question the ways in which scholars have used gnosticism as an overarching category, this does not mean that "biblical demiurgy" is the answer.[41] Such circumscription does not resolve the problem of the diversity of gnostic identity. In fact gnostic identity is complicated because it is an identity that crosses traditional group boundaries and creates new ones that often critique the old. It is an identity that is not so much a group designation as it is a religious orientation towards a transcendent God beyond the conventional God(s).

As such, it is an orientation that is affiliated with multiple groups, which often have other names for themselves. For instance, the Sethians, who call themselves the *Seed of Seth* and the *Standing Ones*, may be some of the earliest people designated as gnostics.[42] We have the Valentinians, who claim to possess knowledge about God that others do not have. Yet they claim to be *Christians*, while they call the Apostolic Catholic Christians *Hebrews* because they still (mistakenly) worship YHWH.[43] We have Basilides, who also teaches about a God who transcends YHWH, saying that the people in his group are "not quite Jews and not as yet Christians (*et Iudaeos quidem iam non esse dicunt, christianos*

---

38  For primary references, see DeConick 2013a.
39  Cf. Clement of Alexandria, *Strom.* 4.21–23 (Stählin 1960, 304–316).
40  Clement of Alexandria, *Strom.* 1.14, 19 (Stählin 1960, 37–41, 58–62); 2.15 (Stählin 1960, 146–151); 5.4 (Stählin 1960, 338–342).
41  Williams 1996, 265–66.
42  Williams 1985.
43  Cf. Gos.Phil. NHC II,3 52.21–25.

*autem nondum)*".[44] We have Justin telling everyone that his initiates are *gnostics* because they have seen the true God, the Good, and he definitely is not the God traditionally worshiped by Jews and Christians.[45] We have Mani creating "true religion" out of his revelations of the true God, a transcendent Father of Light, while viewing all other religions, including Christianity, as "false."[46] The Mandaeans, whose name comes from *manda* or *knowledge*, despise Jesus, considering him a lapsed Mandaean and false prophet.[47] We have the Hermetics with no Jesus at all and a world not quite as dark and maddening as portrayed by other gnostics. In my opinion, we need a construction of the gnostic that can handle this kind of religious diversity and transgression, an identity that can face the countercultural.

## 3 The Invasion of the Centaurs

To be clear, the *counter culture* is a term coined by the American historian Theodore Roszak in his famous 1968 book, *The Making of a Counter Culture*. He did so to try to explain the uprising of the youth, mainly in America and Britain that he observed in the 1960s. He notably defines the counter culture as "a culture so radically disaffected from the mainstream assumptions of our society that it scarcely looks to many as a culture at all, but takes on the alarming appearance of a barbaric invasion."[48] It is like the invasion of the centaurs that Apollo must drive back (although sometimes Apollo does not win).

Roszak does not displace the importance of local society and culture in the youth rebellion against what he identifies as the main culprits: technocracy and the domination of science. Yet he defines the essence of the counterculture in psychological terms as an assault on the reality of the ego as our true identity. The counterculture instead "transcends the consciousness of the dominant culture and runs the risk of appearing to be a brazen exercise in perverse nonsense."[49] It gains its vision and power from that moral and imaginative level of human personality that lies deeper than our ego or intellective consciousness. Although Roszak resists naming it anything but "non-intellective consciousness," he thinks this deep aspect of human personality provides our guiding vision and ultimately determines for us what we regard as sanity.

---

44   Irenaeus, *Haer.* 1.24.6 (Rousseau and Doutreleau 1979, 330).
45   Ps.-Hippolytus, *Haer.* 5.23.3–24.1.
46   Cf. BeDuhn 2015.
47   Cf. Lupieri 2002, 240–253.
48   Roszak 1968, 42.
49   Roszak 1968, 55.

The counterculture emerged, according to Roszak, when people could no longer align this deep aspect, including their moral compass and ideal visions, with the direction of the society. He broadened his definition by declaring that a counterculture emerges when people become alienated from society's institutional structures.[50] The counterculture is reflected in any figure or movement, Roszak argues, that privileges non-intellective knowledge and personal visions of truth over cultural constructions of knowledge. In this way, Roszak was able to take the question of counterculture relative to the hippie generation and suspend it phenomenologically to embrace what, for him, is at stake: the spirit of humanity which underlies social systems and ideologies, and which must serve as the ultimate point of moral reference.[51] Basilides, Valentinus, and their gnostic friends would have exclaimed, "Amen!"

Since Roszak, social scientists speak of the countercultural in terms of a set of norms and values shared by a group that are in sharp contradiction to the dominant norms and values of the larger group or society.[52] Sociologists, psychologists and anthropologists today recognize the fermentation of countercultures in economic disparity and feelings of relative deprivation, the demographic rise of youth, social isolation, and personalities that are impulsive, alienated, narcissistic and antinomian.[53] They have identified a wide variety of types of countercultural groups that emerge, everything from activist institutions to hippie communes (one size does not fit all).[54]

That said, they also critique Roszak's insistence that the counterculture emerges out of the non-intellective consciousness of the human self. Instead, they believe that what is at stake are *socially constructed* worldviews of the true, the good, and the beautiful. Countercultures emerge, they argue, when these cultural worldviews no longer function to help people organize their experiences and deal with crises and ambiguities. When such a rupture happens, people may choose to adopt a drastically different worldview, one that they might believe has been revealed to them experientially.[55] So in the end, their conclusion, like Roszak's, suggests that the counterculture is about the conflict between Apollonian and Dionysian ways of knowing.[56]

---

50   Roszak 1968, 95–96.
51   Roszak 1968, 62.
52   Westhues, 1972, 9–10; Musgrove, 1974, 9; Yinger 1982, 3.
53   Keniston 1960, 56; 1968, 259, 340; Yinger 1982, 51–79.
54   Yinger 1982, 89–95.
55   Yinger 1982, esp. 95–97; cf. Douglas 1973, 81.
56   Musgrove 1974, 40–64.

## 4 Framing the Category *Gnostic* as a Spirituality

In order to explain gnostic diversity, it is necessary to move beyond our previous visions of gnosticism as a heresy, religion, philosophy, (originating) group, typology, or rhetorical fabrication.[57] We need to frame the gnostic in such a way that it can account for multiple origins, affiliations, and identities, some of them not historically linked. Any such conceptualization must begin with how the ancient people first framed the concept for themselves. I have written extensively on how the ancients understood the gnostic to be a person who claimed to have direct knowledge of the transcendent God beyond the conventional God(s), and to be substantially linked to that God.[58] This is a distinctive metaphysical or spiritual orientation. As such, it is not defined by one religion or confined to one religion.

It might be helpful to think of the gnostic and gnosticism as concepts like the fundamentalist and fundamentalism, which identify a very particular orientation toward God and the world. In the case of fundamentalism, it is a perspective that conceives God as an authoritarian patriarch and scripture as a sacred infallible document that is literally true. The human being must conform to God's will as it is revealed literally in the scripture. This leads to an exclusive outlook, where certain people in the group are saved according to their obedience to the scriptures and everyone else outside the group is damned. We have in our world today Christian fundamentalists as well as Jewish, Buddhist, and Muslim. They may not call themselves fundamentalist at all, but Southern Baptist, Catholic, Adventist, Theravada Buddhist, or some similar designation.

Put simply, I think it is valuable to view the gnostic and our modern descriptor gnosticism as identifying its own unique form of spirituality, one that emerged when some ancient religious seekers attempted to make meaning of their experiences of the world in a radically pluralistic environment much like ours today. When I try to imagine what this looked like on the ground, I consider modern New Agers as a parallel. These are religious seekers who, like the ancient gnostics, claim multiple religious affiliations while questing for the God beyond convention. In their quests for the truth behind it all, they consciously draw upon everything from philosophy to astrology, sacred literature, new revelation, and science. They claim to have direct access to knowledge unexpressed by conventional religions, while also being inspired by them.

---

57  For an overview and bibliography of these depictions of the gnostic, see Denzey Lewis 2013.
58  For fuller discussion, see DeConick 2013a; 2013b.

Out of this milieu, these religious seekers produce new scripture, which they believe channels the true message of God. The religious groups that emerge from the modern New Age do so as their own religious movements, although figures like Jesus and scriptures like the Upanishads are not wholly forsaken.[59] Because the sources of inspiration for religious seekers old and new are not necessarily countercultural in and of themselves, I prefer to discuss them in terms of a *revelatory milieu*, instead of the *cultic milieu* postulated by Colin Campbell in 1972.[60] *Revelatory* signals that it was their use and interpretation that was countercultural, putting standard readings of conventional scriptures into reverse or inverse.

Gnostic spirituality emerged as a religious identity in the first century CE when a number of religious people began to claim that they possessed a new kind of spiritual knowledge.[61] *Gnostic* expressed for them, not a new religion, but a new type of spirituality, a new way for them to live in their world as religious people, whatever their current religious affiliations—Egyptian, Greek, Jewish, or Christian. As gnostic spirituality emerged within these different personal contexts, these religious people began to call into question the truth of their regional and ancestral religions, and spun that truth in new and unusual directions.

This means that the real issue for me does not lie in the long-standing debate whether or not gnostic spirituality originated from Judaism or Christianity.[62] The real issue for me is to try to understand what kinds of religious movements develop when gnostic spirituality with its transgressive orientation engages conventional scriptures, ideologies, and practices of Jews and Christians (and others like Buddhists and the followers of Zoroaster).

## 5  The Gnostic as an Emergent Structure

What did this new spirituality look like in the ancient world? Here I rely on the understanding of *emergent structures* theorized by cognitive linguists like Mark Turner and Gilles Fauconnier.[63] What is an emergent structure? It is

---

59  For details about New Age movements, see especially Hanegraaff 1997.
60  Campbell 1972; on the term *religious buffer*, see DeConick 2016a.
61  For this argument, see DeConick 2013a; 2013b; 2016a.
62  The relationship between gnosticism and Judaism is highly contested; much of the discussion focused on dependence issues, on whether or not gnosticism originated from within Judaism or not, on whether or not references to Jewish scriptures are indicative of Jewish origins. For a recent summary of this discussion, see C. Smith 2004 and Lahe 2012.
63  See especially Fauconnier and Turner 2002.

the creation of a new mental concept, an idea that never existed before. New concepts come out of a mental process called *blending*, when we recruit from long-term memory what we already know about a concept and merge it with our experience of something new. What we already know about a concept is called by cognitive linguists a *mental frame* or *schema*.[64] This is knowledge that we have organized into useful categories around ideal attributes.

I like to use the *book* as an example of a frame. What makes a book a book to us, and not something else? We mentally frame the book with ideal characteristics, like a folio of paper bound between two covers. Does a book have to have covers, or can it be a simple folio of paper bound with a string? Usually there is writing inside that we read, but not always. There are blank books to be journaled, as well as unwritten books in our imaginations, or in outline form. There are published and unpublished books, handwritten, typeset, and picture books.

So there is considerable flexibility in the frames we recruit when we think about our world. We recognize that all books are not the same. They do not all have exactly the same properties as the ideal frame. Yet we still recognize them as books. Even more important, the elements that define the book can shift to accommodate new experiences of book-like objects. These new experiences either expand the frame, shift it, or break it open and blend it into something new.

Take the *e-book*, for example. It has no pages, no cover, and virtual words that disappear when the device is turned off. Yet we have come to recognize it as a book because it is an electronic version of a real book. This is an innovation in the concept of the book, what linguists call an *emergent structure*. If this emergent idea stabilizes, as it did with the e-book, it reorganizes the categories we use to think. The e-book allows us to think in new directions about everything from reading to publishing to libraries to other forms of media like magazines and newspapers.

Like the e-book, the *gnostic* is an emergent structure, an innovative concept that some ancient people began to use to describe a new way to be religious. If we look at the gnostic as an emergent structure, what are its characteristics, what are the elements of its frame? I argue that in the ancient memory it is associated with five ideal characteristics.[65]

The first characteristic is framed around direct experiential knowledge of a transcendent God beyond the gods of all the religions (including YHWH), what the gnostics called *gnosis*. In ecstatic moments, the gnostics felt immersed

---

64  Coulson 2001. They are called *idealized cognitive models* by Lakoff 1987.
65  For more details, see DeConick 2013a.

in the overwhelming presence of transcendence, believing that they had been reunited with the Very-Ground-of-Being.

Second, these people were convinced that humans have an innate spiritual nature, a spark of God that is an extension of this transcendence. Most often they called this spark the *pneuma*, or spirit, also the *nous*, or mind. The spirit would survive into eternity, but only if it could be awakened and reconnected with the transcendent God.[66]

Third, these ecstatic states were carefully choreographed in terms of ritual. Gnostic spirituality is oriented toward very particular religious practices that were used to prompt the ecstatic states and unitive experiences of transcendence that gnostics pursued.

Fourth, this was transgressive talk that set gnostics at odds with the conventional religions of their time, which worshiped local deities associated with the earth and the celestial spheres, not the transcendent realms. While some of the Greek philosophers in the first centuries CE also were talking about a transcendent deity beyond Mind and Being (ἐπέκεινα νοῦ καὶ οὐσίας), they did not worship this God as the gnostics were doing.[67] In the second century, several philosophically minded Christians began thinking about a transcendent God too. To resolve the transtheistic problem that the gnostic vision raised—that the true God of worship is the supreme God who lives beyond the cosmos and is not the biblical God—these Christians weld the concept of a transcendent deity with the biblical God.[68] When gnostics engaged conventional theology and traditional religion and its scriptures, they did so by upending normative understandings of the gods and normative readings of texts. They developed a counrercultural hermeneutic that turned conventional worship and scriptures on their edge.

Fifth, to achieve this inversion, they incorporated into their religious discussions everything but the kitchen sink. To reorient religion as *true religion*, they relied on everything from Homer and Plato, to magic and astrology, to ancient brain science and fantastic cosmological speculations about multiworlds. They were embedded within the countercultural even as they sought to reinvent conventional religion to reflect their vision of true religion. Their intellectual engagement was open-ended, their mentality that of seekers.[69] Although we might be tempted to dismiss this kind of eclecticism as a

---

66  Cf. Roig Lanzillota 2013.
67  For a history of this deity "beyond Mind and Being," see Whittaker 1969, who popularized this phrase.
68  Cf. Whittaker 1969, 104.
69  On the seeker mentality, see Roof 1993, 79–83.

"cafeteria-style" spirituality that is totally a function of the religious marketplace, to do so would diminish the fact that gnostics locate spiritual authority in the individual's soul or spirit. So what the individual already knows and comes to know through ecstasy and revelation is what comes into play in their plans to remake religion as true religion.

## 6 Turning the World Upside Down and Inside Out

The current trend in scholarship to deconstruct the gnostic and gnosticism results in a most unfortunate consequence, unintended or not. If we domesticate the gnostic into the Christian, we end up erasing transgressive religious identities from history when, instead, we should be fully exploring their meaning.[70] We end up divorcing from the historical record countercultural identities that have so much to tell us about religion and its power to innovate, stir up, change, and even revolutionize the way we are in our world.

It is something of a paradox that scholars of early Christianity have either declared the gnostics heretics and thus not worthy of study, or have deconstructed them so that the gnostics have been tamed into Christians, with the same result. The gnostic is marginalized or rejected, either as a heretic or as a heretical fabrication, having no worthwhile contribution to make to Western thought and culture. In this discourse, the gnostic has become irrelevant.

Yet sociologists who study deviance have shown that transgression is marked by one group, usually the dominant group, when another group has overstepped a boundary that may not have been evident up until that moment.[71] If the boundary is considered by the dominant group to be significant enough, the dominant group works to naturalize its own position and construe the counterpoint as deviant, wayward and heretical, even to the point of establishing sanctions for future offenses.[72] This is when things get serious, when value judgments about right and wrong get attached to certain positions and reinforced as the natural order of things. This is when the transgressor becomes the heretic.

---

70  For a discussion of gnostic transgression, see DeConick 2013b.
71  For complete literature review, see DeConick 2013b.
72  For an overview of this sociological perspective, see Becker 1963; Schur 1971, 1980; Curra 2000, Clinard and Meier 2008, 11–12, 76–83; Clarke 2008; Franzese 2009 88–101. For sociological studies of deviance and religious groups, see Erikson 1966; Davies 1982, 1032–63; Greenberg 1988; McWilliams 1993. Studies in early Christianity have successfully applied deviance theory to early Christian literature: cf. Malina and Neyrey 1991; Barclay 1995; Still 1999; Pietersen 1997, 2004.

So for me the really interesting questions hinge on this sociological insight. What is it that gnostics were saying and doing that so riled up the emergent Catholics to the point that they began naturalizing their positions? What buttons did gnostics push that lit up the limits and became decisive rallying points for bishops like Irenaeus? What mattered enough to the Apostolic Catholics that they were determined to make gnostics into monsters?

These are particularly important questions given that Jesus and the very first Christians like Paul had their own countercultural programs. It is not insignificant that the author of Acts records that many people in Thessalonica became violent because Paul's preaching about Jesus "has turned the world upside down." Paul's message, they felt, had led to the abuse of Roman laws, replacing Caesar with Jesus as the real king.[73]

While this is not the place to analyze in detail the first Christians as countercultural champions, it is significant that by the second century this countercultural program was beginning to be tamed by many of the Apostolic Catholic Christians who wrote treatises to assure the Roman rulers that they were good citizens. Even though the Apostolic Catholics rejected aspects of Roman society as decadent and heathen (including their gods), they begin to settle in and accommodate their new religion to Rome, especially in terms of advocating for a public form of Christianity that claimed old ancestral customs. For the most part, this domestication did not happen among the gnostic groups who were at odds with both the values of the Romans and the emerging Catholic Christians.

While the Apostolic Catholic Christians began to develop their religion out of a network that interfaced with the traditional values of Rome promoting their religion as "old" and public with customary rites and hierarchies, gnostics prized the new, the revelatory, the unmediated experiences of the God beyond the God of the biblical covenant, beyond the gods of civic duty and the patron-client relationship. Gnostic Christians made little claim to an ancestral past or the God of traditional scriptures, preferring to sever the tie with Judaism and marketing their communities by promoting a new previously unknown deity who wanted nothing whatsoever to do with covenants, traditional sacrifices and other public ceremonies. For them, the practice of religion was not about civic duty and moral obligation, but personal therapy and empowerment. The human being and its needs surpassed the biblical God and the old Greco-Roman and Egyptian gods, and indeed, overturned them and their earthly representatives. This transtheistic perspective cut across not only Judaism and

---

73   Acts 17:6.

Christianity, but also laid the Roman cult to waste. Gnostic spirituality turned the world upside down—and inside out!

Given this orientation, it is not surprising that the evidence reveals that the major transgression that mobilized the emergent Catholics against gnostic groups was the gnostic insistence that the Supreme God of worship is not the biblical LORD called in the scripture by the name YHWH. This allowed gnostics to regard the biblical LORD as a lesser god, a trickster, and demon, on the same level with the Greco-Roman, Syrian and Egyptian gods. He also was an apostate, a rebellious warrior like Satan or the Titans. As such, he controlled this world and the process of birth and death.[74]

This theological crime was connected to another in the writings of the Apostolic Catholics. This is the gnostics' claim to have direct knowledge (gnosis) of the Supreme God who transcends the gods of all the religions of the world, including YHWH. This God does not live in the world, but beyond it, in a special realm of his own.[75] The Catholic concern expressed over these theological crimes suggests that the first Apostolic Catholics had taken for granted that the biblical YHWH is the supreme God of worship. And this was something they were invested in enough that they were willing to fight for it.[76]

Another major transgression identified by the early Catholics, and also by Plotinus, is the gnostic claim to be substantially God, to be mortal gods because a particle of the Supreme God—a seed or a spirit—had been deposited in their souls.[77] This was considered transgressive because it allowed gnostics to claim that they were superior beings to YHWH and all the other gods worshiped conventionally across the Mediterranean.[78] The fallout from this perspective is immense. Because gnostics have nothing to fear from YHWH or the other gods, they were free to live above the laws and were not bound to

---

[74] Irenaeus, *Haer.* 1.pref.1, 1.16.3 (Rousseau-Doutreleau 1979, 18–21,260–265); *Haer.* 2.9.2, 2.13.3, 2.26.1, 2.28.7 (Rousseau-Doutreleau 1982, 84–87, 114–117, 256–259, 284–289); 4 pref.3–4 (Rousseau et al. 1965, 384–390); Tertullian, *Val.* 3.1–2 (Kroymann 1954, 754–755).

[75] Irenaeus, *Haer.* 1.pref.1, 1.4.3, 1.16.3, 1.21.3–4 (Rousseau and Doutreleau 1979, 18–21, 68–69, 260–265, 298–305); Tertullian, *Val.* 1.1–4 (Kroymann 1954, 753–754); Hippolytus, *Haer.* 5.1.4, 5.23.2–3 (Marcovich 1986, 141, 198–199).

[76] Irenaeus, *Haer.* 1.pref.1, 1.10.3 (Rousseau and Doutreleau 1979, 18–21, 160–167); 2.28.2 (Rousseau-Doutreleau 1982, 270–273); Ps.-Hippolytus, *Haer.* 6.41.2–5 (Marcovich 1986, 258–259).

[77] Irenaeus, *Haer.* 2.19.2–4 (Rousseau-Doutreleau 1982, 186–191); 4.19.1 (Rousseau et al. 1965, 614–616); 5.19.2 (Rousseau-Doutreleau-Mercier 1969, 250–252); Tertullian, *Val.* 4.4 (Kroymann 1954, 756–757).

[78] Irenaeus, *Haer.* 2.26.3, 2.30.2 (Rousseau-Doutreleau 1982, 260–263, 302–305); Ps.-Hippolytus, *Haer.* 1.pref.2–3 (Marcovich 1986, 54).

the duties of civic religion.[79] Given this, it is not surprising how often were expressed charges of gnostic hubris and concerns that such attitudes would result in nemesis.[80] This suggests that the Apostolic Catholics had been assuming that the subordinate nature of the human to the gods is natural. They recognized that they were YHWH's servants. They were subject to his rule and his law. Their salvation depended on this.[81]

Yet another transgression identified by the emergent Catholics is the gnostics' contrary reading of scriptures and other texts like Homer—against their conventional hermeneutic.[82] The Apostolic Catholics had been under the impression that their own way to read the scripture was standard because they focused on the natural flow of the narratives and the connections they saw between Jewish prophecy and Christian writings. They dismissed the gnostic preference for focusing on the disjunctures and ambiguities in the scriptures and reading allegorically rather than literally.[83] Ongoing revelation, which the gnostic claimed, was nonsense to the emergent Catholics, who were sure this represented forgery.[84]

The Apostolic Catholics were not happy about gnostic practices either because they perceived them to be secretive, exclusive, and expensive.[85] Clearly the Catholics took for granted that religious practices should be publicly available, rather than performed for a small select group at a cost to the initiate. They also were concerned that some gnostic ceremonies were intentionally made to be similar to their own, or even the same.[86] The transgression of the ritual, however, did not reside in their imitative quality. Rather it resided in

---

79   Irenaeus, *Haer.* 1.6.3, 1.28.2 (Rousseau-Doutreleau 1979, 94–97, 356–357); 2.14.5 (Rousseau-Doutreleau 1982, 136–139); Tertullian, *Presc.* 41.1, 43.3.
80   Irenaeus, *Haer.* 2.30.1 (Rousseau-Doutreleau 1982, 300–303).
81   Cf. Irenaeus, *Haer.* 4.38.4 (Rousseau et al. 1965, 956–960).
82   Irenaeus, *Haer.* 1.3.6, 1.9.4, 1.19.1–2, 1.20.2 (Rousseau and Doutreleau 1979, 60–63, 146–151, 284–289, 290–293); 3.6.5; 3.7.1–2. On gnostic use of John, see Irenaeus, *Haer.* 3.11.1 (Rousseau and Doutreleau 1974, 138–142); 4.41.1–3 (Rousseau et al. 1965, 982–992). On the use and interpretation of John 8:44 in gnostic literature, see DeConick 2013c; 2013d. On gnosticism and John more generally see, Pagels 1973; Hill 2004, 172–293; Turner 2005; Rasimus 2010. On gnostic use of Paul, see Pagels 1975.
83   Irenaeus, *Haer.* 1.1.3 (Rousseau-Doutreleau 1979, 32–35).
84   Irenaeus, *Haer.* 1.20.1 (Rousseau-Doutreleau 1979, 288–289); 3.11.9 (Rousseau-Doutreleau 1974, 170–176).
85   Irenaeus, *Haer.* 1.4.3, 1.21.3–4 (Rousseau-Doutreleau 1979, 68–69, 298–303); 3.15.2 (Rousseau-Doutreleau 1974, 278–282); Ps.-Hippolytus, *Haer.* 1.pref.2–5 (Marcovich 1986, 54–55).
86   Irenaeus, *Haer.* 4.33.3 (Rousseau et al. 1965, 808–10). Cf. Justin Martyr, *1 Apology* 1.26.7; Irenaeus, *Haer.* 1.21.1–3 (Rousseau-Doutreleau 1979, 294–303); Ps.-Hippolytus, *Haer.* 6.41.2–5 (Marcovich 1986, 258–259).

the fact that the liturgies and ceremonies were cued into a different hermeneutic. So Valentinians might confess the same creed as a Catholic, "There is one God the Father and everything comes from him, the Lord Jesus Christ." But the meaning they took from it was different. They were not confessing the Father God to be YHWH. Rather they were confessing the Father God to be the transcendent God.[87]

Prior to its emergence, there was nothing like the extreme gnostic orientation that empowered the individual and subverted religion's traditional purpose to serve the gods. Before gnostic spirituality surfaced, the religions in the Mediterranean basin conceived the human being and God to be vastly different, both in terms of substance and power. These traditional religions understood the human being as a mortal creature made by a powerful god for the sole purpose of obediently serving the god and his appointed king as slaves and vassals. This submissive orientation, what I call *servant spirituality*, clearly is foundational to the assumptions fostered by the Apostolic Catholics about the God YHWH, the scripture, worship, and the nature of the human being.[88]

To the contrary, gnostic spirituality spotlighted the perspective that human beings are more than mortal creatures fashioned by a god to do his bidding. The human being is perceived to be bigger and more powerful than the conventional gods, substantially connected to a divine source that transcends creation.

Gnostic movements and religions that were forged out of this new metaphysical orientation focused on the revival of the divinity that lives at the center of the human being. They conceived this revival as a therapeutic ritual journey of integration, a transpersonal journey to spiritual wholeness. They reoriented the focus of religion from the welfare of the gods to the health and well-being of humans who were not to submit to the gods of this world, but vanquish them.

Gnostic spirituality was not innocuous. Its countercultural program reformatted conventional religions in ways that many traditionalists felt would lead to civil disorder, unrest, and damnation. Yet its call for the liberation of humanity from the tyranny of the gods and their kings did not result in military coups and bloodshed. Gnosticism did not emerge out of political revolt nor did it encourage it.[89]

---

87   Irenaeus, *Haer.* 4.33.3 (Rousseau et al. 1965, 808–810).
88   For a thorough discussion of *servant spirituality*, see DeConick 2016a.
89   Several possibilities for the political origins of gnosticism have been published: unrest in first-century Palestine and Syria (Rudolph 1987, 282–292); Jewish revolt 66–74 CE (Grant 1966, 33–37, 118); unrest from 70–135 CE (Dahl 1980–1981 689–712); Roman suppression of Jews in Egypt 115–117 CE (C. Smith 2004); Bar Kokhba Revolt (Yamauchi 1978,

Rather gnosticism emerges from the life experiences of people who were oppressed but who had no hope for political advantage. Roman colonialism and imperialism had left them despondent and demoralized. Facing brutal oppression on a daily basis, they began to question the value of their religious upbringing, which taught them to submit to the will of the king as the representative of the gods, to suffer divine retribution for their sins, and to endure the fate the gods had cast for them. For some people this was not good enough. These are the people who began searching for truth outside the normal channels. These are the people who were the first gnostics.

This countercultural spirituality was attractive to many ancient people who had never heard anything like it before. It was not long before gnostic spirituality went viral, engaging the conventional religions in ways that turned them inside out. This new spirituality migrated into Greco-Egyptian circles of the Hermetics and the Jewish circles of the Sethians. It moved through Palestine, Samaria, and Asia Minor where it interfaced with emergent Christianity in the letters of Paul and the Gospel of John. By the second century, a variety of gnostic thinkers had interacted with Pythagorean and Platonic philosophy, ancient medical knowledge, as well as the craft of ancient astrology and magic. The result of this religious interchange is the emergence of a large number of unique gnostic grassroots religious movements with wildly networked mythologies, doctrinal systems, and ceremonies.

The relationship between gnostics and conventional religions was tenuous at best. Because of this, gnostics ended up developing reform and separatist movements at the margins of the conventional religions, where they critiqued conventional thought and worship. More often than not, gnostics found themselves beyond the borders of their ancestral religions. Because of this, many gnostic leaders choose to start their own religions altogether, rather than try to reform an existing tradition. One size did not fit all.

Gnostics heavily critiqued claims to authority that traced religious legitimacy to the traditional gods or their human representatives or their scriptures. For the gnostic, authority lay within the heart of each person, and revelation was its succor. This fostered hostile relationships with those people who honored traditional wisdom. The Apostolic Catholic reactions to gnostic spirituality and the movements and religions it generated were disparaging and dangerous. Gnostic transgression galvanized people of the traditional faiths, who sought to control the fall out by sanctioning the gnostics with humiliation, shame, violence, intolerance and accusations of heresy.

---

169–174; Wilson 1995, 206; Segal 1977, 262–265); disaffected Jewish intellectuals (Pearson 1997, 120); alienated Egyptian Jews in first century CE (Green 1985).

## 7     New Age Gnostics

For years, I have been aware of an uncanny similarity between the gnostic movements in antiquity and esoteric movements in our own time, often superficially categorized as the New Age.[90] Both cultivate a form of spirituality that is aggressively countercultural and highly critical of conventionally organized religions. They revel in exposing the errors of conventional religions, religions which they believe to be ineffective. At the center of their transgression is their disapproval of talk-religion, religion that tries to codify God or intellectualize spirituality. For ancient gnostics and modern New Agers, the heart of religion is the subjective experience of the individual meeting a transcendent or transpersonal Reality who is the Source of all existence. Religion is about the God-experience, not God-talk. And so the contemporary spiritual leader Eckhart Tolle says when explaining what God really is, "It's not what you think it is! You can't think about presence, and the mind can't understand it. Understanding presence is *being* present."[91]

Both past and present movements have at their center a transcendent or transpersonal Reality believed to be the Source of our existence. All reality derives from this Source, including us. So this divinity is present within the human being and is recognized as the person's true self. Religion is marketed as a quest for wholeness or, in New Age terms, holism. The way to achieve this transpersonal spiritual integration is envisioned as some kind of sacred psychological therapy, with high-octane contemplation and ritual magic in the mix.

The religions that emerge out of this type of spiritual orientation are vibrantly pluralistic, engaging a wide swath of religious currents, alternative science, magical thinking, and stargazing. Revelation and prophecy are central, providing leaders with authority and legitimacy, and new knowledge to package and market.

Historians are reluctant to make anything out of these types of coincidences because of the long span of time between past and present and the clear lack of historical cause and effect. Without a gnostic church surviving from the ancient times into modern America, the linear track of historical development between the old gnostics and the modern New Agers is reduced to nonsense.

---

90    For overviews of the New Age and its characteristics, see Hanegraaff 1998; Roof 1999; Versluis 2014. Cf. Campbell 1972; Bloom 1996.
91    Tolle 1999, 93.

And yet the similarities are too close to leave to coincidence.[92] Something is going on here, and it begs explanation.

Certainly there are a number of factors at work, including sociological comparatives. Both gnostic and New Age movements arose during historical periods when there was a rapid breakdown of traditional institutions and structures. In antiquity, we had the brutal imperialism of Rome, which advanced the collapse of native cultures and aroused enmity toward the dominant political regime. Likewise, in the 1960s the American romance with traditional politics and cultural structures disintegrated and left a vacuum where countercultural movements could make headway.

It is equally true that in both past and present, there was increased interaction between native and non-native cultures. This expansion in cultural knowledge created a pluralistic environment where eclecticism and inclusiveness allowed for innovation in the realms of spirituality and religion. The ancient Mediterranean world at this time was undergoing internationalization previously unknown due to the increased traffic of merchants, tourists and new residents on Roman built roads, along the Silk Highway, and over the seas. The 1970s witnessed something similar, when there was an explosion of the Asian into America, as well as an explosion into outer space. With our race to the moon, the options for truth expanded to the point that they became alien.

So both eras, the first century CE and the twentieth century CE were the right moments for countercultural religious movements to emerge and take hold. Yet we cannot reduce the similarities to the fact that the countercultural milieu or conditions were spot-on.[93] While the conditions were right, we have to turn elsewhere to explain the meeting of the minds.

## 8  Gnostic Artifacts Left Behind

The solution lies in understanding gnosticism as an emergent religious orientation, an innovative form of spirituality, a new way of being religious that persisted outside conventional religious structures while engaging them in disruptive ways. So where does gnostic spirituality survive physically, if not within its own institutions? Quite simply, it is embedded in the literature our ancestors wrote and the cultural artifacts that they created both as expressions of gnostic spirituality and as attacks to suppress it. Artifacts like literature do not

---

[92]  Similarities between gnostic thought and modern American religion have been noted by others. See Bloom 1992, 1996; Smoley 2006; Burfeind 2014.

[93]  Cf. Kaler 2009.

require a church to pass on a tradition from one generation to the next in an historical chain of transmission. All they require is people at any given time in any given location to pick up the book and read it for themselves. The connection to gnostic spirituality is directly made from text to readers. Time and location are irrelevant. The ancient text speaks directly to its readers, whenever and wherever they are.

In terms of literature that has been accessible to the western world since antiquity, we should mention the great gnostic opponents like Irenaeus, Tertullian, and Augustine. Their writings have been "good reads" for Christians over the centuries. While believing that they were soldiering against the spread of gnosticism, these authors probably never realized that their attacks only preserved gnosticism and redistributed gnostic spirituality into the religious buffer and our communal consciousness every time their condemnations were picked up and reread.

The other texts to mention are the Gospel of John and the letters of Paul. To suppress their gnostic sensibilities and domesticate the texts, the leaders of the Catholic Church imposed strict orthodox interpretations on them. These interpretations were marketed successfully as the *natural* way to read John and Paul. This successful reinterpretation of the texts allowed the leaders of the Catholic Church to canonize the Gospel of John and the letters of Paul within the New Testament. Yet, because the interpretation is the only thing controlling the gnostic spirituality embedded with these texts, the Gospel of John and the letters of Paul are Trojan horses. They await readers who either do not know or do not care about the orthodox interpretation. When these readers engage John or Paul, the door in the Trojan horse opens up and they are confronted with gnostic spirituality head on.

While this brief essay is not the place to map the complex movement of gnostic spirituality from antiquity to the present, explicit gnostic awakenings have taken place, at points when actual literature written by gnostics has resurfaced. These accidents of history have reengaged gnosticism in very public and profound ways. These awakenings have been instrumental in the survival of gnostic spirituality and its ever-widening distribution, as it has been reframed over and over again to meet the needs and interests of new generations of religious people.

There are four major gnostic awakenings that we can mention. The first gnostic awakening probably took place in the medieval period, evident with the emergence of the groups we know of as the Paulicians, Bogomils and Cathars. Although very little, if any, of their literature has survived to impact future generations, legends about them certainly have played heavily into the modern gnostic consciousness. The second gnostic awakening took place in the late fifteenth century when the *Corpus Hermeticum* was translated and became a reservoir for new generations of people to reengage gnosticism in its most cosmic-friendly guise. The third gnostic awakening occurred in the nineteenth century as the result of the recovery of two old gnostic books known as the Bruce and Askew codices, inspiring figures like Helena P. Blavatsky and Carl Jung. The fourth gnostic awakening began in the mid-twentieth century. It was the result of the remarkable accidental finds of several hoards of gnostic texts, including the Nag Hammadi collection, the Berlin and Tchacos codices, and the ongoing flood of Manichaean materials. This renaissance helped build up New Age movements on the old gnostic frame, which has been bent or broken open to accommodate modern sensibilities like Darwinism, environmentalism, and our race into space.

## 9   The Revelatory Milieu

When it comes to the survival of gnostic spirituality, past, present and future, another factor is in constant play. It is a factor that most modern people, scholars included, are uncomfortable discussing because it is irrational. Yet it has happened and still happens and will happen over and over again. It is rapture. The spontaneous religious experience. The sudden overwhelming revelation. The ecstatic encounter with transcendence, with Ultimate Reality, with what the gnostic understands to be the God beyond all gods. Such rapture can be routinized through particular religious rituals and practices, as gnostics did, so that the ecstatic experience of the God beyond all gods is the living source of the gnostic current. Whether we can or ever will be able to explain it, experiences of ecstasy and the transcendence of the self is what continually births gnostic spirituality.

The ecstatic experience of an all-encompassing transcendent Reality prompted many ancient gnostics to seek religious truth beyond their ancestral and regional religions. Because their profound religious experiences did not align with the conventional religions of servitude to powerful capricious gods, they cast traditional religion aside. The gods and religions of the world, they came to believe, were false attempts to capture what cannot be captured, the Reality that is the Source of our being.

In today's global environment, this transtheistic perspective may provide a new solution to religious intolerance and exclusivism. Rather than indulging in the perennialist view that all religions are expressions of the same God, which leaves us with no ability to compare the truth claims of various religions, the transtheistic perspective encourages critique of religions as human constructions. Perhaps Mani said it best when he called all religions false because their organizers were unable to truly capture the God who had been revealed to them through prophets like Moses, Zoroaster, and Jesus.

The survival of gnostic spirituality is linked to this revelatory milieu, when the visions of true religion generated from ecstasy and experiences of self-transcendence give birth to new scriptures as well as new hermeneutics for understanding the old scriptures. Gnostic spirituality survives then in the artifacts left behind. It lives in the gnostic writings themselves, buried in tombs and brought to light by accidents of history. It inhabits the Hermetic literature, exposed with each new renaissance. But it also lies beneath the vehement words of the writings of the Apostolic Catholic leaders, waiting to be resurrected every time they are read. It hides in the letters of Paul and the Gospel of John, which are Trojan horses. While these scriptures are part of the Christian canon, they are also easily drawn upon by people who do not take from them the same meaning as Catholic Christians. It is waiting to be rebuilt by new generations who read the same passages in Genesis and the New Testament gospels, and the same sentences in Plato, and, like the first gnostics, wonder how their own ecstatic and transcendent experiences of the self and God fit into it all. It is the reason that, since the first century, there have always been gnostics among us.

## Bibliography

Barclay, John M.G. 1995. "Deviance and Apostasy: Some Applications of Deviance Theory to First-Century Judaism and Christianity." Pages 114–127 in *Modelling Early Christianity*. Edited by Philip Esler. London: Routledge.

Bauer, Walter. 1971 [1934]. *Orthodoxy and Heresy in Earliest Christianity*. Edited by Robert Kraft and Gerhard Krobel. Philadelphia: Fortress Press.

Becker, Howard. 1963. *Outsiders: Studies in the Sociology of Deviance*. New York: Free Press.

BeDuhn, Jason David. 2015. "Mani and the Crystallization of the Concept of 'Religion' in Third Century Iran." Pages 247–275 in *Mani at the Court of the Persian Kings: Studies on the Chester Beatty Kephalaia Codex*. Edited by Iain Gardner, Jason DeBuhn, and Paul Dilley. Nag Hammadi and Manichaean Studies 87. Leiden: Brill.

Bloom, Harold. 1992. *The American Religion: The Emergence of the Post-Christian Nation*. New York: Simon & Schuster.

Bloom, Harold. 1996. *Omens of Millennium: The Gnosis of Angels, Dreams, and Resurrection*. New York: Riverhead Books.

Bock, Darrell L. 2006. *The Missing Gospels: Unearthing the Truth Behind Alternative Christianities*. Nashville: Nelson.

Boulluec, Alain Le. 1985. *La notion d'hérésie dans la literature grecque II–III siècles*. 2 volumes. Paris: Etudes Augustiniennes.

Boulluec, Alain Le. 2000. "Orthodoxie et hérésie aux premiers siècles dans l'historiographie récente." Pages 303–319 in *Orthodoxie, Christianisme, histoire*. Edited by Susana Elm, Eric Rebillard, and Antonella Romano. Rome: École Française de Rome.

Burfeind, Peter M. 2014. *Gnostic America: A Reading of Contemporary American Culture and Religion According to Christianity's Oldest Heresy*. Pax Domini Press.

Cameron, Averil. 2005. "How to Read Heresiology." Pages 192–212 in *The Cultural Turn in Late Antique Studies: Gender, Asceticism, and Historiography*. Durham, NC: Duke University Press.

Campbell, Colin. 1972. "The Cult, the Cultic Milieu and Secularization." Pages 119–136 in *A Sociological Yearbook of Religion in Britain* 5. London.

Clarke, Edward J. 7th edition, 2008. *Deviant Behavior: A Text-Reader in the Sociology of Deviance*. New York: Worth Publishers.

Clinard, Marshall B., and Robert F. Meier. 2008 (13th edition). *Sociology of Deviant Behavior*. Belmont, CA: Thomson Wadsworth.

Curra, John. 2000. *The Relativity of Deviance*. Thousand Oaks, CA: Sage Publications.

Dahl, Nils. 1980–1981. "The Arrogant Archon and the Lewd Sophia: Jewish Traditions in gnostic Revolt." Pages 689–712 in *The Rediscovery of gnosticism: Proceedings of the International Conference on gnosticism at Yale, New Haven, Connecticut, March 28–31, 1978*. Edited by Bentley Layton. Volume 2. SHR 41. Leiden: Brill.

Davies, Christie. 1982. "Sexual Taboos and Social Boundaries." Pages 1032–63 in *American Journal of Sociology* 87.

DeConick, April D. 2013a. "Crafting Gnosis: Gnostic Spirituality in the Ancient New Age." Pages 285–305 in *Gnosticism, Platonism and the Late Ancient World: Essays in Honour of John D. Turner*. Nag Hammadi and Manichaean Studies 82. Edited by Kevin Corrigan and Tuomas Rasimus. Leiden: Brill.

DeConick, April D. 2013b. "Gnostic Spirituality at the Crossroads of Christianity: Transgressing Boundaries and Creating Orthodoxy." Pages 148–184 in *Beyond the gnostic Gospels: Studies Building on the Work of Elaine Pagels*. Edited by Eduard Iricinschi, Lance Jenott, Nicola Denzey Lewis and Philippa Townsend. Studien und Texte zu Antike und Christentum 82. Tübingen: Mohr Siebeck.

DeConick, April D. 2013c. "Why are the Heavens Closed? Johannine Revelation of the Father in the Catholic-Gnostic Debate." Pages 147–179 in *John's Gospel and Intimations of Apocalyptic Thought*. Edited by Christopher Rowland and Catrin H. Williams. London: T&T Clark.

DeConick, April D. 2013d. "Who is Hiding in the Gospel of John? Reconceptualizing Johannine Theology and the Roots of Gnosticism." Pages 13–29 in *Histories of the Hidden God: Concealment and Revelation in Western Gnostic, Esoteric, and Mystical Traditions*. Edited by April D. DeConick and Grant Adamson. London: Acumen.

DeConick, April D. 2016a. *The Gnostic New Age: How a Countercultural Spirituality Revolutioned Religion from Antiquity to Today*. New York: Columbia University Press.

DeConick, April D. 2016b. "Secret Religion: The Challenge from the Margins." Pages 93–105 in *Religion: Sources, Perspectives, and Methodologies*. Edited by Jeffrey J. Kripal. MacMillan Interdisciplinary Handbooks on Religion. New York: MacMillan.

Denzey Lewis, Nicola. 2013. *Introduction to "Gnosticism": Ancient Voices, Christian Worlds*. New York: Oxford University Press.

Dillon, John M. 1977. *The Middle Platonists: A Study of Platonism 80 BC to AD 220*. London: Duckworth.

Douglas, Mary. 1973. *Natural Symbols*. New York: Penguin.

Erikson, Kai T. 1966. *Wayward Puritans: A Study in the Sociology of Deviance*. New York: Wiley.

Fauconnier, Gilles and Mark Turner. 2002. *The Way We Think: Conceptual Blending and the Mind's Hidden Complexities*. New York: Basic Books.

Franzese, Robert J. 2009. *The Sociology of Deviance: Differences, Tradition, and Stigma*. Springfield, IL: Charles C. Thomas.

Gärtner, Bertil. 1961. *The Theology of the Gospel of Thomas*. Translated by Eric J. Sharpe. London: Collins.

Grant, Robert M. 1966, revised edition. *Gnosticism and Early Christianity*. New York: Harper & Row.

Grant, Robert, and David Noel Freedman. 1960. *The Secret Sayings of Jesus: The gnostic movement which challenged Christianity and its 'Gospel of Thomas' recently discovered in Egypt*. New York: Doubleday.

Green, Henry A. 1985. *The Economic and Social Origins of Gnosticism*. SBL Dissertation Series 77. Atlanta: Scholars Press.

Greenberg, David F. 1988. *The Construction of Homosexuality*. Chicago: University of Chicago Press.

Hanegraaff, Wouter J. 1997. *New Age Religion and Western Culture: Esotericism in the Mirror of Secular Thought*. Albany: State University of New York Press.

Harnack, Adolf von. 1961 [1885]. *History of Dogma*. Vol. 1. Translated from the 3rd German ed. by Neil Buchanan. New York: Dover Publications.

Henderson, John B. 1998. *The Construction of Orthodoxy and Heresy: Neo-Confucian, Islamic, Jewish, and Early Christian Patterns*. Albany: State University of New York Press.

Hill, Charles E. 2004. *The Johannine Corpus in the Early Church*. Oxford: Oxford University Press.

Iricinschi, Eduard, and Holger M. Zellentin, eds. 2008. *Heresy and Identity in Late Antiquity*. Texts and Studies in Ancient Judaism 119. Tübingen: Mohr Siebeck.

Kaler, Michael. 2009. "Cultic Milieu, Nag Hammadi Collectors and Gnosticism." Pages 427–444 in *Studies in Religion* 38.

Keniston, Kenneth. 1960. *The Uncommitted: Alienated Youth in American Society*. New York: Harcourt, Brace and World.

Keniston, Kenneth. 1968. *Young Radicals: Notes on Committed Youth*. New York: Harcourt, Brace and World.

King, Karen L. 2003. *What is Gnosticism?* Cambridge: Harvard University Press.

King, Karen L. 2008. "Social and Theological Effects of Heresiological Discourse." Pages 28–49 in *Heresy and Identity in Late Antiquity*. Edited by Eduard Iricinschi and Holger M. Zellentin. Texts and Studies in Ancient Judaism 119. Tübingen: Mohr Siebeck.

Kroymann, A., ed. 1954. *Tertulliani Opera, Pars II: Opera Montanistica*. Corpus Christianorum: Series Latina 2. Turnhaut: Brepols.

Lahe, Jaan. 2012. *Gnosis und Judentum: Alttestamentliche und jüdische Motive in der gnostichen Literatur und das Ursprungsproblem der Gnosis*. Nag Hammadi and Manichaean Studies 75. Leiden: Brill.

Layton, Bentley. 1995. "Prolegomena to the Study of Ancient Gnosticism." Pages 334–350 in *The Social World of the First Christians: Essays in Honor of Wayne A. Meeks*. Edited by L.M. White and O.L. Yarbrough. Minneapolis: Augsburg Fortress.

Lehtipuu, Outi. 2014. "Who Has the Right to Be Called A Christian? Deviance and Christian Identity in Tertullian's *On the Prescription of Heretics*." Pages 80–98 in *Methods, Theories, Imagination: Social Scientific Approaches in Biblical Studies*. Edited by David J. Chalcraft, Frauke Uhlenbruch, and Rebecca S. Watson. Sheffield: Sheffield Phoenix.

Lupieri, Edmondo. 2002. *The Mandaeans: The Last Gnostics*. Grand Rapids: Eerdmans.

Malina, Bruce J., and Jerome H. Neyrey. 1991. "Conflict in Luke-Acts: Labelling and Deviance Theory." Pages 97–122 in *The Social World of Luke-Acts: Models for Interpretation*. Edited by Jerome H. Neyrey. Peabody, MA: Hendrickson Publishers.

Marcovich, Miroslav, ed. 1986. *Hippolytus Refutatio Omnium Haeresium*. Patristische Texte und Studien 25. Berlin: de Gruyter.

Markschies, Christoph. 2003. *Gnosis: An Introduction*. Translated by John Bowden. London: T&T Clark.

McWilliams, Peter. 1993. *Ain't Nobody's Business If You Do*. Los Angeles: Prelude Press.

Musgrove, Frank. 1974. *Ecstasy and Holiness: Counter Culture and the Open Society*. Bloomington: Indiana University Press.

Nock, Arthur Darby. 1964. "Gnosticism." Pages 255–279 in *Harvard Theological Review* 57.

Pagels, Elaine. 1973. *The Johannine Gospel in Gnostic Exegesis: Heracleon's Commentary on John*. Nashville and New York: Abingdon Press.

Pagels, Elaine. 1975. *The Gnostic Paul: Gnostic Exegesis of the Pauline Letters*. Philadelphia: Fortress Press.

Pagels, Elaine. 1979. *The Gnostic Gospels*. New York: Vintage Books.

Pearson, Birger A. 1997. *The Emergence of the Christian Religion*. Harrisburg: Trinity Press International.

Pietersen, Lloyd K. 1997. "Despicable Deviants: Labelling Theory and the Polemic of the Pastorals." Pages 343–352 in *Sociology of Religion* 58.

Pietersen, Lloyd K. 2004. *The Polemic of the Pastorals: A Sociological Examination of the Development of Pauline Christianity*. Journal for the Study of the New Testament Supplement 264. London: T&T Clark.

Roig Lanzillotta, Lautaro. 2007. "The Early Christians and Human Sacrifice." Pages 81–102 in *The Strange World of Human Sacrifice*. Edited by Jan Bremmer. Leuven: Peeters.

Roig Lanzillotta, Lautaro. 2013. "A Way of Salvation: Becoming Like God in Nag Hammadi." Pages 71–102 in *Numen* 60.

Roof, Wade Clark. 1993. *A Generation of Seekers: The Spiritual Journeys of the Baby Boom Generation*. San Francisco: HarperSanFrancisco.

Roof, Wade Clark. 1999. *Spiritual Marketplace: Baby Boomers and the Remaking of American Religion*. Princeton: Princeton University Press.

Roszak, Theodore. 1968. *The Making of a Counter Culture*. Berkeley: University of California Press.

Rousseau, Adelin, Bertrand Hemmerdinger, Louis Doutreleau, and Charles Mercier, eds. 1965. *Irénée de Lyon, Contre les hérésies, livre IV*. Volume 2. Sources Chrétiennes 100. Paris: Cerf.

Rousseau, Adelin, Louis Doutreleau, and Charles Mercier, eds. 1969. *Irénée de Lyon, Contre les hérésies, livre V*. Volume 2. Sources Chrétiennes 153. Paris: Cerf.

Rousseau, Adelin, and Louis Doutreleau, eds. 1974. *Irénée de Lyon, Contre les hérésies, livre III*. Volume 2. Sources Chrétiennes 211. Paris: Cerf.

Rousseau, Adelin, and Louis Doutreleau, eds. 1979. *Irénée de Lyon. Contre les Hérésies Livre I*. Volume 2. Paris: Les Éditions du Cerf.

Rousseau, Adelin, and Louis Doutreleau, eds. 1982. *Irénée de Lyon. Contre les Hérésies Livre 2*. Volume 2. Paris: Les Éditions du Cerf.

Royalty, Robert M. 2012. *The Origin of Heresy: A History of Discourse in Second Temple Judaism and Early Christianity*. London: Routledge.

Rudolph, Kurt. 1987. *Gnosis: The Nature and History of Gnosticism.* San Francisco: HarperOne.

Schur, E.M. 1971. *Labelling Deviant Behavior: Its Sociological Implications.* New York: Harper & Row.

Schur, E.M. 1980. *The Politics of Deviance: Stigma, Contests and the Uses of Power.* Englewood Cliffs, NJ: Prentice-Hall.

Segal, Alan F. 1977. *Two Powers in Heaven: Early Rabbinic Reports about Christianity and Gnosticism.* Studies in Judaism in Late Antiquity 25. Leiden: Brill.

Smith, Carl A. 2004. *No Longer Jews: The Search for Gnostic Origins.* Peabody: Hendrickson Publishers.

Smith, Geoffrey S. 2015. *Guilt by Association: Heresy Catalogues in Early Christianity.* Oxford: Oxford University Press.

Smith, Morton. 1981. "The History of the Term Gnostikos." Pages 796–807 in *The Rediscovery of Gnosticism: Proceedings of the Conference at Yale March 1978.* Volume 2: *Sethian Gnosticism.* Studies in the History of Religions 49. Edited by Bentley Layton. Leiden: Brill.

Smoley, Richard. 2006. *Forbidden Faith: The Secret History of Gnosticism.* San Francisco: HarperSanFrancisco.

Stählin, Otto. 1960. *Clemens Alexandrinus.* Stromata I-VI. Berlin: Akademie-Verlag.

Still, Todd D. 1999. *Conflict at Thessalonica: A Pauline Church and its Neighbors.* Journal for the Study of the New Testament Supplement 183. Sheffield: Sheffield Academic Press.

Tolle, Eckhart. 1999. *The Power of Now: A Guide to Spiritual Enlightenment.* Novato, CA: New World Library and Vancouver: Namaste Publishing.

Versluis, Arthur. 2014. *American Gurus: From Transcendentalism to New Age Religion.* Oxford: Oxford University Press.

Westhues, Kenneth. 1972. *Society's Shadow: Studies in the Sociology of Counter Cultures.* Toronto: McGraw-Hill Ryerson.

Whittaker, John. 1969. "Epekeina nou kai ousias." Pages 91–104 in *Vigiliae Christianae* 23.

Williams, Michael Allen. 1985. *The Immovable Race: A Gnostic Designation and the Theme of Stability in Late Antiquity.* Nag Hammadi Studies 29. Leiden: Brill.

Williams, Michael Allen. 1996. *Rethinking Gnosticism: Arguments for Dismantling a Dubious Category.* Princeton: Princeton University Press.

Wilson, Stephen G. 1995. *Related Strangers: Jews and Christians 70–170 C.E.* Minneapolis: Fortress Press.

Wisse, F. 1971. "The Nag Hammadi Library and the Heresiologists." Pages 205–223 in *Vigiliae Christianae* 25.

Witherington, Ben, III. 2004. *The Gospel Code: Novel Claims About Jesus, Mary Magdalene, and Da Vinci*. Downers Grove, IL: InterVarsity Press.

Yamauchi, Edwin. 1978. "The Descent of Ishtar, the Fall of Sophia, and the Jewish Roots of Gnosticism." *Tyndale Bulletin* 29: 169–174.

Yinger, J. Milton. 1982. *Countercultures: The Promise and the Peril of a World Turned Upside Down*. New York: The Free Press.

# "I Turned away from the Temple":
# Sethian Counterculture in the Apocryphon of John

*Grant Adamson*
Rice University
*grantadamson1@gmail.com*

## 1   The Johannine Frame Story

The authors of the Apocryphon of John and its related Sethian texts were often involved in conflict with others.[1] This definitely included Christians such as Irenaeus and Origen as well as pagans such as Celsus and Plotinus in the second and third centuries: we have their exposés and critiques of Sethianism.[2] We also likely have a critique of Sethian demiurgic myth in the Valentinian Ptolemy's *Letter to Flora*.[3] Furthermore the conflict must have included Jews despite the lack of any exposé in Jewish literature.[4]

It is with a pseudepigraphical narrativization of such strife that the apocryphon opens. The setting is not the second or third century but the first. John is at the temple in Jerusalem where one of his fellow Jews tells him that his dead master led him into apostasy:

---

1   Sethians, Ophites, classic gnostics: e.g. Schenke 1974; 1981; Stroumsa 1984; B. Layton 1995; Turner 2001; Logan 2006; Rasimus 2009; Brakke 2010; Burns 2014. For a history of the Sethians and their literature in "six phases" and "three distinct but not necessarily mutually exclusive socio-historical religious contexts," namely Judaism, Christianity, and Middle- and Neo-Platonism, see Turner 2001, 255–301. These can be supplemented with a Greco-Egyptian and Hermetic context of early Sethianism: Adamson 2013a; 2013b. Ap. John is the principal treatise in Sethian literature and in the so-called Coptic gnostic codices as a whole, there being one manuscript each in Nag Hammadi codex II, III, and IV, and another in the Berlin codex—that is more than any other text in the codices. Synoptic edition of the four manuscripts: Waldstein and Wisse 1995. Major published studies of the apocryphon: Giversen 1963; Tardieu 1984; Logan 1996; Pleše 2006; King 2006; Luttikhuizen 2006; Barc and Funk 2012.
2   The go-to passages and texts are Irenaeus, *Haer.* 1.29–31; Origen, *Cels.* 6.21–40; and Plotinus, *Enn.* II.9.
3   *Apud* Epiphanius, *Pan.* 33.3–7.
4   E.g. Pleše 2006, 219–221. For the larger issue of early rabbinic reports about 'two powers' in heaven, see Segal 2002/1977. Among Segal's conclusions (2002/1977, 262): "the key factor in separating radical gnosticism from earlier exegesis is the negative portrayal of the demiurge." See also Dahl 1981.

| NHC III | BG | NHC II/IV |
|---|---|---|
| ... did ... | With deception did this Nazarene deceive you, | [With deception did this Nazarene] deceive you, |
| deceive you ... | | |
| your ... he closed [your hearts], | and he filled your ears with [lies], and closed [your hearts and] | and he filled [your ears with lies], and closed [your hearts and] |
| he turned you away from the [trad]itions of your fathers (ⲁϥⲕⲧⲉⲧⲏⲟⲩⲧⲛ̅ ⲉⲃⲟⲗ ⲛ̅[ⲙ̅ⲡⲁⲣⲁ]ⲇⲟⲥⲓⲥ ⲛ̅ⲛⲉⲧⲛ̅ⲉⲓⲟⲧⲉ). | turned you [away from] the traditions of your [fathers] (ⲁϥⲕⲧⲉ ⲧⲏⲩⲧⲛ̅ ⲉⲃ[ⲟⲗ ϩⲛ̅] ⲙⲡⲁⲣⲁⲇⲟⲥⲓⲥ ⲛ̅ⲛⲉⲧⲛ̅ⲉⲓ[ⲟⲧ]ⲉ). | turned you] away from the traditions [of your fathers] ([ⲁϥⲕⲧⲱⲧⲛ ⲉ]ⲃⲟⲗ ⲛ̅ⲙ̅ⲡⲁⲣⲁⲇ[ⲟⲥⲓⲥ ⲛⲛⲉⲧⲛⲉⲓⲟⲧⲉ]).[5] |

John's Jewish antagonist here could easily represent multiple groups of Sethian opponents.[6] What is more important than the precise identity of the opponents is that the authors of the apocryphon did not deny that they turned away from the traditions of their fathers. Instead their response to the charge of apostasy was that those traditions were wrong to begin with, going all the way back to the Genesis creation accounts.

So in the frame story, John abandons the house of 'God' to hear the Savior repeatedly say that Moses was mistaken:

---

5   Ap. John NHC III,1 1.12–15 / BG 2 19.17–20.3 / NHC II,1 1.13–17 (Waldstein and Wisse 1995, 12–15; translation modified). Passage not extant in NHC IV,1.

6   In Tardieu's commentary 1984, 31, 38, the design of the apocryphon is "fondamentalement antijuif," and the opponents are "à la fois les judéochrétiens et les chrétiens." John's Jewish antagonist is supposed to be a Pharisee. His name, Arimanias, could also have pagan significance: the 'evil spirit' in Greco-Roman conceptions of Zoroastrianism; see e.g. Giverson 1963, 152–153. This seems more likely to me than the idea in Barc and Funk 2012, 184, that the name refers to Joseph of Arimathea.

| NHC III | BG | NHC II/IV |
|---|---|---|
| And [when] I heard these things, I turned away from the temple (ⲁⲉⲓⲕⲟⲧ ⲉⲃⲟⲗ [ⲙⲡϩⲓ]ⲉⲣⲟⲛ) to a mountain ... place ... | When I heard these things, I turned away from the temple (ⲁⲓⲕⲟⲧ ⲉⲃⲟⲗ ϩⲙ ⲫⲓⲉⲣⲟⲛ) to the mountain, a desert place. | [When] I, [John], heard these things, [I turned] away from the temple ([ⲁⲓⲕⲱⲧⲉ] ⲉⲃ[ⲟ]ⲗ ϩⲙ̄ ⲡⲉⲣⲡ[ⲉ]) [to a mountainous and desert place].[7] |

The Savior appearing next in the Johannine frame story is not the Jesus of the Gospel of Mark who says that Moses was necessarily lenient in legislation.[8] Nor is this the Jesus of the Gospel of Matthew who says that as a new Moses he has come to fulfill the law by intensifying its ethical demands.[9] Much less is this the Jesus of the Gospel of Luke or the Gospel of John who says that Moses wrote about him.[10] Rather the Savior contradicts Moses over and over.[11]

---

7  Ap. John NHC III,1 1.16–17 / BG 2 20.4–6 / NHC II,1 1.17–19 (Waldstein and Wisse 1995, 14–15). Passage not extant in NHC IV,1.

8  Mark 10.2–9.

9  Matt 5.17–20. King 2006, 239–240, argues: "In its revisionary mode, the *Secret Revelation of John* fits solidly within the Christian hermeneutical project. ... If we moderns should feel the audacity of this sweeping cultural project more fiercely in the pages of the *Secret Revelation of John* than we do with Paul or the *Gospel of Matthew*, that is only because the latter's historical success has domesticated their boldness." But neither Paul nor Matthew ever vilified the biblical creator. And King 2006, 241 goes on to recognize: "Certainly its ridicule of the God of *Genesis* as an arrogant and ignorant pretender strikes at the core of Jewish piety. ... [I]t is impossible to gainsay the willingness, even gleefulness, of the *Secret Revelation of John*'s ridicule of the most cherished beliefs of Jews. Surely this must be evidence of some kind of real animosity." I think the bitterness would have been towards most Christians also given that they too believed in and worshipped the God of Genesis.

10 Luke 24.27, 44; John 1.44; 5.39–47. Pleše 2006, 8–9, 17, highlights Luke 24.13–53 as the "ultimate source" or "model for the Gnostic type of paradosis. ... Christ's hermeneutical strategy, as described in Luke, is therefore not much different from the Savior's exegesis of *Genesis* and Wisdom literature in the 'core document,' or 'Ur-text', of the *Apocryphon of John*." With respect to form, I agree. The substance of the tradition that the Sethian Jesus hands down is not at all what the Lukan Jesus teaches, though; cf. Luttikhuizen 2006, 27: "Just like other early Christians, Ap. John's mythopoets were convinced that the true significance of the Jewish Scriptures was disclosed when they were read in the light of the Christian revelation. The agreement is, however, purely formal because early Christians had very divergent ideas about the actual content and meaning of the revelation brought by Christ."

11 Ap. John BG 2 45.8–13 / NHC II,1 13.18–23; NHC III 29.4–7 / BG 2 58.16–59.1 / NHC II,1 22.22–25 / NHC IV,1 34.31–35.3; NHC III,1 29.21–22 / BG 2 59.17–18 / NHC II,1 23.3 / NHC IV 35.22–24; NHC III,1 37.22–23 / BG 2 73.4–5 / NHC II,1 29.6; NHC IV,1 45.1–2. These occasional

If John's Jewish antagonist in the opening scene represents Sethian opponents, John is assumed to be the latest human founder of the true religion of Adam, Eve, and their son Seth, the first gnostics.[12] John further represents potential Sethian converts and neophytes, while the Savior speaks for those who have already been initiated and hence know that much of Jewish and Christian scripture is a demonic version of sacred history calculated to oppress them from the beginning.

## 2   The Myth

Sethian conflict with others is not just narrativized in the frame story, which may be a secondary textual component after all; it is fundamental to the myth itself.[13] The authors of the Apocryphon of John interpreted and rewrote the Genesis creation accounts by rearranging and combining them into alternate sequences and structures. They read certain passages more than once and at more than one cosmological level. They paid attention to divine plurals and double entendre. They grappled with interpretive problems such as descriptions of God that were all too human. No doubt they participated in the same overarching exegetical conversations as Greek-speaking Jews like Philo of Alexandria, and Aramaic-speaking Jews like those whose interpretations and rewritings of Genesis were recorded in the targums, as well as Christians.[14] But they went much further.

---

contradictions of Moses by name are hardly the only or even the most vigorous contradictions of the Torah and Judeo-Christian scripture in the apocryphon; they are merely the most explicit ones.

12   The authors of the texts in the Coptic gnostic codices (Askew, Berlin, Bruce, Nag Hammadi) do not refer to themselves as gnostics in those texts—a longstanding challenge to definitions of gnosticism, narrow and broad. This remains the case, even after the publication of the Tchacos codex. There is, however, an oblique reference to a Sethian author's possession of divine gnosis in Gos. Jud. TC3 54.8–12 (Kasser et al. 2007, 227; translation modified): "But God [i.e. the transcendent far above the biblical creators] caused knowledge (ⲅⲛⲱⲥⲓⲥ) to be brought to Adam and those with him, in order that the kings of Chaos and Hades might not rule over them." Note also Ap. John NHC II,1 4.5, 23.26. Furthermore there is good second-hand evidence that Sethians and others called themselves gnostics; see e.g. DeConick 2013a, 295–296.

13   Pleše 2006, 18, and Luttikhuizen 2006, 19, stress the continuity between the frame story and the myth, and they tend to understand the authors of both as Christians. Logan 1996 argues for a Christian understanding of the myth in the apocryphon and its related texts too. I am stressing a general continuity of Sethian conflict with others, although I think it's possible that the myth was written against Jewish tradition first, then Christian tradition also, with the added Johannine frame story; cf. Barc and Funk 2012, 34.

14   For the apocryphon as a rewriting of Genesis, and for its overall Jewish component, whether mediated through Christianity or not, see King 2006, 95–110, 215–234; also Luttikhuizen, 2006, 44–107; Barc and Funk 2012, 30–32; King 2013.

The authors of the apocryphon claimed that Moses was wrong, chiefly about God and creation. God was not the anthropomorphic biblical creator worshipped by Jews in the temple in Jerusalem and later by Christians. God was far above the biblical creator, who came into being by mistake and who was initially ignorant of God, then led a rebellion against his mother Sophia and ultimately against God as he obscured their existence so that he could enslave humanity to his own worship. The creation of heaven and earth, humans, and ultimately Judeo-Christian tradition was all part of this original apostasy.[15] Thus the Sethians were not the apostates; to their minds, the apostates were the biblical creator and by extension his worshippers.[16]

It was not just that the authors of the apocryphon exploited the divine plurals in Genesis in order to exalt God above the biblical creator or insulate God from the undesirable results of creation and from the advent of evil. They did that along with other Jewish and Christian interpreters.[17] But what is more, they vilified and mocked the biblical creator, which was also to vilify and mock the deity of their opponents. Not only did they portray him as an embarrassingly ill-begotten apostate, they called him Saklas and Samael ("fool" and "blind god" in Aramaic) as well as Ialdabaoth, which perhaps derives from divine names in Hebrew scripture: YHWH Elohim Adonai Sabaoth, the Lord God of Hosts.[18] According to the myth in the apocryphon, he was ignorant and boastful. When he and his angels created Adam, and when the biblical creator was subsequently tricked into animating that molded psychic body with the light-power/spirit he had stolen from his mother and the transcendent God's

---

15 M. Williams 2013 argues that despite their negative view of the creator, the authors of texts such as the apocryphon did not have a negative view of creation and life on Earth but lived lives 'full of meaning and purpose.' To be sure, according to the apocryphon the creation of humans was providential enough, and the molded psychic body was created in the divine image before it was remolded and clothed in darkness. There is also some correspondence, however weak, between the cosmos and the realm of the transcendent God. I don't think this or Pronoia's continued mundane activity, though, establishes that the world and its inhabitants—much less the birth of their creator—were intended to be. If the authors of the apocryphon did believe their lives were full of meaning and purpose, apparently this kind of life was only a recent possibility for them. Human history from the time after the Flood to the narrative present is described dismally in the longer manuscripts (Ap. John NHC II 30.2–7 / IV 46.10–15 [Waldstein and Wisse 166–167]): "They (the people) became old without having enjoyment. They died, not having found truth and without knowing the God of truth. And thus the whole creation became enslaved forever, from the foundation of the world until now."

16 In Gos. Jud. TC 51.12–15 (Kasser et al. 2007, 221), Nebro a.k.a. Ialdabaoth is even said to be ⲁⲡ[ⲟⲥ]ⲧⲁⲧⲏⲥ.

17 E.g. M. Williams 1996, 64–75.

18 E.g. Pearson 2007, 107; Rasimus 2009, 105, 125–126; also Barc and Funk 2012, 246.

domain, Adam turned out to be their superior. Adam was luminous, intelligent, and wise. Jealous, they stripped him of his perfection, entombing him and enchaining him in a remolded elemental body. Not wanting Adam to realize what they had done to him, next the biblical creator and his angels deceived Adam about the trees in the garden from which he should and should not eat, and they anaesthetized him in order to remove the spirit inside. After Eve woke Adam up, Ialdabaoth ignorantly put him in charge of her and clothed them both in gloomy darkness. The chief archon even raped Eve, thereby fathering Cain and Abel.[19]

Again it was not just that the authors of the apocryphon speculated on Adam's lost garment of light. They did that along with other Jewish and Christian interpreters.[20] But what is more, they blamed the loss of it on the jealousy of the biblical creator and his angels, not any failing of Adam or Eve.[21]

---

19  Ap. John NHC III 22.1–31.20 / BG 48.6–62.20 / NHC II 14.30–24.25 / NHC IV 23.9–38.12.
20  J. Smith 1978; DeConick and Fossum 1991; Lambden 1992; Anderson 2001. For the interpretation of the garment of skin in Genesis 3.21 as the physical body, a reading popularized by Origen and his followers along with the interpretation of the molded 'body' in Genesis 2.7 as the vehicle of the soul, see Simonetti 1962; Crouzel 1977; Beatrice 1985; Dechow 1988, 297–347; Bammel 1989; Clark 1992, 85–158; Schibli 1992; R. Layton 2004, 85–113; Reuling 2006, 72–77. The soul's vehicle, not to be confused with the light garment, is arguably a Middle- and Neo-Platonic invention; see e.g. Kissling 1922; Dodds 1992/1933; A. Smith 1974, 152–158; Finamore 1985. Alternatively Bos 2003 argues that it was invented already by Aristotle himself. Drawing on Bos' study, Luttikhuizen 2006, 64–65, understands the light-power in the apocryphon to be the nous, mind or intellect, and he understands the molded psychic body to be its temporary ethereal vehicle. Whether or not Bos is correct about Aristotle's psychology, the discourse on the fate of souls in the apocryphon is about the fate of *the soul*, the molded psychic body in other words, not the fate of the light-power as breath of life or spirit or mind. Hence in the pleromic aeon of Seth and his seed are found *the souls* of the saints, just as in the aeon below it are found *the souls* that were tardy in their repentance. It seems to me, then, that the molded psychic body is not the soul's vehicle; if anything in the apocryphon, that would be the remolded elemental body. I think one of the best comparanda for the apocryphon's psychology is Justin Martyr in his *Dial.*, esp. 6.1–2, where the human soul can die but is animated by God's spirit for as long as God wants it to live in or out of the body. The soul is also mortal according to Gos. Jud. TC3 43.11–44.7, 53.17–25.
21  Ap. John NHC III,1 28.6–15 / BG 2 57.8–19 / NHC II,1 22.3–8. Passage in NHC IV damaged. The light garment was maliciously taken from Adam; he did not lose it. And it was taken from him before he ever ate the fruit, not after. The double entendre of the garment of skin/light has not received the attention it deserves in major studies of the apocryphon; but see Rasimus 2009, 164–165. Tardieu 1984, 327, alone comments, "l'exégète gnostique inverse la valeur du jeu de mots rabbinique," that is, the words for light (אוֹר) in Genesis 1.3 and skin (עוֹר) in Genesis 3.21. I think the word play is subverted though not inverted. In the apocryphon, the light garment is still good, as it is in other Jewish and Christian interpretations of Genesis, while the skin garment is much more negative. The subversion

Once again, it was not just that they believed an evil angel seduced Eve, and that the watchers did the same to subsequent women. They read Genesis that way along with other Jewish and Christian exegetes.[22] But what is more, they identified that evil angel as the biblical creator worshipped by most all Jews and Christians![23]

For their part, the gnostics who wrote the apocryphon worshipped a different God far above the biblical creator, even as they vilified the deity of their opponents. They were well aware of what they were doing and the hazards involved. According to the myth, once Adam and Eve ate the fruit and consequently knew they had already fallen into the chaos and darkness of the biblical creator's realm, they "withdrew" from him and "were afraid to curse him and to reveal his ignorance:"

| NHC III | BG | NHC II/IV |
|---|---|---|
| Now Ialdabaoth noticed [that] they withdrew from him (ⲭⲉ] ⲁⲩⲥⲁϩⲱⲟⲩ ⲉⲃⲟⲗ ⲙ̄ⲙⲟϥ). He [cursed them]. In addition, he added about the woman, 'Your | Ialdabaoth noticed that they withdrew from him (ⲭⲉ ⲁⲩϩ̄ⲧⲟⲩ ⲛ̄ⲥⲁⲛⲃⲟⲗ ⲙ̄ⲙⲟϥ). He cursed them. And in addition, he adds about the woman that the husband is to | And when Ialdabaoth noticed that they withdrew from him (ⲭⲉ ⲁⲩⲥⲉϩⲱⲟⲩ ⲉⲃⲟⲗ ⲙ̄ⲙⲟϥ), he cursed his earth. He found the woman as she was |

---

involves who's to blame for the loss of the garment of light—Adam and Eve, or the biblical creator—which in turn affects the value of the eating of the fruit. The light garment also appears in the myth that Irenaeus had access to; see *Haer.* 1.30.9.

22  For the watchers traditions, see e.g. Harkins, Coblentz Bautch, and Endres 2014.
23  As Tardieu 1984, 327, comments, "le diable traditionnel a été remplacé par le Dieu de la *Genèse*." Luttikhuizen 2006, 58, is starker: "In his wickedness and ferocity he [Ialdabaoth] even surpasses the Satan of apocalyptic Jewish and (non-Gnostic) Christian traditions." King 2006, 170–172, compares and contrasts the apocryphon with Justin Martyr's anti-pagan use of the watchers traditions, and with the cosmic struggle in the New Testament book of Revelation, stating: "However much other Christians might object, the framers of the *Secret Revelation of John* placed themselves within the Christian camp, not least by making the Savior the hero of their story." But it seems to me that by having the Savior identify the leader of the fallen angels as the biblical creator, the gnostic authors of the apocryphon hoisted Christians like Justin Martyr with their own petard.

"I TURNED AWAY FROM THE TEMPLE"

(*cont.*)

| NHC III | BG | NHC II/IV |
|---|---|---|
| husband will rule over you,' [for he does] not know the mystery which [came to pass] through the holy decree from on high. And they were afraid to curse him, to reveal his ignorance to his angels. | rule over her, for he does not know the mystery which came to pass through the holy decree from on high. And they were afraid to curse him and to reveal his ignorance. | preparing herself for her husband. He was ruler over her though he did not know the mystery which had come to pass through the holy decree. And they were afraid to blame him. And he showed his angels his ignorance which is in him.[24] |

Adam and Eve withdraw from (ⲥⲟⲟϩⲉ, ⲥⲁϩⲱ⸗ ⲉⲃⲟⲗ ⲛ-; ϩⲓⲛⲉ, ϩⲛⲧ⸗ ⲥⲁⲃⲟⲗ ⲛ-) the biblical creator just as John turns away from (ⲕⲱⲧⲉ, ⲕⲟⲧ⸗ ⲉⲃⲟⲗ ϩⲛ-) the temple in Jerusalem.[25] Adam and Eve's fear of cursing/blaming Ialdabaoth and exposing his ignorance probably expresses the authors' own sentiment and has to do with their use of mythopoesis and pseudepigraphy; they did not write under their own names because, among other reasons, they were wary of calling the biblical creator a fool in the open in the company of other Jews and Christians. In a Christian context, it was safer and more authoritative, not to mention more shocking, to have the Savior and John reveal his ignorance for them.[26] But even if the frame story is a postscript to the myth, Sethian conflict

---

24  Ap. John NHC III,1 30.23–31.3 / BG 2 61.8–18 / NHC II,1 23.35–24.6 / NHC IV,1 37.4–14 (Waldstein and Wisse 1995, 136–137; translation modified).
25  Notably Crum 1962/1939, 125b, 380a, 689b, lists ἀφιστάναι among the Greek equivalents for all three Coptic verbs. Even if other Greek verbs stand behind the Coptic, there is a conceptual link here. This important point of continuity between the frame story and the myth has not received the attention it deserves in major studies of the apocryphon.
26  Tardieu 1984, 327, comments: "Ce qui sous-entend que cette timidité du couple promordial ne doit plus avoir cours aujourd'hui car la révélation écrite de la gnose proclame l'ignorance et la malédiction du démiurge." The authors of the apocryphon did proclaim the ignorance and cursedness of the demiurge. If it were the case that Adam and Eve's timidity no longer ought to apply, though, I think the authors would have written under their own names without fear.

with others must have started sooner than later—as hard as it is to document before the mid second century.

## 3 Irenaeus, Celsus, Origen, Plotinus and Porphyry

Their opponents were also fairly well aware of what the authors of the Apocryphon of John and its related Sethian texts were doing. Irenaeus wrote against them, referring to them as gnostics. He had access to a version of the rewritten creation accounts in the apocryphon. Besides the rape of Eve he went on to add in his exposé of gnostic myth that the biblical creator made a covenant with Abraham, gave the law to Moses, and had Jesus killed.[27] This was beyond the pale for the Christian bishop. Irenaeus tentatively hoped that a few of the gnostics and those influenced by them "might be saved (*saluari possint*) as they do penance (*paenitentiam agentes*) and convert to the one sole creator God and maker of the universe (*et conuertentes ad unum solum conditorem deum et factorem uniuersitatis*)."[28] Naturally we do not have to side with Irenaeus in considering the Sethians and those influenced by them to be sinful heretics in need of repentance, but he is not off the mark when he writes that he and they worshipped different deities.

Sethian theology was itself influenced by Greek philosophy, mostly Platonizing but also some Aristotelian and Stoic. This does not account for the difference, however. Several Greek philosophers and other Jews and Christians influenced by Greek philosophy posited a more or less transcendent God, without vilifying the creator. In Platonic thought in particular, to hold a thoroughly negative view of the creator and creation was unspeakable, as Plato put it in the *Timaeus*:

> Hence to discover the maker and father of this universe (τὸν ... ποιητὴν καὶ πατέρα τοῦδε τοῦ παντός) is a task indeed; and having discovered him, to declare him to all people is impossible. However, let us return and inquire further concerning the cosmos—After which of the models did its architect (ὁ τεκταινόμενος) construct it? Was it after that which is self-identical and uniform, or after that which has come into existence? Now if this

---

27  Irenaeus, *Haer.* 1.29–30. In 1.30.7, it is not Ialdabaoth himself but his lackeys that rape Eve. For the biblical creator's remote-control execution of Jesus, compare 1.30.13 with Gos. Jud. TC, where the betrayal is astrologically determined; see e.g. Adamson 2009.

28  *Haer.* 1.31.3 (Rousseau and Doutreleau 1979, 388; Unger and Dillon 1992, 103; translation modified).

cosmos is beautiful and its craftsman is good (εἰ μὲν δὴ καλός ἐστιν ὅδε ὁ κόσμος ὅ τε δημιουργὸς ἀγαθός), then it is plain that he was looking at the eternal; but if otherwise (εἰ δέ), which is not right for anyone even to say (ὃ μηδ' εἰπεῖν τινὶ θέμις), then he was looking at that which has come into existence. To everyone in fact it is obvious (παντὶ δὴ σαφὲς) that he was looking at the eternal; for the cosmos is the most beautiful (κάλλιστος) of all that has come into existence, and the craftsman is the best (ἄριστος) of all causes.[29]

The authors of the apocryphon rewrote the *Timaeus* alongside the Genesis creation accounts, and in the process they did the unspeakable.[30] Holding a thoroughly negative view of the creator, they fused their ignorant, boastful, jealous and apostate Ialdabaoth with the demiurge. The situation in the apocryphon is far more ghastly than Plato's worst case scenario because, as Samael, the Sethian demiurge was not looking at any model when he created the world.[31] According to the longer manuscripts, he depended on thieved memories from his mother Sophia.[32]

So it is not surprising to find Celsus and Origen, both Platonists or at least strongly influenced by Platonism, agreeing with one another against the Sethians almost despite themselves. The pagan Celsus wrote against Christianity, which for him included Sethianism; the Christian Origen wrote against the Sethians and against Celsus in reply.

Celsus referred to the Sethians as Christians. He critiqued them for their belief "that the god of the Jews is an accursed god (θεὸν κατηραμένον τὸν Ἰουδαίων), the one who sends rain and thunder, and who is the craftsman of this cosmos (τοῦδε τοῦ κόσμου δημιουργὸν), and who is the god of Moses, described in his creation account."[33] The cursedness (κατηραμένον) of the biblical creator here

---

29   *Tim.* 28c–29a (Bury 1929, 50–53; translation modified).
30   For the apocryphon as a rewriting of *Tim.*, and for its overall Greek philosophical component, see Plcše 2006, esp. 49–66, 271–272; also Luttikhuizen 2006, 29–43; King 2006, 191–214; Barc and Funk 2012, 32–34; King 2013.
31   Pleše 2006, 199: "Ialdabaoth is a 'blind' and incompetent pretender, moved by the impulses of his irrational soul and therefore capable of producing only deceptive semblances of ideal forms."
32   Ap. John NHC II,1 13.1–5 / IV,1 20.15–18. For proto-Sethian and Sethian developments leading up to the apocryphon's break in the chain of being, see Adamson 2013a, esp. 76–80. The creation of the first human is another matter. Ialdabaoth and his angels were looking at the eternal, but only indirectly as the eternal was reflected on water; see Ap. John NHC III,1 22.1–6 / BG 2 48.6–14 / NHC II,1 14.30–15.4 / NHC IV,1 23.9–20.
33   Origen, *Cels.* 6.27.16–19 (Borret 1969, 246; Chadwick 1965/1953, 343; translation modified); see also 6.28.7–10.

picks up on the cursedness (ἐπικατάρατος) of the serpent as well as the ground in Genesis.[34] There is a similar exchange in the passage from the apocryphon, where Ialdabaoth curses (ⲥⲁϩⲟⲩ, ⲥⲟⲩϩⲱⲣ, ⲥϩⲟⲩⲱⲣ⸗) Adam and Eve, and where they in turn are afraid to curse (ⲥⲁϩⲟⲩ, ⲥⲁϩⲱ⸗) him and reveal his ignorance.[35]

Addressing the Sethians in the singular, Celsus thought they were "most impious (ὦ δυσσεβέστατε)" for believing the creator was an accursed god, and for "pouring abuse on him." Interestingly Celsus seems to have had information about Sethians who were afraid to curse the biblical creator and reveal his ignorance in front of a Jewish audience, like Adam and Eve are afraid to do in the apocryphon: "But when you are put in difficulties by the Jews (ἀλλ' ὅταν μὲν ὑπὸ τούτων βιάζῃ), you allow that you worship the same god (τὸν αὐτὸν θεὸν σέβειν ὁμολογεῖς)."[36] If so, and if Sethians dissembled in their conflict with Jews face to face when their Jewish opponents had the upper hand, it is nonetheless clear that behind the relative privacy and security of a pseudonym the authors of the apocryphon believed Moses was wrong about God, and that most all Jews as well as Christians worshipped a foolish apostate.

In his response to Celsus, Origen referred to the Sethians as Ophians or Ophites. He critiqued them much the way Celsus did, as he distanced himself and his Christianity from them. Charging Celsus with misrepresenting Christian belief, Origen agreed that it would be most impious to curse and pour abuse on the creator, something that Christians would never do, according to Origen, not in their debates with Jews, and not in their debates with each other. Only the heretical Ophians would do that, Origen wrote, and he did not regard them as Christians.[37]

We do not have to side with Celsus and Origen in considering the Ophite-Sethians to be impious, any more than we do with Irenaeus in considering them to be heretics. Still Celsus himself is proof that their theology could be as shocking to pagans as it was to Jews and Christians—not just Christians like Irenaeus but even Christians like Origen who had been strongly influenced by Platonism.

Further proof comes from the Neo-Platonic philosopher Plotinus and his student Porphyry. Porphyry referred to the Sethians as Christians and philosophical heretics. He was Plotinus' literary executor and editor, and he gave a short title to part of his teacher's writings against them. It was "Against the

---

34  Genesis 3.14, 17.
35  Ap. John NHC III,1 30.23–31.3 / BG 2 61.8–18 / NHC II,1 23.35–24.6 / NHC IV,1 37.4–14 (Waldstein and Wisse 1995, 136–137). Crum 1962/1939, 387b lists καταρᾶσθαι and ἐπικαταρᾶσθαι among the Greek equivalents.
36  Origen, Cels. 6.29.4–17 (Borret 1969, 250; Chadwick 1965/1953, 345).
37  Origen, Cels. 6.24–40, esp. 6.29.

Gnostics." But the extended title strikes at the heart of the issue: "Against those who say that the craftsman of the cosmos and the cosmos are evil (Πρὸς τοὺς κακὸν τὸν δημιουργὸν τοῦ κόσμου καὶ τὸν κόσμον κακὸν εἶναι λέγοντας)."[38] In other words, Plotinus was writing against the Sethians for doing what was unspeakable per the *Timaeus*. Plotinus wrote that they poured abuse on the cosmos as well as its craftsman, that they despised the lower deities, and that their characterization of the demiurge as rebellious (ἀποστάντα) was purposely very much abusive.[39] He also wrote that they would "recommend their own opinions to their audience by ridiculing and insulting the Greeks," and that they would "pull to pieces what godlike men of antiquity have said nobly and in accordance with the truth," those godlike men being Plato in particular.[40]

Plotinus even summed up the Sethians' evangelizing strategy. He has them say to the potential convert and neophyte: "You are God's offspring, and the other people whom you used to admire are not, and neither are the beings they venerate according to the tradition received from their fathers (οὐδ' ἃ τιμῶσιν ἐκ πατέρων λαβόντες); but you are even better than the heaven, without having taken any trouble to become so."[41]

The Sethians and especially the authors of the apocryphon would not have said it quite like that. For one thing, although they engaged in harsh polemic with others, their soteriological thinking was ultimately universalist, believing as they did that only apostates from Sethianism would not be saved; non-Sethians would be converted eventually, even if it was only after death.[42]

But on the whole, Plotinus accurately summarized what the Savior tells John in the apocryphon. He tells him that he and his fellow spirits, the seed of Seth, have been created in the divine image above the biblical creator. He tells him that the spirit animating them is not the creator's own spirit but one that Ialdabaoth had stolen from the transcendent God's domain. Thus, like Adam, John is superior to his celestial though evil makers. And like Adam and Eve, John should withdraw from the biblical creator. He should turn away from the temple in Jerusalem, and turn away from the traditions of his fathers. The Savior tells John that Moses was wrong about God, and therefore so are Jews and Christians. Plotinus was not Jewish or Christian, and he may have never read the apocryphon itself. Even so he got the Sethian gospel message

---

38  Porphyry, *Vit. Plot.* 16, 24 (Armstrong 1966, 1:44–45, 76–77; translation modified).
39  Plotinus, *Enn.* II.9.8, 9, 10 (Armstrong 1966, 2:252–253, 258–261, 266–267; translation modified and paraphrased).
40  Plotinus, *Enn.* II.9.6, 10 (Armstrong 1966, 2:247, 265).
41  Plotinus, *Enn.* II.9.9 (Armstrong 1966, 2:260–261; translation modified).
42  See e.g. M.A. Williams 1996, 195–198.

clear enough: his admired Plato was also wrong, and the demiurge was no good after all.

## 4 Sethian Counterculture

So how are we to understand this Sethian portrayal of the Platonic demiurge and the traditional biblical creator? To repeat, we do not have to side with the Sethians' opponents in considering their vilification of him to be heresy or impiety. But that doesn't mean it wasn't sociologically transgressive or countercultural. It was.[43] It clearly shocked Christians such as Irenaeus and Origen as well as pagans such as Celsus and Plotinus. It was no less shocking to the Valentinian Ptolemy.[44] We could hardly expect otherwise from the ignorant, boastful, jealous and apostate Ialdabaoth, Saklas, Samael, featured in the Apocryphon of John and its related Sethian texts. To vilify the creator also would have been shocking to most all Jews, even if we do not have any exposés or critiques of Sethianism as such from them.

By countercultural I am suggesting it was against previous tradition, both Judeo-Christian and Platonic.[45] Most Jews and Christians believed the biblical creator was good, not evil; this holds for those Jews and Christians who believed in a sort of transcendent God and attributed the work of creation to one or more demiurgic figures. In Platonic thought, following the *Timaeus*, it was forbidden to say the craftsman was not good. Even a general survey of Greek

---

43  For transgressive and countercultural gnosis, see DeConick 2013a, 300–301; 2013b; 2016; plus her article in this volume.

44  In *Flor.*, Ptolemy critiqued unnamed 'others' who identified the Mosaic lawgiver as the devil and equated him with the craftsman. Ptolemy had Sethians in mind, not Marcionites, it seems. His shock is evident in his scorn. He concluded (apud Epiphanius, *Pan.* 33.7.1–5 [Holl, Begermann and Collatz 2013, 456; F. Williams 1987, 203; translation modified) that the law was given by a just demiurge rehabilitated from Sethian myth, "not by the perfect God himself, and surely not by the devil (μήτε μὴν ὑπ' τοῦ διαβόλου), which is not even right to say (ὃ μηδ' θεμιτόν ἐστιν εἰπεῖν)." Note Ptolemy's allusion to Plato, *Tim.* 29a (Bury 1929, 50): ὃ μηδ' εἰπεῖν τινὶ θέμις.

45  Cahana 2014, 60, discusses Ap. John as an example of what he calls 'gnostic antitraditionalism,' which he understands to be the rejection of the Greco-Roman cultural premise that older is better and more reliable. About the Johannine frame story he states: "Christ seems to imply … that one should indeed turn away from tradition." I concur that the authors of the apocryphon did not deny the charge of apostasy from Judaism and Christianity. But I don't think they were against tradition qua the old. They claimed that their beliefs—revealed again however lately by the Savior—were those of the first humans, before Moses, before Plato. For the classic gnostic appeal to Seth, see Rasimus 2009, 194–198.

philosophy before the Common Era reveals that the notion of a bad creator was rare at best.[46]

I don't want to suggest that because of Sethian counterculture the gnostic authors of the apocryphon were not thoroughly embedded in the very traditions they turned away from. I also don't want to suggest that they were not shaped by, and involved in the shaping of, those traditions. They were. Yet they vilified the biblical creator along with the Platonic demiurge. So we cannot treat them as any other variety of Christians, for one, unless we recognize that they venerated a different God.

Definitions and categorizations of gnosticism have been debated perennially and are not without their challenges. In the last few decades, scholarship has tended to avoid and even proscribe the term. We could dismantle gnosis, gnostic, and gnosticism altogether and instead experiment with other categories, such as a category of biblical traditions in which there is a demiurgic figure, as there is in Platonism.[47] But the Sethian creator is simply unlike most others. We could focus our study on individual texts within the hybridity of early Christian and ancient Mediterranean literature as a whole, apart from any definition and categorization of gnosticism.[48] But the central text in the so-called Coptic gnostic codices, the Apocryphon of John, resists categorization as Jewish or Christian, precisely because its authors vilified the traditional biblical creator. To lump the apocryphon and its gnostic authors in with their fellow Jews and Christians as well as their fellow Platonists might excuse us from having to define and categorize gnosticism any longer as something different from the rest. This would be to miss the Sethians' own point, however, which was not just rhetorical or discursive. It would be, from their perspective, to re-enslave them to the worship of a foolish apostate who raped Eve and had Jesus' killed.

## 5   Why Ialdabaoth

I have focused on the vilification of the creator in the Apocryphon of John as a primary example of Sethian counterculture. There is, of course, much more to the story of the Sethians, the Ophites, the classic gnostics, their myths and rituals. I will merely conclude with a brief speculative hypothesis about how

---

46   See Mansfeld 1981.
47   M.A. Williams 1996.
48   King 2003.

and why the authors of the apocryphon and its related texts may have come to vilify the creator in the first place.[49]

An evil creator is paramount among the features of Sethianism that distinguish classic gnostics from other Jews, Christians, and Platonists, as well as any proto-Sethians that we might reconstruct. Some of the proto-Sethains must have been deeply invested in biblical tradition, it seems to me—so deeply that they could not write off the investment once the cost of maintaining their membership in the tradition outweighed any returns they had once enjoyed or could hope for in the future.[50] They had participated in the same overarching exegetical conversations as their fellow Jews and Christians, all of whom were Hellenized to one extent or another. Hellenization had made proto-Sethians painfully cognizant of interpretive problems such as the descriptions of an anthropomorphic creator. Influenced by Greek philosophy including Platonism, they had persisted in pointing out these problems to their fellows as they ventured preliminary solutions and sought partners in a bold project of theological renovation. Some, maybe most of their fellows turned them down, however. Talk of the problems, the solutions, was not welcome. Proto-Sethians were even vilified by their co-religionists. As relations deteriorated, they came to vilify the deity of their opponents, which had also been the God they themselves worshipped initially. Proto-Sethians became Sethians. They rewrote the Genesis creation accounts both in order to solve interpretive problems and in order to get back at their rivals.

Having vilified the biblical creator—in part due to the influence of Greek philosophical thought which is what had highlighted for them the interpretive problems in scripture from the get go—they did likewise to the Platonic demiurge. In the *Timaeus*, Plato himself acknowledged the notion of a bad creator,

---

49  For scholarship on the vilification or demonization of the demiurge in the apocryphon and elsewhere, a topic that can be tantamount to the origin of gnosticism, see e.g. Fossum 1985, 2–24, 213–220, 332–338; M.A. Williams 1996, 213–234; Rasimus 2009, 171–188.

50  King 2006, 162, applies the cross-cultural comparative work of social scientist James C. Scott to her study of the apocryphon: "Scott has argued that resistance is more likely to arise from among those who have bought heavily into a society's dominant ideology and feel betrayed than from those who reject the values of their society. The myth of the *Secret Revelation of John* expresses this sensibility of betrayal." For King 2006, 167, the apocryphon's social critique is largely aimed at Rome, even though she admits that the text "doesn't actually mention any local or imperial figure or office." It seems to me too that the resistance arose from among insiders. But I think they were Jews and Christians invested in biblical tradition, and that the critique of the biblical creator and his angels is first and foremost a critique of Judaism and Christianity.

albeit unapprovingly and only as an elliptical 'if on the other hand....' After him, no pagan Middle- or Neo-Platonist vilified the demiurge. I do not think the gnostic authors of the apocryphon would have either except for their failed investment in biblical tradition.

## Bibliography

Adamson, Grant. 2013a. "The Old Gods of Egypt in Lost Hermetica and Early Sethianism." Pages 58–86 in *Histories of the Hidden God*. Edited by April D. DeConick and Grant Adamson. Durham: Acumen/Routledge.

Adamson, Grant. 2013b. "Astrological Medicine in Gnostic Traditions." Pages 333–358 in *Practicing Gnosis*. Edited by April D. DeConick, Gregory Shaw, and John D. Turner. Nag Hammadi and Manichaean Studies 85. Leiden: Brill.

Adamson, Grant. 2009. "Fate Indelible: The *Gospel of Judas* and Horoscopic Astrology." Pages 305–324 in *The Codex Judas Papers*. Edited by April D. DeConick. Nag Hammadi and Manichaean Studies 73. Leiden: Brill.

Anderson, Gary A. 2001. "The Garments of Skin in Apocryphal Narrative and Biblical Commentary." Pages 101–143 in *Studies in Ancient Midrash*. Edited by James L. Kugel. Cambridge, Mass.: Harvard Center for Jewish Studies.

Armstrong, A.H., ed. 1966. *Plotinus I–II*. Loeb Classical Library 440–441. Cambridge, Mass.: Harvard University Press.

Bammel, C.P. 1989. "Adam in Origen." Pages 62–93 in *The Making of Orthodoxy*. Edited by Rowan Williams. Cambridge: Cambridge University Press.

Barc, Bernard, and Wolf-Peter Funk. 2012. *Le livre des secrets de Jean, recension brève (NH III,1 et BG,2)*. Bibliothèque copte de Nag Hammadi, section «Textes» 35. Québec: Les presses de l'Universite Laval.

Beatrice, Pier Franco. 1985. "Le tuniche di pele: Antiche letture di Gen. 3,21." Pages 433–484 in *La tradizione dell'enkrateia*. Edited by Ugo Bianchi. Rome: Edizioni dell'Ateneo.

Borret, Marcel, ed. 1969. *Origène, Contra Celse, tome III*. Sources chrétiennes 147. Paris: Les Éditions du Cerf.

Bos, A.P. 2003. *The Soul and Its Instrumental Body: A Reinterpretation of Aristotle's Philosophy of Living Nature*. Studies in Intellectual History 112. Leiden: Brill.

Brakke, David. 2010. *The Gnostics: Myth, Ritual, and Diversity in Early Christianity*. Cambridge, Mass.: Harvard University Press.

Burns, Dylan M. 2014. *Apocalypse of the Alien God: Platonism and the Exile of Sethian Gnosticism*. Philadelphia, Pa.: University of Pennsylvania Press.

Bury, R.G., ed. 1929. *Plato IX*. Loeb Classical Library 234. Cambridge, Mass.: Harvard University Press.

Cahana, Jonathan. 2014. "None of Them Knew Me or My Brothers: Gnostic Anti-traditionalism and Gnosticism as a Cultural Phenomenon." Pages 49–73 in *Journal of Religion* 94.1.

Chadwick, Henry, ed. 1965/1953. *Origen: Contra Celsum*. Cambridge: Cambridge University Press.

Clark, Elizabeth A. 1992. *The Origenist Controversy: The Cultural Construction of an Early Christian Debate*. Princeton, N.J.: Princeton University Press.

Crouzel, Henri. 1977. "Le theme platonicien du 'véhicule de l'âme' chez Origène." Pages 225–238 in *Didaskalia* 7.

Crum, W.E., ed. 1962/1939. *A Coptic Dictionary*. Oxford: Oxford University Press.

Dahl, Nils A. 1981. "The Arrogant Archon and the Lewd Sophia: Jewish Traditions in Gnostic Revolt." Pages 689–712 in *The Rediscovery of Gnosticism*. Edited by Bentley Layton. Studies in the History of Religions 41.2. Leiden: Brill.

Dechow, Jon F. 1988. *Dogma and Mysticism in Early Christianity: Epiphanius of Cyprus and the Legacy of Origen*. Patristic Monograph Series 13. Macon, Ga.: Mercer University Press.

DeConick, April D. 2013a. "Crafting Gnosis: Gnostic Spirituality in the Ancient New Age." Pages 285–305 in *Gnosticism, Platonism and the Late Ancient World*. Edited by Kevin Corrigan and Tuomas Rasimus. Nag Hammadi and Manichaean Studies 82. Leiden: Brill.

DeConick, April D. 2013b. "Gnostic Spirituality at the Crossroads of Christianity: Transgressing Boundaries and Creating Orthodoxy." Pages 148–184 in *Beyond the Gnostic Gospels*. Edited by Eduard Iricinschi, Lance Jenott, Nicola Denzey Lewis, and Philippa Townsend. Studien und Texte zu Antike und Christentum 82. Tübingen: Mohr Siebeck.

DeConick, April D. 2016. *The Gnostic New Age: How a Countercultural Spirituality Revolutionized Religion from Antiquity to Today*. New York, N.Y.: Columbia University Press.

DeConick, April D., and Jarl Fossum. 1991. "Stripped before God: A New Interpretation of Logion 37 in the Gospel of Thomas." Pages 123–150 in *Vigiliae Christianae* 45.2.

Dodds, E.R. 1992/1933. "Appendix II: The Astral Body in Neoplatonism." Pages 313–321 in *Proclus, The Elements of Theology*. Oxford: Clarendon Press.

Finamore, John F. 1985. *Iamblichus and the Theory of the Vehicle of the Soul*. American Classical Studies 14. Chico, Calif.: Scholars Press.

Fossum, Jarl E. 1985. *The Name of God and the Angel of the Lord: Samaritan and Jewish Concepts of Intermediation and the Origin of Gnosticism*. Wissenschaftliche Untersuchungen zum Neuen Testament 36. Tübingen: Mohr Siebeck.

Giversen, Søren. 1963. *Apocryphon Johannis*. Acta Theologica Danica 5. Copenhagen: Munksgaard.

Harkins, Angela Kim, Kelley Coblentz Bautch, and John C. Endres, eds. 2014. *The Fallen Angels Traditions: Second Temple Developments and Reception History*. Catholic Biblical Quarterly Monograph Series 53. Washington, D.C.: Catholic Biblical Association of America.

Holl, Karl, Marc Bergermann, and Christian-Friedrich Collatz, eds. 2013. *Epiphanius I*. Die Griechischen Christlichen Schriftsteller der ersten Jahrhunderte 10.1. Berlin: De Gruyter.

Kasser, Rodolphe, Gregor Wurst, Marvin Meyer, François Gaudard, eds. 2007. *The Gospel of Judas: Critical Edition*. Washington, D.C.: National Geographic.

King, Karen L. 2003. *What Is Gnosticism?* Cambridge, Mass.: Harvard University Press.

King, Karen L. 2006. *The Secret Revelation of John*. Cambridge, Mass.: Harvard University Press.

King, Karen L. 2013. "A Distinctive Intertextuality: Genesis and Platonizing Philosophy in the *Secret Revelation of John*." Pages 3–22 in *Gnosticism, Platonism and the Late Ancient World*. Edited by Kevin Corrigan and Tuomas Rasimus. Nag Hammadi and Manichaean Studies 82. Leiden: Brill.

Kissling, Robert Christian. 1922. "The ΟΧΗΜΑ-ΠΝΕΥΜΑ of the Neo-Platonists and the *De insomniis* of Synesius of Cyrene." Pages 318–330 in the *American Journal of Philology* 43.4.

Lambden, Stephen N. 1992. "From Fig Leaves to Fingernails: Some Notes on the Garments of Adam and Eve in the Hebrew Bible and Select Early Postbiblical Jewish Writings." Pages 74–90 in *A Walk in the Garden*. Edited by Paul Morris and Deborah Sawyer. JSOT Supplement 136. Sheffield: JSOT Press.

Layton, Bentley. 1995. "Prolegomena to the Study of Ancient Gnosticism." Pages 334–350 in *The Social World of the First Christians*, edited by L.M. White and O.L. Yarbrough. Minneapolis, Minn.: Fortress Press.

Layton, Richard A. 2004. *Didymus the Blind and His Circle in Late-Antique Alexandria: Virtue and Narrative in Biblical Scholarship*. Urbana; Chicago, Ill.: University of Illinois Press.

Logan, Alastair H.B. 1996. *Gnostic Truth and Christian Heresy: A Study in the History of Gnosticism*. Edinburgh: T&T Clark.

Logan, Alastair H.B. 2006. *The Gnostics: Identifying an Early Christian Cult*. London: T&T Clark.

Luttikhuizen, Gerard P. 2006. *Gnostic Revisions of Genesis Stories and Early Jesus Traditions*. Nag Hammadi and Manichaean Studies 58. Leiden: Brill.

Mansfeld, Jaap. 1981. "Bad World and Demiurge: A 'Gnostic' Motif from Parmenides and Empedocles to Lucretius and Philo." Pages 261–314 in *Studies in Gnosticism and Hellenistic Religions*. Edited by R. van den Broek and M.J. Vermaseren. Études préliminaires aux religions orientales dans l'empire romain 91. Leiden: Brill.

Pleše, Zlatko. 2006. *Poetics of the Gnostic Universe: Narrative and Cosmology in the Apocryphon of John*. Nag Hammadi and Manichaean Studies 52. Leiden: Brill.

Pearson, Birger A. 2007. *Ancient Gnosticism: Traditions and Literature*. Minneapolis, Minn.: Fortress Press.

Rasimus, Tuomas. 2009. *Paradise Reconsidered in Gnostic Mythmaking: Rethinking Sethianism in Light of the Ophite Evidence*. Nag Hammadi and Manichaean Studies 68. Leiden: Brill.

Reuling, Hanneke. 2006. *After Eden: Church Fathers and Rabbis on Genesis 3:16–21*. Jewish and Christian Perspectives 10. Leiden: Brill.

Rousseau, Adelin, and Louis Doutreleau, eds. 1979. *Irénée de Lyon, Contre les hérésies, livre I*. Sources chrétiennes 264. Paris: Les Éditions du Cerf.

Schenke, Hans-Martin. 1974. "Das sethianische System nach Nag-hammadi-Handschriften." Pages 165–173 in *Studia Coptica*. Edited by Peter Nagel. Berliner Byzantinische Arbeiten 45. Berlin: Akademie Verlag.

Schenke, Hans-Martin. 1981. "The Phenomenon and Significance of Gnostic Sethianism." Pages 588–616 in *The Rediscovery of Gnosticism*. Edited by Bentley Layton. Studies in the History of Religions 41.2. Leiden: Brill.

Schibli, Hermann S. 1992. "Origen, Didymus, and the Vehicle of the Soul." Pages 381–391 in *Origeniana Quinta*. Edited by Robert J. Daily. Leuven: Peeters.

Segal, Alan F. 2002/1977. *Two Powers in Heaven: Early Rabbinic Reports about Christianity and Gnosticism*. Leiden: Brill.

Simonetti, Manlio. 1962. "Alcune osservazioni sull'interpretazione origeniana di Genesi 2,7 e 3,21." Pages 370–381 in *Aevum* 36.

Smith, Andrew. 1974. *Porphyry's Place in the Neoplatonic Tradition: A Study in Post-Plotinian Neoplatonism*. The Hague: Martinus Nijhoff.

Smith, Jonathan Z. 1978. "The Garments of Shame." Pages 1–23 in *Map Is Not Territory: Studies in the History of Religions*. Leiden: Brill.

Stroumsa, Gedaliahu A.G. 1984. *Another Seed: Studies in Gnostic Mythology*. Nag Hammadi and Manichaean Studies 24. Leiden: Brill.

Tardieu, Michel. 1984. *Écrits gnostiques: Codex de Berlin*. Paris: Les Éditions du Cerf.

Turner, John D. 2001. *Sethian Gnosticism and the Platonic Tradition*. Bibliothèque copte de Nag Hammadi, section « Études » 6. Québec: Les presses de l'Universite Laval.

Unger, Dominic J., and John J. Dillon, eds. 1992. *St. Irenaeus of Lyons, Against the Heresies, Volume 1*. Ancient Christian Writers 55. New York, N.Y.: Paulist Press.

Waldstein, Michael, and Frederik Wisse. 1995. *The Apocryphon of John: Synopsis of Nag Hammadi Codices II,1; III,1; and IV,1 with BG 8502,2*. Nag Hammadi and Manichaean Studies 33. Leiden: Brill.

Williams, Frank, ed. 1987. *The Panarion of Epiphanius of Salamis, Book 1*. Nag Hammadi and Manichaean Studies 35. Leiden: Brill.

Williams, Michael A. 1996. *Rethinking "Gnosticism:" An Argument for Dismantling a Dubious Category*. Princeton, N.J.: Princeton University Press.

Williams, Michael A. 2013. "A Life Full of Meaning and Purpose: Demiurgical Myths and Social Implications." Pages 19–59 in *Beyond the Gnostic Gospels*. Edited by Eduard Iricinschi, Lance Jenott, Nicola Denzey Lewis, and Philippa Townsend. Studien und Texte zu Antike und Christentum 82. Tübingen: Mohr Siebeck.

# Transgressing Boundaries: Plotinus and the Gnostics

*John D. Turner*
University of Nebraska-Lincoln
jturner2@unl.edu

April DeConick has defined gnostics as a type of religious person who claims to possess and teach gnosis, aspects of which afford a direct insight into the nature of ultimate reality and its divine ground as well as the means of the self-realization of one's own essential divine affinity, accessible only to a community initiated into its secrets. Aspects of this knowledge were contingent upon transgressive hermeneutics and metaphysical speculations radically different from those widely accepted as traditional. Although they often employed the same authoritative texts, myths, philosophies, and even rituals sanctioned by tradition, they conceived of the world, humans, and God in non-standard, even subversive terms that challenged more traditional understandings by drawing upon the hidden implications of a variety of well-known but under-developed late antique philosophical and religious traditions, often without any regard for commonly accepted philosophical and religious boundaries.[1]

Since one of the questions of this conference is "what is it about the gnostic that opens us up to a deviance so subversive that it reverses and redefines whatever it contacts?" I have chosen to focus on what might be thought of as Plotinus's "love-hate" relationship with second and third century gnostic thought. It was "love" in the sense that, as fellow devotees of "Plato's mysteries," certain of these gnostics developed original interpretations of Platonic thought similar to Plotinus's own and may have actually contributed to his metaphysics at some crucial points.[2] It was "hate" in the sense that, at the same time, Plotinus could assert, "they falsify Plato's account of the manner of the [world's] making, and a great deal else, and degrade the great man's teachings."[3]

In the latest study of the relation between Plotinus and the gnostics, Jean-Marc Narbonne observes that throughout the course of a roughly twenty-five-year teaching career in Rome beginning around 244 CE and ending abruptly

---

[1] DeConick 2013a and 2013b.
[2] Puech 1960, 182–3.
[3] Plotinus, *Enn.* II.9[33].6.24–6.

in 269, Plotinus developed a number of positions reflecting confrontations with various opponents, among whom the gnostics certainly took precedence.[4] Porphyry's *Life of Plotinus* tells us that among the gnostic apocalypses circulating in his Roman seminar, there were two, Zostrianos and Allogenes, discovered in 1945 within the corpus of Sethian or "classical" gnostic treatises from Nag Hammadi. According to Porphyry, Plotinus himself delivered refutations of such treatises many times in his courses, traces of which surface throughout most of his entire corpus, but which came to a head during the years 263–268 in a tetralogy of consecutive treatises—the so-called *Großschrift*[5]—that culminates in his most explicit critique of gnostic doctrines and practices in *Enneades* II.9[33], *Against the Gnostics*. Since some of those close to Plotinus, whom he called "friends," had fallen under the spell of these rival doctrines and were defecting, he also mandated even more thoroughgoing refutations of them by his principal disciples, Amelius and Porphyry.[6]

In the course of his refutations, Plotinus accuses the gnostics of many sorts of transgressions, not merely violations of moral or ethical behavioral norms, but also of accepted cultural and aesthetic values, and of the fundamental metaphysical principles upon which Plotinus believed these other areas depended. In his contribution to the new Budé edition of *Enneades* II.9,[7] Zeke Mazur numbers among ethical and moral transgressions: immoral conduct and excessive discontent with perceived defects and inequalities in the subintelligible world. Cultural transgressions include: arrogantly claiming extraordinary contemplative abilities available only to the initiated elect, plagiarizing

---

4   Narbonne 2011, 115–16. As early as 2001, Corrigan (2001a, 42) stated: "I propose that we should be alive to the real possibility that all of the treatises after the *Großschrift*, especially those with cognate interests such as VI.7[38] and VI.8[39], will bear similar traces of such a dialogue. In which case, and in the sense we have specified, Plotinus is certainly influenced by the Gnostics, for some of his most mature thought is shaped by an implicit conversation with them."

5   *Enn.* III.8[30], V.8[31], V.5[32], II.9[33].

6   According to Puech 1960, 182–3, the friends would be fellow partisans of Plato's "mysteries": Plotinus, *Enn.* II.9.10.3–11: "We feel a certain regard for some of our friends who happened upon this way of thinking before they became our friends, and, though I do not know how they manage it, continue in it.... But we have addressed what we have said so far to our own acquaintances, not to them [i.e. the Gnostics] (for we could make no further progress towards convincing them), so that they might not be troubled by these latter, who do not bring forward proofs—how could they?—but make arbitrary, arrogant assertions." See Edwards 1989, 228–232, who suggests that Plotinus here attacks the Gnostic Platonism of his former colleagues in Ammonius Saccas's school or another study-group in Alexandria, who joined him in Rome around the same time as Porphyry; but unlike Plotinus continued to espouse it rather than rejecting it.

7   Mazur 2016, 229.

from and insulting Plato and other ancient Hellenic authorities, as well as violating the accepted norms of philosophical discourse and reasoned argument in favor of divine revelations, while their major aesthetic transgression was the disparagement of the order and beauty of the sensible world and its stellar and celestial divinities. Perhaps most serious all were the violations of the metaphysical principles upon which the others depended, such as the economy of transcendent principles, and the non-arbitrary constancy of the divine necessity governing the entire cosmos, and especially what Mazur has called the "axiom of continuous hierarchy" that underlies the basic ontological framework of the ultimate reality upon which the status and function of everything else depends: it is the principle of an unbroken, continuous procession or unfolding of all realities, such that what is ontologically and causally prior, and thus more powerful, is by necessity axiologically and ethically superior to its product.[8]

## 1 The Generation of Reality in Plotinian and Gnostic Metaphysics

This axiom of continuous hierarchy is central to Plotinus's monistic doctrine of three principal hypostases, the One, Intellect and Soul, in which the realm of true being and intellect, followed by that of Soul and Nature itself, continuously unfold from their source in the One, a transcendent, only negatively conceivable ultimate unitary principle which is itself beyond being. Every reality subsequent to the One is eternally generated in three continuous phases: first, an initial identity of the product with its source, a sort of potential or prefigurative existence; second, an indefinite procession or spontaneous emission of the product from its source; and third, a contemplative visionary reversion of the product upon its own prefiguration within its source, in which the product becomes aware of its separate existence and thereby takes on its own distinctive form and definition.

> It is because there is nothing in it (the One) that all things come from it: in order that Being may exist, the One is not being, but the generator of being. This, we may say, is the first act of generation: *the One, perfect because it seeks nothing, has nothing, and needs nothing, overflows, as it were, and its superabundance makes something other than itself.* This, when it has come into being, turns back upon the One and is filled, and becomes Intellect by looking towards it. Its halt and turning towards the One

---

8  Mazur 2005a.

constitutes Being; its gaze upon the One, Intellect. Since it halts and turns towards the One that it may see, it becomes at once Intellect and Being.[9]

The later Neoplatonists named these three stages *permanence* or *remaining*, *procession* and *reversion*, and often characterized the three successive modes of the product's existence during this process by the terms of the noetic triad of Being, Life and Intellect.

Although Plotinus has often been credited as the first major philosopher to elaborate such a scheme of ontogenesis, it is clear that similar models of dynamic emanation were beginning to develop in gnostic thought and expressed in various texts, some lost, some extant, and even some known to Plotinus, such as the Nag Hammadi Platonizing Sethian treatises Zostrianos and Allogenes and, as seems increasingly likely, even the Valentinian Tripartite Tractate.[10] For most gnostic models of ontogenesis, including that of the Tripartite Tractate, the supreme principle engages in a direct self-reflexive thinking that becomes instantiated in the second principle,[11] whereas in

---

9  Plotinus, *Enn.* V.2[11].1.8–13 (Armstrong 1966–88).
10  See Turner and Corrigan, 2015; Turner 2013 and 2015.
11  Thus at the beginning of the Tri. Trac., the ineffable Father has a thought of himself, which is the Son (Tri. Trac. NHC I,5 56.16–57.3). Likewise in Clement of Alexandria, *Exc.* 7 (Casey 1934), the Unknown Father is said to emit the second principle, the Monogenes-Son, "as if knowing himself" (ὡς ἂν ἑαυτὸν ἐγνωκώς, … προέβαλε τὸν Μονογενῆ). In both Eugnostos and its nearly identical but Christianized version, the Wis. Jes. Chr., the divine Forefather sees himself "within himself as in a mirror", and the resultant image is the second principle, the Self-Father. Eugnostos NHC III,3 74.21–75.12 (Parrott 1996): "The Lord of the Universe is not rightly called 'Father' but 'Forefather.' For the Father is the beginning (*or* principle) of what is visible. For he (the Lord) is the beginningless Forefather. He sees himself within himself, like a mirror, having appeared in his likeness as Self-Father, that is, Self-Begetter, and as Confronter, since he is face to face with the Unbegotten First Existent. He is indeed of equal age with the one who is before him, but he is not equal to him in power." Also 72.10–11: "It looks to every side and sees itself from itself." Cf. The Wis. Jes. Chr. NHC III,4 98.24–99.13 & 95.6. In Hippolytus of Rome's account in *Haer.* VI.13 of Simonian doctrine, the pre-existent first principle abides in absolute unity, but gives rise to an intellectual principle through self-manifestation: "manifesting himself to himself, the one who stood became the second." (my translation of Marcovich 1986). According to the initial theogony of Ap. John, the supreme Invisible Spirit emanates an overflow of luminous water in which he then sees a reflection of himself; this self-vision then becomes the second, intellectual, principle, Barbelo, the divine First Thought. Ap. John BG 2 8502.2 (cf. also NHC II,1; III,1; and IV,1) 26.1–30.4: "For it is he (the Invisible Spirit or Monad) who contemplates himself in his own light that surrounds him, which is he himself, the source of living water…. The fountain of the Spirit flowed from the living luminous water and provided all aeons and worlds. In every direction he contemplated his own image (εἰκών), beholding it in the pure luminous water that surrounds him. And his Thought (ἔννοια) became active and appeared and stood at rest before him in the brilliance of the light. She

the ontogenetic model underlying Plotinus and the Platonizing Sethian treatises, only the spontaneous efflux from the One, but not the One itself, knows or reflexively acts upon itself. To better understand Plotinus's critique of gnostic metaphysics, I offer the following sketch of the transcendental metaphysics of both the Sethian Platonizing treatises and the Valentinian Tripartite Tractate.

## 2    The Metaphysics of the Sethian Platonizing Treatises

The metaphysical hierarchy of the Platonizing Sethian treatises is headed by a supreme and pre-existent Unknowable One, often called the Invisible Spirit.[12] As in Plotinus, this One is clearly beyond being, and can be described only in negative terms mostly derived from the second half of Plato's *Parmenides*, especially its first hypothesis.[13]

Below the supreme One, at the level of determinate being, is the Barbelo Aeon, conceived along the lines of a Middle Platonic tripartite divine Intellect as posited by Numenius and Amelius.[14] At its highest level, Kalyptos is the contemplated intellect (the νοῦς νοητός) in which are "hidden" the paradigmatic ideas or authentic existents.[15] At its median level, Protophanes is the

---

[is the Providence (πρόνοια) of the All] the likeness of the light, the image of the invisible One, the perfect power Barbelo" (my translation).

12    From certain earlier Sethian treatises (Ap. John, Three Forms, and the Gos. Eg.), the Platonizing treatises have inherited a tendency to identify the supreme deity by the somewhat Stoicizing name "the Invisible Spirit". While the Steles Seth NHC VII,5 125.23–5) calls this supreme pre-existent One a "single living Spirit", Zost. identifies this One as "the Triple Powered Invisible Spirit". On the other hand, Allogenes tends to distinguish this One from both the Invisible Spirit and the Triple Powered One, while Marsanes supplements them all with a supreme "unknown silent One".

13    Plato, *Parm.* 137c–142a.

14    These functional distinctions within the divine intellect were justified by a reading of the *Timaeus*'s (Plato, *Tim.* 39e) doctrine of a transcendent model contemplated by a demiurge who then orders the universe in accord with the model (Jowett 2010): "According, then, as Reason (the Demiurge) perceives Forms existing in the Absolute Living Creature (the Model), such and so many as exist therein did he deem that this world also should possess," reflected in Numenius, Frag. 11, 13, 15, 16 (des Places 1973), Amelius (Proclus, *In Tim.* 1.306.1–14; 1.309.14–20; 1.431.26–28), and the early Plotinus (*Enn.* III.9[13].1, but rejected in *Enn.*I 1.9[33].1).

15    See Allogenes XI,3 46.6–35. In Zost. NHC VII,1 82.5–13 Kalyptos emerges as the second knowledge of the Invisible Spirit (the first being Barbelo): "And they appeared [through the one (Barbelo)] who foreknows him, being an eternal space, having become a secondary form of his knowledge, even the duplication of his knowledge, the ingenerate Kalyptos" (Turner 2009); In 119.12–13 Kalyptos is associated with his ἰδέα: "And there is Kalyptos, having [joined] with his Idea" (Turner 2009).

contemplating intellect (the νοῦς θεωρητικός) in which these contemplated ideas now "first appear" "all together" in union with the minds that contemplate them.[16] At the lowest level, Autogenes is the "self-generated" demiurgic mind (νοῦς διανοούμενος) who shapes the individuated realm of Nature below him according to the forms in Kalyptos that are contemplated and made available to him by Protophanes.[17] As the equivalent of the Plotinian Soul, Autogenes analyzes these forms in a discursive fashion and thus comes to contain the "perfect individuals," that is the ideas of particular things as well as individual souls. In fact the names of these intellectual principles, Kalyptos, Protophanes, and Autogenes, suggest that they could have designated, not just the ontological levels of the Barbelo Aeon, but also the dynamic process by which the Barbelo Aeon gradually unfolded from its source in the Invisible Spirit as a divine Intellect: at first "hidden" (*Kalyptos*) or latent within the Spirit as the prefiguration of a distinct intellect, then "first appearing" (*Prōtophanēs*) as

16  Apparently to be distinguished both from ideas of particular things (in Autogenes) and from the uncombinable authentic existents in Kalyptos; the status of Plato's "mathematicals" cited in Aristotle, Metaph. 987b14–18; 1080a11–b14. On the phrase "all together" (Coptic ϩιογμα) cf. Plotinus, *Enn*. IV.1[42].1.5–6 (Armstrong 1966–88): "There the whole of Intellect is all together and not separated or divided, and all souls are together" (ἐκεῖ δὲ (i.e. ἐν τῷ νῷ) ὁμοῦ μὲν νοῦς πᾶς καὶ οὐ διακεκριμένον οὐδὲ μεμερισμένον, ὁμοῦ δὲ πᾶσαι ψυχαί); V.8[31].10.16–22 (Armstrong 1966–88): "the gods individually and together (οἱ θεοὶ καθ' ἕνα καὶ πᾶς ὁμοῦ), and the souls who see everything there and originate from everything ... are present there (in the intelligible realm) so long as they are naturally able, but often times—when they are undivided—even the whole of them is present." Cf. Corpus herm., Frag. 21 (Nock and Festugière 1946): "The preexistent one is thus above those that exist and those that truly exist, for there is a preexistent one through which the so-called universal essentiality of those that truly exist is intelligized together, while those that exist are intelligized individually (προὸν [ὂν] γάρ ἐστι, δι' οὗ ἡ οὐσιότης ἡ καθόλου λεγομένη κοινῇ νοεῖται τῶν ὄντως ὄντων καὶ τῶν ὄντων τῶν καθ' ἑαυτὰ νοουμένων, translation mine)." The name Protophanes is derived from a philosophical interpretation of the Orphic figure of Phanes, firstborn from his mother Night; cf. *Orphicorum Hymni* 52.5–6 (Quandt 1973, 1–57); *Papyri Magicae* IV.943–4; IV.1716–1870 (Preisendanz and Henrichs 1973–74), and the Orphic *Argonautica*, line 16 (Dottin 1930): Φάνητα ... καλέουσι βροτοί· πρῶτος γὰρ ἐφάνθη. See Thomassen 2013, 63–71.

17  On the demiurgic activity of Autogenes, see Allogenes XI,3 51.25–32 (Armstrong 1966–88): the Barbelo Aeon is "endowed with the divine Autogenes as an image that knows each one of these (individuals), acting separately and individually, continually rectifying defects arising from Nature." Cf. Untitled BC 3 242.24–253.2 (Schmidt and MacDermot 1978): "Moreover the power that was given to the forefather is called first-visible because it is he who was first manifest (πρωτοφανής). And he was called unbegotten because no one had created him. And he was (called) the ineffable and the nameless one. And he was also called self-begotten (αὐτογενής) and self-willed because he had revealed himself by his own will."

the initially indeterminate emergence of the Spirit's self-thinking, and finally "self-generated" (*Autogenēs*) as a distinct and fully formed demiurgical mind.[18]

Yet when it came to working out the actual dynamics of the emanation of the Barbelo Aeon from the supreme Invisible Spirit, these Platonizing treatises employ a different terminology, namely a version of the noetic triad of Being, Life and Mind.[19] Now Plotinus himself occasionally used this triad to illustrate how the One gives rise to something other than itself, as in the generation of being and intellect from a trace of life emitting from the One.[20] But just as the Sethians confined the Kalyptos–Protophanes–Autogenes triad to the Barbelo Aeon as their second hypostasis, Plotinus too mostly confined the activity of this noetic triad to his second hypostasis, the self-thinking Intellect, where Mind (νοῦς) denotes the thinking subject; Being denotes the object of its thinking; and Life (ζωή) denotes the activity of thinking itself.[21]

In the Platonizing Sethian treatises, the noetic triad appears as the supreme Invisible Spirit's three powers of Existence, Vitality, and Mentality or Blessedness (ὕπαρξις or ὀντότης, ζωότης, and νοότης or μακαριότης) rather than

---

18    In *Ad Candidum* 14.11–14, Victorinus hints at a similar progression: "For what is above ὄν is hidden (cf. Kalyptos) ὄν; indeed the manifestation (cf. Protophanes) of the hidden is generation (cf. Autogenes), since ὄν in potentiality generates ὄν in act" (my translation). Corrigan 1996, 54, raised the possibility of an echo of the Sethian figures Kalyptos, Protophanes and Autogenes in Plotinus, *Enn.* v.5[32].7.31–5 (Armstrong 1966–88): "Thus indeed Intellect, veiled (καλύψας) itself from all the outer, withdrawing to the inmost, seeing nothing, beholds—not some other light in some other thing but the light within itself alone, pure, suddenly apparent (φανέν), so that it wonders whence it appeared (ἐφάνη), from within or without, and when it has gone forth, to say 'It was within; yet no, it was without.'"

19    On the Platonic sources of the triad itself see the seminal article of Hadot 1960a, esp. 199–201.

20    E.g. Plotinus, *Enn.* VI.7[38].17.13–26 (Armstrong 1966–88): "Life, not the life of the One, but a trace of it, looking toward the One was boundless, but once having looked was bounded (without bounding its source). Life looks toward the One and, determined by it, takes on boundary, limit and form … it must then have been determined as (the life of) a Unity including multiplicity. Each element of multiplicity is determined multiplicity because of Life, but is also a Unity because of limit … so Intellect is bounded Life."

21    Hadot 1960a, 130–132. Justified by Plato, *Sophist* 248e–249b (Jowett 2010): "Are we really to be so easily persuaded that change, life, soul and intelligence have no place in the perfectly real (παντελῶς ὄν), that is has neither life (ζωή) nor intelligence (νοῦς), but stands aloof devoid of intelligence (φρόνησις)?" and *Tim.* 39e (Jowett 2010): "the Nous beholds (καθορᾷ) the ideas resident in the veritable living being (ὅ ἐστι ζῷον); such and so many as exist therein he planned (διενοήθη) that the universe should contain." Intellect is not a lifeless being, but an act (Plotinus, *Enn.* v.3[49].5.33–44; cf. II.4[25].3.36; II.9[33].6.14–19; v.5[32].2.9–13; VI.9[9].9.17). The restriction of the triad to Intellect perhaps owes to his aversion to Middle Platonic and Gnostic theologies that multiply the number of transcendental hypostases beyond three.

Being, Life, and Mind (τὸ ὄν, ζωή and νοῦς). This triad serves as the means by which the supreme Unknowable One generates the Aeon of Barbelo in three phases. In its initial phase, (1) the Triple Powered One is a purely static but indeterminate Existence latent within and identical with the supreme One; in its emanative phase it is (2) an indeterminate Vitality that proceeds forth from One; and in its final phase it is (3) a Mentality that contemplates its prefigurative source in the supreme One, an act by which it delimits itself as the fully determinate being of a new and distinct entity, the Aeon of Barbelo.[22]

Moreover, in Allogenes, these descending ontogenetic phases in reverse order also demarcate the phases through which its central character Allogenes contemplatively ascends to reunite with his own primordial prefiguration in the Unknowable One. That is, his mystical ascent retraces the ontogenetic sequence of the phases by which the Invisible Spirit's Triple Power unfolds into the Aeon of Barbelo. The ascent consists of successive contemplative self-withdrawals into his primordial self or "originary manifestation" still resident in the supreme One, and ends in an utter cognitive vacancy where knower and known become completely assimilated to one another, as narrated on pages 60–61 of Allogenes:[23]

> There was within me a stillness of silence, and I heard the Blessedness whereby I knew <my> proper self. And I withdrew to the Vitality as

---

[22] E.g. Zost. NHC VIII,1 81.6–20 (Turner 2009): "She (Barbelo) [was] existing [individually] [as cause] of [the declination]. Lest she come forth anymore or get further away from perfection, she knew herself and him (the Invisible Spirit), and she stood at rest and spread forth on his [behalf] ... to know herself and the one that pre-exists."; Allogenes XI,3 45.22–30 (trans. mine): "For after it (the Barbelo Aeon) [contracted, it expanded] and [spread out] and became complete, [and] it was empowered [with] all of them, by knowing [itself in the perfect Invisible Spirit]. And it [became an] aeon who knows [herself because] she knew that one"; Allogenes NHC XI,3 48.15–17 (trans. mine): "it is with [the] hiddenness of Existence that he provides Being, [providing] for [it in] every way, since it is this that [shall] come into being when he intelligizes himself"; Allogenes NHC XI,3 49.5–26 (trans. mine): "He is endowed with [Blessedness] and Goodness, because when he is intelligized as the Delimiter (D of the Boundlessness (B) of the Invisible Spirit (IS) [that subsists] in him (D), it (B) causes [him (D)] to revert to [it (IS)] in order that it (B) might know what it is that is within it (IS) and how it (IS) exists, and that he (D) might guarantee the endurance of everything by being a cause for those who truly exist. For through him (D) knowledge of it (IS) became available, since he (D) is the one who knows what it (IS; or he, D?) is. But they brought forth nothing [beyond] themselves, neither power nor rank nor glory nor aeon, for they are all eternal." Cf. Ap. John, see note 11 above, where the living waters of the baptismal rite have become a transcendent emanation of luminous, living and self-reflective thinking.

[23] On primary revelation of originary manifestation, see Mazur 2005b.

I sought <myself>. And I joined it and stood, not firmly but quietly. And I saw an eternal, intellectual, undivided motion, all-powerful, formless, undetermined by determination. And when I wanted to stand firmly, I withdrew to the Existence, which I found standing and at rest. Like an image and likeness of what had come upon me by means of a manifestation of the Indivisible and the Stable, I was filled with revelation; by means of an originary manifestation (ⲟⲩⲙⲛ̄ⲧ`ϣⲟⲣⲛ̄ ⲛ̄ⲟⲩⲱⲛϩ̄ ⲉⲃⲟⲗ, perhaps rendering the Greek προφάνεια) of the Unknowable One, [as though] unknowing him, I [knew] him and was empowered by him. Having been permanently strengthened, I knew that [which] exists in me, even the Triple-Powered One and the manifestation of his uncontainableness. [And] by means of an originary manifestation of the universally prime Unknowable One—the God beyond perfection—I saw him and the Triple-Powered One that exists in them all. I was seeking the ineffable and unknowable God of whom—should one know him—one would be completely unknowing, the mediator of the Triple-Powered One, the one who subsists in stillness and silence and is unknowable.[24]

Significantly, in *Enn.* III.8, Plotinus too describes the contemplative ascent to the One as a withdrawal into one's prenoetic, primordial self, which, rather than "originary manifestation," he denominates as the "first life":[25]

What is it, then, which we shall receive when we set our intellect to it? Rather, the intellect must first withdraw, so to speak, backwards, and give itself up, in a way, to what lies behind it—for it faces in both directions; and there, if it wishes to see that First Principle, it must not be altogether intellect. For it is the first life, since it is an activity manifest in the way of outgoing of all things (Ἔστι μὲν γὰρ αὐτὸς ζωὴ πρώτη, ἐνέργεια οὖσα ἐν διεξόδῳ τῶν πάντων·); outgoing not in the sense that it is now in process of going out but that it has gone out. If, then, it is life and outgoing and holds all things distinctly and not in a vague general way—for [in the latter

---

24   Allogenes NHC XI,3 60.14–61.22.
25   Elsewhere Plotinus frequently imputes a kind of transcendent "life" to the activity intrinsic to the One, cf. *Enn.* VI.8[39].7.51 and V.3[49].16.40. On self-vision, see *Enn.* V.8[31].11.1–8 (Armstrong 1966–88): "Further, one of us, being unable to see himself, when he is possessed by that god brings his contemplation to the point of vision, and presents himself to his own mind and looks at a beautified image of himself; but then he dismisses that image, beautiful though it is, and comes to unity with himself, and, making no more separation, is one and all together with that god silently present, and is with him as much as he wants to be and can be."

case] it would hold them imperfectly and inarticulately—it must itself derive from something else, which is no more in the way of outgoing, but is the origin of outgoing, and the origin of life and the origin of intellect and all things (ἀρχὴ διεξόδου καὶ ἀρχὴ ζωῆς καὶ ἀρχὴ νοῦ καὶ τῶν πάντων.).[26]

Moreover, the technique of "learned ignorance" like that found in Allogenes, by which the mystical aspirant knows the One by "unknowing" him,[27] is also invoked, though not further developed, by Plotinus, as in *Enn.* IV.9:[28]

> Abandoning all external things, it [the soul] must revert completely towards the interior, and not be inclined to any of the external things, but un-knowing (ἀγνοήσαντα) all things—both as it had at first, in the sensible realm, then even in that of the forms—and even "un-knowing" itself (ἀγνοήσαντα δὲ καὶ αὐτόν), come to be in the contemplation of that one; and, having come together and having had as it were sufficient intercourse with that, must come to proclaim the communion up there, if possible, also to another.[29]

In this connection, it is worth noting that in *Enn.* VI.7,[30] Plotinus's discussion of the soul's contemplative ascent through Intellect towards the One names the three aspects of Intellect to which the aspirant must become assimilated prior

---

26   Plotinus, *Enn.* III.8.[30].9.29–39.
27   Allogenes NHC XI,3 60.38–61.8 (trans. mine): "As if I were incognizant of him, I [knew] him [i.e. the Unknowable One] ... I knew the (Triple Powered One) that exists in me." Cf. also the anonymous *Parmenides* commentary, Frag. II and IV, and Porphyry *Sent.* 25 (Lamberz 1975, my translation): "By intellection (κατὰ νόησιν) much may be said about that which transcends intellect (τοῦ ἐπέκεινα νοῦ), but it is better contemplated by incognizance than intellection (θεωρεῖται δὲ ἀνοησίᾳ κρείττονι νοήσεως)."
28   Cf. also Plotinus, *Enn.* VI.9[9].6.50–52; VI.7[38].39; V.3[49].12.48–53.
29   Plotinus, *Enn.* VI.9[9].7.16–22.
30   Plotinus, *Enn.* VI.7[38].36.4–12 (Armstrong 1966–68): "The greatest thing is knowledge of or contact with the Good. Plato says that it is "the greatest study," meaning by 'study' not the actual vision but learning something about It beforehand. We learn about It by comparisons and negations and knowledge of the things which proceed from It and intellectual progress by ascending degrees; but we advance towards It by purifications and virtues and adornings of the soul and by gaining a foothold in the world of *Nous* and settling ourselves firmly There and feasting on its contents. Anyone who attains to this at once contemplates himself and everything else and is the object of his contemplation; *he becomes real being and intellect and the Perfect Living Being* (οὐσία καὶ νοῦς καὶ ζῷον παντελές, οὐσία καὶ νοῦς καὶ ζῷον παντελές, cf. Plato, *Tim.* 39e7–9 and *Soph.* 248c–e) and does not look at it any more from outside. When he becomes this he is near; the Good is next above him, close to him, already shining over the whole intelligible world. Then letting all study go, led by his instruction to *Nous* and firmly established in beauty, he raises

to union with the One at the penultimate phase of the contemplative ascent to the Good as "substance and intellect and all—perfect living being" (οὐσία καὶ νοῦς καὶ ζῷον παντελὲς), nearly the exact terms the Platonizing Sethians use to designate the powers of Existence-Vitality-Mentality by which the Invisible Spirit gives rise to the Barbelo Aeon, the same phases traversed by Allogenes as he ascends from the Barbelo Aeon to union with the supreme One. As Zeke Mazur notes, the appearance of these two triads—the contemplated, contemplating, planning intellects of *Enn.* II.9.6.19–23 and the Being-Mind-Life triad of VI.7.36.10–12 cannot be coincidental, and is of profound importance for the debate concerning the provenance of the noetic triad, since Plotinus himself provides evidence for its use by pre–Plotinian gnostics.[31]

## 3   The Metaphysics of the Tripartite Tractate

Despite its absence from the list of the mostly Sethian apocalypses named in Porphyry's *Life of Plotinus* as circulating in Plotinus's circle, the ontogenetic metaphysics of the Tripartite Tractate has recognizable similarities to Plotinus's own. Unlike the Sethian Platonizing treatises, its emanative process is inaugurated by the first principle's direct self-reflexive thinking, described largely through metaphors of flowing, growth, and embryology, rather than through the agency of a hierarchy of ontogenetic principles like the Being-Life-Mind triad. Yet like Plotinus, the Tripartite Tractate also employs the notions of the freedom of the divine will and self-causation,[32] of the physical cosmos as a product of natural wisdom,[33] and that the second principle, spiritual beings are simultaneously present in their entirety as a "one-all" or "one-many."[34]

In the Tripartite Tractate, the generation of all reality other than the supreme principle begins with the emergence of a second principle, the Son, who comes to exist "by the Father having him as a thought, that is, his thought

---

his thought to that in which he is, but is carried out of it by the very surge of the wave of *Nous* and, lifted high by its swell, suddenly sees without knowing how."

[31]   Mazur 2016, 74–76. The main parties to this debate: the case for a post-Plotinian (Porphyrian) origin of the triad have been made by Abramowski 1983, followed by Majercik 1992 and 2005. The case for a pre-Plotinian origin of the triad is made in Corrigan 2001b, while the case for a specifically Sethian origin was made most recently by Rasimus 2010.

[32]   Cf. Plotinus, *Enn.* VI.8[39].16.17–39 with Tri. Trac. NHC I,5 65.34–35; 71,36–72.5; 76.23–25.

[33]   Compare Plotinus, *Enn.* V.8[31].5.1–8 with Tri. Trac. NHC I,5 75.17–76.23.

[34]   Compare Plotinus, *Enn.* V.3[49]. 3,43–46; 15.18–24 with Tri. Trac. NHC I,5 58.21–59.16; 66.34–67.12.

about himself."[35] As in Plotinus, the ambiguity in the antecedents of self-reflexive pronouns, which can refer to either the Father or the Son, is necessary, since the object of the self-perception of both the first and the second principle are one and the same, namely the pre-existent prefiguration of the second in the first. Thus in *Enn.* v.1[10].7, the subject of self-perception can be properly called neither One nor Intellect, but is rather a subject that starts out as the One, but by perceiving itself, ends up as Intellect:

> But we say that Intellect is an image of that Good; for we must speak more plainly; first of all we must say that what has come into being must be in a way that Good, and retain much of it and be a likeness of it, as light is of the sun. But Intellect is not that Good. How then does it generate Intellect? Because by its return to it, it sees: and this seeing is Intellect.[36]

Moreover, the Tripartite Tractate may have provided a clear antecedent for Plotinus's theory of emanation as an undiminished giving. On pages 51, 60, 68, and 74, it likens the supreme Father's emanation of the pleromatic aeons to the effluence of water from an undiminished spring, the sprouting of blossoms from a vine, or branches that spread out from the root of a tree.[37] Significantly,

---

35  Tri. Trac. NHC I,5 56.1–57.3: "Nor it is truly his ineffable self that he (the Father) engenders. It is self-generation, where he conceives of himself and knows himself as he is. He brings forth something worthy of the admiration, glory, praise, and honor that belong to himself, through his boundless greatness, his inscrutable wisdom, his immeasurable power, and his sweetness that is beyond tasting. It is he himself whom he puts forth in this manner of generation, and who receives glory and praise, admiration and love, and it is also he who gives himself glory, admiration, praise, and love. This he has as a Son dwelling in him, keeping silent about him, and this is the ineffable within the ineffable, the invisible, the ungraspable, the inconceivable within the inconceivable. This is how he exists eternally within himself. As we have explained, *by knowing himself in himself the Father bore him (the Son) without generation, so that he exists by the Father having him as a thought—that is, his thought about himself,* his sensation of himself and ... of his eternal self-standing." See also the Val. Exp. NHC XI,2 22.31–9, where it is unclear whether the generation of the second principle is due to the second thinking the first or the first thinking the second.

36  Plotinus, *Enn.*v.1[10].7.1–6.

37  Trip. Trac. NHC I,5 51.8–19: "The Father is singular while being many.... That singular one who is the only Father is in fact like a tree that has a trunk, branches, and fruit"; 60.1–15: "The aeons existed eternally in the Father's thought and he was like a thought and a place for them. And once it was decided that they should be born, he who possesses all power desired to take and bring what was incomplete out of ... those who [were within] him. But he is [as] he is, [for he is] a spring that is not diminished by the water flowing from it"; 62.6–13: "For the Father produced the All like a little child, like a drop from a spring, like a blossom from a [vine], like a ..., like a shoot ..., so that they needed [nourishment],

*Enn.* III.8 is the only other source I can find that combines all three of these images of water and plants together.[38] Although can be found *individually* in Macrobius and the *Corpus Hermeticum*,[39] it is only in Plotinus and the Tripartite Tractate that they are *all* combined together.

## 4  Plotinus's Debate with the Gnostics: Acceptance and Rejection

For the sake of brevity, I will focus only on those features of these gnostic treatises reflected in the first ten chapters of *Enn.* II.9, perhaps completed in the year 265, which, despite their similarity to Plotinus's own, he deems as transgressive, namely their treatment of the supreme principle and divine Intellect, the Soul and demiurge as cosmogonic agents, the ascent of the soul, and their apparent transgression of philosophical tradition and etiquette.

### 4.1  *The Supreme Principle and Primary Ontogenesis*

At many points Plotinus's notion of the supreme One and its generation of subsequent reality is more or less in agreement with and perhaps even indebted to the gnostics. He seldom objects to the general schemes of the unfolding of the transcendent world implemented in the treatises we have examined. Thus he can use the same constellation of natural processes of growth and flowing to illustrate his principle of undiminished giving as does the Tripartite Tractate. When in *Enn.* II.9 3.10–11 Plotinus insists that each successive ontological level from the One through Intellect and Soul on down to the sensible realm is

---

growth, and perfection"; 74.1–18: "the true aeon also is single yet multiple.… Or, to use other similes, it is like a spring that remains what it is even if it flows into rivers, lakes, streams, and canals; or like a root that spreads out into trees with branches and fruits; or like a human body that is indivisibly divided into limbs and limbs—main limbs and extremities, large ones and small."

38  *Enn.* III.8[30].10.3–14 (Armstrong 1966–88, with alterations): "What is above life is cause of life, for the activity of life which is all things is not first; it itself flows forth, so to speak, as if from a spring. Imagine a spring that has no other origin; it gives itself to all the rivers, yet is never used up by the rivers, but remains itself at rest; the rivers that proceed from it remain all together for a while before they run their several ways, yet all, in some sense, know beforehand down what channels they will pour their streams. Or: think of the life coursing throughout some huge plant while its origin remains and is not dispersed over the whole, since it is as it were firmly settled in its root: it is the giver of the entire and manifold life of the tree, but remains unmoved itself, not manifold but the origin of that manifold life."

39  Macrobius, *Somn. Scip.* 2.6.23 (Willis 1970): "fons … qui ita principium est aquae, ut cum de se fluvios et lacus procreet, a nullo nasci ipse dicatur". Cf. *Corp. herm.* 4.10 (Nock and Festugière 1972): ἡ γὰρ μονάς, οὖσα πάντων ἀρχὴ καὶ ῥίζα, ἐν πᾶσίν ἐστιν ὡς ἂν ῥίζα καὶ ἀρχή.

necessarily vivified by its superiors, he seems to be invoking the Platonizing Sethian treatises' own notion that the boundless vitality overflowing from the supreme principle results in the generation of the Barbelo Aeon as a divine intellect. Here, just as in Allogenes (NHC XI,3) 48.29–49.1,[40] Plotinus refers to both a primary and secondary life or vitality as virtual synonyms for his well-known doctrine of two activities (ἐνέργειαι), an 'internal' primary activity by which an entity is what it is, and an incidental 'external' or secondary activity that it emits as an image or trace of its primary internal activity.[41]

Moreover, both Plotinus and Allogenes portray the practice of mystical ascent as a series of contemplative self-withdrawals through primary life of the divine Intellect ending in an unknowing union with the supreme One. Yet, despite these similarities, in *Enn.* II.9.9.45–49, Plotinus's first explicit reference to the gnostic practice of contemplative or visionary ascent accuses them of "boorishness" (ἀγροικία, cf. 9.26) in claiming the ability to ascend beyond even Intellect itself to a point alongside or immediately after the First principle;[42] thus exceeding the natural limit of human capability and situating themselves in a class apart from all other aspirants, whether human or divine.

In the opening chapter of *Enn.* II.9, Plotinus criticizes the gnostics' unnecessary multiplication of distinguishable transcendent hypostases beyond simply the One, Intellect, and Soul. This multiplication of entities is reflected in many pre-Plotinian sources, including the fragments of Numenius's *On the Good*, the *Chaldaean Oracles*, and even the speculations of his disciple Amelius,[43] but most clearly in the doctrine of transcendent triads found in the Platonizing Sethian treatises, namely the Kalyptos–Protophanes–Autogenes levels of the Barbelo Aeon,[44] or at the highest level, the emanative powers of Existence,

---

40   Allogenes NHC XI,3 48.29–49.1 (Turner 2009): "Yet he is a provider of provisions and a divinity of divinity—but whenever they apprehend they participate the First Vitality (ⲧϢⲟⲣⲡ ⲘⲘⲚⲦⲰⲚϨ <*πρώτη ζωότης) and an undivided activity (ἐνέργεια) and a hypostasis of the First One from the One who truly exists. And a second activity (ἐνέργεια) …"; cf. Plotinus, *Enn.* III.8[30].8–10; VI.7.17.13–26.

41   E.g., Plotinus, *Enn.* IV.8[6].6.1–2; V.4[7].2.21–37; V.1[10].6.28–53; IV.5[29].7.13–23; II.9[33].8.11–19; VI.2[43].22.26–29; V.3[49].7.13–3; and VI.8[39].16 V.9[5].8.

42   Plotinus, *Enn.* II.9.45–49 (Armstrong 1966–88): "Then the man of real dignity must ascend in due measure, with an absence of boorish arrogance, going only so far as our nature is able to go, and consider that there is room for the others at God's side, and not set himself alone next after God." Plotinus, however, insists elsewhere that Intellect too must be transcended: *Enn.* VI.9[9].7.16–23; VI.9[9].11.38–45; VI.7[38].22.14–22; VI.8[39].15.14–23.

43   Cf. Amelius cited in Proclus, *In Tim.* I.306.2, 10–14; I.431.26–28; III 103, 18ff.

44   Corrigan 1996, 54, raised the possibility of an echo of the Sethian figures Kalyptos, Protophanes, and Autogenes in Plotinus's treatment of the veiling, "first appearing" and "self-appearing" of intellect in *Enn.* V.5[32].7.31–5 (Armstrong 1966–88): "Thus indeed Intellect, veiled (καλύψας) itself from all the outer, withdrawing to the inmost, seeing

Vitality and Mentality by which the fully-fledged Barbelo Aeon emerges from the supreme Unknowable One.

For Plotinus, the One is entirely transcendent to the second principle Intellect; no hypostatic entity can exist between them as mediator. While the Tripartite Tractate expresses no such mediating entity between the Father and Son, the Sethian concept of the Invisible Spirit's Triple Power of Existence-Vitality-Mentality would certainly qualify as an object of Plotinus's objection. While Zostrianos tends to portray this entity as the Invisible Spirits inherent three-fold power, Allogenes tends to portray it as a quasi-hypostasis interposed between the Unknowable One and the Aeon of Barbelo. As Existence it is essentially identical with the supreme One and as Mentality it is identical with the Barbelo Aeon, while its processional phase of Vitality certainly does mediate between these two. Yet Plotinus too portrays the generation of Intellect as the result of a traversal of vitality or life from its source in the supreme One.[45] Perhaps Plotinus has in mind also the Triple Power's initial phase of Existence when he forbids one to distinguish between One in act and another One in potency, since to posit a potential prefiguration of the second principle in the first would imply an internal complexity within the One that would compromise its absolute simplicity. Yet in less polemical contexts than the *Großschrift*, Plotinus too frequently alludes to a certain minimal subject-object duality in any act of intellection, including the reflexive self-apprehension by which the second principle emerges from the first.[46]

### 4.2   *The Second Principle: Intellect*

In chapter 9 of *Enn.* II.9, Plotinus forbids any partitioning of Intellect:[47] one may not distinguish between an intellect at rest containing all realities

---

nothing, beholds—not some other light in some other thing but the light within itself alone, pure, suddenly apparent (φανέν), so that it wonders whence it appeared (ἐφάνη), from within or without, and when it has gone forth, to say 'It was within; yet no, it was without.'"

45   Cf. Plotinus, *Enn.* III.8[30].8–10; VI.7.17.13–26; cf. Allogenes NHC XI,3 49.5–21.

46   Plotinus, *Enn.* III.9[13].6–9; V.6[24].1–6; III.8[30].8.31–38; VI.7[38].16.9–13, 41; VI.6[34].9.29–42; VI.2[43].6.9–20; V.3[49].1, 10–13.

47   For Plotinus spiritual beings, the Platonic ideas as minds united with their objects of thought, are simultaneously present in their entirety as "all together" in the Intellect. For example, *Enn.* V.3[49].15, 18–24 (Armstrong 1966–88): "For that (Intellect) which comes immediately after it (the One) shows clearly that it is immediately after it because its multiplicity is a one-everywhere (*hen pantachou*); for although it is a multiplicity it is at the same time identical with itself and there is no way in which you could divide it, because "all things are together" (ὁμοῦ πάντα, Anaxagoras Frag. B1 DK); for each of the things also that come from it, as long as it participates in life, is a one-many (*hen panta*), for it cannot

(τὰ ὄντα) and another in motion that contemplates them.[48] Likewise, in chapter 6, he forbids the positing of three intellects—one at rest and containing the Forms (νοῦς νοητός), one contemplating (θεωροῦντος), and one that plans using discursive reason (διανοούμενος) as a faulty interpretation of *Tim.* 39e7–9:

> Generally speaking, some of their ideas have been taken from Plato but others—all the new ideas they have brought in to establish a philosophy of their own—are things they found outside the truth. For the judgments too, and the rivers in Hades and the reincarnations come from Plato. And the making a plurality in the intelligible world—Being and Intellect and the other Maker and the Soul—is taken from the words in the *Timaeus* (39e7–9), for Plato says: "The maker of this universe thought that it should contain all the forms that intelligence discerns contained in the truly living being." But they did not understand, and took it to mean that there is one mind in repose that contains all realities, and another mind different from it which contemplates them, and another which plans, but often they have soul as the maker instead of the planning mind, and they

---

reveal itself as a one-all (*hen polla*), but (Intellect) does reveal itself as a one-all (*hen panta*), since it comes after its origin, for its origin is really and truly one." Cf. Plotinus, *Enn.* V.3.43–46; V.8[31].7–9; VI 7[38] 32, 12–14. Allogenes and Zostrianos express this notion by the phrase "those who are united" in Protophanes: Allogenes NHC XI,3 45.7–8; 46.21; 48.6–8; 55.14–15 and Zost. NHC VIII,1 21.10–11: "undivided, with living thoughts" and 116.1–6 (Turner 2009): "All of them exist in unity, unified and individually, perfected in fellowship and filled with the aeon that truly exists." For the Tripartite Tractate, the Pleromatic aeons are similarly unified: Tri. Trac. NHC I,5 66.34–67.12: "And in the same unitary way they (the aeons) are simultaneously this single *one as well as all* of them.... Rather, he is entirely himself forever; [he is] each and every one of the members of the All eternally at the same time. He is what all of them are, as Father of the All, and the members of the All are the Father as well." Cf. Tri. Trac. NHC I,5 58.21–59.16 (trans. Thomassen, *NHS*): "His offspring, the ones who are, are without number and limit and at the same time indivisible. They have issued from him, the Son and the Father, in the same way as kisses, when two people abundantly embrace one another in a good and insatiable thought—it is a single embrace but consists of many kisses. This is the Church that consists of many people and exists before the aeons and is justly called 'the aeons of the aeons.' ... These [are a] community (*politeuma*) [formed] with one another and [with the ones] who have gone forth from [them and] with the Son, for whom they exist as glory."

48  Even though elsewhere Plotinus suggests that the pre-noetic efflux that emerges from the One to form Intellect either *is* or *is in* a kind of motion. Cf. Plotinus, *Enn.* II.4[12].5.31–34; V.6[24].5.8–9; VI.7[38].16.16–17. Indeed, during his ultimate ascent through these three powers depicted in Allogenes NHC XI,3 59–61, Allogenes finds Vitality, the intermediate term of the triad, to be in motion, while the supreme term, Existence, abides in absolute stasis and silence.

think that this is the maker according to Plato, being a long way from knowing who the maker is.[49]

These three intellects clearly correspond to the three principal subaeons of Barbelo in the Platonizing Sethian treatises, Kalyptos, Protophanes, and Autogenes, each of which emerges through the contemplation of its superior. But rather than regarding this partitioning of Intellect as an accidental misinterpretation of *Tim.* 39e7–9, Plotinus accuses the gnostics of a deliberate falsification of Plato's teaching, a clear instance of transgressive hermeneutics.

Despite Plotinus's reservations, the close, though certainly not exact, similarity of such gnostic transcendental metaphysics to Plotinus's own surely raises the question of the extent to which the doctrines he read in these Platonizing Sethian treatises may have made positive contributions to his own metaphysical philosophy.

### 4.3    The Role of Soul/Wisdom in Cosmogenesis

Plotinus attacks the gnostic idea that in order to produce the physical cosmos, Soul or Sophia had to decline.[50] On the contrary, in *Enn.* v.8[51] he had just argued that the primal wisdom is "neither a derivative nor a stranger in something strange to it," but is constantly consubstantial with true being and thus with Intellect itself, not a departure from it. Plotinus's critique of the gnostic portrayals of Sophia's creative role focuses on two notions: first, that of Wisdom's transgressive descent portrayed in various Sethian, Ophite, and Valentinian sources;[52] and second, the notion that Sophia herself did not decline, but merely looked down and illuminated the lower darkness, especially as portrayed in Zost. (NHC VIII,1) 9.17–10.20, from which he virtually cites about eleven lines.[53]

---

49   Plotinus, *Enn.* II.9[33].6.11–24.
50   Plotinus, *Enn.* II.9.10.19–24. The two seem to be distinct, since Plotinus asks whether both descended together or one was the instigator of a shared transgression.
51   Plotinus, *Enn.* v.8[31].5.
52   Sethian: Ap. John NHC II,1 13.13–14.13; Ophite: Irenaeus, *Haer.* 1.30, Orig. World, Eugnostos, etc.; Valentinian: Tri. Trac. NHC I,5 75.17–76.23; Irenaeus, *Haer.* 1.2.2.13–23.
53   Cf. Zost. NHC VIII,1 9.17–10.20 (Turner 2009): "When Sophia looked [down], she saw the darkness, [illumining it] while maintaining [her own station], being [a] model for [worldly] things, [a principle] for the [insubstantial] substance [and the form]less form [...] a [shapeless] shape. [It makes room] for [every cosmic thing ...] the All [... the corrupt product. Since it is a rational principle that persuades] the darkness, [he sows from his] reason. Since it [is im]possible [for the archon] of [creation] to see any of the eternal entities, he saw a reflection, and with reference to the reflection that he [saw] therein, he created the world. With a reflection of a reflection he worked upon the world, and then even

For they say that *Soul declined to what was below it, and with it some sort of 'Wisdom,'* whether Soul started it or whether Wisdom was a cause of Soul being like this, or whether they mean both to be the same thing, and then they tell us that the other souls came down too, and as members of Wisdom put on bodies, human bodies for instance. *But again they say that very being for the sake of which these souls came down did not come down itself, did not decline, so to put it, but only illumined (supplied form to) the darkness, and so an image from it came into existence in matter. Then they form an image of the image somewhere here below,* through matter or materiality or whatever they like to call it—they use now one name and now another, and say many other names just to make their meaning obscure—*and produce what they call the Maker,* and make him revolt from his mother *and drag the cosmos which proceeds from him down to the ultimate limit of images.*[54]

The notion that Soul or Wisdom descended certainly appears in the Tripartite Tractate's account of the descent of the Logos that results in the creation of irrational and antidivine offspring, to which Plotinus's responds to such a notion is by simply disagreeing with it.[55] The second notion, found in Zostrianos and the Gospel of the Egyptians,[56] neither of which regards Sophia as the creator's mother,[57] holds that, rather than descending, Soul or Sophia remains above and merely illumines the darkness. Since Plotinus largely agrees with

---

*the reflection of the appearance was taken from him.* But Sophia was given a place of rest in exchange for her repentance. *In consequence, because there was within her no pure, original image, either pre-existing in him or that had already come to be through him, he used his imagination and fashioned the remainder,* for the image belonging to Sophia is always corrupt [and] deceptive. *But the Archon—*[*since he simulates*] *and embodies by* [*pursuing the image*] *because of the superabundance* [*that inclined downward*]*—looked down.*" This dependence was first discovered by Tardieu 2005.

54  Plotinus, *Enn.* II.9[33].10.19–32.
55  Plotinus, *Enn.* II.11.1–9, 12.30–44. Instead, according to *Enn.* IV.8[6].1–6, Soul remains above in a primary contemplation of Intellect, which gives rise to a secondary activity that issues in the rise of particular souls as its image, who make a voluntary, spontaneous, sometimes even audacious but necessary descent (*Enn.* IV.8[6].5.16–27) in order to insure that the world's body be inhabited by a soul (cf. *Tim.* 34b8). Various Gnostic sources have Sophia, roughly equivalent to Plotinus's soul transgressively descend: e.g., Ap. John NHC II,1 13.13–14.13, Tri. Trac. NHC I,5 75.17–76.2, and Irenaeus' reports on the Valentinian (*Haer.* 1.2.2,13–23) Ophite (*Haer.* 30.3) myths of the fall of Sophia.
56  Gos. Eg. NHC III,2 56.26–57.5.
57  Unlike Ap. John and Three Forms.

this alternative,[58] he merely moves on to a critique of the gnostic demiurge himself.

### 4.4 The Demiurge

According to Zost. 9.17–10.20, Sophia's illumination of lower darkness or matter generates an initial 'material' image" of herself—itself deceptive and intermittent[59]—that serves as the archetype on which the demiurge attempts to model the cosmos as "an image of an image."[60] But when Sophia repents and is restored to the Pleroma, her image reflected in matter similarly vanishes, leaving the demiurge to rely upon on his own imagination of Sophia's now missing image in order to create the cosmos, a notion Plotinus ridicules earlier.[61] For Plotinus, unlike Nature's "tranquil vision" of the things above,[62] such a creator figure, unable to perceive true being or even his own archetype, can pursue only its secondary images.

In *Enn.* 10.31–32 and elsewhere,[63] Plotinus complains that the gnostics impugn the Demiurge by conflating him with a lowly human artist. Zeke Mazur suggests that this notion is based upon a juxtaposition of Plato's image in the *Timaeus*[64] of a demiurge creating the sensible world as an imitation of the Forms with the *Republic*'s implication that God himself—the Good—*directly* generates the paradigmatic Forms, thereby reading the *Timaeus* and *Republic against* one another, so as to emphasize the vast separation between the true God and the incompetent demiurge along with his mediocre creation, thus subverting what was likely Plato's original intention, a clear case of hermeneutical transgression.[65]

---

58  See *Enn.* II.9.12.31–44; IV.3[27].9.21–26; I.1[53].12.25–27.
59  Zost. NHC VIII,1 10.16.
60  Cf. Plotinus's own version of this in *Enn.* III.9[13].33.7–16 where the image of the "partial soul" descends to generate matter, and descends a "second time" to illumine or inform it.
61  Plotinus, *Enn.* 4.14–15 and 5.5–7 and later in 12.9–16. In *Enn.* 12.6–12, Plotinus writes, "but this image (of Sophia, i.e., the demiurge), even if dimly—as they say—still manages to form a conception (ἐνθυμηθῆναι, cf. Ap. John NHC III,1 14.10–12; Irenaeus, *Haer.* 1.4.1) of the intelligible realities when it has just come into being, whether itself or even its mother, a material image, and not only to conceive them and form an idea of a world and of that world, but to learn the elements from which it could come into being? What could have been the reason why it made fire first?" To such a claim that "there was within her (i.e. Sophia) no pure, original image" (Zost. NHC VIII,1 9.10–11), Plotinus elsewhere objects that "there is in the Nature-Principle itself an ideal archetype of the beauty that is found in material forms" (*Enn.* V.8[31].3.1–3).
62  Plotinus, *Enn.* III.8[30].4, 8.6; cf. II.9.2.
63  Plotinus, *Enn.* 4.14–15; 5.5–7; 12.18–19.
64  Plato, *Tim.* 29a–e.
65  Mazur 2016, 208.

## 4.5  The Ascent of the Soul

Another point of contact between Plotinus and Zostrianos occurs in the critique of the Sethian nomenclature for the psychic aeonic levels extending below the intelligible Barbelo Aeon, namely the Repentance and Sojourn, which Plotinus takes to refer to passions of the soul, as well as Aeonic Copies (ἀντίτυποι), which he correctly takes to refer to images of yet higher realities.[66]

> And what ought one to say of the other beings they introduce, their "Sojourns" and "Antitypes" and "Repentances"? For if they say that these are affections of the soul, when it has changed its purpose, and "Antitypes," when it is contemplating, in a way, images of realities and not the realities themselves, then these are the terms of people inventing a new jargon to recommend their own school. They contrive this meretricious language as if they had no connection with the ancient Hellenic school (αἵρεσις), though the Hellenes knew all this and knew it clearly, and spoke without delusive pomposity of ascents (ἀναβάσεις) from the cave and advancing gradually closer and closer to a truer vision (θέαν ἀληθεστέραν*t* ).[67]

Rather than psychic affections, Sethian sources use these terms to designate distinct aeonic levels between the moon—what Zostrianos calls the "airy earth"—and the Self-generated Aeons in the lowest level of the Barbelo Aeon, inhabited by souls, whether as temporary way-stations during the soul's visionary ascent or as its postmortem destination.[68] Just outside the periphery of the

---

66  Plotinus, *Enn.* 6.1–7. Plotinus lists these terms in the plural, παροικήσεις, μετάνοιαι, and ἀντίτυποι, perhaps because according to Zost. NHC VIII,1 11.2–12.22, these realms exist on two levels, the truly existing Self-generated Aeons, Repentance, and Sojourn as well as their copies (antitypes); thus souls, apparently in the process of reincarnation work their way from the the level of the copies to the level of their exemplars, in order to enter the Self-generated Aeons, where the reincarnational cycle ends; cf. Turner 2001, 109–11, 558–70, and Untitled BC 3 263.11–264.6. He also rejects the sort of magical incantations and sounds found in the Platonizing Sethian treatises generally (*Enn.* II.9[33].14.2–9; cf. Zost. NHC VIII,1 52; 85–88; 118; 127.1–6; Allogenes XI,3 53.32–55.11; 126.1–17; Marsanes NHC X 25.17–32.5). Yet this criticism is offset by his own quasi-incantational etymologies in *Enn.* v.5[32].5.21–27 (Armstrong 1966–88): "Thus that which came to exist, substance and being, has an image of the One since it flows from its power; and the [soul] which sees it and is moved to speech by the sight, imaging what it saw, cried out "ὤν" and "εἶναι," and " οὐσία" and "ἑστία" For these sounds intend to signify the real nature of that produced by the birth pangs of the utterer, imitating, as far as they are able, the generation of real being." and even by the appeal to nondiscursive Egyptian hieroglyphs in *Enn.*v.8 [31].6.1–9.

67  Plotinus, *Enn.* II.9[33].6.1–10.

68  Zost. NHC VIII,1 24.30–25.15, Marsanes NHC X 2,26–3,17 and Untitled BC 3 263.11–264.6.

Barbelo Aeon come the repentant, that is, those who have rejected worldly concerns and fully accepted *gnōsis*;[69] and below these come the sojourners, that is, those loosely affiliated with but not fully included among the Sethian elect in the Self-generated Aeons,[70] having no fixed dwelling place or power and following the practices of others.

## 5 Cultural Transgression

### 5.1 Non-Hellenic Terminological Jargon

Drawing on the work of Denise Buell,[71] Dylan Burns connects such Sethian nomenclature as "sojourners" and an "airy earth" as well as other terms of self-identity such as "ἀλλογενεῖς," literally "stranger," "of another kind or race,"[72] or the "unshakeable race" of "Seth's seed," with ethnic reasoning, specifically the Judaeo-Christian "resident alien motif" applied by scripture to both non-Israelites dwelling in Israel and to Israelites in exile from their own land, by Philo to the soul exiled in a physical body, as well as by elect Christians and gnostics to themselves as aliens sojourning in an inhospitable world.[73] Burns concludes that for Plotinus, such ethnic language culled from the traditions of Jewish literature must have signalled a rejection of Hellenic heritage in which ethnicity was defined chiefly by one's mastery of the Greek classics.[74]

---

69  According to the *de anima* passage in the Ap. John NHC II,1 9.18–23, those who repent seem to correspond to those who, although not generically included among the seed of Seth in the third luminary Daveithai, nevertheless shall finally repent and enter the fourth luminary Eleleth.

70  Cf. Apoc. Adam NHC V,5 73.13–24 (MacRae and Parrott 2009): "Then others from the seed of Ham and Japheth will come, four hundred thousand men, and enter into another land and sojourn (ϭⲟⲓⲗⲉ) with those men who came forth from the great eternal knowledge (i.e., the angels of 72.10–11, identified as the heavenly seed of the heavenly Seth in 65.5–9). For the shadow of their power will protect those who have sojourned with them from every evil thing and every unclean desire."

71  Buell (2005, 139) argues in part that "ethnic reasoning allowed Christians not only to describe themselves as a people, but also to depict the process of becoming a Christian was one of crossing a boundary from membership in one race to another."

72  Derived from the σπέρμα ἕτερον of Gen. 4:25; cf. Pi-Geradamas perhaps "the stranger (Heb. gēr) Adamas."

73  Burns 2014, 102–104, referring to Dunning 2009, 25–40.

74  Burns 2014, 88: "When we recall that for the Neoplatonists, ethnicity was defined chiefly by one's mastery of the Greek classics. More strikingly, the Sethian texts describe their in-group and its teaching not simply as superior to other races or nations, but as 'elect,' 'saved,' in contrast to souls that will be destroyed. Surely members of the Sethian

In chapters 5 and 11 of *Enn*.II.9[75] Plotinus objects to the concept of a certain supernal "New Earth" that can be found in various gnostic sources, no doubt the same as the "Airy Earth" (ⲕⲁϩ ⲛ̄ⲁⲏⲣ) mentioned in Zostrianos.[76] While Plotinus thinks his opponents have invented this "airy earth" as a *destination* for either a visionary or postmortem ascent of their souls, the gnostic sources actually portray it as a place intermediate between the physical cosmos and the superior aeons that serves as a kind of 'staging area'—perhaps the moon itself— for souls during their ascent to yet higher realms.[77] According to Zostrianos,[78] souls ascending from the perceptible earth to the Self-generated Aeons in the lower extremity of the Barbelo Aeon must traverse first, the thirteen cosmic aeons presided over by the world ruler up to the Airy Earth, followed by the Aeonic Copies or antitypes, the Sojourn (παροίκησις), and the Repentance (μετάνοια), whence they finally enter the Self-generated Aeons.

Zeke Mazur has pointed out that Plotinus may have perceived here yet another transgressive juxtaposition of independent passages from Plato, namely that the gnostic's Airy Earth must have been derived from a transgressive conflation of two distinct locations successively described by Socrates in Plato's *Phaedo*,[79] the "true earth"[80] located just beyond the cosmic sphere that serves as the imperishable paradigm of our inferior earth, and its opposite, the fiery rivers of the Hades as places of postmortem judgments and torments, which by Plotinus's time had been transposed into the heavens.[81] For Plotinus, such illegitimate grafting together of originally independent motifs not only impugns the physical cosmos as a the equivalent of Hell, but also demotes Plato's

---

elect were educated in the Hellenic schools, but there is no sign in the texts that they continued to identify as Hellenes, and many signs that they regarded themselves as something much more—'the living, the Seed of the holy Seth'!"

75  Plotinus, *Enn*. 11.9.5.26–32, 11.8–15; cf. v.8[31].3.27–4.19.
76  In Zost. NHC VIII,1 5.17–18; 8.11; 9.3; 130.1 as well as in Gos. Eg. NHC III,2 50.10 // NHC IV,2 62.9 and Untitled BC 3 20.263.16–17. Cf. also the "new earth" in Untitled BC 3 12.249.21 and the Manichaean *Kephalaia* §55.
77  According to Proclus, *In Plat. Tim. comm*. 2.16.1–7. Porphyry claimed that the "Egyptians"— whoever this means—consider the Moon to be an "aetherial Earth" (γῆ αἰθερία) into which the demiurge sows souls who gestate there for a certain period of time prior to their descent into bodies. In *In Tim*. 2.48.15–21, Proclus attributes to the "Pythagoreans" a similar doctrine in the form of an ostensibly Orphic fragment (Frag. 91; Kern 1922, 161) to the effect that the Moon is an "aetherial Earth" with innumerable mountains, cities and mansions. Cf. also Macrobius, *Somn. Scip*. 1.11.7.
78  Zost. NHC VIII,1 4.21–5.23; cf. 5.10–29; 8.9–16; 12.4–21 etc.
79  Plato, *Phaed*. 109e–111c.
80  Plato, *Phaed*. 110a1.
81  Mazur 2016, 58–61.

true Earth to a mere way station on the way to the loftier intelligible realm of the Barbelo Aeon, a realm to which the Sethian elect have exclusive access, but of which Plato had no knowledge.

### 5.2  Transgression of Philosophical Tradition and Etiquette

Conceiving of these intermediate aeonic levels to represent further superfluous gnostic "hypostases" whose names are merely "terms of people inventing a new jargon to recommend their own school," Plotinus continues in chapter 6 with what seems to be his fundamental criticism, that the gnostics plagiarize and then falsify Plato's teaching:

> And in general they falsify Plato's account of the making and a great deal else, and degrade the great man's teaching as if they had understood the intelligible nature, but he and the other blessed philosophers had not.... (here Plotinus summarizes his doctrine of the One, Intellect, and Soul) ... They themselves have received from them (the godlike ancient authorities) what is good in what they say—the immortality of the soul, the intelligible universe, the first god, the necessity for the soul to shun fellowship with the body, the separation from the body, the escape from becoming to being—for these doctrines are there in Plato, and when they state them clearly in this way they do well. If they wish to disagree on these points, there is no unfair hostility in saying to them that they should not recommend their own opinions to their audience by ridiculing and insulting the Greeks but that they should show the correctness on their own merits of all the points of doctrine which are peculiar to them and differ from the views of the Greeks, stating their real opinions courteously, as befits philosophers, and fairly on the points where they are opposed, looking to the truth and not hunting fame by censuring men who have been judged good from ancient times by men of worth and saying that they themselves are better than the Greeks. For what is said by the ancients about the intelligible world is far better, and is put in a way appropriate to educated men (πεπαιδευμένως), and it will be easily recognized by those who are not utterly deceived by the delusion that is rushing upon men that these teachings have been taken by them later from the ancients, but have acquired some entirely inappropriate additions. On the points, at any rate, on which they wish to oppose the ancient teachings they introduce all sorts of comings into being and passings away, and disapprove of this universe, and blame the soul for its association with the body and censure the director of this universe, and identify its maker with the soul,

and attribute to this universal soul the same affections as those which the souls in some parts of the universe have.[82]

Here Plotinus claims that whatever the gnostics happen to get right, they have taken from Plato, and whatever remainder of their doctrine was not derived from Plato has no claim to authority and is therefore simply false. As Burns has argued at length,[83] while Plotinus is aware of the serious debt that the gnostics owe to Plato for their own doctrines, he is unwilling to consider them good-faith philosophical rivals due to what he perceives to be their lack of acceptable philosophical etiquette.[84] Because they attribute their knowledge of Platonic metaphysical structures and conceptions to visionary revelations from various heavenly angels, glories, and luminaries and defer to the authority of Judaeo-Christian antediluvian sages like Adam and Seth, Plotinus can accuse his opponents of founding their own philosophical sect, dissociating themselves from the authority of the Platonic school, and "ridiculing the Greeks," i.e., those who do speak in an educated, cultured manner (πεπαιδευμένως).[85]

Apparently these gnostics latched upon Platonic metaphysical doctrines as virtual revelations because they furnished a precise, respected philosophical vocabulary for constructing propositions about the divine. Yet in situations of open disputation like Plotinus's seminars, asserting such propositions could threaten to upset established patterns of social authority, especially when

---

82  Plotinus, *Enn.* II.9[33].6.24–53.
83  Burns 2014, 42–47, esp. 46: "Plotinus says they are stupid and that they speak like bumpkins, that is, not like Hellenes, who speak in an educated and cultured manner, despite their claim that gnosis is philosophical. What Plotinus means is not that they are incapable of engaging in technical metaphysics … rather that they eschew the contemporary culture of philosophy, a way of life that goes back to ancients [Greeks] like Pythagoras, and that encourages civic activity and respect for traditional cultic practices. The situation was exacerbated by the pseudepigraphical appeal to the authority of Judaeo-Christian antediluvian sages in their apocalypses."
84  They neither discourse courteously and philosophically (εὐμενῶς καὶ φιλοσόφως) and fairly (δικαίως), nor learn with good will (II.9. 6.37, 48; 8.6). Burns 2014, 43 n.83 notes that "Plotinus never explicitly spells out what a proper approach to philosophical problems and 'ancient authorities' looks like, but we can imagine it probably resembled something like his remarks at the beginning of On Time and Eternity (3.7 [45] 1.13–17): 'Now we must consider that some of the blessed philosophers of ancient times have found out the truth (i.e., about time and eternity); but it is proper to investigate (ἐπισκέψασθαι) which of them have attained it most completely, and how we could reach an understanding (συνήσις) about these things.'"
85  In his *Vit. Plot.* 16.8–9, Porphyry even says that in their opinion, Plato failed to penetrate "intelligible being," although no extant gnostic treatise claims this.

appropriated by self-taught men who had not been socialized into an ethos subordinating individual advantage to "the common good" as defined by the formally educated. Such autodidacts might indeed flout the conventions of their society, which stipulated gentlemanly tranquility and social privilege as the fundamental requirements for attaining true elevated knowledge and the competence to discourse on issues concerning ultimate reality. Since contemplation of the higher order through human reason alone was regarded as a fundamentally impossible proposition,[86] it is perhaps natural that they might resort to the agency of angelic mediators as essential to securing and authenticating knowledge of the divine world. Unfortunately, such revelations would tend to describe what for Plotinus is a continual and spontaneous generation of reality through endless contemplation[87] by means of a theogony that narrated conceptually distinguishable phases in the generation of reality as a temporal sequence of episodes involving distinct acts and *dramatis personae*.

## 6  Hermeneutical Innovation

Given the number of similarities between the metaphysics of the gnostics and that of Plotinus,—some of which seem to indicate instances of his own indebtedness to gnostic thought—one must raise the question whether the degree of transgressiveness he attributes to gnostic thought rises to the level of true countercultural conflict with the larger dominant culture in the sense of a "deviance so subversive that it reverses and redefines whatever it contacts." These similarities and interdependencies between the transcendental metaphysics of Plotinus and the gnostics seem to me actually to be cases of mutual hermeneutical innovation rather than countercultural protests, except perhaps on the part of certain members of Plotinus's rather privileged circle. The designation countercultural vis-à-vis the broader, educated Greco-Roman stratum of society might more appropriately be applied to the gnostics' preference for assertion rather than deliberation, their use of non-Hellenic, Judaeo-Christian terminology to describe the contents of the sub-Pleromatic world, and their reliance on revelation rather than reasoned argument. Time has not permitted any discussion of transgressions that are more indicative of a

---

86   As Plato says in *Tim.* 28c (Jowett 2010): "Now to discover the Maker and Father of this Universe were a task indeed; and having discovered Him, to declare Him unto all men were a thing impossible."

87   Plotinus, *Enn.* III.8[30].7.14–27.

gnostic violations of the dominant social and ethical norms of Plotinus's time: possible licentious or antinomian conduct, arrogant claims to a privileged status and extraordinary contemplative abilities exclusive to themselves alone, and excessive discontent with perceived defects and inequalities in the sub-intelligible world and human society that suggest a failure to accept the natural hierarchical ordering of the entire cosmos by the divine necessity. Perhaps here one may indeed speak of a genuine counterculturalism.

## Bibliography

Abramowski, Luise. 1983. "Marius Victorinus, Porphyrius und die römischen Gnostiker." *Zeitschrift für dir Neutestamentliche Wissenschaft* 74.1–2: 108–128.

Armstrong, A. H. 1966–1988. *Plotinus. Text with an English Translation*. 7 vols. LCL. Cambridge: Harvard University Press.

Buell, Denise Kimber. 2005. *Why This New Race: Ethnic Reasoning in Early Christianity*. New York: Columbia University Press.

Burns, Dylan. 2014. *Apocalypse of the Alien God: Platonism ad the Exile of Sethian Gnosticism*. Philadelphia: University of Pennsylvania Press.

Casey, Robert P., ed. 1934. *The Exerpta Ex Theodoto of Clement of Alexandria*. Studies and Documents 1. London: Christophers.

Corrigan, Kevin. 1996. "The Anonymous Turin Commentary on the Parmenides and the Distinction between Essence and Existence in Middle Platonism, Plotinus's Circle, and Sethian Gnostic Texts." Paper presented at the Annual Meeting of the Society of Biblical Literature. New Orleans, LA, 24 November.

Corrigan, Kevin. 2001a. "Positive and Negative Matter in Later Platonism: The Uncovering of Plotinus's Dialogue with the Gnostics." Pages 19–56 in *Gnosticism & Later Platonism: Themes, Figures, and Texts*. SBL Symposium Series 12. Edited by John D. Turner and Ruth Majercik. Atlanta: The Society of Biblical Literature.

Corrigan, Kevin. 2001b. "Platonism and Gnosticism. The Anonymous Commentary on the *Parmenides*: Middle or Neoplatonic?" Pages 141–177 in *Gnosticism & Later Platonism: Themes, Figures, and Texts*. SBL Symposium Series 12. Edited by John D. Turner and Ruth Majercik. Atlanta: The Society of Biblical Literature.

DeConick, April D. 2013a. "Crafting Gnosis: Gnostic Spirituality in the Ancient New Age." Pages 285–305 in *Gnosticism, Platonism and the Late Ancient World. Essays in Honour of John D. Turner*. Edited by Kevin Corrigan and Tuomas Rasimus. Nag Hammadi and Manichaean Studies 82. Leiden/Boston: Brill.

DeConick, April D. 2013b. "Gnostic Spirituality at the Crossroads of Christianity: Transgressing Boundaries and Creating Orthodoxy." Pages 148–184 in *Beyond the Gnostic Gospels. Studies Building on the Work of Elaine Pagels*. Edited by Eduard

Iricinschi, Lance Jenott, Nicola Denzey Lewis and Philippa Townsend. Tübingen: Mohr Siebeck.

des Places, Édouard. 1973. *Numénius Fragments*. Paris: Société d'Éditions "Les Belles Lettres."

Dottin, Georges. 1930. *Les argonautiques d'Orphée*. Paris: Société d'Éditions "Les Belles Lettres."

Dunning, Benjamin H. 2009. *Aliens and Sojourners. Self as Other in Early Christianity, Divinations: Rereading Late Antique Religion*, Philadelphia: University of Pennsylvania Press.

Edwards, Marc J. 1989. "*Aidôs* in Plotinus: Enneads II.9.10." *Classical Quarterly* 39.1: 228–232.

Hadot, Pierre. 1960a. "Être, Vie, Pensée chez Plotin et avant Plotin." Pages 107–141 in *Les sources de Plotin, Entretiens sur l'Antiquité classique 5*. Edited by E. R. Dodds et al. Vandoeuvres – Genéve: Fondation Hardt.

Hadot, Pierre. 1960b. *Marius Victorinus: Traitées théologiques sur la Trinité: texte établi par Paul Henry, introduction, traduction et notes par Pierre Hadot*. 2 vols. Sources chrétiennes 68–69. Paris: Cerf.

Jowett, Benjamin. 2010. *The Dialogues of Plato: Translated into English with Analyses and Introduction* 4 vols. Cambridge: Cambridge University Press.

Kern, Otto. 1922. *Orphicorum fragmenta, collegit Otto Kern*. Berlin: Weidemann.

Lamberz, Erich, ed. 1975. *Porphyrii sententiae ad intelligibilia ducentes*. Leipzig: Teubner.

MacDermot, Violet, trans. 1978. *The Books of Jeu and the Untitled Text in the Bruce Codex*. Edited by Carl Schmidt. Nag Hammadi Studies 23. Leiden: Brill.

MacRae, George W. and Douglas M. Parrott. 1996. "Apocalypse of Adam." Pages 260–268 in *The Nag Hammadi Library in English*, 4th Revised Edition. Edited by James M. Robinson. Leiden: Brill.

Majercik, Ruth. 1992. "The Existence—Life—Intellect Triad in Gnosticism and Neoplatonism." *Classical Quarterly* 42.2: 475–488.

Majercik, Ruth. 2005. "Porphyry and Gnosticism." *Classical Quarterly* 55.1: 277–292.

Marcovich, Miroslav, ed. 1986. *Hoppolytus Refutatio Omnium Haeresium*. Patristische Texte Und Studien 25. Berlin: De Gruyter.

Mazur, Zeke. 2005a. "Plotinus' Philosophical Opposition to Gnosticism and the Axiom of Continuous Hierarchy." Pages 95–112 in *History of Platonism: Plato Redivivus*. Edited by John Finamore and Robert Berchman. New Orleans: University Press of the South.

Mazur, Zeke. 2005b. "Primordial Self-Reversion and the Gnostic Background of Plotinian Procession." Unpublished paper presented at the Annual Meeting of the International Society for Neoplatonic Studies. New Orleans, LA, June 2005.

Mazur, Zeke. 2016. "Notes pour Plotin, Traité 33 (II 9) Contre les Gnostiques. Draft 1." Forthcoming in *Plotin: Oeuvres complètes*. Tome 7. Collection des Universités de

France-Association Gillaume Budé. Edited by Jean-Marc Narbonne, Mauricio Pagotto Marsola, Lorenzo Ferroni, Kevin Corrigan, and John D. Turner. Paris: Les Belles Lettres.

Narbonne, Jean-Marc. 2011. *Plotinus in Dialogue with the Gnostics*. Leiden: Brill.

Nock, Arthur D. and André-Jean Festugière. 1946. *Corpus hermeticum*. Tomo 1, Pimander. Trattati II–XII. Edited by Arthur D. Nock. Translated by André-Jean Festugière. Paris: les Belles Lettres.

Parrott, Douglas M. 1996. "Eugnostos the Blessed." Pages 220–243 in *The Nag Hammadi Library in English*, 4th Revised Edition. Edited by James M. Robinson. Leiden: Brill.

Preisendanz, Karl and Albert Henrichs, eds. 1973–72. *Papyri Graecae Magicae. Die griechischen Zauberpapyri*. 2 vols. (1: 1973; 2: 1974) 2nd ed. Stuttgart: Teubner.

Puech, Henri-Charles. 1960. "Plotin et les Gnostiques." Pages 161–174 in *Les Sources de Plotin: dix exposés et discussions*. Entretiens sur l'Antiquité classique. Edited by E.R. Dodds et al. Geneva: Fondation Hardt.

Quandt, Wilhelm. 1973. *Orphei hymni*, 3rd ed. Berlin: Weidmann.

Rasimus, Tuomas. 2010. "Porphyry and the Gnostics: Reassessing Pierre Hadot's Thesis in Light of the Second- and Third-Century Sethian Treatises." Pages 81–110 in *Plato's Parmenides and its Heritage*. Vol. 2: *Its reception in Neoplatonic, Jewish, and Christian Texts*. Edited by John D. Turner and Kevin Corrigan. Atlanta: The Society of Biblical Literature.

Rasimus, Tuomas. 2013. "Johannine Background of the Being-Life-Mind Triad." Pages 369–401 in *Gnosticism, Platonism and the Late Ancient World. Essays in Honour of John D. Turner*. Nag Hammadi and Manichaean Studies 82. Edited by Kevin Corrigan and Tuomas Rasimus. Leiden: Brill.

Schmidt, Carl and Violet MacDermot, eds. 1978. *The Books of Jeu and the Untitled Text in the Bruce Codex*. Nag Hammadi Studies 13. Leiden: Brill.

Tardieu, Michel. 2005. "Plotin citateur du Zostrien." Unpublished paper for the "Colloquium on Thèmes et problèmes du traité 33 de Plotin contre les Gnostiques." Collège de France, Paris, 7 June.

Thomassen, Einar. 2013. "Sethian Names in Magical Texts: Protophanes and Meirotheos," Pages 63–78 in *Gnosticism, Platonism and the Late Ancient World. Essays in Honour of John D. Turner*. Nag Hammadi and Manichaean Studies 82. Edited by Kevin Corrigan and Tuomas Rasimus. Leiden: Brill.

Turner, John D. 2009. Allogenes the Stranger in *The Nag Hammadi Scriptures: The International Edition*. Edited by Marvin Meyer. New York: Harper Collins Publishers.

Turner, John D. 2009. "Zostrianos." Pages 537–584 in *The Nag Hammadi Scriptures: The International Edition*. Edited by Marvin Meyer. New York: Harper Collins Publishers.

Turner, John D. 2013. "Plotinus and the Gnostics: The *Tripartite Tractate*?" Paper presented at the Annual Meeting of the Society of Biblical Literature. Baltimore, MD, 17 November 2013.

Turner, John D. 2016. "Self-Reflexive Ontogenesis in the Tripartite Tractate and Plotinus." Forthcoming in *Defining Platonism: Essays on Plato, Middle and Neoplatonism, and Modern Platonism*. Edited by John Finamore and Sarah Wear. New York: Cambridge University Press.

Turner, John D. and Kevin Corrigan. 2015. "Plotinus and the Gnostics: the Peculiar Impact of the Tripartite Tractate and Later Works." in *Estratégias anti-gnósticas nos escritos de Plotino. Atas do colóquio internacional realizado em São Paulo em 18–19 de março 2012*. Serie Classica. Edited by Mauricio Marsilio. São Paulo: Rosari et Paulus.

Willis, Jacob. 1970. *Ambrosii Theodosii Macrobii Commentarii in Somnium Scipionis*. Leipzig: Teubner.

# Forbidden Knowledge: Cognitive Transgression and "Ascent Above Intellect" in the Debate Between Plotinus and the Gnostics

Zeke Mazur
Université Laval
zekemazur@gmail.com

In his treatise *Against the Gnostics*, Plotinus repeatedly complains that the gnostics claim to possess some propensity for contemplation that allows them unique access to the divine Intellect.[1] At one point he even implies that they go so far as to presume to be able to *surpass the Intellect altogether* and thus to attain a privileged place for themselves alone next to the transcendent deity at the apex of a visionary ascent. Not only (according to Plotinus) does such phantasmagorical hubris preclude any possibility of divinization, it also results in a catastrophe:

> [T]he dignified person must ascend in a measured fashion, without boorishness, going just as far as one's nature is able, but one also must consider there to be space beside God for the others, and not rank oneself alone right next to him (it is just like flying in one's dreams!), thus depriving oneself of becoming god even insofar as it is possible for a human soul. *One is able to go as far as Intellect leads, but to go above Intellect is immediately to fall outside of it!* (δύναται δὲ εἰς ὅσον νοῦς ἄγει· τὸ δ' ὑπὲρ νοῦν ἤδη ἐστὶν ἔξω νοῦ πεσεῖν).[2]

What is most peculiar about Plotinus's axiomatic injunction—namely, that an ascent *above* intellect inevitably results in a catastrophic fall *outside* of it—is its apparent hypocrisy.[3] For central to Plotinus's own life and thought is a contemplative ascent towards union with a supreme principle, the One or the

---

1 Plotinus, *Enn.* II.9[33].5.1–8, 6.28–34, 9.45–60, 9.75–83, 18.30–38; see also Porphyry, *Vit. Plot.* 16.6–9.
2 Plotinus, *Enn.* II.9[33].9.45–52. For the Greek critical edition of Plotinus see Henry and Schwyzer 1964–1983. This and all subsequent translations mine unless otherwise noted.
3 This perplexity has been remarked by certain scholars. For instance, Narbonne (2011: 103–116) suggests that in treatises written after his midcareer anti-gnostic tetralogy, Plotinus rejects the solitary ascent above intellect in reaction to gnostic claims; and yet, while it is certainly true that later accounts of ascent tend to de-emphasize the rejection or transcendence of

Good, which explicitly abides *beyond both Being and Intellect*. According to Porphyry, Plotinus attained some kind of mystical union with this principle four times during the time that the two men were together,[4] and at several points throughout his own oeuvre, Plotinus himself describes the contemplative ascent to the One in terms of the transcendence of Intellect,[5] in one case even μόνος πρὸς μόνον, "alone with the alone."[6] Although many passages necessarily imply a hyper-noetic phase of ascent, perhaps the clearest explicit statement—which I will quote here simply to illustrate the contrast—occurs in his 38th treatise, written at some point after his great anti-gnostic tetralogy (chronologically treatises 30 to 33); here, Plotinus insists that the soul, having been inspired by an initial glimpse of the supreme principle,

> naturally rises upwards, raised up by the provider of love; and *it rises up above intellect* (νοῦ ... ὑπεραίρει), but it is not able to run up above the Good, because there is nothing lying 'above' it; but if it remains in intellect, it beholds beauties and noble things, yet still does not entirely have what it seeks.[7]

We might note here the radical nature of Plotinus's own claim, within a Greek philosophical context, to surpass the intellect during a contemplative ascent.[8] Yet precisely such an ascent beyond intellect is described with meticulous detail in the Platonizing Sethian gnostic 'ascent pattern' tractates Zostrianos (NHC VIII,1) and Allogenes (NHC XI,3) that are homonymous with those gnostic apocalypses said by Porphyry to have been read and critiqued at length in Plotinus's circle,[9] as well as in the closely related tractate Marsanes

---

    intellect at the final phase, one nevertheless can find instances of this in later, post-tetralogical passages such as VI.7[38].22.17–22 and VI.8[39].15.14–23.

4  Porphyry, *Vit. Plot.* 23.7–18.
5  Plotinus, *Enn.* I.6[1].7.1–19; VI.9[9].7.1–26, 11.4–25, 11.35–45; III.8[30].9.19–32; VI.7[38]. 34.1–4, 35.1–7, 36.10–26.
6  Plotinus, *Enn.* VI.9[9].11.51.
7  Plotinus, *Enn.* VI.7[38].22.17–22.
8  Even once pre-Plotinian Platonists began to postulate a transcendent first principle distinctly beyond intellect and being, modeled upon the Good ἐπέκεινα τῆς οὐσίας of Plato, *Resp.* 509d9—a principle accessible only through various negative-theological acts of abstraction and mental privation—there was never any sense that the ultimate vision of the Good required the transcendence of intellect; indeed, in the academic Platonism prior to Plotinus, it is the intellect *itself* which is typically the beneficiary of the ultimate vision of the Good. Plotinus is thus the first within the academic philosophical tradition *sensu stricto* to claim the transcendence of the *nous* during an ascent.
9  Porphyry, *Vit. Plot.* 16.5–7.

(NHC X,1).¹⁰ Each of these tractates purports to be the first-hand account of an ascent undertaken by an eponymous visionary, each of whom respectively claims to have ascended beyond not only the cosmic spheres but even beyond the various strata that comprise the metaphysical superstructure by which all reality had originally unfolded—namely, the Barbelo Aeon, more or less equivalent to the intelligible realm—and thereby to have attained some kind of apprehension of the hyper-transcendent principle(s) beyond Intellect and even Being itself. And it is surely to this body of thought that Plotinus is reacting with this particular critique of the hubristic ascent 'above Intellect.' Yet Plotinus's apparent self–contradiction in II.9[33] remains perplexing. What, we may wonder, *really* lies behind Plotinus's peculiar, even paradoxical, outrage at a gnostic conception which he himself apparently shared? What, more generally, is *really* at stake in this debate over the nature of the ascent to the first principle?

In what follows I would like to propose an answer that presupposes a far more problematic or even antagonistic relationship than is usually assumed to have obtained between the academic Platonist milieu and that of the Platonizing Sethian gnostics. Beforehand, however, I should contextualize the present study. It is often repeated that history is written by the victors. In this case the 'victors' are certainly Plotinus and his circle, who are, in some sense, the direct ancestors of the European intellectual lineage to which we are all heirs; we therefore risk being substantially biased in favor of the self-interested view of Plotinus and his circle. Indeed, so complete has been Plotinus' 'victory' over the gnostics that many modern commentators attempt to understand Plotinus' anti-gnostic critique with only a very superficial reading, if any, of the available gnostic texts themselves, or even, more importantly, by neglecting or minimizing any indication *in Plotinus's own text* that the gnostics had real generative agency or intellectual self-determination.¹¹

---

10   See Zost. NHC VIII,1 22.1–24.17; 44.1–22; 129.4–14; Allogenes NHC XI,3 59.9–61.22; Marsanes NHC X 6.17–12.23. In previous studies, I have made the case that Plotinus derived his own notion of mystical ascent from the Platonizing Sethian gnostic milieu, with which, I conjectured, he was once associated in his youth, but which he later rejected in favor of a purified form of Platonism, now purged (at least for the most part) of any explicitly gnostic themes or technical terminology; see Mazur 2010 and 2013b.

11   One ramification of this bias has been the tendency among historians of philosophy to understand any similarity in doctrine between a gnostic text and an academic Platonist source as the result of the servile dependence of the former upon the latter. Another has been to conceal the degree to which the gnostics were creatively interpreting actual Platonic dialogues themselves, unmediated by the lens of academic Platonism. In a number of studies over the past several years—esp. Mazur 2013a, and Mazur forthcoming a and forthcoming b, all of which are largely inspired by John Turner—I have attempted to

Some time ago, in reaction against this attitude, I developed the opinion that the system of the Sethian authors of tractates such as Zostrianos and Allogenes were virtually indistinguishable, in all but superficial literary style, from that of their more conventional academic-Platonist contemporaries, and that the only truly salient bone of contention was a more or less accidental conflict of identity, one which Plotinus possibly even exaggerated for polemic effect, in order to legitimate his claim to be a more authentic heir of Plato. Here, however, in light of my more recent research on Plotinus's critique of the gnostics in *Enneades* II.9[33], I would like to take a slightly different approach—one, incidentally, that is perhaps more appropriate to the present theme of "gnostic counterculture"—by suggesting that Plotinus's indignation concerning the transcendence of intellect is motivated by his recognition—his *correct* recognition—that the gnostic claim to possess some unique propensity for visionary ascent was intentionally associated with, or even *predicated upon*, a concomitant denigration of Plato and thus of the Platonic philosophical milieu from which these sectaries had themselves emerged. Plotinus, I submit, was simply responding to a prior provocation.

## 1 Whence Plotinus' Complaint that the Gnostics Abuse Plato?

Let us begin, then, by considering a repeated, but often underappreciated, complaint running throughout Plotinus's anti-gnostic treatise *Enneades* II.9[33], but concentrated especially in chapter 6: namely, that the gnostics abuse Plato and the venerable tradition of Greek philosophy.[12] This complaint in fact may be subdivided into several elements, some of which might indicate no more than Plotinus's own inference from ideas such as those we can easily find in the extant Platonizing Sethian corpus. For instance, the gnostics (1) plagiarize

---

demonstrate that the Platonizing Sethians were actively engaged in a gnostic exegesis of a number of Platonic passages quite at variance with those commonly proffered by contemporaneous philosophical schools. My challenge in those studies was to prove to a rather skeptical audience that these gnostics, once considered to be unphilosophical intellectual 'parasites,' were in fact among the most creative interpreters of canonical philosophical texts in late antiquity, and had been unfairly excluded from the history of philosophy due to widespread but erroneous assumptions about the nature of 'gnosticism.'

12  Underappreciated, for instance, by Jackson 1990, 254 n. 4 who inexplicably asserts that Plotinus "does not necessarily imply open and actual ridicule of Plato; Plotinus's words are as likely to be the product of his own righteous indignation as accurate representation either of his opponents' position or even that of the authors of the apocalypses."

from Plato's thought,[13] while nevertheless (2) misunderstanding it,[14] they (3) contaminate genuine Platonic doctrine with extraneous additions,[15] and they (4) coin deliberately obscure neologisms to conceal the Hellenic (and, by implication, Platonic) source of their thought.[16] Other elements of this complaint, however, appear to suggest a slightly more active and self-conscious denigration of Plato by the gnostics, a denigration of a sort which is not immediately evident in the Platonizing Sethian tractates themselves. Thus Plotinus complains, curiously, that the gnostics somehow (5) demote the status of Plato's intelligible realm,[17] and also, perhaps more importantly, (6) they consider their own grasp of the intelligible to be superior to that of Plato and the other venerable Hellenic authorities, while (7) insulting the latter: thus, for instance, "they *drag the worthy man's (i.e., Plato's) doctrines towards the inferior* (πρὸς τὸ χεῖρον ἕλκουσι τὰς δόξας τοῦ ἀνδρός), as if they had understood the intelligible nature, and he and other blessed men had not."[18] The significance of this latter claim is reinforced by Porphyry's (often underappreciated) statement that the fundamental motivation for Plotinus's entire anti-gnostic project was the fact that the gnostics were "misleading many, themselves misled, that Plato had not attained to the depth of intelligible essence, *whence* (ὅθεν) [Plotinus] made several refutations in the meetings, and wrote the book which we entitled *Against the Gnostics*."[19]

However, if one glances only superficially at the Platonizing Sethian tractates, it is not immediately evident where one might find the stimulus for the latter two complaints, namely that the gnostics actively disparage Plato and elevate themselves above him; Plato's name, after all, does not occur anywhere in the extant Sethian corpus. It is of course possible that Plotinus simply infers this disparagement from the evident complexity of the Platonizing Sethian conception of the structure of the Barbelo Aeon, which certainly goes beyond anything one can find in Plato.[20] Yet Plotinus's emphatic and unequivocal

---

13   Plotinus, *Enn.* II.9[33].6.10–19, 6.54–56, 17.1–3.
14   Plotinus, *Enn.* II.9[33].6.14–24, 18.38–40.
15   Plotinus, *Enn.* II.9[33].6.10–12, 6.56–57.
16   Plotinus, *Enn.* II.9[33].6.5–6, 10.27–30.
17   Plotinus, *Enn.* II.9[33].6.25–31.
18   E.g., Plotinus, *Enn.* II.9[33].6.25–28; see also 6.36, 6.44, 10.13.
19   Porphyry, *Vit. Plot.* 16. 9–11.
20   In previous studies I have attempted to show that one of these complaints—(5) the demotion of Plato's intelligible realm—can be discerned in tacit form in our extant Zostrianos NHC VIII,1 in at least two respects. First, it appears that pseudo-Zostrianos has transformed Plato's mythical description of the luminous region outside the cosmos in the *Phaed.* (110a–111c)—an image undoubtedly intended to represent the intelligible realm—into an inferior nth-generation copy of a copy of the true Intelligible—referred

language nevertheless suggests that he is referring to something quite specific: "They should not substantiate their own opinions to their audience *by savaging and insulting the Greeks* (τοὺς Ἕλληνας διασύρειν καὶ ὑβρίζειν) ... nor should they hunt fame by censuring (ψέγειν) those men who, since ancient times, have been judged to be good by men who are not worthless, declaring they themselves [i.e., the gnostics] to be better then them [i.e., the Greeks]."[21] To what, we may wonder, do these statements refer?

To begin with, I would suggest that the most fundamental issue on which the gnostics claim superiority over the Platonists concerns the visionary ascent. This is initially suggested by the fact that in *Enneades* II.9[33], chapter 6, Plotinus introduces his entire critique of the gnostic abuse of Plato with the complaint that the gnostics plagiarize from him the notion of an "ascent from the cave towards a progressively more accurate vision."[22] In several other passages, including the one with which we began, he complains rather defensively that the gnostics claim to have a unique propensity for ascent that surpasses not only that of the stars but also other human beings as well.[23] Thus, for instance, later in the same treatise Plotinus insists that the person who truly loves God

> honors each [person] according to his worth, and always strives towards that to which all who are able, strive—for many are striving there, and some who are blessed, attain it, while others have the share appropriate to their ability—while not according himself alone that ability. For it is not by proclaiming to have what one claims to have that one has it, yet many things that they (i.e. the gnostics) too know they do not have, they

---

to as the "Aerial Earth"—which the mediocre demiurge uses as the immediate model for the material cosmos, thus mocking one of Plato's more mythological and less properly 'philosophical' illustrations of the intelligible realm. More importantly, in a lengthy disquisition (Zost. NHC VIII,1 44–46) about the fate of the individual soul that is capable of being saved, pseudo-Zostrianos seems to have adapted Plato's myth of the cyclical transmigration and reincarnation of souls in the *Phaedr.* (248a–d) by transposing the home of the soul (at least the soul of one who can be saved) to the realm of Forms itself, not the intra–cosmic heaven, and by suggesting that the fall into birth occurs not, as in the *Phaedrus*, when one fails to follow in the train of one's tutelary deity in the hyper-cosmic realm (the realm of Forms), but rather when one makes a quixotic but ultimately futile attempt to apprehend what is *beyond* the intelligible—i.e., the hyper-noetic transcendentalia—without benefit of the salvific powers unique to the Sethian elect.

21  Plotinus, *Enn.* II.9[33].6.49–52.
22  Plotinus, *Enn.* II.9[33].6.8–10, alluding, of course, to Plato *Resp.* 514a–518b.
23  See *supra* n. 1.

say that they do have, while not having them, and [they say that] they *alone* [have] what they alone do *not* have.[24]

Given that the contemplative ascent towards a vision of the supreme principle was especially associated with Platonism among all Greek philosophical schools,[25] it seems reasonable to assume that Plotinus' insistence on this point targets a specific gnostic claim to surpass the Platonists themselves. This impression is reinforced by the centrality of visionary ascent to the Platonizing Sethian corpus. We may begin to suspect that at least from Plotinus' perspective, the gnostic claim to possess a superior capacity for visionary ascent is somehow profoundly intertwined with the denigration of Plato.

Indeed, although we do not find any explicit skepticism of the Platonists' capability for visionary ascent anywhere in the Platonizing Sethian corpus, Plotinus's assertion that the gnostics claim for *themselves alone*—that is to say, for their own spiritual 'race'—a unique capacity for contemplation, is amply demonstrated by the texts themselves. Thus in Zostrianos, it is the Sethian elect alone—the "self-generated" ones—who are said to possess certain luminous, salvific "thoughts" or "impressions" (τύποι) which enable an ascent beyond the cosmos and all the aeons.[26] In Allogenes and Marsanes, the transcendent deity has invested the eponymous visionary with a special power that permits the apprehension of the transcendentalia beyond knowledge.[27] In both Zostrianos and Allogenes, this ultimate apprehension is enabled by a particular faculty—referred to as a "first thought" or a "primordial revelation"—which abides uniquely within the souls of the elect,[28] and which appears to be an indwelling reflection or residue of the hyper-transcendent first principle's own reflexive self-apprehension at the very first moment of ontogenesis.[29] This ingeniously conflates the notion of a faculty of transcendental apprehension unique to the elect with the more traditional theme of divine revelation, and it is relatively easy to imagine Plotinus reacting against both the exclusivity inherent in the notion of election and the conception of a Sethian revelation that is, it is implied, superior to that of Plato. It is for this reason, we may surmise, that Plotinus emphasizes throughout *Enneades* II.9[33] that the ultimate vision

24  Plotinus, *Enn.* II.9[33].9.75–83.
25  Ultimately deriving from, *inter alia*, Plato, *Symp.* 210c–212c., *Resp.* 515e–518a, and *7th Letter* 341c. That Platonism *in particular* was popularly associated with the vision of God is suggested by Justin Martyr, *Dial. with Tryph.* 2.6.7–10.
26  E.g., Zost. NHC VIII,1 23.17–24.25, 46.17–21.
27  Allogenes NHC XI,3 45.10–11, 50.21–36, 52.9–33, 57.32–39; Marsanes NHC X 110.7–23.
28  Zost. NHC VIII,1 24.10–13, 60.10–21; Allogenes NHC XI,3 48.13, 59.28–32, 60. 39–61.1. 61.9–11.
29  As I have argued in Mazur 2010.

of the divine is at least potentially accessible to all people, and not just an elect subset.[30]

## 2 Cognitive Transgression in Platonizing Sethian Eschatology

This, of course, still does not explain Plotinus's claim that the gnostics actively disparage Plato. At this point, therefore, I suggest we pause to consider a feature of Platonizing Sethian thought that might not immediately appear relevant, but, as we will see, may eventually prove useful. In several passages of Zostrianos we find an explicit correlation between a complex hierarchy of essential 'types' of human souls, on the one hand, and, on the other hand, various degrees of innate (or divinely conferred) aptitude for visionary ascent that are distinctly associated with different prospects for salvation. According to this eschatological schema, those disincarnate souls with any potential for salvation are stratified according to several successive domains intermediary between the "aerial Earth" at the superior boundary of the cosmos and the very threshold of the Barbelo Aeon; these include, in ascending order, a series of "copies" or "antitypes" (ἀντίτυποι) of the superior strata, then the strata themselves, consisting of the "Exile" (παροίκησις), the "Repentance" (μετάνοια), and finally the "self-generated" (αὐτογενής) aeons, the latter being the abode of the disincarnate, perfected souls of the Sethian elect.[31] It is therefore significant that *Enneads* II.9[33], chapter 6—the primary locus of Plotinus' defense of Plato from gnostic reprobation—opens with a condemnation of precisely this notion:

> And what should one say about the other hypostases (ὑποστάσεις) which they introduce, the "exiles" (παροικήσεις) and the "antitypes" (ἀντίτυποι) and the "repentances" (μετάνοιαι)? For they say that these (i.e. the "exiles" and "repentances") are the passions of the soul when it should enter into a state of repentance, and "antitypes" when it contemplates images of the [true] beings, as it were, and not yet those beings themselves.[32]

---

30  E.g. Plotinus, *Enn.* II.9[33].9.26–29, 9.75–79; 16.14–17.
31  During the initial phases of ascent at Zost. NHC VIII,1 5.17–29, the eponymous visionary ascends through the Airy Earth, the Antitypes, the Exile, and the Repentance, undergoing a series of baptisms on each stratum. The Exile and Repentance are subsequently mentioned at 8.13–16, 11.29–12.18, 24.21–25.18, 27.9–28.16, 31.5–11 (fragmentarily), and 43.13–26.
32  Plotinus, *Enn.* II.9[33].6.1–5.

Despite apparent references to these "hypostases" in one or possibly two other Sethian tractates,[33] Zostrianos is almost certain to be the earliest source to mention them, and discusses them at length; no similarly extensive discussion occurs elsewhere in Sethian literature. As an ensemble, therefore, they seem to be a Zostrianian innovation.[34] No scholarly consensus exists on the precise role and nature of the ἀντίτυποι, παροίκησις and μετάνοια, although various Jewish and Christian as well as earlier Sethian antecedents for one or another individual term have been proposed.[35] What we seem to be able to determine from the few lacunose passages in Zostrianos is as follows. Much as in Plato's *Phaedrus*, souls undergo repeated transmigratory cycles, and are classified hierarchically according to their (more or less immutable) essence. Certain types of "immortal" souls—those intermediary between those that are "dead" (and thus have no possibility for salvation) and the elect, "self-generated" (αὐτογενής) souls—are said to have respectively "taken root" upon the Exile or upon the Repentance.[36] The former, those in the Exile, have apparently

---

33  Untitled BC 3 263.11–264.6 (Schmidt-MacDermot 1978); possibly Marsanes NHC X 3.15–17.
34  Thus also Turner in Funk *et al.* 2000, 165 n. 85.
35  Turner (in Barry *et al.* 2000, 107–111, 536, 539–543, and in Turner 2001, 110–112, 557–568) sees here an echo of the Platonic conception of the judgment of souls during their transmigration, and takes these domains to be largely for the purpose of the expiation of sin. Burns (2014, 96–101) adduces Christian and gnostic parallels that valorize alien-ness (which Burns takes to be largely synonymous with the concept of 'exile'). Abramowski 1983, Brankaer 2009, and Tardieu 2013 similarly understand these regions in a more positive, less punitive sense.
36  Zost. NHC VIII,1 27.9–25 (Barry *et al.* 2000): "And other immortal souls commune with all these souls on account of the Sophia who inclined downward (ϭⲱϣⲧ̄ ⲉⲡⲉⲥⲏⲧ). For there are three species of immortal souls. There are those who take root upon the Exile, for they have no power of self-generation; they follow the works of others. This is a single species, which is self-contained. Then there are those who stand upon the Repentance, who were not ambivalent toward sin, knowledge (*gnōsis*) being sufficient for them; (but) they are (still) neophytes [...]." Note that the Coptic expression ϭⲱϣⲧ̄ ⲉⲡⲉⲥⲏⲧ, "inclined downward," at Zost. NHC VIII,1 27.12 certainly can be rendered "*look* down," as previous translators have thought, but I prefer "*incline* downward" because it almost certainly translates some variant of νεύειν κάτω, which can ambiguously mean either "to look down" or "to incline downward." Plotinus himself confirms this to have been the original Greek term (note νεῦσαι κάτω at *Enn.* II.9[33].10.19); he understandably expresses some confusion, in the subsequent lines (10.24–25), as to whether this means that Sophia actually descends or merely illuminates what lies below her (presumably with her gaze). It remains unclear whether souls "rooted" upon the Exile or the Repentance can eventually progress up to the suprajacent level; Turner suggests it is possible after repeated reincarnations (as with the types of lives in the *Phaedrus*), but the text of Zost. itself leaves this ambiguous; the only upward progression that is described explicitly (other than Zostrianos's own visionary ascent) is the elevation of one in a given "antitype" of the Exile or Repentance to the actual hypostasis itself following its period of "training" in the antitype

"sinned"[37] and "follow the works of the others"[38] (whatever this means), while the latter, those in the Repentance, have repented, and possess "sufficient knowledge," but remain "neophytes."[39] Only the truly "autogenous" (self-generated) souls, those of the Sethian elect themselves, who possess a "word of immutable truth,"[40] have access (it is implied) to the Barbelo Aeon and thence to the supreme principle itself.

The παροίκησις and μετάνοια thus appear to be penal repositories for various universal classes of imperfect human souls who have "sinned," some of whom eventually repent. Previous commentators have understood this "sin" in a rather general sense,[41] yet there remains a more specific possibility worth considering. That the issue of *cognitive transgression* underlies this schema is initially suggested by the fact that the "Exile" and "Repentance" appear to represent the hypostatization of the paradigmatic vicissitudes of the figure of Sophia in classic Sethian and Valentinian myth: in particular, her expulsion from the Pleroma—thus her *exile*—and her subsequent atonement and restoration—i.e., her *repentance*.[42]

To be precise, according to several variants of a widespread gnostic myth, the last of the aeons, Sophia, undertakes an audacious cognitive or reproductive overreach in an attempt to attain the transcendent first principle, and is thus responsible for the very first rupture in the hitherto perfect process of ontogenesis. This failure results in (1) the emergence of passion,[43] or matter itself, and thus evil, and (2) the generation of the congenitally mediocre Demiurge, as well as (3) Sophia's own extrusion from the Pleroma, only after which she eventually repents (i.e., undergoes μετάνοια) and is ultimately restored to her former place.[44] In Valentinian sources, Sophia's failure is typically

---

(Zost. NHC VIII,2 12.1-18). However, Zost. NHC VIII,1 43.13-27 seems to suggest that a certain degree of self-improvement, including the discovery of the truth within oneself, is possible for one in the Exile.

37  Zost. NHC VIII,1 24.31-25.5, 27.25, 28.1-6.
38  Zost. NHC VIII,1 25.3-5, 27.18-19.
39  Zost. NHC VIII,1 27.25.
40  Zost. NHC VIII,1 28.10-14.
41  See the references in note 35 above.
42  For Sophia's original *metanoia*, see Zost. NHC VIII,1 10.7-9; for the explicit association of Sophia with these eschatological domains, *ibid.* 27.9-19.
43  Plotinus betrays his awareness of the gnostic myth of Sophia's experience of primordial passion when he describes these hypostases as "the passions of the soul" (ψυχῆς ... πάθη) at *Enn.* II.9[33].6.3.
44  For an example of this schema in classic Sethianism, Ap. John NHC III,1 14.9-15.16; II,1 9.25-21 and parallels; among the 'Barbeloites,' Irenaeus, *Haer.* I.29.4 (Rousseau and Dutreleau 1979); for Valentinian examples: Irenaeus, *Haer.* I.1.2.13-3.13 (Rousseau and

understood in primarily cognitive terms; it is a failure resulting from the noble but ultimately futile attempt to know the unknowable Father. In classic Sethian sources, the failure is expressed in more reproductive or even embryological terms, as a failure to find an appropriate (male) consort: specifically, the supreme deity himself. This entails an abnormal (monogenetic) conception, which in turn results in the birth of a malformed, theriomorphic demiurge. Thus in either case, the event that precipitates Sophia's exile from the Pleroma is *a failed attempt to attain the supreme, unknowable principle*.

We might therefore consider the possibility that the "sin" of those individual souls who wind up within, or "rooted upon," the Exile or the Repentance, was intended in a very particular, circumscribed sense, as robustly analogous to its divine prototype, the "sin" of Sophia: specifically, that these souls are guilty of an inappropriate, hubristic attempt to apprehend what is *beyond knowledge* without the benefit of a special kind of divine providence. Although this is not stated explicitly, there are several hints in Zostrianos in favor of this interpretation, of which the following seem to me to be the most important.

First, in a remarkable passage running from Zost. (NHC VIII,1) 23.17 to 24.17 we find the clearest expression of Platonizing Sethian transcendental epistemology anywhere in the corpus, in which an ascending sequence of ever more exalted principles—beginning with the subaeons of Barbelo—is correlated with a series of increasingly refined faculties of apprehension by which the elect soul may apprehend them:

> On the one hand, one sees in a perfect soul those of Autogenes; on the other hand, in intellect, those of the Triple Male; in a pure spirit, those of the Protophanes. One hears about Kalyptos through the powers of the Spirit which emerged in a vastly superior manifestation of the Invisible Spirit. By the thought that now exists in Silence (and) by the First Thought (one learns) about the Triple Powered Invisible Spirit; it is, then, an audition and a power of silence which is purified in a vivifying spirit, perfect, first–perfect, and all–perfect. Therefore, glories are set upon them, as vivifiers. Those who receive baptism of truth, (i.e.,) in knowledge, and those who are worthy, are kept safe. But those who are not from this race are (mere) 'things,' and they return to their own root.[45]

---

Doutreleau 1979); Tri. Trac. NHC I,5 77.11–25; Tertullian, *Val.* 9.1–3; Gos. Truth NHC I,3 16.4–20; Clement of Alexandria, *Exc.* 31.3 (Sagnard 1948).

45   Zost. NHC VIII,1 24.1–25 (Barry *et al.* 2000).

From this passage, it is evident that Pseudo-Zostrianos intends to contrast the salvation of the elect, on the basis of their extraordinary epistemic capacity, with the fate of the non-elect: while the former enjoy protected status—i.e., are "kept safe" (ϩⲁⲣⲉϩ)—during such a perilous visionary ascent,[46] the latter—it is implied—attempt but fail to apprehend the transcendentalia and therefore are punished with an expulsion. Although the passage is unfortunately damaged by a lacuna at that point, the term "root" recalls the punitive hypostases of the Exile and Repentance on which souls of the non-elect have "taken root," and in fact, after four unintelligible lines of text, the discussion has returned to the fate of those fallen souls who nevertheless manage to "strip off the cosmos and put nature aside"[47]—i.e., undertake ascetic exercises propaedeutic to visionary ascent—and yet still "follow the works of others," and consequently wind up in the Exile or Repentance. Cognitive failure thus appears to be the cause, as well as the result, of the soul's banishment to the intermediary hypostases.

Second, in a passage beginning at Zost. NHC VIII,1 27.11, certain souls among the three immortal kinds of soul (those respectively in the Exile, the Repentance, and the self-generated aeons) are, in fact, explicitly said to "associate" or "commune" with the souls in these domains "*because of* (ⲉⲧⲃⲉ) the Sophia who inclined downward."[48] That there is a substantive relation between the condition of the individual human soul and Sophia's 'original sin' would appear to be supported by a lacunose passage outlining a complex taxonomy of souls on the next page, Zost. NHC VIII,1 28, where we find three subcategories of repentant souls—i.e., those in the Repentance—consisting of (1) "those who have committed all sins, and then repented, or (2) those who are 'parts,' or (3) those who desired on their own."[49] Although the interpretation of this phrase is contested,[50] these latter two subcategories, it seems, refer

---

46 We are reminded of the potential danger that confronts the visionary in the Hekhalot literature.
47 Presumably through contemplative practice.
48 Zost. NHC VIII,1 27.11–12 The entire passage is quoted above, note 36.
49 Zost. NHC VIII,1 28.4–7.
50 The *Bibliothèque copte de Nag Hammadi* team (in Barry et al. 2000) takes the term ϩⲉⲛⲙⲉⲣⲟⲥ "(indefinite) parts," to refer to sins rather than souls, and thus translate to the effect of "those who commit only *some* sins" as opposed to "those who commit *all* sins" etc., but even if we accept this lexical peculiarity, this would still leave the last category, "those who desired on their own," problematic. Turner himself suggests (in the same work) translating this "those who only desired" (to sin, but failed to do so), thus making a trichotomy between those who commit all sins, those who commit some sins, and those who only wanted to sin but did not. This proposal would be more compelling if there was any precedent for such a tripartite schema in ancient literature. It seems to me more likely

to the souls' motivation for "sin": either, I would suggest, they are "parts" of Sophia, in which case responsibility for their sin—cognitive hubris—accrues back to Sophia herself, on account of her own desire to know what is beyond knowledge, or these souls are responsible for their *own* desire for this forbidden knowledge.

Finally, we may note that elsewhere in Zostrianos (NHC VIII,1 44–46), in a remarkable account of cyclical metempsychosis, the individual soul appears to replicate, so to speak, 'microcosmically,' the paradigmatic schema of the vicissitudes of Sophia, involving (1) cognitive overreach, (2) cognitive failure, (3) fall or expulsion from the divine, and (4) eventual restoration. This is the case even for an elect soul, which, on occasion, finds itself imprisoned in a body.[51] Here Pseudo-Zostrianos understands the fall of the "self-generated" (i.e., elect) soul into incarnation to be the result of a prior attempt and failure to apprehend the transcendentalia beyond intellect without the benefit of sufficient salvific assistance. An elect soul in this unfortunate situation can nevertheless ultimately attain salvation once it has rediscovered within itself the luminous "impression" (τύπος) that is the unique property of autogenous souls.[52]

It therefore appears that the archetypal paradigm of *all* sin, for the Platonizing Sethians, is cognitive transgression, whether divine or human. Elsewhere I have made the case that the more general gnostic myth of the fall of Sophia—involving cognitive overreach, failure, and fall—was developed at least in part on the basis of a remarkable but underappreciated passage from the pseudo-Platonic *2nd Letter*.[53] This passage immediately follows the much more famous, indeed notoriously enigmatic, passage concerning the so-called "three kings" (which itself was certainly used as a source text by various gnostic thinkers)—in which "Plato" reveals begrudgingly to Dionysius the fact that the very "cause of all evils" (ὁ πάντων αἴτιόν ... κακῶν) is the soul's inquiry after, and unsuccessful search for, the unknowable "King of All," with which

---

that ⲙⲉⲣⲟⲥ describes the souls rather than the sins, and is non-coincidentally related to (1) the mention of an association of certain souls with Sophia at the beginning of the passage, on the previous page, (2) the more general notion of the souls of the elect as "parts" earlier, esp. at Zost. 22.1–4, and (3) Plotinus's testimony that the gnostics considered certain souls to be "members" (μέλη) of Sophia. The complexities of the entire passage are discussed by Turner (in Barry *et al.* 2000, 542–543).

51  See Mazur, forthcoming a.
52  That Pseudo-Zostrianos is well aware of the implicit structural parallel with the fall of Sophia is also intimated by the subtly ironic tone in Zostrianos' initial question concerning the fate of human souls, addressed to the revealer Ephesech: "Can your *wisdom* instruct me about the 'sowing' of the human who is saved ...?" (45.3–5).
53  Mazur, forthcoming b.

the soul has no kinship and therefore no means of apprehending.[54] I further suggested that the Platonizing Sethians allude to this putative proof text with regard to the condition of the *individual* soul as well. Beneath the Platonizing Sethian emphasis on the unique possession by the elect of a special power for transcendental apprehension, we may begin to detect the underlying concern with the avoidance of the kind of cognitive overreach—the "sin"—that condemns to exile both Sophia and also, as I suggest, those human souls that find themselves banished to the intermediary hypostases.

Support for this hypothesis may be found elsewhere throughout the Platonizing Sethian corpus, in which we find anxiously repeated assurances that it is "fitting" or "appropriate" for the aspirant to receive a given revelation or vision.[55] At the apex of the narrative ascent in Zostrianos itself, for instance, the eponymous visionary admits that his ultimate search for the supreme Triple-Powered Invisible Spirit is an act of audacity (τόλμα).[56] Similarly, in Allogenes, the eponymous narrator at one point declares, "the thought which is within me distinguished those things which are beyond measure and those things that are unknowable; on this account I was afraid lest what I learn *become something beyond what is appropriate*" (ⲁⲥⲉⲓⲣⲉ ⲛ̄ⲟⲩⲗⲁⲁⲩ ⲡⲁⲣⲁ ⲡⲉⲧⲉϣϣⲉ).[57] An allusion to the injunction of the *2nd Letter* may be found later in the same tractate, in a passage in which the so-called Luminaries of Barbelo inform Allogenes that an attempt to comprehend the supreme principle, the Unknowable, through conventional philosophical methods, in the absence of an extraordinary cognitive faculty or revelation ("the eye of revelation"), will necessarily result in condemnation:

> If [i] [one should claim that one sees] the manner in which [the unknowable deity] is *unknowable*, or [ii] that one sees the manner in which he (i.e., the deity) *exists in every respect*, or [iii] one should claim that he (the deity) exists as *something like* knowledge, then one has committed an impiety against him, and for this person there is condemnation because he

---

54  Pseudo-Plato, *2nd Letter* 212e4–313a6.
55  E.g., Zost. NHC VIII,1 60.16, 62.11–13, possibly 73.4; Allogenes NHC XI,3 49.38–50.36, 52.22–28, 56.27–34 (fragmentary), 57.32–39, 67.20–38; Marsanes NHC X 39.18–24.
56  Zost. NHC VIII,1 128.19–23.
57  Allogenes NHC XI,3 50.12–17. Note also the fact that the Luminaries of Barbelo advise Allogenes what to do if, during his final ascent through the three powers of the Triple-Powered, he should become "afraid": the two instances of such potential fear—59.17–18 and 59.32–33—occur precisely at the two *hyper-noetic* self-withdrawals, i.e., those that respectively correspond to the Vitality and the Existence (which are both implicitly *above* Intellect = Blessedness / Mentality).

did not know God. He will not be condemned by that [deity, since the latter] does not have concern about anything, nor does [the latter] have any desire, but rather [the person] will be [condemned] *by himself* because he has not found the truly existing principle. He (the person) was blind apart from the 'eye of revelation' that is at rest, that which is activated from the triple power of the First Thought of the Invisible Spirit.[58]

If I am correct thus far, then, it appears that the Platonizing Sethians believed themselves to possess a unique faculty that allows both the visionary ascent towards the ultimate apprehension of the transcendentalia during life, and potential residence among the vaunted autogenous aeons after death, while maintaining that the "others"—the non-elect, so to speak—not only have no such faculty, but necessarily *fall into sin* if they should attempt such an ascent. Furthermore, in what amounts to a circular argument, Zostrianos explains the congenital differences in visionary aptitude between the elect and the non-elect by invoking in return the differential eschatological conditions of various classes of human beings, some of whom have "dead souls," while others, perhaps less abject, although still mediocre, are rooted in the intermediary zones of the Exile and the Repentance.[59] That pseudo-Zostrianos understood

---

58   Allogenes NHC XI,3 64.14–36 (Funk *et al.* 2004). This passage contains a derisive echo of the three conventional ways of apprehending the Good (the so–called *via negationis, via eminentiae,* and *via analogiae*) that were standard in Middle Platonic school tradition, and of which examples can be found in Origen, *Cels.* VII.42 and Alcinous, *Didask.* 10.5–6. Here we have a specific and self-conscious instance of a Platonizing Sethian critique of a conventional academic formula, which, in a great irony, tacitly invokes Plato, or what was at least thought to be Plato (i.e., the injunction of the *2nd Letter*), against the Platonic school tradition, and follows Zostrianos in understanding the attempt to apprehend the transcendentalia unaided, without the benefit of Sethian revelation, to be an act of impiety and a sin worthy of condemnation, although of course in this case—unlike the more mythological postmortem punishments that we have seen in Zost.—one condemns *oneself*. Note that my translation here differs slightly from those of other translators. There is an evident grammatical problem in the text: specifically, a lack of a necessary verb in the conditional phrase beginning on line 14, which has led the *Bibliotheque copte de Nag Hammadi* team (as well as the *Coptic Gnostic Library* editors in Wire 1990) to suspect a line of text has been accidentally omitted (on the other hand, King 1995 takes all of these clauses to be questions). Both the CGL and the BCNH editions supply "sees" from line 16, but it makes more sense in this context to imagine a verb of *saying*, hence my "would claim," which anticipates the verb ⲛⲁϫⲟⲟⲥ (the future of "to say,") on line 19.

59   Interestingly, in an early, pre-tetralogical treatise, at *Enn.* V.9[5].1.7–21, Plotinus himself characterizes various philosophical schools according to a tripartite hierarchical schema, each school being associated with a progressively greater capability for ascent towards the vision of the Good, and described by a different type of bird (flightless, those that can fly a little bit, and those that soar over the clouds and enjoy exceptional keen-sightedness).

these conditions to be essential characteristics of souls rather than merely temporary states is suggested by fact that the heavenly revealer (Ephesech) introduces the first substantial discussion of the various types of soul in the Exile and Repentance by admonishing the eponymous visionary, "do not be amazed at the *differences between souls*" (ⲆⲒⲀⲪⲞⲢⲀ ⲆⲈ ⲚⲦⲈⲚⲒⲮⲨⲬⲎ).[60]

## 3 Zostrianian Eschatology as a Critique of Academic Platonism

Of course it is impossible to know precisely how the Platonizing Sethians defined their own putative spiritual "race," but it is most likely a conventional discourse that reflects voluntary affiliation with a tradition of textual exegesis and ritual practice (the "works") rather than an actual biological lineage. And while it is certainly possible that pseudo-Zostrianos intended the "different types of souls" to represent various universal categories of human being, it seems more likely that he or she had some well-defined communities of people in mind, especially because those 'rooted upon' the Exile and Repentance—those non-elect still in possession of "immortal souls"—are nevertheless vastly superior to the majority of humans, which includes several additional categories of "dead" souls. One might begin to suspect that the inhabitants of the Exile and the Repentance are intended to represent the members of a rival subgroup—the "others"—within a larger community: although those in the inferior category (the Exile) still "follow the *works* (i.e., the practices, doctrines or writings) *of others*," those in the superior category (the Repentance) have attained "sufficient *knowledge*" (γνῶσις) but remain "neophytes," apparently excluded, perhaps permanently, from the benefits bestowed through divine providence or revelation upon the autogenous individuals alone.

At this point I would like to make explicit the principal hypothesis of this paper, which has been thus far only an inexorably growing suspicion: specifically, that *the categories of soul that are, according to the Platonizing Sethians, 'rooted' in the Exile or the Repentance, subtly allude to Plato or the academic Platonists*. We have already seen circumstantial evidence that the Platonizing Sethians considered Plato and his followers to have a lesser propensity than themselves for visionary ascent, and further, that they maintained that such propensity is intrinsically correlated with the eschatological prospects for one's soul. Remarkably, this suspicion is explicitly confirmed by a hitherto neglected and otherwise inexplicable passage of Plotinus that occurs in the continuation of the very same chapter of II.9[33] in which he mentions

---

60  Zost. NHC VIII,1 26.19–20.

the Exile, Repentance, and Antitypes, and in which he attempts to defend Plato against gnostic abuse (ch. 6). In this passage, Plotinus echoes verbatim the Zostrianian phraseology concerning the "difference between souls" in a rejection of the gnostic claim that the venerable Greek philosophical authorities—i.e., the academic Platonists—possess *souls of an essentially inferior status*:

> [The gnostics should] trace *the differences in souls* (διαφοράς δὲ ψυχῶν) to (differences) in experiences or in nature, *without ripping to shreds* (μηδὲν ... διασύροντας) those divine men (i.e., Plato and other Greek philosophers), but rather receiving their doctrines graciously, since they are more venerable, and since they (i.e., the gnostics) take from there what they themselves say correctly.[61]

There is, moreover, one final clue as to the nature of this debate: one so obvious, in fact, it seems to be, so to speak, hiding in plain sight. Pseudo-Zostrianos explicitly states, and Plotinus repeats, that certain human souls have some ambiguous connection with Sophia. As we have seen, in Zostrianos, certain immortal souls "associate" with those in the Exile and Repentance "on account of" or "because of" (ⲉⲧⲃⲉ) Sophia; this passage defies any obvious interpretation. Similarly, Plotinus describes a gnostic schema in which human souls ambiguously "descended together with" (συγκατεληλυθέναι) Sophia, and thus acquired bodies, but he then admits uncertainty whether (according to the gnostics) it is Sophia or the soul who is at fault, and he even presents a variant in which Sophia, she "for the sake of whom" the souls descend, does not herself descend.[62] Behind all this confusion, surely there is an allusion, at very least, to the paradigmatic nature of the fall of Sophia for the fate of the human soul in general; but is it not also possible to imagine, behind both of these ambiguous texts, a Platonizing Sethian critique of a particular subset of human souls, specifically those whose fallen condition is a result of their own veneration of Sophia, which is to say, the souls of those who practice *philo-sophia*?

This suspicion is strengthened by Plotinus's curious report that the gnostics refer to certain incarnated souls as "members of Sophia" (μέλη τῆς σοφίας), a phrase that has no exact parallel in any other gnostic or Platonist source, but might instead be understood as a construction parallel to the frequent Pauline use of "*members* of Christ" to refer to the emergent Church, the 'followers of

---

61  Plotinus, *Enn.* II.9[33].6.35–38.
62  Plotinus, *Enn.* II.9[33].10.19–26.

Christ,'[63] thus indicating the 'followers of Sophia' (i.e., the philosophers). The Platonizing Sethians, it appears, have turned the academic Platonists' own claim to practice "philosophy" against them,[64] mischievously impugning the object of the latters' pursuit—*sophia*, "wisdom"—as a principle characterized by cognitive inability *par excellence*.

## 4    Platonizing Sethians as Apostate Platonists

At this point we must confront a final question concerning the historical circumstances behind the Platonizing Sethians' paradoxical approach to Plato. We know from Porphyry's account that the gnostic apocalypses (ἀποκαλύψεις) of Zostrianos and Allogenes, among others, were proffered (or composed) by a particular subset of "Christians," namely certain gnostic "heretics" or "sectarians" (αἱρετικοί) who had "departed from" or "emerged from" (ἀνηγμένοι) Greek, presumably Platonic, philosophical schools, but who maintained that Plato himself "had not attained the depths of intelligible essence."[65] In addition, we know from Plotinus's own account that he himself had gnostic friends.[66] It is therefore safe to assume, both on the basis of this testimony and of the content of the extant tractates themselves, that the Platonizing Sethian authors were originally trained in academic Platonist circles and perhaps even once considered themselves 'Platonists,' whatever other simultaneous affiliations they may have had.

Let us therefore try to conceptualize an unprovable but nevertheless plausible scenario that explains both how the Platonizing Sethians could have come to turn against their former academic milieu and why Plotinus might have taken it upon himself to refute so vigorously the doctrines of his "friends". We may begin by supposing that both Plotinus and the Platonizing Sethians emerged from a common academic Platonist milieu in Alexandria, perhaps all being pupils in the school of Ammonius Saccas.[67] Within this school, let us assume, are participants in one or more of the many traditional Hellenistic or Greco-Egyptian cults, but also other sectarians who might variously identify as Jewish, Christian, gnostic, Sethian, and so forth. Indeed, all of these identities

---

63    1 Cor 16:15, 12:27; Rom 12:5.
64    Interestingly, the term "philosophy" and its cognates do not occur in the Platonizing Sethian corpus.
65    Porphyry, *Vit. Plot.* 16.1–18.
66    Plotinus, *Enn.* 11.9[33].10.3–5.
67    Plotinus' statement that he has gnostic "friends" is,—this, incidentally, the only mention of any of his contemporary associates anywhere in his oeuvre.

could plausibly be superimposed upon a rather ecumenical Platonism. Now let us suppose that some of these sectarians are seeking definitive solutions to certain philosophical and spiritual problems raised, but not resolved, by Plato's own corpus, and as a consequence produce new (and yet supposedly ancient and pre-Platonic, hence more authoritative) interpretations in the form of pseudepigraphic 'revelations' that are meant to be read *in addition to* the works of Plato and other classical philosophical authorities. These sectarians are profoundly embedded within a Platonic world-view, and yet remain convinced that their own revelations allow access to the Transcendent that had remained inaccessible to Plato himself. For this fraction of the school community, the more traditional Platonists are not the enemy; indeed, they are close to the truth, but congenitally unable to attain the ultimate vision of the supreme principle.

Now we may further imagine that an increasingly acrimonious, internecine opposition emerges within the school, between, on the one hand, the Platonizing gnostics who invoke Sophia's own catastrophic failure to apprehend that principle as the paradigm of the failure of traditional Greek philosophy, and, on the other hand, the more traditional Platonists—the putative 'followers of Sophia,' so to speak—who maintain that Platonic philosophy alone, involving dialectic and intellectual cogitation, is sufficient.[68] Assuming our scenario is taking place during the period immediately before Plotinus's departure from Alexandria, in the mid 240s, this schism is perhaps exacerbated, if not precipitated, by the first ominous premonitions of the widespread intercommunal violence in that city, which will culminate in the Decian persecution of 250. It is at this point that Plotinus firmly chooses a side in this debate, aligning himself with the venerable 'Hellenic' tradition rather than with those who produce new parabiblical revelations (who themselves were considered, rightly or wrongly, to rank among the much-reviled 'Christians'), and he abandons the school. Eventually Plotinus establishes his own school in Rome, and reconstructs himself anew, as the ostensibly 'pure' Platonist we now assume him to have always been, by veiling his past—which had involved an embarrassing proximity to the gnostics—in extreme reticence and even deliberate secrecy.[69]

---

68   This division into intramural scholastic camps might account for the repeated use of the curious term "the others" by both the Platonizing Sethians and by Plotinus to refer to their unnamed, but certainly well-known, opponents. On Plotinus's use of an enigmatic and otherwise unexplained "others" at *Enn.* IV.8[6].8.1 to refer to the gnostics, see Narbonne 2011, 64–69.

69   See Porphyry, *Vit. Plot.* 1.1–4, 2.37–38, 3.24–29, 10.1–14, 14.21–25.

In the mid 260s, however, certain Platonizing Sethian books from Alexandria—the writings of the 'others'—reappear in Rome and begin to circulate among Plotinus's students. These tractates now seem to Plotinus to be the height of arrogance—substantially dependent upon, yet tacitly insolent towards, Plato—and Plotinus comes to see them—*correctly*—as an insult to the Platonic tradition itself, the very tradition with which he has self-consciously come to identify. It is in defense of this tradition, and of those of his contemporaries who adhere to it, that Plotinus writes his anti-gnostic treatise: as he himself explicitly insists, the purpose is *not* to persuade the gnostics themselves (since they are beyond persuasion), but rather so that his own students "might not be troubled" (ἵνα μὴ ... ἐνοχλοῖντο) by the insults directed at those just like them by their own teacher's erstwhile gnostic friends.[70]

## Conclusion

The scenario that I have suggested here is quite different from the typical notion of the relation between Plotinus and the gnostics, and suggests that the Platonizing Sethians maintained a rather more willfully eristic or even 'countercultural' attitude towards Greek philosophy than is usually assumed. Yet it is not difficult to find a precedent in gnostic literature for this kind of self-conscious irreverence towards one's own spiritual or intellectual genealogy.[71] Nearly a century before Plotinus wrote his anti-gnostic tetralogy, the Platonist Celsus attempted to attack Christianity in general by citing the arrogant claim of what must have been a Platonizing gnostic sect: "Some Christians, misunderstanding the meaning of the Platonists, boast of a supercelestial God, ascending up above (ὑπεραναβαίνοντας) the heaven of the Jews."[72] In the very same way in which this claim to ascend beyond the god of the Jews both elevates the gnostic visionary, and, simultaneously, denigrates both the Jews and most Christians, so also the Platonizing Sethians elevated themselves at the expense of more traditional Platonists. Indeed, the Platonizing Sethian claim to transcend the intellect during a visionary ascent concomitantly asserts cognitive superiority over not only the divine soul (Sophia) but also her putative "members," the Platonist philosophers. These sectarians assimilate themselves instead to Sophia's more exalted counterpart, Barbelo, who, by contrast with

---

70  Plotinus, *Enn.* II.9[33].1.7–14.
71  On widespread gnostic 'anti-traditionalism,' see most recently Cahana 2014.
72  Origen, *Cels.* VI.19.1–3.

Sophia, is uniquely capable of apprehending the unknowable[73] [see Table 1]. What is more, according to the Platonizing Sethians' own subversive interpretation of Plato himself (or at any rate an author thought to be Plato), the academic Platonists' own futile attempts to apprehend the 'Good-beyond-Being' will condemn them to purgatory. Might not even Plato himself, perhaps, still be languishing in the miserable Exile or Repentance? And this, of course, explains the vehemence of Plotinus's reaction. Indeed, that he is aware of the fundamental issue underlying the Platonizing Sethian attitude is evident in his original, perhaps hypocritical, admonition that "One is able to go as far as Intellect leads, but to go above Intellect is immediately to fall outside of it." With these words, Plotinus is turning the gnostics' own injunction back against them, paraphrasing the Valentinian heresiarch Theodotus (as quoted by Clement): "The aeon (i.e. Sophia) *who wished to grasp that which is above knowledge* (ὁ δὲ βουληθεὶσ αἰὼν τὸ ὑπὲρ τὴν γνῶσιν λαβεῖν) came to be in ignorance and shapelessness."[74]

TABLE 1   Hypothesized Zostrianian view of the status of Sethians vis-à-vis that of the academic Platonists

| Community | Associated with | Characterized by | Eschatological 'root' in |
|---|---|---|---|
| Sethian Elect | Barbelo | Ability to apprehend First Principle 'beyond Intellect' | Autogenous Aeons |
| Academic Philosophers | Sophia | Inability to apprehend First Principle 'beyond Intellect' | Exile/Repentance |

---

73   E.g. Zost. NHC VIII,1 112.1, where the aspirant is said to "become a Barbelo." On the close structural interrelation between Sophia and Barbelo in this tractate, see Sieber 1981. On Barbelo as a principle that can apprehend the supreme Invisible Spirit, Zost. NHC VIII,1 81.10–83.1, 83.8.
74   Clement of Alexandria, *Exc.* 31.3 (Sagnard 1948).

## Bibliography

Barry, Catherine, Wolf-Peter Funk, Paul-Hubert Poirier, and John D. Turner, ed. 2000. *Zostrien*, (NH VIII, 1). Bibliothèque copte de Nag Hammadi, Section: « Textes » 24. Québec: Les presses de l'Université Laval; Leuven: Peeters.

Brankaer, Johanna. 2011. "Der Begriff *metanoia* in gnostischen Schriften." *Zeitschrift für Antikes Christentum* 13.1:87–97.

Burns, Dylan. 2014. *Apocalypse of the Alien God: Platonism and the Exile of Sethian Gnosticism*. Divinations: Rereading Late Ancient Religion. Philadelphia: University of Pennsylvania Press.

Cahana, Jonathan. 2014. "None of Them Knew Me or My Brothers: Gnostic Antitraditionalism and Gnosticism as a Cultural Phenomenon." *The Journal of Religion* 94.1: 49–73.

Funk, Wolf-Peter, Paul–Hubert Poirier, and John D. Turner, ed. 2000. *Marsanès (NH X,1)*. Bibliothèque copte de Nag Hammadi, Section: "Textes" 25. Québec: Les Presses de l'Université Laval; Leuven: Peeters.

Funk, Wolf-Peter, Paul-Hubert Poirier, Maddalena Scopello, and John D. Turner. 2004. *L'Allogène* (NH XI, 3). Bibliotèque copte de Nag Hammadi, Section "Textes" 30. Québec: Les presses de l'Université Laval; Louvain: Peeters.

Henry, Paul and Hans-Rudolf Schwyzer. 1964–1983. *Plotini opera*. 3 volumes. Scriptorum classicorum bibliotheca Oxoniensis. Oxford: Clarendon Press.

Jackson, Howard M. 1990. "The Seer Nicotheus and his Lost Apocalypse." *Novum Testamentum* 32: 250–277.

King, Karen. 1995. *Revelation of the Unknowable God: With Text, Translation and Notes to NHC XI,3, Allogenes*. California Classical Library. Santa Rosa, CA: Polebridge.

Mazur, Zeke. 2010. "The Platonizing Sethian Gnostic Background of Plotinus' Mysticism." Ph.D. Dissertation, University of Chicago.

Mazur, Zeke. 2013a. "The Platonizing Sethian Gnostic Interpretation of Plato's *Sophist*." Pages 469–93 in *Practicing Gnosis: Ritual, Magic, Theurgy, and Other Ancient Literature. Essays in Honor of Birger A. Pearson*. Edited by April D. DeConick, Gregory Shaw, and John D. Turner. Nag Hammadi and Manichaean Studies 85. Leiden: Brill.

Mazur, Zeke. 2013b. "'Those Who Ascend to the Sanctuaries of the Temples': The Gnostic Context of Plotinus' First Treatise, 1.6[1] *On Beauty*." Pages 329–68 in *Gnosticism, Platonism, and the Late Ancient World. Essays in Honour of John D. Turner*. Edited by Kevin Corrigan and Tuomas Rasimus in collaboration with Dylan M. Burns, Lance Jenott, and Zeke Mazur. Nag Hammadi and Manichaean Studies 82. Leiden: Brill.

Mazur, Zeke. Forthcoming a. "Traces of the Competition Between the Platonizing Sethian Gnostics and Plotinus' Circle: The Case of *Zostrianos* 44–46." In *Estratégias anti-gnósticas nos escritos de Plotino. Atas do colóquio internacional realizado em*

*São Paulo em 18–19 de março 2012.* Edited by Mauricio Pagotto Marsola and Lorenzo Ferroni. São Paulo: Rosari et Paulus.

Mazur, Zeke. Forthcoming b. "A Gnostic Icarus? Traces of the Controversy Between Plotinus and the Gnostics over a Surprising Source for the Fall of Sophia: the Pseudo-Platonic *2nd Letter*." *International Journal of the Platonic Tradition*.

Narbonne, Jean-Marc. 2011. *Plotinus in Dialogue with the Gnostics*. Studies in Platonism, Neoplatonism, and the Platonic Tradition 11. Leiden: Brill.

Sagnard, François. 1970. *Clément D'Alexandrie, Extraits de Théodote*. Sources chrétiennes 23. Paris: Cerf.

Schmidt, Carl, and Violet MacDermot. 1978. *The Books of Jeu and the Untitled Text in the Bruce Codex*. Nag Hammadi Studies 13. Leiden: Brill.

Sieber, John. 1981. "The Barbelo Aeon as Sophia in *Zostrianos* and Related Tractates." Pages 788–95 in *The Rediscovery of Gnosticism, Proceedings of the International Conference on Gnosticism at Yale, New Heaven, Connecticut, March 28–31, 1978*, vol. 2, *Sethian Gnosticism*. Studies in the History of Religions, 41. Edited by Bentley Layton. Leiden: Brill.

Tardieu, Michel. 1996. "Echo et les antitypes." Pages 427–42 in *Gnosticism, Platonism, and the Late Ancient World. Essays in Honour of John D. Turner*. Nag Hammadi and Manichaean Studies 82. Edited by Kevin Corrigan and Tuomas Rasimus in collaboration with Dylan M. Burns, Lance Jenott, and Zeke Mazur. Leiden: Brill.

Turner, John D. 2001. *Sethian Gnosticism and the Platonic Tradition*. Bibliotèque copte de Nag Hammadi, Section "Études" 6. Québec: Les presses de l'Université Laval; Louvain: Peeters.

Wire, Antoinette Clark, John D. Turner, and Orval S. Wintermute. 1990. "Allogenes." Pages 173–267 in *Nag Hammadi Codices XI, XII, and XIII*. Nag Hammadi Studies 28. Edited by Charles W. Hedrick. Leiden: Brill.

# The Apocalypse of Paul (NHC V,2): Cosmology, Anthropology, and Ethics

*Lautaro Roig Lanzillotta*
University of Groningen
*f.l.roig.lanzillotta@rug.nl*

Despite the obvious disdain shown by the first scholarly approaches for the Gnostic Apocalypse of Paul in the fifth codex of the Nag Hammadi corpus, the text is very interesting in many respects.[1] To begin with, it is interesting from an intertextual perspective, since even if not explicitly the text presents itself as a continuation of Paul's reference of his rapture to the third heaven in 2 Cor 12:2–4.[2] Apocalypse of Paul provides an nice example of how later Christian generations combined tradition and innovation in dealing with their textual tradition.[3] While Pauline lore is preserved as authoritative, this authority is used as a starting point for something new, for a creative interpretation of this tradition.

Apocalypse of Paul is also interesting due to its subject matter, since it describes the ascent of the soul not as something taking place after the death of the individual, but as an out-of-body experience.[4] It provides the testimony of a witness, of a spectator who describes what he was allowed to see (probably) during a mystical or ecstatic experience. And the Apocalypse of Paul is intriguing from the history of religions perspective due to its inclusion of a description of the punishment of sinners. The Greek background of the scene is clear, I think, not only in the description of both sinner and his punishment in the form of reincarnation[5] but also in the fact that it takes place in heaven, and especially in that the lot of the sinners is not presented as a counterpart of the bliss of the righteous.[6] No less exciting is the Apocalypse of Paul's relationship

---

1  Schenke 1966, 25; See also the opinion by the Berliner Arbeitskreis in Tröger 1973, 43. In the same line, Böhlig 1963, 15 15.
2  Klauck 1985.
3  Kaler, Painchaud and Bussieres, 2004 173–93; see also Harrison 2004. On the relationship between first-century Paul and its reception during the second century, see more recently Kaler 2008, 77–119.
4  Wright 2000, 163.
5  On which see Solmsen 1982 and, more recently, Riedweg 2015.
6  On the emphasis of this contrast in Christian texts see Roig Lanzillotta 2003.

to the *Visio Pauli*. Some years ago[7] I compared the Coptic version to the Greek[8] and Latin versions[9] of the text. Presently I am working with the Coptologist J. Van der Vliet from the University of Leiden on a new edition of the Coptic text of the *Visio*.[10]

The most interesting aspect, however, is no doubt the cosmological framework behind the text, which includes many transgressive elements. And this is not simply for the peculiarity of its inclusion of ten heavens instead of eight heavens—as one might normally expect in a Gnostic text[11]—nor the fact that the text structures the cosmos into three clear, separate regions, nor that it omits any reference to the first two heavens. The cosmology behind the text is especially fascinating, on the one hand, because of its close connection with the text's anthropology, which conceives of man in the light of the cosmological framework, and, on the other, for its description of Paul's ascension as an ethical progress. Besides, in depicting this cosmological whole, Apocalypse of Paul introduces several polemical and transgressive elements, such as the attribution of the traits of the Biblical God to the demiurge, and the view of the apostles as inhabitants of the archontic region, as "psychics" inferior to the apostle Paul. In the next pages I will focus mainly on Apocalypse of Paul's cosmology and the anthropological, theological, and ethical implications of its worldview, but will point in passing to the transgressive elements included in this text. After a first section that describes the text, its context, character, and condition, the second provides the promised analysis of the text's cosmology. I will close my paper with some remarks regarding the character affiliation of the text.

---

7    Roig Lanzillotta 2007.
8    Tischendorf 1866 [1966], XIV–XVIII, 34–69.
9    Silverstein and Hilhorst 1997.
10   The Coptic text was first edited by Wallis-Budge, 1915, 534–74, 1043–84.
11   The entire corpus of Gnostic testimonies, from the polemical treatises to the Nag Hammadi writings, unanimously conceive of the heavenly region as formed by seven heavens. See, for example, Corp. herm. 1.9; 9.18–20 (Nock and Festugière 1945–1954); 13; 10.19–11.5; 24–26 (Nock and Festugière 1945–1954); Ap. John NHC II,1 11.23–35 Nat. Rulers NHC II,4 95.1–5; Orig. World NHC II,5 101.9–102.16, on which Tardieu 1974, 62–65; in general, see Festugière 1932, 101–15. The only notable exception affirming the rule is Pistis Sophia AC 136, which apparently refers to only five heavens. Yarbro Collins 1996, 52, contends that even if the seven planets might be implied here, unexpectedly Sun and Moon have been omitted.

## 1 Text and Contents of the Gnostic Apocalypse of Paul

The Coptic version of Apocalypse of Paul is the second text of codex V, a codex which, if we exclude *Eugnostos*, is of a marked apocalyptic nature.[12] It occupies seven pages between folios 17 and 24 of a manuscript of very poor papyrus quality, as a result of which the text is now and then very damaged:[13] In addition to the first pages, the top and bottom of each page generally include lacunae.[14] The Sahidic dialect of codex V presents some peculiarities, which according to Alexander Böhlig are due to Fayyumic influences[15] and according to H.M. Schenke to the strong Subachmimic features of the pre-classical Sahidic of the text.[16] As far as Apocalypse of Paul is concerned, Funk has pointed out that the Boharicisms of the text seems to indicate that it circulated in Bohairic before being translated into Sahidic.[17] The original text was presumably written in Greek in the second century, while Trevijano Echeverría would date it with yet more precision to between 150 and 170.[18]

Despite the fact that the first scholarly approaches to Apocalypse of Paul do not consider it to be an important text,[19] the last two decades have seen a renewed interest in the apocalypse, with new assessments of its numerous intriguing aspects, such as genre, structure, character and intention, and affiliation.[20] As far as the literary genre of the text is concerned, its pseudonymity, the report of the vision that includes the *angelus interpres* and its depiction of the other world allows us to classify it, in spite of Kurt Rudolph,[21] as an apocalyptic text and, more precisely, in the subcategory of heavenly journey texts.[22]

In terms of its structure, the text has been divided into two or three sections. William Murdock and George MacRae distinguish three main episodes, namely an epiphany scene, a scene of judgment and punishment, and a heavenly

---

12  Indeed, besides Apoc. Paul, the MS includes three other apocalypses, namely 1 Apoc. Jas NHC V,3, 2 Apoc. Jas NHC V,4, and Apoc. Adam NHC V,5.
13  Murdock and MacRae 1979.
14  See Rosenstiehl and Kaler 2005, 12–14.
15  Böhlig 1963, 11–14.
16  Schenke 1966.
17  Funk 1995, 107–47.
18  Trevijano Etcheverría 1981.
19  See note 1 above.
20  For an overview of the literature on all these aspects, see the two most recent and excellent studies by Rosenstiehl and Kaler 2005 and Kaler 2008, passim.
21  Rudolph 1968, 99, prefers the description "Gnostic Dialogue," since the text includes this dialogue after the description of the vision of the heavens.
22  Krause 1983, 626–28, on the basis of the criteria offered by Vielhauer 1975; See also Fallon 1979, 138; and Klauck 1985, 159–60.

journey.[23] Martin Krause, however, prefers to distinguish only two, namely the epiphany and the ascension, which in view of the text's message and implications seems to make, in my view, more sense.[24] When assessing the text's character, earlier studies originally considered it the "result of popular syncretism" due to an alleged mixture of Jewish and Hellenistic elements,[25] an opinion that seemed to be reinforced by Rodolphe Kasser's view of the text as a result of redactional reworking of diverse sources.[26] Murdock and Kaler, however, have attempted to undermine its alleged syncretic character by claiming that the Jewish apocalyptic current was already a syncretic phenomenon.[27] Despite early scholarly hesitation as to the affiliation of the text, recent studies finally describe it as (early) Valentinian.[28]

The text relates Paul's spiritual ascent to heaven. After the lacuna-filled beginning, Paul meets a revealer in the form of a little child,[29] who might incarnate the polymorphic Jesus.[30] Later the revealer is referred to as either Spirit[31] or the Holy Spirit.[32] Paul's *angelus interpres* takes him directly to the third heaven, in what seems to be an intentional continuation of 2 Cor 12:2–4. After a brief description of the punishment of sinners in the fourth and fifth heavens, and a short reference to the light of the sixth, the text describes Paul's encounter in the seventh heaven with an old man, the demiurge, who attempts to impede his ascent. After giving him the password, however, Paul further proceeds to the *ogdoad*, after which he reaches the ninth and the tenth heaven, where he finally becomes pure spirit.

## 2  A Tripartite View of the Cosmos

The cosmos in Apocalypse of Paul consists of three large regions. The first of them, symbolically referred to as the mountain of Jericho, is the material world where Paul and the apostles live, and where Jesus' epiphany as a small child actually takes place.[33] This is followed by the celestial region, the

---

23  Murdock and MacRae 1979, 48.
24  Krause 1983, 625.
25  Murdock and MacRae 1979, 48; Böhlig 1963; Klauck 1985, 178–187; MacRae 1976, 285–88.
26  Kasser 1965, 76.
27  Murdock 1968, 237, cited in Kaler 2008, 38–39.
28  Trevijano Etcheverría 1981; Kaler 2008, 40.
29  Apoc. Paul NHC V,2 18.6, 8, 13.
30  Roig Lanzillotta 2013.
31  Apoc. Paul NHC V,2 20.4; 22.1.
32  Apoc. Paul NHC V,2 19.21; 19.26; 21.22.
33  Apoc. Paul NHC V,2 18.6; 18.13–14. See Rosenstiehl and Kaler 2005, 70–77.

hebdomad symbolically associated with Jerusalem, the region inhabited by "principalities and authorities and archangels and powers and the whole race of demons"[34] and, of course, the demiurge; finally, there is the divine region, or *pleroma*, which consists of three levels beginning with the ogdoad and ending with the tenth heaven, to which Paul's spirit actually belongs.

The text does not show any special interest in the lower realm. The little child simply associates the physical world with the mountain of Jericho,[35] an allegory that Paul should be able to understand if his intellect is awakened, as the child puts it, "so that you may know the hidden things in those that are visible."[36] Rosenstiehl and Kaler are right in pointing out that the importance of the mountain is as a place of revelation.[37] In the present context of Paul's ascension, however, I think it is more interesting to interpret the mountain in line with the Heracleon fragment 20 as the material world: Paul's point of departure is the lower realm, the sphere of influence of the Devil (below).[38]

The tangible world is consequently referred to as "the earth,"[39] as "the creation,"[40] as the "world of the dead,"[41] or else simply as "the world."[42] It is the place in which both Paul's and the apostle's likenesses remain while *angelus interpres* and Paul are traveling through the heavens, something that the text emphasizes by expressions such as "and he looked down"[43] or "he gazed

---

[34] Apoc. Paul NHC V,2 19.2–5.
[35] References in Rosenstiehl and Kaler, 2005, 26–34.
[36] Apoc. Paul NHC V,2 19.13–14.
[37] Rosenstiehl and Kaler 2005, 26–29. The "elaborate and ingenious" explanation is, according to Kaler (2008, 9 n. 17), due to Rosenstiehl. Kaler comments it in extenso at 2008, 198–201.
[38] According to Orbe 1983, 91, we find here an allegorical reading of Luke 10:30 that inverts the terms of the story. Rosenstiehl and Kaler 2005, 27 n. 159, consider Orbe was probably thinking of Heracleon's exegesis of John 2:12. This is even more likely taking into consideration Heracleon's interpretation in Frag. 20 (of John 4:21), of the mountain as the material world: "The mountain represents the Devil, or his world, since the Devil was one part of the whole of matter, but the world is the total mountain of evil, a deserted dwelling place of beasts, to which all who lived before the law and all Gentiles render worship. But Jerusalem represents the creation or the Creator whom the Jews worship.... The mountain is the creation which the Gentiles worship, but Jerusalem is the creator whom the Jews serve. You then who are spiritual should worship neither the creation nor the Craftsman, but the Father of Truth. And he (Jesus) accepts her (the Samaritan woman) as one of the already faithful, and to be counted with those who worship in truth". See Wucherpfennig 2002, 130–131.
[39] Apoc. Paul NHC V,2 19.29.
[40] Apoc. Paul NHC V,2 20.4, *ktisis*; 23.27.
[41] Apoc. Paul NHC V,2 20.19–20; 23.13–14.
[42] Apoc. Paul NHC V,2 21.5, *kosmos*.
[43] Apoc. Paul NHC V,2 19.29–30.

down and saw."[44] From an anthropological perspective, this region is associated with the body, which is mentioned three times and is always equated with sin.[45] From an ethical perspective, it is the scenario in which lawless deeds, murder, and concupiscence take place. From an epistemological one, finally, we may say that it is the realm of darkness,[46] where torpor of the mind obstructs knowledge and from which consequently one must awake.[47] In short, it is the realm of the captivity (αἰχμαλωσία), which Paul mentions by means of a polyptoton in his answer to the Demiurge in the seventh heaven:

> I am going down to the world (κόσμος) of
> the dead in order to lead captive (αἰχμαλωτίζειν)
> the captivity (αἰχμαλωσία)
> that was led captive (αἰχμαλωτίζειν)
> in the captivity (αἰχμαλωσία) of Babylon.[48]

This is all we can derive from the text about the earthly realm. There is no further cosmographical interest, no reference, for example, to the higher, bordering region between the sublunary world and the celestial region, sometimes described in other texts as the "firmament" or "the air," as in the Ascension of Isaiah,[49] or "the region in the middle of the air," as in the Coptic Asclepius.[50] In my view, this lack of interest shows that despite the clear separation between both spheres there is a given continuity between them: it seems as if Apocalypse of Paul conceives the lower and the celestial realms as parts of an organic whole.

From the mountain of Jericho, Paul is taken directly to the third heaven. Maybe due to its being a continuation of Second Corinthians, or to the fact that the focus of the text is neither the netherworld nor the celestial region but the pleroma, the first two heavens are simply omitted.[51] The second region of this tripartite cosmic whole is the celestial realm, which is symbolically referred to

---

44   Apoc. Paul NHC V,2 20.1–2.
45   Apoc. Paul NHC V,2 20.22–23; 20.29; 21.20.
46   Apoc. Paul NHC V,2 21.13.
47   Apoc. Paul NHC V,2 18.22; 19.10.
48   Apoc. Paul NHC V,2 23.13–17. On the use of the term αἰχμαλωσία 'captivity' and derivatives in the context of Nag Hammadi, see Klauck 1985, 177–178.
49   See Ascen. Isa. 7.9–11; 10.30, on which Roig Lanzillotta 2016, 1.3.1 and n. 22.
50   Perf. Disc. NHC VI,8 76.22–37.
51   Against the view of Kasser 1969, 260, who surmises a complicated textual history for the text in order to explain the silence regarding the first two heavens, Kaler 2008, 60–61, already surmised that 2 Cor 12:2–4 as point of departure may sufficiently explain this omission.

as Jerusalem.[52] Heracleon's fragment 13 allegorizes the way up to Jerusalem as the ascension from the material to the psychic.[53] The already mentioned fragment 20 further associates the city with both the creator god and the psychic region.[54] I think consequently that the Jerusalem of Apocalypse of Paul cannot be put in connection with the Valentinian ogdoad, as described by Irenaeus.[55] As is also the case in (First) Revelation of James, Jerusalem "gives the cup of bitterness to the sons of the light. She is the dwelling place of a great number of archons."[56]

In comparison to elementary level of the mountain of Jericho, Jerusalem represents a higher stage of development, which in the present context is the realm that the apostles, as "elect spirits,"[57] are said to attain (but not to trespass.[58] The little child in fact refers to Jerusalem as the apostles' domain.[59] When Paul starts his way up, their psychic component is already there since, when Paul looks up, he sees them greeting him,[60] and they are also said to accompany Paul during his travel through the hebdomad.[61] In spite of the question raised by earlier scholars as to whether or not the apostles ascend with Paul,[62]

---

52   Apoc. Paul NHC V,2 18.5; 18[18].
53   See Heracleon's Frag. 13 (on John 2:13–16): "The ascent to Jerusalem signifies the ascent of the Lord from material realm things to the animate (psychic) place, which is an image of Jerusalem". On the issue Wucherpfennig 2002, 51–53 and 64–67.
54   See above note 34.
55   See Kaler in Rosenstiehl and Kaler (2005, 271–272), in reference to Irenaeus, Haer. 1.5.3.
56   1 Apoc. Jas. NHC V,3 25.16–19. trans. Schoedel 1979. On Jerusalem as the habitat of the archons, see also DeConick 2009, 276–8.
57   Apoc. Paul NHC V,2 19.17.
58   Apoc. Paul NHC V,2 24.1–4.
59   Apoc. Paul NHC V,2 18.18–19.
60   Apoc. Paul NHC V,2 19.18–20.
61   Apoc. Paul NHC V,2 21.29–30; 22.14–16. In contrast to Paul's mobility, which takes him from the lower to the highest realm, the figure of the Apostles is rather static. In the beginning they are already in the celestial region, in Jerusalem, since they greet Paul from there when he is preparing himself to ascend (19.18–20). At the end, they also greet Paul from the seventh heaven, once he proceeds to the ogdoad.
62   See Tröger 1973, 43, who refers to Schenke's opinion according to which 20.4 with its reference to the "creation" seems to imply a negative answer. Apoc. Paul NHC V,2 20.18–20, however, clearly shows that the apostles are already in the celestial region, since it says that Paul raises his eyes and sees them greeting him. I think the text intentionally distinguishes between Paul's and the apostles's "likeness," which remains in the lower realm, and the soul, which ascends to the archontic region. As for the third, divine region only Paul's spirit is allowed to enter. Thus also Klauck, 1985, 169. See also Kaler, 2008, 11 n. 37, who provides two additional reasons for denying that the apostles accompany Paul beyond the ogdoad: 1) to begin with, the frame story from Galatians places the apostles in Jerusalem; 2) secondly, the apostles are always explicitly mentioned whenever they are referred to.

I think they do but only up to the upper border of the celestial region, namely to the confines of the hebdomad. In a last analysis the heavenly Jerusalem is the apostle's proper region. Consequently they not only greet Paul from there when he is still on earth; they also accompany him during his ascent, and when Paul finally abandons the hebdomad, while entering the ogdoad he looks (back) at them and sees them greeting him, as it were to wish him fare-well.[63]

I think this interpretation fits well in the view developed by April DeConick of the apostles as archons in the Gospel of Judas. As she has clearly shown, there is amply testimony in a wide array of early Christian writings as to both the (negative or positive) view of the apostles' relationship to the zodiac and their equation to the archontic powers populating the astral region.[64] At any rate we seem to be dealing here with a highly polemical statement about the status and character of the apostles, who are not only hierarchically inferior to *the* apostle Paul but are also associated with the passions that characterize the psychic realm. Most transgressive, however, are the implications of such a statement: while Paul's authority is based on the *pleroma*, that of the apostles is derived from their service to the rule of the demiurge.

Another important polemical aspect is perhaps the portrayal of the demiurge[65] with its reminiscences of Daniel 7. Even if he remains a negative figure, apparent in his hostility to Paul and his obstructing his way up, it is interesting that the text does not include other typically negative aspects belonging to the demiurge's description, such his beast-like countenance or his presumptuous arrogance. Apocalypse of Paul rather describes him as an "old man"[66] and refers both to the bright white clothes he wears and his throne, seven times brighter than the sun, which contributes to the overall neutral presentation. In my view, this description intends to emphasize even more clearly that we are dealing here with the "divinity who was considered by Jews and non-gnostic Christians to be the supreme deity," but was seen as an inferior or subaltern god by gnostics.[67] Once again then we encounter a transgressive element: despite his magnificent countenance, "the old man" in the seventh heaven is

---

63  Given that the apostles, according to Apoc. Paul 22.14–16, accompany Paul during his ascent, it is incorrect to say that the Spirit's promise to take Paul to the Apostles (in 19.17–18) is only fulfilled when they reach the ogdoad (Rosensthiel and Kaler 2005, 271). Rather, when reaching the ogdoad Paul looks (back) at the apostles and they greet him in order to bid him farewell.
64  DeConick 2009.
65  Apoc. Paul NHC V,2 22.25–23.28.
66  Apoc. Paul NHC V,2 22.25.
67  See Kaler's commentary in Rosenstiehl and Kaler 2005, 252. *Contra* Rosenstiehl's introduction in Rosenstiehl and Kaler 2005, 55–62.

the creator god, and is the lord of the authorities and principalities ruling the lower heavens and the sublunary world.

Other important inhabitants of this region are the various angels in charge of the judgment and punishment of sinners in the fourth and fifth heavens,[68] of course the souls of the sinners,[69] the "toll collectors"[70] who control the gates of the heavens, and the demiurge's "principalities and authorities."[71]

The password Paul gives the demiurge in any case clearly shows that we have reached a climactic point before proceeding to the divine region. From a cosmological perspective, this momentous turning point in the seventh heaven emphasizes that the hard divide between the celestial and divine realms is here and not in the ogdoad, as numerous scholars seem to believe.[72] The ogdoad in the Apocalypse of Paul is clearly seen as antechamber of the pleroma and thus as belonging to the divine region.

As far as the cosmographical description is concerned, not all the heavens receive such a detailed description. The third heaven is mentioned in passing, and the actual description of the hebdomad begins in the fourth heaven with the judgment of a soul. If we exclude the mention of the gates[73] and the bright light of the sixth heaven, there are no further descriptions of the region. From an anthropological perspective, however, the description is richer. The archontic region is, of course, the psychic region. If the description of the first earthly realm abounds in references to the body and materiality, the psychic region now includes numerous references to both the soul and passions. In the same way that the earth is the setting for factual sins and crimes, such as iniquity, promiscuity, and murder, the psychic realm includes the passions that gave rise to them: anger, rage, envy, and desire.[74] Although there is no reference to the origin of passions—, which might be due to either the lack of references to the planets or to the archons responsible for them, or both—, it is interesting that the three witnesses that accuse the soul of her sins are in fact

---

68  Apoc. Paul NHC V,2 20.5–12; 22.2–10. Three angels, who under the leadership of the great angel goad the souls, might according to Murdock, 1965, 76, be inspired by the Erinyes (see Virgil, *Aen.* VI, 570–572) of Greek mythology. As support, he adds the alleged etymological relationship between the Greek verb ἐρίζειν "compete, to be rival" and the name of the Ἐρινύες. However, in spite of Klauck 1985, 183, and Rosenstiehl and Kaler 2005, 48–50, there is no such etymological relationship: Both words have completely different roots. See Pierre Chantraine, *Dictionnaire étymologique*, s.v. ἔρις and Ἐρινύες.

69  Apoc. Paul NHC V,2 20.8–21.22; 22.9–10.

70  Apoc. Paul NHC V,2 20.16; 22.20.

71  Apoc. Paul NHC V,2 23.20–22; 23.28.

72  Thus for example Kaler's commentary in Rosenstiehl and Kaler 2005, 272–273 n. 381.

73  Apoc. Paul NHC V,2 20.10; 21.27; 22.12, πύλη.

74  Apoc. Paul NHC V,2 21.1–9. See DeConick, 2013.

personifications of the urges behind these passions. This is the reason why, in my view, there is no relationship whatsoever between Apocalypse of Paul and the Testament of Abraham 10.[75] From an ethical perspective, it is interesting to note that the soul appears to be responsible for yielding to their impulses and for the wrong course of action based on them.

The last divine region consists of three heavens, namely the ogdoad, the ninth heaven, and the tenth heaven. Apocalypse of Paul's description of this realm is reduced to a minimum. There is neither a special denomination for it nor a description of its inhabitants. We simply hear who is allowed to enter and who is not. While Paul and the Spirit-child proceed to the new region, as indicated by Paul's restrictive use of "we" (to refer to himself and the Spirit), the apostles remain behind (see below), greeting Paul from the seventh heaven.[76] This is also emphasized by the fact that it is only Paul who gives the old man the password necessary to be allowed to continue the ascension. No further mention is made of the inhabitants of the eighth heaven. In the ninth, Apocalypse of Paul simply makes a reference to "those who are in the ninth heaven." As for the inhabitants of the tenth heaven, Paul describes them as my "fellow spirits."[77]

No further cosmographical details are added. The special place the divine region occupies in the overall cosmological structure is more derived from its highest hierarchical position than from its intrinsic description. From an anthropological perspective, the divine is the realm of the intellect (*nous*). It is

---

[75] In spite of the scholarly opinions that, on the basis of Murdock and MacRae 1979, claim a relationship between the judgment scenes in Apoc. Paul and T. Ab. 10 (long recension and Coptic version, see See G.W. MacRae 1976, 334–335), in my view the similarities should not be overstated. In fact the only common motif between both scenes is the appearance of *three witnesses* who testify against the soul. Despite MacRae 1976, closer analysis reveals important structural differences among the scenes: (1) First of all, there is an important difference between the character and function of the witnesses. In Apoc. Paul in fact they seem to be personifications of the urges behind the passions (see also Klauck 1985, 171); in T. Ab. they are real witnesses who accuse the soul of the sins actually committed. (2) The place of judgment is different: the fourth heaven (Apoc. Paul) and Paradise (T. Ab.). (3) The order of the elements in the narration is also different: in Apoc. Paul, Paul sees first the judgment of one soul and then the angels conducting numerous souls to judgment; in T. Ab. it is the other way around: first thousands of souls are brought and one of them is chosen for judgment. (4) The intention is different as well: While Apoc. Paul simply shows the punishment of sins, T. Ab. contrasts right and wrong. (5) Accusations are worded differently: Not only what they say, but also the sins of which they accuse the soul are of a rather different nature. (6) The motif of the books does not imply textual relationship, since it is a rather common object in the context of judgments.

[76] Apoc. Paul NHC V,2 24.1–3.

[77] Apoc. Paul NHC V,2 24.8.

the part Paul needs to awaken in order to know the "hidden thing in those that are visible"[78] and is the only human component that is allowed in the highest region, which is then, however, described as "spirit" (*pneuma*).[79] The lack of any other description plausibly points to both simplicity as main characteristic of the divine and to the necessary silence regarding the revelations the neophyte has received.

## 3 Continuity and Discontinuity among the Realms

The three realms which make up the cosmos—earthly, celestial, divine—are arranged according to an implicit ascending hierarchy. The lower realm is inferior to the celestial one, which in turn is inferior to the divine abode. However, can we say something more about how the spheres are articulated? In my view, the study of how the borders between the regions are described may help us to refine the analysis. To begin with, the lack of interest in the border between the earthly realm and the hebdomad, and the absence of references either to firmament or air of this area, shows that both realms are conceived of as a continuum. This fluidity seems to be confirmed by the fact that there is visibility between the realms. When Paul looks up or down he is able to see what is happening either in the heavens or on the earth.[80] The continuity between both realms is also stressed by the fact that Paul is taken directly from the earth to the third heaven, without intermediary stations. Furthermore, the conception of the earthly mountain of Jericho and celestial Jerusalem as point of departure and goal of the journey, respectively, clearly shows that the text conceives both realms as belonging together, as a continuum. This seems to be confirmed by the ambiguity of the term for "creation" (*ktisis*, 20.4) that in Apocalypse of Paul at the same time refers to the lower and celestial realms as parts of the same creation of the lower deity.

This continuum is interrupted, however, when Paul reaches the seventh heaven. As already pointed out, the momentous speech with the old man, his magnificent description, Paul's password, and the apostles' greeting from that region underline the hard divide between celestial and divine regions. When Paul proceeds to the ogdoad he enters a new realm, a new space, the difference of which is marked off by its special name (no longer just adding a

---

78  For, *nous*, see Apoc. Paul NHC V,2 19.10.
79  Apoc. Paul NHC V,2 24.8.
80  Thus in Apoc. Paul NHC V,2 19.18–20 Paul looks up and sees the apostles greeting him from the hebdomad; in 19.27–32; 20.1–4, he looks down and sees their likenesses on earth.

numeral to a heaven but by a special name, namely the ogdoad), by its simplicity, and by the text's silence regarding both its characteristics and inhabitants. In contrast to the detailed description of the two lower realms, the divine region belongs to the revelatory part of the journey; it needs to be protected by esoteric transmission.

## 4    Why Ten Heavens?

In marked difference from the more widespread cosmological patterns including three or seven heavens, Apocalypse of Paul apparently includes ten heavens, and all commentaries point out the anomaly.[81] It is important to note, however, that in so doing Apocalypse of Paul is not as anomalous as commentators seem to assume. Apocalypse of Paul includes a seven-plus-three pattern, which means that it in fact combines the regular seven heavens of the hebdomad with three layers of the divine realm. This is, by the way, not that strange among Nag Hammadi writings: witness, for example, the systems of the Secret Book of John, which also includes ten heavens,[82] or On the Origin of the World and Nature of the Rulers, which, besides describing the creation of the demiurge, also provide an overview of the higher divine region, albeit without clearly distinguishing layers within it.[83]

Due to Apocalypse of Paul's silence concerning the upper three layers, which is not that strange either—see, for example, the similar case of the Orig. World[84]—we cannot know the specific characteristics peculiar to them. In any case, the author attempted to organize and give structure to the Gnostic aeons, expressing by means of hierarchically disposed heavens that which other texts express by means of highly poetic descriptions. In this sense, it is plausible to think that Apocalypse of Paul was trying to adapt his view of the cosmos to standard ancient cosmology and that, in so doing he created a hybrid product that conflates cosmology with theology, similarly to the Aristotelian system of the *Metaphysics Lambda*. In fact, Aristotle adds to the seven planetary orbits and the outer circle of the fixed stars, inherited from Plato's *Timaeus*, a divine

---

81   Murdock and MacRae 1979, 47; Rosenstiehl and Kaler 2005, 28; Kaler 2008, 60–62.
82   Ap. John NHC II,1 14.1–14.
83   Orig. World NHC II,5 102.1–2; 104.30–35; Nat. Rulers NHC II,4 94.8–95.21.
84   Also referred to by Bethge 2015: "The complete absence of any description of the upper world or any account of its development is striking."

region allotted to the Unmoved Mover.[85] The only difference from Apocalypse of Paul's system is that the fixed stars are included in the divine region and that it, moreover, divides the transcendent layer into two.

A similar combination of cosmology and theology can be found in three interesting Hermetic tracts, two of them in the Corpus Hermeticum, and one in the Nag Hammadi library. I am referring to Poimandres, the thirteenth Hermetic treatise,[86] and the Discourse on the Eighth and the Ninth.[87] Interestingly enough, they all also include the same seven-plus-three pattern.[88] After enumerating the seven heavens and the seven vices (implicitly) associated with the planets,[89] Poimandres also describes the divine region as consisting of three layers, the ogdoad, the ninth, and the tenth heaven:[90]

> Then, stripped of the activities of the cosmos, he enters the substance of the eighth plain with his own power, and he sings praises to the Father with those who are present; those who are near rejoice at his coming. Being made like to those who are there together, he also hears certain powers which are above the eighth sphere, singing praises to God with sweet voice. Then in due order, they ascend to the Father and they surrender themselves to the powers, and becoming the powers they are merged in God.[91]

Whether Poimandres provides here an eschatological description, as Nock and Festugière surmised,[92] or whether it offers a commentary on the previous visions described in Poimandres chapters 4 through 7, as Wouter Hanegraaff perhaps more likely interprets[93] is irrelevant for our present purpose. What interests us here is that even if the ascension described in Poimandres takes place after death,[94] the ethical dimension is obvious, since the individual leaves

---

85   The system Aristotle adapts is of course that of Eudoxus with the corrections included by Callipus. See Mendell 2000. However, Plato's *Tim.* (38C–40C), albeit in a mythical exposition, already implies the same cosmological structure. See Leinkauf and Steel 2005.
86   Corp. herm. 13.10.
87   Disc. 8–9 NHC VI,6.
88   Dirkse, Brashler and Parrott 1979, 342.
89   See Nock and Festugière 1945–1954, 28.
90   Corp. herm. 1.26 (Nock and Festugière, 1945–1954).
91   Trans. Salaman et al. 1999.
92   Nock and Festugière, 1945, Corp. herm. 1.2–6; and notes to chapters 23–26.
93   Hanegraaff 2008, 141–142.
94   Nock and Festugière, 1945, Corp. herm. 1.6; Tröger, 1971, 140. Van den Broek 2006, 66; Hanegraaff 2008, 149.

behind the passions and vices that bothered the soul during its life.[95] At the end of that process, we find the fusion with the divine, the final *homoiosis theo*.

A similar process is involved in the Disc. 8–9, but in this case we see an out-of-body experience. The ecstatic experience allows the disciples to reach the eighth and ninth levels. That the ascension is at the same time conceived of as an ethical progress can be seen in the fact that, in order to reach the divine region, the individual surpasses first the *heimarmene* governed by the *Ousiarches* and then the vices associated with them.[96] Interestingly the *Discourse* describes the divine region in a similar way to Poimandres. Not only is the tenth heaven not explicitly mentioned, but we also see that the increasing degree of perfection of the three highest heavens is expressed by means of the praises that each heaven sings to the next one.[97] As for the silence regarding God's abode in the tenth heaven, it is its omission that makes it all the more present.

By contrast, the thirteenth Hermetic treatise does mention the tenth level of ascent explicitly,[98] even if its exposition is more schematic. This is probably due to the mainly ethical description of the ascension here set forth, which consequently shuns every reference to planets or to heavens. The ascension of the soul includes ten levels, the first nine of which are associated with vices that, when counteracted by the opposite virtues,[99] allow access to the following level. Once the soul passes through all nine levels, the ethical progress culminates in the assimilation to the divine, the rebirth, or *palingenesia*, in the tenth, the divine realm.[100] Interestingly, as Bousset, Ferguson, and Nock and Festugière have rightly noticed we also seem to have behind the thirteenth Hermetic tractate a seven-plus-three pattern, since to an original list of seven

---

95  The ethical character of the ascent's description was also noticed by Dirkse, Brashler and Parrott 1979, 342.

96  Disc. 8–9 NHC VI,6 63.19. On the topic see Scott 1936, vol. 3, 115, who, relating it with Stoicism, interprets the term *heimarmene* as a divinity who "presides over (some kind of) material substance." In my view, Festugière 1967, 127, rightly points out that these are the seven archons governing the seven planetary regions. See more recently, Mahé 1978 133–134.

97  Disc. 8–9 NHC VI,6 59.28–60.1, trans. Salaman et al.: "And I see the eighth (ὀγδοάς) and the souls (ψυχή) that are in it and the angels singing a hymn (ὑμνεῖν) to the ninth (ἐννεάς) and its powers (δύναμις). And I see him who has the power (δύναμις) of them all, creating those <that are> in the spirit (πνεῦμα)." According to Mahé, 1978, 120, we have here a parallel to the explicit mention of the tenth level in Corp. herm. 13.

98  See Mahé 1978, 120.

99  See Mussies 1981.

100 Corp. herm. 13.10, "You know now, o son, the manner of rebirth. And with the arrival of these ten, spiritual birth is complete and it drives out the twelve, and by this birth we have become divine. Whoever, then, by God's mercy attains a divine birth is freed from the bodily senses and is made whole by these powers. He knows himself and rejoices."

vices and their opposed virtues the text adds the good, life and light to reach the number ten, the δέκας that will counteract the power of the Twelve.[101]

## 5 Intention of Apocalypse of Paul

In my view, Apocalypse of Paul shares with the Hermetic tracts something more than the number of heavens. In the same way as in the Hermetic treatises, the ascension in Apocalypse of Paul is presented as an ethical progress, which begins upon his leaving Jericho, the realm of the body and physical existence, and culminates in Jerusalem, the higher psychic level. With Poimandres, Apocalypse of Paul shares both the negative view of the hebdomad, the ogdoad as the beginning of the divine region, and the description of the ascending degrees of glory of the following two layers. With *Disc. 8–9*, Apocalypse of Paul shares a view of the ascension as an ecstatic experience that at the same time is conceived of in terms of ethical progress. This is also the case in the thirteenth Hermetic treatise which, however, leaves the heavens aside, retaining only their significance and presenting a more abstract sequence of ten levels of purification.

If Apocalypse of Paul was composed vis-à-vis Jewish apocalyptic texts, it seems obvious that its writer was attempting to redefine, if not the genre, at least the character and the goal of the revelation presented in it. To begin with the latter, the goal of the revelation is not the vision of God or his throne, but something much more radical, namely the fusion with God. Significantly, the Biblical God appears in the text but not as a goal, rather as an obstacle Paul easily transcends. The character of the apocalypse is also redefined: the ascent shows a typically ethical nature, since it symbolizes the steps that the gnostic has to fulfil to transcend both his body and soul and become pure spirit.

This is the reason why Apocalypse of Paul includes a seven-plus-three heaven pattern. The ascent through the hebdomad is necessary to provide the ethical purification by means of which the individual frees himself from soul altogether. The last three levels focus on the progressive process of transformation before attaining the final assimilation. As all three Hermetic texts also do, Apocalypse of Paul conceives of the tenth level as the highest point and ultimate goal of the ascent. It is at that point—once Paul has liberated himself from all the accretions of both body and soul—that he can fuse with the

---

[101] Bousset 1973 [1907], 364 in reference to Reitzenstein; Ferguson cited in Scott 1936, 388; Nock and Festugière 1945–1954, 213. See, however, more recently DeConick 2013; and 2009.

divine, attaining the desired *homoiosis theo* that Apocalypse of Paul laconically describes as Paul greeting his "fellow spirits."

## Summary

As far as Apocalypse of Paul's cosmology is concerned, first, one of the most important aspects of the text is its tripartite conception of the universe. Not only do the three cosmological regions show that we are dealing with a text heavily influenced by a typically Greek worldview, but it is especially the continuity between earthly and celestial realms, and the discontinuity between the latter and the divine realm, which do as well. To begin with, the three realms seem to echo Aristotle's distinguishing, as found in the *Metaphysics*, of three sorts of substance: perishable, movable-eternal, and immovable.[102] The hard divide between the celestial and divine realms seems to betray the influence of the Aristotelian system, since it combines the Eudoxian model of the cosmos with the view of the external cause of the Unmoved Mover of *Metaphysics Lambda*. All these aspects seem to point to a Greco-Roman background rather than to a specifically Jewish one, as has been assumed in recent scholarship.

Second, it is important to note that Apocalypse of Paul's interest in the heavens is rather more anthropological than cosmological, which means that the heavens are significant for the influence they might exert on human beings. Consequently, Greek cosmology is adapted to suit the anthropological and ethical views of the text. In spite of Apocalypse of Paul's silence regarding the planets, the reference to the toll collectors and the demiurge clearly show that the hebdomad is seen as the realm of the *heimarmene*, the psychic realm that oppresses humans by means of passions and vices. The personifications of the urges behind the affections, which appear as witnesses to testimony against a sinner's soul in the fourth heaven, further complete this framework. Most interestingly and transgressively, Apocalypse of Paul conceives of this region as station of the apostles, who in this way are presented as lackeys of the demiurge and his creation. Differently, Paul, the gnostic, transcends all this and speeds to the divine region, from which his authority emanates.

This is the reason why Apocalypse of Paul describes the ascension as an ethical progress in which the individual leaves behind the passions belonging to the psychic level. Incidentally, this mainly ethical view of the ascent may allow one to explain the alleged anomalous pattern of ten heavens. From an ethical perspective, the seven-plus-three pattern is perfectly understandable,

---

102   See Aristotle, *Metaph.* 1069AB.

since it focuses on both the preparatory ethical progress towards the goal—the purificatory ascension through the seven heavens culminates with the *homoiosis theo* in the divine region. This ethical focus of the text is clear in that it culminates not in the vision of God or the throne of God as in Jewish apocalyptic currents, but in the fusion with the divine, with divinization of the individual. Most transgressive is the use of a description of the Biblical god evoking Daniel 7 to present the demiurge, whom Paul leaves behind staring at his creation.

Finally, in my view the previous conclusions leave little room for hesitation. It seems clear that the goal of Paul's ascension is more ethical than apocalyptic. What I mean is that the goal of the revelation transmitted by the text is not so much the description of an otherworldly journey and its stations as it is the ethical progress experienced by the initiate and the fact that its culmination is equated to the fusion with the divine. Interesting in this context is the fact that the vision of the sinners is not intended to contrast with the fate of the righteous. The interest is not so much in the punishment of the faults as it is in the very passions that generated them.

The countercultural message is, I think, obvious: While conventional Christians follow the apostles and remain trapped in the purgatory of the archontic region, dealing with passions and the oppression of the *heimarmene*, gnostics go far beyond all this, knowing as they do the way to dispose of the accretions of both body and soul and how to supersede the cosmic realms related to them.

## Bibliography

Bethge, Hans-Gebhard. 2000–04. "On the Origin of the World (OTOOTW)." *The Coptic Gnostic Library—A Complete Edition of the Nag Hammadi Codices.* Editor in Chief: James M. Robinson. Brill Online, 2015. Reference. http://referenceworks.brillonline.com/entries/ coptic-gnostic-library/on-the-origin-of-the-world-otootw-aOTOOTW.

Böhlig, Alexander. 1963. "Die Apokalypse des Paulus." Pages 15–26 in *Koptisch-gnostische Apokalypsen aus Codex V von Nag Hammadi im Koptischen Museum zu Alt-Kairo.* Edited by Alexander Böhlig and Pahor Labib. Halle-Wittenberg: Martin-Luther-Universität.

Bullard, Roger A. 1990. "Paul, Apocalypse of (NH)." Page 664 in I *Mercer Dictionary of the Bible*, edited by Watson E. Mills et al. Macon: Mercer University Press.

Bousset, Wilhelm. 1973 [1907]. *Hauptprobleme der Gnosis* (Forschungen zur Religion und Literatur des Alten und Neuen Testaments 10; Göttingen: Vandenhoeck und Ruprecht.

DeConick, April D. 2009. "Apostles as Archons. The Fight for Authority and the Emergence of Gnosticism in the Tchakos Codex and Other Early Christian Literature." Pages 243–288 in *Codex Judas Papers: Proceedings of The International Congress On The Tchacos Codex Held At Rice University, Houston, Texas, March 13–16, 2008*. Edited by April D. DeConick. Leiden: Brill.

DeConick, April D. 2013. "The Road for the Souls Is through the Planets: The Mysteries of the Ophians Mapped." Pages 37–74 in *Practicing Gnosis Ritual, Magic, Theurgy and Liturgy in Nag Hammadi, Manichaean and Other Ancient Literature Essays in Honor of Birger A. Pearson*. Edited by April D. DeConick, Gregory Shaw and John D. Turner. Leiden: Brill.

Dirkse, Peter A., James Brashler, and Douglas M. Parrott. 1979. "The Discourse on the Eighth and the Ninth." Pages 341–73 in *Nag Hammadi Codices V, 2–5 and VI with Papyrus Berolinensis gnosticus*. Edited by Douglas M. Parrott. Leiden: Brill.

Fallon, Francis T. 1979. "The Gnostic Apocalypses." *Semeia* 14: 123–158.

Festugière, André-Jean. 1932. *L'idéal religieux des Grecs et l'Évangile*. Paris: Gabalda.

Festugière, André-Jean. 1967. *Hermétisme et mystique païenne*. Paris: Aubier Montaigne.

Funk, Wolf-Peter. 1989. "Koptisch-gnostische Apokalypse des Paulus." Pages 628–33 in *Neutestamentliche Apokryphen in deutscher Übersetzung, II Band: Apostolisches Apokalypsen und Verwandtes*. Edited by Wilhelm Schneemelcher and Edgar Hennecke. 5. Aufl.; Tubingen: Mohr-Siebeck.

Funk, Wolf-Peter. "The Coptic Gnostic Apocalypse of Paul," in W. Schneemelcher & R. McL. Wilson (eds.), *New Testament Apocrypha II: Writings Related to the Apostles, Apocalypses and Related Subjects* (Cambridge: James Clarke and Louisville: Westminster/John Knox, 1992) 695–700.

Funk, Wolf-Peter. 1995. "The Linguistic Aspect of Classifying Nag Hammadi Codices." Pages 107–47 in *Les textes de Nag Hammadi et le problème de leur classification: Actes du Colloque tenu à Québec du 15 a 19 septembre 1993*. Edited by Louis Painchaud and Anne Pasquier. Québec: Presses de l'Université Laval; Louvain: Peeters, 1995.

Funk, Wolf-Peter. 1997. "Koptisch-gnostische Apokalypse des Paulus." Pages 628–633 in *Neutestamentliche Apokryphen in deutscher Übersetzung*, II: Apostolisches Apokalypsen und Verwandtes. Edited by Wilhelm Schneemelcher. 6. Aufl.; Tübingen: Mohr-Siebeck.

Hanegraaff, Wouter J. 2008. "Altered States of Knowledge: The Attainment of Gnōsis in the Hermetica." *The International Journal of the Platonic Tradition* 2: 128–163.

Harrison, J.R. 2004. "In Quest of the Third Heaven: Paul & His Apocalyptic Imitators." *Vigiliae Christianae* 58: 24–55.

Kaler, Michael. 2008. *Flora tells a Story: the Apocalypse of Paul and Its Contexts*. Waterloo, ON: Wilfrid Laurier University Press.

Kaler, Michael, Painchaud, Louis and Bussieres, Marie-Pierre. 2004. "The Coptic *Apocalypse of Paul*, Irenaeus' *Adversus Haereses* 2.30.7, and the Second-Century Battle for Paul's Legacy," *Journal of Early Christian Studies* 12: 173–193.

Kasser, Rodolphe. 1965. "Textes gnostiques. Remarques à propos des éditions récentes du Livre secret de Jean et des Apocalypses de Paul, Jacques et Adam," *Museon* 78:71–98; 299–306.

Kasser, Rodolphe. 1969. "Bibliothèque gnostique VII: *L'Apocalypse de Paul*." *Revue de théologie et de philosophie* 19: 259–263.

Klauck, Hans-Josef. 1985. "Die Himmelfahrt des Paulus (2 Kor 12:2–4) in der koptischen Paulusapokalypse aus Nag Hammadi (NHC V/2)," *Studien zum Neuen Testament und seiner Umwelt* 10: 151–190.

Krause, Martin. 1983. "Die literarischen Gattungen der Apokalypsen von Nag Hammadi." Pages 621–637 in *Apocalypticism in the Mediterranean World and the Near East*. Edited by David Hellholm. Tübingen: Mohr Siebeck.

Leinkauf, Thomas and Carlos G. Steel. 2005. *Platons Timaios Als Grundtext Der Kosmologie in Spätantike, Mittelalter und Renaissance*. Leuven: Leuven University Press.

MacRae, George W. 1976. "The Judgment Scene in the Coptic Apocalypse of Paul." (ed.), Pages 285–288 in *Studies on the Testament of Abraham*. Edited by George W.E. Nickelsburg, Jr. SBL Septuagint and Cognate Studies 6; Missoula, MT: Scholars Press, 1976.

Mahé, Jean-Pierre. 1978–1982. *Hermès en Haute-Égypte*. Québec: Les presses de l'Université Laval; Leuven: Peeters.

Mendell, Henry. 2000. "The Trouble with Eudoxus." Pages 59–138 in *Ancient and Medieval Traditions in the Exact Sciences*. Edited by Patrick Suppes, Julius Moravcsik, and Henry Mendell. Stanford, CA: Center for the Study of Language and Information.

Murdock, William R. 1965. *The Apocalypse of Paul from Nag Hammadi*. Th.D. dissertation, School of Theology at Claremont.

Murdock, William R. and George W. MacRae. 1979. "The Apocalypse of Paul." Pages 47–63 in *Nag Hammadi Codices V,2–5 and VI with Papyrus Berolinensis 8502, 1 and 4*. Edited by Douglas M. Parrott. Leiden: Brill.

Mussies, Gerard. 1981. "Catalogues of Sins and Virtues Personified (NHC II, 5)." Pages 314–336 in *Studies in Gnosticism and Hellenistic Religions presented to Gilles Quispel on the Occasion of his 65th Birthday*. Edited by Roelof van den Broek and Maarten Jozef Vermaseren. Leiden: Brill.

Nock A.D. and Festugière, André-Jean. 1945–1954. *Corpus Hermeticum*, I: *Traités I–XII*; II: *Traités XIII–XVIII; Asclépius*; III–IV: *Fragments extraits de Stobée (I–XXIX); Fragments divers*. Paris: Société d'Edition "Les Belles Lettres".

Orbe, A. 1983. "Gli apocrifi cristiani a Nag Hammadi." *Augustinianum* 23: 81–109.
Riedweg, Christoph. 2015. "Soul, migration of the." *Brill's New Pauly*. Antiquity volumes edited by: Hubert Cancik Helmuth Schneider and Christine F. Salazar. Brill Online. http://referenceworks.brillonline.com/entries/brill-s-new-pauly/soul-migration-of-the-e1106520.
Roig Lanzillotta, Lautaro. 2003. "Does Punishment Reward the Righteous? The Justice Pattern Underlying the Apocalypse of Peter." Pages 127–157 in *The Apocalypse of Peter*. Edited by Jan N. Bremmer and István Czachesz. Leuven: Peeters.
Roig Lanzillotta, Lautaro. 2007. "The Coptic Apocalypse of Paul in Ms. Oriental 7023." Pages 158–197 in *The Visio Pauli and the Gnostic Apocalypse of Paul*. Edited by Jan N. Bremmer and István Czachesz. Leuven: Peeters.
Roig Lanzillotta, Lautaro. 2013. "El polimorfismo divino en la literatura apócrifa cristiana primitiva y en Nag Hammadi." Pages 1–27 in *Actas del I Congreso Internacional de Estudios Patrísticos: "La identidad de Jesús: unidad y diversidad en la época de la patrística."* Edited by Á. Hernández, S. Villalonga and P. Ciner. San Juan, Argentina: Universidad Católica de Cuyo.
Roig Lanzillotta, Lautaro. 2016. "The Cosmology of the *Ascension of Isaiah*: Analysis and Re-Assessment of the Text's Cosmological Framework." Pages 259–288 *The Ascension of Isaiah*. Edited by in Jan N. Bremmer, T.R. Karmann and T. Nicklas. Leuven: Peeters.
Rosenstiehl, Jean-Marc and Michael Kaler. 2005. *L'Apocalypse de Paul (NH V,2)*. Bibliothèque copte de Nag Hammadi, 31; Québec: Les Presses de l'Université Laval; Leuven: Peeters.
Rosenstiehl, Jean-Marc. 2006. "La montagne de Jericho (NH v, 2,19, IIB): Contribution a l'étude de *l'Apocalypse copte de Paul.*" Pages 885–892 in *Coptica-Gnostica-Manichaica: Mélanges offerts à Wolf-Peter Funk*. Edited by Louis Painchaud and Paul-Hubert Poirier. Leuven: Peeters.
Rudolph, Kurt. 1968. "Der gnostische Dialog als literarisches Genus." Pages 85–107 in *Probleme der koptischen Literatur*. Edited by P. Nagel. Halle-Wittenberg: Halle: Saale.
Salaman, Clement, Dorine Van Oyen, William D. Wharton, and Jean-Pierre Mahé. 2000. *The Way of Hermes. New Translations of The Corpus Hermeticum and The Definitions of Hermes Trismegistus to Asclepius*. Rochester, Vermont: Inner Traditions.
Schenke, Hans-Martin. 1966. "Rez. A.Böhlig- P. Labib, Apokalypsen," *Orientalische Literaturzeitung* 61: 23–34.
Schoedel, William R. 1979. "The (First) Revelation of James." Pages 66–103 in *Nag Hammadi Codices V, 2–5 and VI with Papyrus Berolinensis 8502, 1 and 4*. Edited by Douglas M. Parrott. Leiden: Brill.
Scott, Walter. 1936–1945. *Hermetica: the Ancient Greek and Latin Writings which contain religious or philosophic teachings ascribed to Hermes Trismegistus*. Oxford: The Clarendon Press.

Silverstein, Theodore, and Anthony Hilhorst. 1997. *Apocalypse of Paul. A New Critical Edition of Three Long Latin Versions.* Geneva: P. Cramer.

Solmsen, Friedrich. 1982. "Reincarnation in Ancient and Early Christian Thought." Pages 465–494 in *Kleine Schriften* 3. Edited by Friedrich Solmsen. Hildesheim: Olms.

Tardieu, Michel. 1974. *Trois mythes gnostiques: Adam, Éros et les animaux d'Égypte dans un écrit de Nag Hammadi (II,5)*. Paris: Études Augustiniennes.

Tischendorf, Constantin von. 1966 [1866]. *Apocalypses Apocryphae, Mosis, Esdrae, Pauli, Iohannis, item Mariae Dormitio, additis evangeliorum et actuum apocryphorum suplementis.* Hildesheim: G. Olms.

Trevijano Etcheverría, R. 1981. "El Apocalipsis de Pablo (NHC V2: 17,19–24,9). Traduccion y Comentario." Pages 217–236 in *Quaere Paulum. Miscelánea a Monseñor Dr. Lorenzo Turrado.* Edited by A. Díez Macho et al. Salamanca: Universidad Pontificia de Salamanca.

Tröger, Karl-Wolfgang. 1971. *Mysterienglaube und Gnosis in Corpus Hermeticum XIII.* Berlin: Akademie-Verlag.

Tröger (ed.), Karl-Wolfgang. 1973. *Gnosis und Neues Testament. Studien aus Religionswissenschaft und Theologie.* Gütersloh: Gütersloher Verlagshaus.

Van den Broek, Roelof. 2006. *Hermes Trismegistus: Inleiding, Teksten, Commentaren.* Amsterdam: Pelican.

Vielhauer, Philipp. 1975. *Geschichte der urchristlichen Literatur: Einleitung in das Neue Testament, die Apokryphen und die apostolische Väter.* Berlin: de Gruyter.

Wallis-Budge, E.A. 1915 [1966]. *Miscellaneous Coptic Texts in the Dialect of Upper Egypt. Edited, with English Translations.* Oxford: Oxford University Press.

Wilson, R.McL. 1975. "Paul, Apocalypse of." Pages 623–4 in *The Zondervan Pictorial Encyclopedia of the Bible*, IV. Edited by Merrill Chapin Tenney et al. Grand Rapids: Zondervan.

Wallis-Budge, W.E.A. 1915. *Miscellaneous texts in the dialect of Upper Egypt.* Edited with English translations 534–74, 1043–84. London.

Wucherpfennig, Ansgar. 2002. *Heracleon Philologus. Gnostische Johannesexegese im zweiten Jahrhundert.* Tübingen: Mohr Siebeck.

Wright, J. Edward. 2000. *The Early History of Heaven.* Oxford: Oxford University Press.

Yarbro Collins, Adela. 1996. *Cosmology and Eschatology in Jewish and Christian Apocalypticism.* Leiden: Brill.

# Gnosis Undomesticated: Archon-Seduction, Demon Sex, and Sodomites in the Paraphrase of Shem (NHC VII,1)

*Dylan M. Burns*
Freie Universität Berlin, Ägyptologisches Seminar
*dylan.burns@fu-berlin.de*

Gnosticism used to be considered dangerous stuff—a religious current associated with reverse exegesis, parasitism, anticosmic world-rejection, hatred of the body, sexual libertinism, and deterministic elitism. Readers of Michael Allen Williams's now-canonical study *Rethinking "Gnosticism": An Argument for Dismantling a Dubious Category* will recognize these characteristics of Gnosticism as "clichés," false allegations about the individuals and movements associated with "Gnosticism," which only lead us astray.[1] Williams has done us a great service in exposing these misleading construals about "Gnosticism" and showing how they simply do not add up when applied to our sources, particularly the Coptic works discovered at Nag Hammadi in 1945.[2]

Perhaps the least-invoked cliché of all is that of Gnostic sexual "libertinism." It is undeniable that it was common in antiquity (as today) for polemicists to denigrate their opponents by accusing them of sexual immorality.[3] Thus the occasional charges of licentiousness laid by Christian heresiographers at the feet of the Gnostics—and particularly Epiphanius of Salamis's wild tale of the Borborite *agapē* ("love-feast"), wherein semen and menstrual blood are substituted for the Eucharistic bread and wine—are generally regarded as falsehoods, thanks in part to Williams's analysis.[4] Indeed, Williams's work (and the wave of scholarship that followed it) stands at the tail end of a longer process of normalizing "Gnostic" sources, which began with the translation and interpretation of the Nag Hammadi evidence itself, as it appeared in no way

---

1  M.A. Williams 1996, esp. 263–65.
2  On the Nag Hammadi codices, see Emmel 2008.
3  Grant 1981 remains the classic study; see now Knust 2006, esp. 15–50.
4  M.A. Williams 1996, 179–84, 184: "we probably are dealing with instances in the life history of a rumor, much like other widely circulated and richly embroidered rumors about obscene practices among Christians and others in antiquity"; similarly, see Knust 2006, 3; van den Broek 2008, 2; Rasimus 2009, 253–54 regarding "libertines," his term for "Borborites." For skepticism specifically regarding the veracity of Epiphanius's report about the sexual rites of the Borborites, see Rudolph 1987, 250; Layton 1987, 200.

to corroborate the heresiological reports of Gnostic licentiousness and sexual rites.[5] Moreover, our other Coptic Gnostic evidence actually disparages individuals who engage in spermatophagy.[6] This "domesticization of Gnosis," as Henry Chadwick put it at the International Conference at the International Conference on Gnosticism at Yale University in 1978, leads scholars to read much of the Nag Hammadi literature as ascetic and even encratite.[7]

One work from Nag Hammadi, however, is far less easy to domesticate: the Paraphrase of Shem (NHC VII,1). It contains narratives that are not only the most sexually explicit passages in all extant Gnostic literature, but also exhibit clear signs of indebtedness in this work to the mythology and school of thought that Epiphanius claimed inspired Gnostic love-feasts. These passages severely mitigate the thesis of a "domesticated" Gnosticism beholden to strictly puritan concerns. Moreover, they invite us to revisit the possibility that some adherents of Gnostic myths practiced sexual rites of the sort mentioned by Epiphanius—and saw these myths not only as ancient fiction but lived reality.

1    The Seduction of Nature and Demon Sex in the 'Paraphrase of Shem'

The Paraphrase of Shem is often passed over in discussions of Gnosticism because it is a long and frustrating text. The Coptic is at times unclear—likely the product of corruption via translation—and its content bewildering.[8] It begins with a lengthy description of the primordial activities of three first principles—Light, Spirit, and Darkness—which are mixed together, and the repeated attempts of a celestial savior-revealer, named Derdekeas, to descend into the deep and liberate the divine light mired in the dark. Darkness here has a consort—Womb (*mētra*).

Early in the text, Darkness copulates with the Womb, ejaculating inside of her and filling her with "every form," endowing her with demiurgic capacity.[9]

---

5   M.A. Williams 1996, 165, 184.
6   Pistis Sophia AC 147; 2 Jeu BC 43. Again, M.A. Williams 1996, 184, argues that these passages are simply "once again polemical accusations, not advocacy by practitioners."
7   Chadwick 1981, 11: "I fear I owe my audience some apology," he continues, "for having made gnosticism more credible but the subject duller."
8   In 1987, Tardieu famously declared Paraph. Shem to be "le chef-d'œuvre de l'obscurité gnostique," 411. Wisse, 1996a, 20, its English translator for the Coptic Gnostic Library, despaired that he had perhaps imparted more sense to the text than is actually there.
9   Paraph. Shem NHC VII,1 4.25–5.6. All translations of ancient literature offered in this contribution are my own, unless noted. With regards to Paraph. Shem, I have both consulted the

Meanwhile, she collides with a hot vapor, which splits her into four sub-vapors or clouds (*cloole*): "*Hymen* (outer membrane), *Chorion* (inner membrane), Power, and Water."[10] These sub-vapors comprise Nature (*physis*), and, indeed, throughout the rest of the text, the terms *Nature* and *Womb* are used more or less synonymously,[11] and with a negative connotation—for Nature is characterized throughout the text by her "prurience" (*akatharsia*, or "impurity"), i.e., her desire to have sex, and her association with putrid water.[12]

Introducing their respective translations of the work, Frederik Wisse and Hans-Martin Schenke note its sexual language without comment.[13] Meanwhile, Michel Roberge has done much to elucidate the background of this imagery by rightfully contextualizing it in terms of contemporary gynecology, although he, like Wisse and Schenke, persists in rendering the names of the first two sub-vapors as "Hymen" and "Chorion"—as if they were proper names—rather than translating them as the gynecological terms they are: the outer and inner membranes encapsulating a fetus in the womb, which is entirely appropriate since the text is, after all, discussing a womb.[14]

So, why a womb? The womb constitutes an apt metaphor for generation, and was thus used in the ancient Mediterranean world to talk about the origins of the universe.[15] It is then only natural that some Gnostics, having reservations about the goodness of the cosmos and its origins, were known to characterize the evil demiurge not as a male, lion-faced demon, but a womb: Irenaeus of Lyons, writing in the later second century CE, accuses the "others"—who, he says, claim kinship with Cain, Esau, and the Sodomites—of pursuing the goal of "dissolving the works of the Womb" (*solvere opera hysterae*), whom "they call the creator of heaven and earth."[16] Like the followers of Carpocrates,

---

critical texts of Wisse 1996b and Roberge 2000b (although they rarely diverge, given the fine condition of the MS), in addition to the translation of Schenke 2003b.

10   Paraph. Shem NHC VII,1 5.22–6.4.

11   Paraph. Shem NHC VII,1 5.9, 8.26–33, 24.29–34, and in the passages on pages 19–23 discussed below.

12   On Nature's (sexual) impurity, see Paraph. Shem 7.17–22, 8.26–33, 18.27–35, 23.3–6, 32.2–5, 34.19–22 (repeated at 47.3–5). On Nature as dwelling in putrid water, see 15.1–6; as identified with "dark water," see 38.19–21.

13   Wisse 1996a, 18; Schenke 2003a, 547.

14   Roberge 2006, 864–68. See further Burns 2015, 90–94, regarding Porphyry, *Gaur.* 10.3 (Wilberding 2011).

15   For survey of womb-metaphors in ancient Mediterranean religious literature, see Iricinschi 2013, although the study brackets those of Paraph. Shem (ibid., 765). For discussion of the use in Gnostic literature (although not Paraph. Shem) of one important Greek term for the womb (*hystera*), see Fredriksen 1979.

16   Irenaeus, *Haer.* 1.31.1–2 (Rousseau and Doutreleau 1979).

he continues, these individuals (dubbed "Cainites" by scholars, although the actual existence of such a sect is questionable),[17] consider their unlawful sexual practices to be divinely ordained, implying that they consider antinomian sex a chief means to "dissolving the works of the Womb."[18]

Irenaeus does not relate how the Cainite womb goes about creating, but the Paraphrase of Shem, the sole extant Gnostic work that identifies a malevolent demiurge as a womb, does.[19] According to the Paraphrase of Shem, Womb produces the world as a reaction to Derdekeas's effort recover the divine light possessed by Darkness and Womb, or Nature. In the opening theogony, Derdekeas performs this recovery by delving into Darkness repeatedly while wearing robes of fire, resulting in the emission of Light, which rises back up to heaven.[20]

At a certain point, though, Derdekeas changes his strategy:

> I put on the (guise of) the beast, and I made a great request of her [Womb], so that heaven and earth would come into being, so that all the light might rise up; for by no other method would the power of the Spirit be saved from bondage, except that I appear to her in animal form. For this reason, she was gracious to me, as if I were her son, and because of my request, Nature rose up, since she possesses (something),[21] from the power of the Spirit, and darkness and fire. For she divested herself of her forms. Once she had cast it off, she breathed upon the water. The heaven was created. And from the foam of heaven, the earth came into being.[22]

---

17  For an overview of the evidence (and conclusion that no such "Cainites" existed), see Pearson 1990, followed by M.A. Williams 1996, 172; Pearson 2006a; cf. Grypeou 2005, 143–45.
18  As noted by Benko 1967, 114.
19  Recognized by Good 1997, 203. See also Tardieu 1987, 423.
20  I have elsewhere argued that these scenes are largely intelligible in the context of contemporary Greco-Egyptian alchemical language (Burns 2015, 87–96), although some of their characteristics also recall the Orphic cosmogonies extant in the Pseudo-Clementine Homilies (6.13–13) and Recognitions (10.17–19.30), as well as some of our evidence regarding the teaching of Bardaisan. On these sources, see recently Roig Lanzillotta 2010, 117–31, and Ramelli 2009, 173–82, 312–14, respectively. These contexts are hardly mutually exclusive; rather, they are indebted to similar complexes of pre-Socratic and Stoic physics, in this case circulating in second–fourth century Syria. In a future contribution, I hope to revisit both Paraph. Shem and Paraph. Seth with reference to our evidence regarding Orphic and Bardaisanite cosmogonies in their Syrian context.
21  Thus Paraph. Shem NHC VII,1 1.20.3–4, per Roberge 2000b ("puisqu'elle avait (quelque chose) provenant de la puissance …") and Schenke 2003b ("da sie (etwas) von der Kraft … besaß"). Cf. Wisse 1996b ("since she possesses of the power …").
22  Paraph. Shem NHC VII,1 1.19.26–20.10.

Flora and fauna appear. But Derdekeas is not yet finished with Nature:

> I came forth to her from the water for the second time. For my face pleased her. Her face, too, was glad, and I said to her, "let a seed and power come forth from you upon the earth." And she obeyed the will of the Spirit, so that she might become barren. Now, when her forms returned, they beat their tongue(s) against one another; they made love, birthing winds and demons and the power which comes from the fire, and (from) the darkness and Spirit. Now the shape that remained alone pushed the beast off herself. She did not have intercourse; rather, it is she who rubbed herself, alone, and she gave birth to a wind who possesses power from the fire and the darkness and the Spirit.[23]

It suffices to observe that the womb here, who produces by "rubbing herself, alone," likely recalls the Sophia of the Apocryphon of John, who produces without "her consort," a grave error resulting in the creation of the demiurge.[24] Nature here, meanwhile, already is a kind of demiurge figure, so the text moves on to describe further these winds and demons:

> Now, so that the other demons might become devoid of the power which they possessed thanks to the impure copulation (*t-koinōnia et-jahem*), a womb came into being with the winds, in a liquid form. And an impure penis (*u-prosthema n-akarthaton*) came into being with the demons, according to the model of the darkness, just as it had rubbed on the womb from the beginning. And when the forms of Nature came into being with one another, they separated from one another, casting off the power, being amazed by the deceit which had befallen them. They were terribly, eternally upset, covering themselves with their power.[25]

The text here becomes corrupt, and then takes up the exaltation of intellect (which has been released from darkness), before Derdekeas returns to the activity of the demons:

> Now, the winds that exist, being demons, having come from water and fire and darkness and light, engaged in intercourse unto perdition

---

23   Paraph. Shem NHC VII,1 21.13–36.
24   Ap. John NHC II,1 9.28–31, 13.15–17, 13.34–36, and parallels; cf. Grypeou 2005, 253–54.
25   Paraph. Shem NHC VII,1 21.36–22.16. The passage is described by Grypeou 2005, 254 and Roberge 2006, 870, more or less without comment.

(*au-r-koinōni a-pteko*). And from this intercourse, the winds received in their womb a foam (*hbēte*, i.e., seminal fluid) from the penis of the demons. They conceived a power in their orifice (*tapro*). The wombs of the winds shielded one another from the respiration (*a<na>pnoē*), until the times of birth arrived. They descended to the water.... When the times of birth approached, all the winds from the water which is near the earth gathered together. They birthed every sort of prurience (*akatharsia*). And the place to which the wind went by itself was filled with prurience. Barren wives have come from it, along with sterile husbands; for just as they will be begotten, so do they beget.[26]

Sexually explicit as the tale may be, it brings us to the mundane (if obscure) conclusion that "sterility" is the result of concupiscence. Roberge dubs these impure, sterile individuals the "psychics," since they have a soul and a body, but no share of the spiritual light (*pneuma*) and no share of intellect (*nous*), and so will not be saved.[27]

But what about the rest of the story? Why does Derdekeas become a beast? Why does he seduce Nature? And what is happening with all that demon sex?

## 2   Archon-Seduction in the Paraphrase of Seth

First, why does Derdekeas adopt the guise of a "beast" to seduce Nature? As is well known, the author of the *Refutation of all Heresies*, often referred to in scholarship as Hippolytus of Rome,[28] assigns to a group of Gnostics he calls "Sethians" a cosmology that, he says, derives from Orphic teachings contained in a work known as the *Bacchica*.[29] He recounts their myth, many of whose

---

26   Paraph. Shem NHC VII,1 23.9–24.2. Note that Roberge, 2000a, 80, hypothesizes that this wind that acts on its own is Molychtas, since he is said later in the text (NHC VII,1 34.9–11) to have engendered everything on earth.

27   Roberge 2000a, 80, recalling Hippolytus, *Haer.* 5.8 (Marcovich 1986), which reports that the Naassenes call "sterile" those who do not possess reason; see also Roberge 2006, 870. On the three classes of the saved in Paraph. Shem, see Roberge 1986.

28   For a recent overview of the question of the authorship of the *Refutatio*, see van den Broek 2013, 129–30. The problem has no bearing on the present article, which remains agnostic regarding it, referring simply to the author of the *Refutatio*.

29   *Haer.* 5.20.4–8; for commentary and bibliography on this passage, see Herrero de Jáuregui 2010, 160–64. These Sethians have, apparently, no relation to the system of thought, largely attested at Nag Hammadi, that scholars, following Schenke, refer to as "Sethian" (on which, see Turner 2001; cf. Rasimus 2009, 9–62).

features—a three-power doctrine, the mixing of light and darkness, use of a uterine metaphor, the demonization of water, and the description of male sexual vigor as "wind"—are very similar to what we find in the Paraphrase of Shem.[30] Moreover, he says, the teachings of the Sethians are to be found in a work entitled the Paraphrase of Seth.

Thus some scholars have posited that there must be some relationship between the lost Paraphrase of Seth known to author of the *Refutatio* and the Paraphrase of Shem we have recovered from Nag Hammadi.[31] In any case, as Jean-Marie Sevrin observes,[32] Derdekeas's seduction of Nature is paralleled quite precisely in the Sethian cosmology from the *Refutatio*, as follows:

> And so, after the light and the spirit have been taken, they say, into the impure and baleful, disordered womb (*tēn akatharton kai polupēmona mētran atakton*), and the serpent—the wind of the darkness, first-begotten[33] of the waters—has entered it, it begets humanity, and the impure womb does not love nor recognize any other form. Therefore, the perfect word of the light on high, having taken on the guise of a beast—the serpent—went inside of the impure womb, tricking her with the disguise of the beast, in order to remove the bonds surrounding the perfect mind, which had been begotten in the impurity of the womb by the first-begotten of <the> water—the serpent, wind, beast. This—so they say—is "the form of the servant,"[34] and it is the reason that the Word of God must enter the womb of a virgin. But, they say, it is not sufficient for the Perfect Human—<the> Word—to have entered the womb of a virgin and "alleviate the birth-pangs" that were in that darkness.[35] But after the entrance <into the> foul mysteries of the womb, he was washed, and drank the cup "of the living water," "bubbling"—which was necessary for him to drink, he who was about to divest himself of the servile form and don celestial raiment.[36]

---

[30] See inter alia Sevrin 1975, 72–73; Krause 1977, 105; Roberge 2000a, 107–13.
[31] See Krause 1977, 108; Schenke, 2003a, 544. Early scholarship, such as Sevrin 1975, 75, identified the first part of Paraph. Shem with Paraph. Seth, holding that the two works probably came from the "same school."
[32] Sevrin 1975.
[33] Cf. Paraph. Shem NHC VII,1 20.1: "as if I were her son".
[34] Phil 2:7.
[35] Cf. Paraph. Shem NHC VII,1 24.10–15, on the pains of the womb.
[36] *Haer.* 5.19.19–21; see Sevrin 1975, 73.

As Tuomas Rasimus has argued, the author of the *Refutatio* may be correct that some of this imagery—particularly the association of a serpent with wind and creation—stems from Orphic sources.[37] Regardless, we can say that the Paraphrase of Shem is certainly the product of the same school as the Paraphrase of Seth, interested in an exegesis of Genesis and ideas reckoned by some in antiquity to be of Orphic provenance, and that is why Derdekeas takes on the form of a beast—because in the Paraphrase of Seth, the *logos* becomes a beast—a demiurgic, Orphic serpent.

## 3   Archon-Seduction amongst Manichaeans ...

Why the seduction of Nature? Why would a divine principle like Derdekeas descend to mate with what is sub-divine? The author of the *Refutatio* does not say but, fortunately, we have been blessed with several other accounts in our sources associated with "Gnosticism" in which a celestial figure seduces an

---

37   Rasimus 2009, 84–85, recalling the sixth-century Platonist Damascius' discussion of a serpentine, winged (i.e., borne on "wind"), demiurgic deity named Chronos-Hercules known, Damascius says, from an Orphic theogony transmitted by "Hieronymus or Hellanicus" (*Princ.* ch. 123; for translation and commentary, see Ahbel-Rappe 2010, 416–17; text in Ruelle 1889, 1:317–18). Meanwhile, several Church Fathers complain that Orphic myths tell of Zeus having intercourse in the form of a serpent (Athenagoras, *Leg.* 20; Clement of Alexandria, *Protr.* 2.16.1; Arnobius, *Adv. nat.* 5.21, cited in Rasimus 2009, 85 n. 71). See also Roig Lanzillotta 2010, 136. Herrero de Jáuregui 2010, 161–62, meanwhile, speculates that "If Hippolytus," in his notice on the *Bacchica* in *Haer.* 5.20.4, "was referring to a more specific work than the *Orphica* in general, it might have been the *Rhapsodies*. The 'womb, the serpent, and the navel that is a virile member' of the Sethians refer back to earlier paragraphs that described the Sethian doctrine according to which a serpent fertilizes the womb of a virgin and also to the way that the heavens and the earth are similar in form to a womb with an *omphalos* at its center (5.19.19–21). If there is anything similar to this related to Orpheus, it is doubtless the theogonic poetry, with the primordial couple of Uranus and Gaia and with Zeus's intercourse with Core in the form of a serpent."
    What kind of bestial form Derdekeas adopts in Paraph. Shem is not clear. Immediately prior to the seduction, intellect is said to possess "the likeness of a fish that has a drop of fire and firey power"; Derdekeas dons the light of the spirit, "and I rested with my garment upon the sight of the fish" (Paraph. Shem NHC VII,1.19.2–4, 11–13). Roberge therefore hypothesizes that Derdekeas becomes a fish when he seduces Nature, with reference to the mermaid-like Syrian Goddess Atargatis, whose cult worshipped fish and prohibited their consumption (Roberge 2000a, 77 n. 226, 76 n. 224). One might add that Ephrem Syrus condemns the "sons of Bardaisan" for holding that "something flowed out and descended from that Father of Life, and the Mother, in the likeness of a fish, conceived and gave birth to him; he was called, 'the Son of Life, Jesus, the holy one' " (*Hymns against Heresies* 55.1, text in Beck 1957, 207).

agent of darkness. The most famous of these is found in a complex of excerpts from Manichaean sources for whose content the term "archon-seduction" was coined.[38] In the interests of brevity, we will focus on the account given in an eighth-century epitome of the thought of Mani, penned by the Syrian heresiographer Theodore bar Konai, which describes the envoy to the archons of a being known as the "Third Emissary." First, however, the Living Spirit, after having his three sons create the heavens and earths, "revealed his forms to the sons of darkness, and he strained out light from the light that had been gulped down by them, out of the five luminous deities, making the sun and the moon."[39] Then the Father of Greatness sends his messenger, the Third Emissary, an androgynous being:

> The Emissary revealed his forms—male and female—and became visible to all the archons, the sons of darkness—male and female. And at the sight of the Messenger, who was gorgeous in his forms, all the archons went mad with lust—the males for the female image, and the females for the male image—and began, thanks to their lust, to discharge that light which they had gulped down from the five luminous deities.[40]

Bar Konai continues:

> And he (Mani) says that these daughters of darkness were already pregnant of their own nature. And, due to the beauty of the forms of the

---

38  Cumont 1912, although Jackson (1932, 236 n. 61) held the term "seduction" to be a misnomer. For discussion of this complex of evidence, see van Oort 2016a and van Oort 2016b, as well as the notes below. The two most lengthy and well-preserved passages include Theodore bar Konai, *Liber Scholiarum* 2:311.12–318.4 (Scher 1910–12), and Augustine, *Nat. bon.* 44 (quoting Mani's *Thesaurus*). Sadly, our Coptic evidence about the mytheme is obscure or fragmentary; van Oort (2016a, n. 83–84) suggests "reminisces" of the scene in the *Psalm-Book* (Allberry 1938, 2.27–31, 10.6–9) and the *Kephalaia* (Böhlig and Polotsky 1940, 30–34). Further Coptic parallels are discussed in the following. Better preserved but brief is a Middle Persian fragment (M268, on which see Sundermann 1991).

39  *Lib. Schol.* 2:315.19–20 (Scher 1910–1912). This proleptic seduction carried out by the Living Spirit is also preserved in M268, as discussed in Sundermann 1991.

40  *Lib. Schol.* 2:316.12–18 (Scher 1910–1912). Differences with the archon-seduction scene Augustine quotes from Mani's *Thesaurus* are minor; in both accounts, the heavenly forms taken on male and female forms to accommodate the gender of female and male archons, respectively, and the ejaculation of divine essence results in its release to heaven (see figure 1, below). In the *Thesaurus*, the Emissary is absent (instead, the Father sends his "forms"), and we are told about the hot and cold qualities belonging to the divine essence which is still (despite having been released from the archons) too intertwined with matter to ascend to heaven.

> Emissary they had seen, their fetuses miscarried and fell upon the earth. And they ate the buds of the trees. The abortions took counsel with one another, and recalled the form of the Emissary that they had seen, and said: "where is the form that we saw?"[41]

The King of Darkness responds to their question by creating Adam and Eve.

This scene has a strong parallel at Nag Hammadi, in the untitled treatise usually referred to by scholars as On the Origin of the World (NHC II,5). Here, too, the celestial human being appears to the Prime Begetter and his archons as a way of condemning his blasphemous claim to be the first principle.[42]

> When this light manifested, a human image appeared within it, being very splendorous, and nobody saw it, except for the Prime Begetter alone and Providence, who was with him … Once Providence saw this Emissary, she fell in love with him; but he despised her, because she was on darkness. Now, she wanted to embrace him, but she was not able to. When she was unable to cure her desire, she poured out her light upon the earth. From that very day, that angel is called, "Adam-Light," whose translation is, "luminous man of blood," and the earth <upon which it (her light)> is spread (is called), "Holy Adam," whose translation is "holy adamantine earth."[43]

From this blood grows Eros; the story thus relates the origin of sexuality.[44]

Now, scholars have long recognized that Providence's prurience at the sight of the luminous Adam, resulting in her emission of light, recalls Theodore bar

---

41  Lib. Schol. 2:317.2–8 (Scher 1910–1912). Cf. the Coptic Kephalaia (§48; Böhlig and Polotsky 1940, 122.24–123.11), where the Messenger reveals his image to the archons; in response, they emit light, which he removes back to the heavens. They also emit matter (a sort of byproduct of the reaction), which falls upon the earth. Abortions appear, but they do not eat from the trees.

42  "For he had been afraid, lest they might recognize that there had indeed been another one before him, and condemn him. Well, he, being thoughtless, despised the condemnation, and grew reckless, saying, 'If one exists prior to me, let him appear, so that we might see his light!' And lo and behold, light came from the ogdoad which is above, making its way through all the heavens of the earth. When the Prime Begetter saw the light, that it was beautiful, shining, he was amazed, and he was very ashamed" (Orig. World NHC II,5 107.31–108.7, following the text of Painchaud 1995b, with reference to that found in Bethge and Layton 1989).

43  Orig. World NHC II,5 108.7–25, adopting the emendation proposed by Bethge and Layton 1989, 52–53. Cf. Nat. Rul. NHC II,4 87.13–14.

44  Orig. World NHC II,5 109.1–22; for exhaustive analysis, see Tardieu 1974, 140–214; recently, Dunning 2009, 63–64; Denzey Lewis 2013, 41–43.

## GNOSIS UNDOMESTICATED

Archon-Seductions in Gnostic and Manichaean Sources

| | Divine seducer: | Guise adopted for seduction: | Sub-divine, desiring subject: | Divine Substance produced via ...: | Resulting products: |
|---|---|---|---|---|---|
| Paraph. Shem (NHC VII,1): | Derdekeas | Beast (male; fish?) | Nature-Womb (female) | Pregnancy, birth | Recovery of divine power; humanity; heaven, earth |
| Paraph. Seth (Hippolytus, *Haer.* 5.19.19ff): | Logos | Beast (male serpent) | Nature-Womb (female) | Pregnancy, birth | Humanity |
| Orig. World (NHC II,5): | Light-Adam ("Emissary") | Self (male) | Lower Pronoia (female) | Blood "poured out" | Sex, desire |
| Nicolatians (Epiph., *Pan.* 25): | Barbelo | Self (female) | Archons (male) | Ejaculation | Recovery of divine power |
| Borborites (Epiph., *Pan.* 26): | Norea | Self (female) | Archons (male) | Ejaculation | Recovery of divine power |
| Manichaeans (T. bar Konai), I: | Living Spirit | "Forms" | Archons (male and female) | Light "strained out" | Sun, moon (i.e., heaven) |
| Manichaeans (T. bar Konai), II: | Third Emissary | "Forms" (male and female) | Archons (male and female) | Ejaculation; pregnancy, birth | Recovery of divine power; humanity |
| Manichaeans (*Thesaurus*, ap. Augustine) | "Powers" | "Forms" (male and female) | Archons (male and female) | Ejaculation; pregnancy, birth | Recovery of divine power; humanity |

Konai's account of the Third Messenger's seduction of the archons, resulting in their emission of light. Louis Painchaud has thus speculated that this passage in NHC II,5 is a Manichaean interpolation.[45] Timothy Pettipiece rightly points out that we might be dealing with an earlier Gnostic myth, extant in On the Origin of the World, which was also known to Mani and appropriated by him.[46] The Paraphrase of Shem (and, for that matter, the Paraphrase of Seth) appears to draw from a similar, if not the same, literary tradition.

## 4    ... And Amongst 'Libertine Gnostics'

Meanwhile, Epiphanius, writing in the later 370s CE, also describes several myths of archon-seduction, myths that, he claims, are the basis for rites involving the consumption of human semen and menses.[47] One he assigns to a sect he dubs the "Nicolaitans,"[48] some of whom employ a theology which, to our modern eyes, bears a striking resemblance to the tri-dynamic system of the Paraphrase of Shem (and the Paraphrase of Seth):[49]

---

45  In a note to his translation provided in Mahé and Poirier 2007, 436, with reference to bar Konai; Painchaud's commentary (1995b, 347), does not comment on the possibility of a Manichaean interpolation. Cf. the reading of Stroumsa 1984, 63–65, which sees the story as a stage in the evolution of a single Gnostic sexual mythos prior to that attested by Epiphanius and Manichaeism, wherein a female divinity seduces male archons.

46  Pettipiece 2012, 50–51.

47  For this dating of the *Panarion*, see F. Williams 2009, xx. Worth mentioning is Epiphanius's allegation that the "Simonians" spin a myth where a celestial female being ("they call her Prunicus, but she is called Barbero or Barbelo by other sects") seduces the archons, driving them into a lustful frenzy where they slaughter one another, and draws the divine essence from their blood to bring back to heaven (*Pan.* 21.2.5). I bracket this evidence given the absence in *Pan.* 21 of other similarities to Paraph. Shem. It is likely that Epiphanius freely interprets some source about archon-seduction here to suit his rhetorical ends, namely the disparagement of Simon Magus, whose consort, an ostensible avatar of Prunicus, claimed to be a reincarnation of Helen of Troy (*Pan.* 21.2.4)—hence the archons' civil war over a female deity. Such a source could be that which he mentions in *Pan.* 25–26 (cf. Grypeou 2005, 108–9).

48  For summaries of evidence about the "Nicolaitans," see M.A. Williams 1996, 170–71; Grypeou 2005, 112–14; Pearson 2006b; Rasimus 2009, 240 n. 42. M.A. Williams contests the "relation" of the Nicolaitans "to the category 'gnosticism,' as the latter is normally constructed" (1996, 171). Yet he does not mention Epiphanius's report that the Nicolaitans found authoritative myths dealing with the Barbelo and malevolent agents of the demiurge called "archons," which would merit at least a provisional association with Gnosticism (or, if one prefers, "Biblical demiurgical myths").

49  *Pan.* 25.5.1–3 (I translate the text of Holl 1915 with reference to F. Williams 2009, and use the latter's numbering of the passages): "And certain others from amongst them devise

For some of them glorify a certain Barbelo, who, they say, is above in the eighth heaven, and, they say, was emanated from the Father. And some attest that she is the mother of Yaldabaoth; others, of Sabaoth. And her son has ruled the seventh heaven insolently and tyrannically, saying to those below him, they maintain, "I am the first and the last, and there is no god other than myself." Now, Barbelo heard this statement and wept. And she constantly appears to the archons with some pleasing form, and divesting them of their seed through their orgasm and ejaculation, ostensibly so that she might once again recover her power that had been sown into a number of them.[50]

Thus they explain, says Epiphanius, "'we gather the power of Prounikos from their bodies and through their emissions'—that is, I say, through the semen and menses!"[51]

A similar myth is recounted in the following chapter of Epiphanius, which he says, addresses the "Borborites," or simply "Gnostics," a group he says is an offshoot of the Nicolaitans.[52] He finds their teaching ridiculous, since they "speak of a 'Womb' and shameful things and other matters." They claim to possess revealed wisdom from Norea, the daughter of Noah, who "showed that what has been stolen from the Mother above by the archon who created the world, and by the other gods, angels, and demons who are with him, must be gathered out of the power that is in their bodies, through the emission of the males and females."[53] This is the purported rationale behind the infamous Eucharist Epiphanius alleges they practice, a "love-feast" (*agapē*) wherein

---

new names, saying that there was Darkness and Depth and Water, and the Spirit, above, made a border in-between them. And the Darkness became angered and spiteful at the Spirit, wherefore Darkness rose up, embraced it, and begat, so they say, a certain so-called "Womb," which became pregnant by the same Spirit that had given birth to it ... And after all these things, it emanated a certain shameful aeon, and that one mated with the aforementioned Womb. And from this shameful aeon and the Womb were born gods, angels, demons, and seven spirits." F. Williams 2009, 88 n. 22–24, rightly recalls Paraph. Shem's descriptions of the three powers and the cosmic womb, as well as Irenaeus, *Haer.* 1.31 (on the "Cainite" demiurgical womb); we may add the archon-seduction performed by the logos-"beast" of Paraph. Shem and Paraph. Seth (*Pan.*'s "ignoble aeon"), and the proliferation of demons that follows in Paraph. Shem (as discussed above).

50   *Pan.* 25.2.2–2.4; see also van den Broek, 2008, 13.
51   *Pan.* 25.3.2; see also Benko 1967, 117; van den Broek 2008, 13.
52   For summaries of evidence about the "Borborites," see Gero 1986, 292–301; Grypeou 2005, 115–36; van den Broek 2006; Rasimus 2009, 47n138, discussing "Borborites" as "libertines"; cf. M.A. Williams 1996, 179–84. On the Borborites as an offshoot of the Nicolaitans, see *Pan.* 25.7.1–2, 26.1.1, 1.3.
53   *Pan.* 26.2.1.

bread and wine are replaced with semen and menstrual blood.[54] Similarly, the Borborites believe that the flesh belongs to the archons (and so will not rise), but *psychē* inhabits menstrual fluid and sperm: "'the power is the soul-essence (*psychē*) that is in the menses and in the semen,' they say, 'which we gather and eat. And as regards whatever we eat—whether it be meat or vegetables or bread or anything else—we do a favor to these creatures, gathering the soul-essence from them and taking them with us back to the heavens.'"[55]

Many scholars doubt the veracity of Epiphanius's testimony and even the very existence of "Nicolaitan" or "Borborite" sects in antiquity.[56] Others have argued that, Epiphanius's biases notwithstanding, his report is entirely believable if one accepts the veracity of Epiphanius's report of Nicolaitan theology, which centers on Barbelo's seduction of the archon(s) to recover the creative power stolen and misused.[57] (The story is essentially a sexualization of a scene attested in many Gnostic myths, wherein the demiurge is tricked into yielding the creative power he has stolen from Sophia.)[58] As Stephen Benko states, on the basis of this story we could surmise in what salvation would consist: "it is the gathering and collecting of the power of Barbelo and leading it back to its original condition. Since this power is physically available in the generating substances of men, it is clear that the collecting and offering of these serve salvation in the most perfect way."[59] In this reconstruction, the Borborites would have been Gnostics who found some kind of myth resembling those found in Irenaeus *Adversus Haereses* 1.29, the Apocryphon of John, or the Paraphrase of Shem authoritative, and who took literally the metaphor of "seed" to describe the presence of the divine in humanity.[60] Williams objects

---

54  *Pan.* 26.4.5–7.
55  *Pan.* 26.9.3. As Buckley observes, this practice is to be distinguished from Manichaean practices of processing divine light through the body. The Borborites are open to eating anything in their love-feasts, seeking to strengthen their bodies and so produce more fluids (divine substance); the Manichaean Elect purifies light through all meals, but the source and type of food are much more narrowly circumscribed. Buckley 1994, 20, 23.
56  Regarding the Nicolaitans, see M.A. Williams 1996, 171, followed by Knust 2006, 233n47. Pearson 2006b, 868, holds that "virtually nothing of historical value can be learned" from Epiphanius's evidence about them; similarly Rasimus 2009, 290, on the Borborites ("libertines").
57  Goehring 1988, 340–43. Buckley 1994, 15–17.
58  See e.g. Irenaeus, *Haer.* 1.30.6; Ap. John NHC II,1 19.21–32 and parallel; Nat. Rul. NHC II,4 87.20–88.11.
59  Benko 1967, 117; similarly, van den Broek 2006, 195; DeConick 2011, 108–10.
60  Van den Broek 2006, 196; idem 2008, 17.

that such an approach "shows only how one might *imagine* a connection between the myths and these sexual practices."[61]

What is certain, however, is that Epiphanius has access to some Gnostic sources (regardless of how he may confuse them),[62] and that these include accounts of archon-seduction that are borne out by our primary sources about Gnosticism (Paraph. Shem, Paraph. Seth, Orig. World) and Manichaeism (as recounted by bar Konai). What these stories have in common is that they are mythological creation accounts regarding the presence or absence in things of divinity—the light-substance, represented by sexual fluid(s), as shown in figure 1. They differ in many ways, as suits the diverse rhetorical situations of these diverse texts, but can be broken down into three loose groups:

First, the Paraphrase of Shem and Paraphrase of Seth use (possibly Orphic) imagery, where the seducer is a male beast, and the seduced is a womb, who produces by giving birth. Similar in some respect is the myth recounted in On the Origin of the World, where the seducer is the luminous light-Adam, and the seduced is the female "lower providence." Second, in the myths reckoned by Epiphanius to the Nicolaitans and Borborites, the divine seducer is a female, and the seduced is male. He attributes language about a "womb" to both parties. Finally, the Manichaean myth known to Theodore bar Konai appears to synthesize elements of these myths, for the Emissary appears as both male and female (depending on the gender of the archon to which it appears), and the divine light is emitted both through ejaculation and birth (or, rather, miscarriage). Despite this diversity, the object of the seduction in each of these myths is to release the divine creative energy stolen from the celestial world by the archons (the byproduct of the release, meanwhile, being the object of further creation).[63]

Epiphanius claims that such stories form the mythic substratum to the licentious practices that involve the worship of their own bodily fluids, practices employed by sects which adhered to myths of Gnostic valence. Augustine of Hippo says much the same of a sect of Manichaeans he calls the "Catharists."[64] The Paraphrase of Shem, too, draws from this mythic substratum that, Epiphanius and others say, provides the rationale for the libertine love-feast. But does it describe such sexual practices themselves?

---

61  M.A. Williams 1996, 182.
62  On Epiphanius's treatment of Gnostic sources, see F. Williams 2009, xxvii–viii.
63  The myths teach about the presence or absence of divine substance in the cosmos, people, sexuality, etc.
64  *Haer.* 46.9–10, on which see van Oort 2016a.

## 5 Demon Sex and Sodomites

We might tackle this problem by first pursuing our third initial question about sexual imagery in the Paraphrase of Shem: why the extended description of copulating demons? An answer may be found, again, in On the Origin of the World (NHC II,5). Here, the Prime Begetter observes the enthronement and favoring of his son, Sabaoth, by Pistis Sophia, and grows jealous. His response is to create Death, who breeds:

> Next, Death, being androgynous, copulated (*tōh*) with his nature, producing seven offspring, androgynous. These are the names of the males: Jealousy, Wrath, Tears, Sighing, Suffering, Lamentation, Bitter Weeping. And these are the names of the females: Wrath, Sorrow, Pleasure, Sighing, Curse, Bitterness, Bellicosity. They copulated (*koinōnei*) with one another, [and] each begot seven (more) offspring, so that they number forty-nine androgynous demons. Their names and their influences shall you find in The Book of Solomon.[65]

These seven malignant pairs of malignant forces are then opposed to seven good forces, created by Life:

> And in the presence of all these events, Life, who was with Sabaoth, created (*tamio*) seven powers that are good, (also) androgynous. The names of the males are these: He who is without Jealousy, The Blessed, The Joyful, The True, He who is without Envy, The Beloved, The Trustworthy. The female ones, too—these are their names: Peace, Joy, Rejoicing, The Blessed, Truth, Love, Faith. And from these derive many good and innocent spirits. Their influences and their effects shall you find in The Signs of Celestial Fate which are Under the Dodecad.[66]

As Painchaud observes, the generation of these evil and good forces is described with contrasting terminology of sexuality and of creation, respectively—i.e., death produces through copulation, while life produces through a non-sexual creation.[67] Indeed, this is what we find in the Paraphrase of Shem: the story skips over the creation of humanity entirely but ends by observing that, just as the demons breed out of prurience, humans who copulate in the same way

---

65 Orig. World NHC II,5 106.27–107.3.
66 Orig. World NHC II,5 107.4–17.
67 Painchaud 1995b, 335–36.

are actually "sterile." Yet here we reach a hermeneutic juncture, for barrenness is a *good thing* in the rest of the Paraphrase of Shem—it is the object of the descents of Derdekeas, who repeatedly states that he wants to make Nature barren.[68] By implication, he wishes to put a stop to the cycle of birth and death—what Irenaeus's "others" called "dissolving the works of the womb."

How can sterility and barrenness be both good and bad? The text must mean that they are not the same thing. Indeed, the words used in the Coptic are not the same: the desired "barrenness" of the womb is denoted with the Egyptian *ouasǯ*; "sterile," the Greco-Coptic *steiras*. It is then likely that the "sterility" of the psychics is metaphorical, not physical. Like demons, their physical copulation only begets physical birth (which necessarily entails physical death), as they do not transmit the divine light mixed in with matter. The text is clear on their fate: these "psychics" will be destroyed at the end of time.[69]

But what of the elect? Derdekeas unfortunately relates no details as to what sort of things the elect practices, but he does tell us a bit about what they are like—they are Sodomites:

> I shall appear to those who shall acquire the thought of the light—the Spirit ... [in] the place that shall be called "Sodom."[70] But quickly, you, proclaim to the Sodomites your universal teaching. For they are members of your congregation.[71] Now, the demon, in human form, shall part from that place by my will, being ignorant. He shall withhold this news; but the Sodomites, according to the will of the Majesty, shall bear witness to the universal testimony. They shall come to rest with a pure conscience, in the place of their repose—the Unbegotten Spirit. Now ... Sodom will be burned, unjustly, by perverse Nature. For evil shall not cease ...[72]

Sevrin observed long ago that this exaltation of the Sodomites is paralleled in the Gospel of the Egyptians, where Sodom is said unequivocally to be the land of the savior, the Great Seth.[73] Guy Stroumsa has remarked further that the Revelation of Adam, in its description of Saklas's attempt to destroy the elect by fire (following his first try, by the Flood), almost certainly refers (if not by name) to the destruction of Sodom, and thus implies that the elect

---

68   Paraph. Shem NHC VII,1 21.22, 22.22, 26.25–28.
69   Paraph. Shem, NHC VII,1 35.31–36.1.
70   Paraph. Shem NHC VII,1 28.31–29.1.
71   Lit. "they are your members" NHC VII,1 29:14. Thus Wisse 1996b; Roberge 2000b; Schenke 2003b.
72   Paraph. Shem NHC VII,1 29.12–31.
73   Sevrin 1975, 80n63, Gos. Eg. NHC IV,2 71.22–30 = (III,2) 60.12–18.

of Abraham's age were Sodomites.[74] As he observes, these tales play into wider, well-known Jewish traditions that view humanity as having survived two cataclysms—water and fire—and awaiting a third.[75]

The authors of the Gospel of the Egyptians, Revelation of Adam, and the Paraphrase of Shem may then have identified the Sodomites as the elect because they were known to be persecuted by the God of the cosmos—a case of genuine Gnostic "reverse exegesis."[76] This much is sure. Any further valence as to what constitutes a Sodomite in the Paraphrase of Shem—beyond possession of the "universal teaching," and their lack of "sterility"—can only be guessed. Ancient Jewish and Christian traditions nigh-universally condemned the inhabitants of Sodom for their "very grave" sin (Gen 18:20; see also 13:30), but what precisely constituted the sin of Sodom differs across ancient authors. Most famously, the sins of the Sodomites were regarded, by both ancient Jewish and Christian writers, as being of a sexual nature.[77] Other writers considered the Sodomites to have committed "social sins," i.e., behaving uncharitably, inhospitably, and violently as a result, according to some, of their excess wealth.[78] Still others saw Sodomites as guilty of all of these sins.[79]

## 6   Libertine Gnostics

Arrogance, hospitality, and violence do not come into question in the Paraphrase of Shem, but sexuality does, since the treatise draws upon the myth of the seduction of the archons, particularly as known in our evidence about the

---

74   Stroumsa 1984, 106, Apoc. Adam NHC V,5 75.9–28.
75   Stroumsa 1984, 106–10; cf. Sevrin 1975, 80: "Comme le déluge, l'incendie de Sodome sert d'allégorie à l'action des puissances mauvaises contre la révélation salutaire. Ce peut n'être que l'utilisation assez libre d'images de destruction totale prises dans le patrimoine culturel du judaïsme.... Si l'on voulait pourtant que ce texte se réfère à la Bible avec des intentions plus précises, il faudrait que ce soit à rebours, de façon polémique, par une sorte de processus de dé-judaïsation."
76   M.A. Williams 1996, 74–76 argues that we find no consistent pattern of "reversal of value" in Gnostic exegesis, but rather that such reversals focused on "problem passages." Yet this argument does not address these passages about the Sodomites in Gnostic literature.
77   Homosexuality: Gen 19:4–5. Adultery: Jer 23:14. General "sexual profligacy": Jub 16:5–6, 20:5; T. Levi 14:6; T. Naph. 3:4–5; T. Benj. 9:1; 2 Pet 2:6–8; Jude 1:7; Augustine, *Civ.* 16.30. For these citations I am indebted to Kugel 1998, 331–33, Lietaert-Peerbolte 2004, 75–77, and Knust 2006, 120–27. See also 4Q172 Frag. 4, discussed in Tigchelaar 2004, 50–52.
78   Ezek 16:49–50. Arrogance: Sir 16:8; 3 Macc. 2:5. Inhospitability: Wis 19:14; Jos. *Ant.* 1.194–5 (Niese); Matt 10:14–15; m. Abot 5:13; Pirqe R. El. 25. See here Kugel 1998, 334; also García Martínez 2004, Tg. Neof. Gen 13:13; Tg. Ps.-J. Gen 13:13; b. Sanh. 109a–b.
79   Philo, *Abr.* 133–35, Kugel 1998, 334; see also Knust 2006, 58.

lost Paraphrase of Seth, but also Gnostic myth associated with the Nicolatians and Borborites, On the Origin of the World, and Manichaeism. Use of language about the "womb" also recalls Irenaeus's comments on the "others" who valorize Cain, Esau, et al., practice sexual licentiousness to "dissolve the works of the womb," and identify themselves with Sodomites. Epiphanius's "Nicolatians" and "Borborites," too, engage in speculations about a cosmic "womb," and, in the former case, the tri-dynamic cosmology we know from the Paraphrase of Shem and the Paraphrase of Seth.

It is then clear that the Paraphrase of Shem belongs to a complex of traditions associated by the heresiographers with Gnostic sects scholarship once called "libertine": Irenaeus's "others" (the so-called "Cainites"), "Nicolatians," and "Borborites." The Nag Hammadi documents thus do not contain merely "domesticated" sources at home in the mainstream of early Christian ascetic literature. Rather, the first tractate of Nag Hammadi codex VII is a lengthy, well-preserved work which explicitly identifies the demiurge as a "womb," divine intervention in creation as a seduction of the demiurge, salvation history as the emptying of divine light from the world, human reproduction as demonic activity, and the elect as Sodomites. The Nag Hammadi evidence therefore confirms the veracity of the heresiographers' claim that such transgressive ideas circulated amongst some of their contemporaries.

Does this mean that the Paraphrase of Shem is a "libertine Gnostic" text that espouses the *agapē* of semen and menses? Initially, one would be inclined to say "certainly not": the Paraphrase of Shem speaks in clear and harsh terms about what it calls "the impure rubbing," a copulative act associated with the unquestionably negative characters of Darkness and the Womb.[80] Moreover, it designates the elect as individuals who will "shield their thinking from the impure rubbing."[81] On this reading, even if the Paraphrase of Shem teaches the myth of the seduction of the archons, it does not subscribe to the sexual practices Epiphanius assigns to the Nicolaitans and Borborites.

At the same time, it must be observed that the "impure rubbing" is associated with the "works of Nature," i.e., the demiurgic Womb, which means that it is associated with worldly birth—precisely what Irenaeus says the "others" (so-called "Cainites") were trying to overcome. In other words, if "impure rubbing" creates birth (and death), is there then room in the Paraphrase of

---

80  Paraph. Shem NHC VII,1 4.29–32, 10.19–25, 14.13–16, 18.31–35, 21.30–36, 22.5–9, 23.22–24, 27.2–6; see also Grypeou 2005, 254, and following note.
81  Paraph. Shem NHC VII,1 35.5–6. Similarly, 34.19–22, and 38.3–9: "For I prophesy it to those who possess understanding: they shall cease persisting in the utterly impure baptism, and those who have understanding from the light of the Spirit shall not co-mingle with the prurient rubbing."

Shem for such a thing as "the pure rubbing," which does not create birth but liberates light through the release of sexual fluids? The evidence does not permit a clear answer either way, but the question must be asked, for even if the Paraphrase of Shem does not describe for us the "libertine" Gnostic *agapē*, it does describe a version of the mythological framework to which such a practice is fitted in our heresiographical evidence—which means the first treatise of Nag Hammadi Codex VII would complement an "undomesticated" *agapē* very well indeed.[82]

## Bibliography

Ahbel-Rappe, Sarah. 2010. *Damascius' Problems and Solutions Concerning First Principles*. AAR Religion in Transformation. The American Academy of Religion/Oxford University Press: Oxford.

Allberry, C.R.C., ed. and tr. 1938. *A Manichaean Psalm-Book. Part II*. Stuttgart: Kohlhammer.

Beck, Edmund, ed. 1957. *Des Heiligen Ephraem des Syrers Hymnen Contra Haereses*. Sorpus Scriptorum Christianorum Orientalium 169; Scriptores Syri 76. Louvain: L. Durbecq.

Benko, Stephen. 1967. "The Libertine Gnostic Sect of the Phibionites According to Epiphanius." *Vigiliae Christianae* 21:103–19.

Bethge, Hans-Gebhard. and Bentley Layton, et al., eds. 1989. "Treatise Without Title: On the Origin of the World." Pages 28–134 in *Nag Hammadi Codex II, 2–7*. Vol. 2. Edited by Bentley Layton. Nag Hammadi Studies 21. Leiden: Brill.

Böhlig, Alexander and Hans Jakob Polotsky, eds. 1940. *Kephalaia, Band I, 1. Hälfte (Lieferung 1–10)*. Stuttgart: Kohlhammer.

Broek, Roelof van den. 2006. "Borborites." Pages 194–96 in *Dictionary of Gnosis and Western Esotericism*. Edited by Wouter J. Hanegraaff, et al. Leiden: Brill.

Broek, Roelof van den. 2008. "Sexuality and Sexual Symbolism in Hermetic and Gnostic Thought and Practice (Second–Fourth Centuries)." Pages 1–22 in *Hidden Intercourse: Eros and Sexuality in the History of Western Esotericism*. Edited by Wouter J. Hanegraaff and Jeffrey J. Kripal. Aries Book Series 7. Leiden: Brill.

---

[82] The parallel with Manichaeism is instructive again: Manichaean myths describe the cosmological framework undergirding the ascetic practices which constitute the salvific enterprise, but do not describe a proper Manichaean diet. Similarly, Paraph. Shem is not a church order or liturgical manual, but a theological work providing metaphysical justification compatible to what we find in Borborite as well as Manichaean cosmogonies.

Broek, Roelof van den. 2013. *Gnostic Religion in Antiquity*. Cambridge: Cambridge University Press.

Buckley, Jorunn Jacobsen. 1994. "Libertines or Not: Fruit, Bread, Semen and Other Body Fluids in Gnosticism." *Journal of Early Christian Studies* 2:15–31.

Burns, Dylan M. 2015. "μίξεώς τινι τέχνῃ κρείττονι—Alchemical Metaphor in the *Paraphrase of Shem* (NHC VII,1)." *Aries* 15:79–106.

Chadwick, Henry. 1981. "The Domestication of Gnosis." Pages 3–16 in *The Rediscovery of Gnosticism: Proceedings of the International Conference on Gnosticism, 1: The School of Valentinus*. Edited by Bentley Layton. Numen Book Series. Leiden: Brill.

Cumont, Franz. 1908. *La Cosmogonie Manichéenne d'après Théodore bar Khôni*. Recherches sur le Manichéisme 1. Bruxelles.

DeConick, April D. 2011. *Holy Misogyny: Why the Sex and Gender Conflicts in the Early Church Still Matter*. New York: Continuum.

Denzey Lewis, Nicola. 2013. *Cosmology and Fate in Gnosticism and Graeco-Roman Antiquity: Under Pitiless Skies*. Nag Hammadi and Manichaean Studies 81. Leiden: Brill.

Dunning, Benjamin H. 2009. "What Sort of Thing Is This Luminous Woman?: Thinking Sexual Difference in On the Origin of the World." *Journal of Early Christian Studies* 17:55–84.

Emmel, Stephen. 2008. "The Coptic Gnostic Texts as Witnesses to the Production and Transmission of Gnostic (and Other) Traditions." Pages 33–50 in *Das Thomasevangelium: Entstehung-Rezeption-Theologie*. Edited by Jörg Frey et al. Beihefte zur Zeitschrift für die neutestamentliche Wissenschaft 157. Berlin: De Gruyter.

Fredriksen, Paula. 1979. "Hysteria and the Gnostic Myths of Creation." *Vigiliae Christianae* 33:287–90.

García Martínez, Florentino. 2004. "Sodom and Gomorrah in the Targumim." Pages 83–96 in *Sodom's Sin: Genesis 18–19 and its Interpretations*. Edited by Ed Noort and Eibert Tigchelaar. Themes in Biblical Narrative 7. Leiden: Brill.

Gero, Stephen. 1986. "With Walter Bauer on the Tigris." Pages 287–307 in *Nag Hammadi, Gnosticism, and Early Christianity*. Edited by Charles W. Hedrick and Robert Hodgson Jr. Peabody, MA: Hendrickson.

Goehring, James E. 1988. "Libertine or Liberated? Women in the So-Called Libertine Gnostic Communities." Pages 329–44 in *Images of the Feminine in Gnosticism*. Edited by Karen King. Philadelphia: Fortress Press.

Good, Deirde. 1997. "Cainites." Page 203 in *The Encyclopedia of Early Christianity*, 2nd ed. Edited by Everett Ferguson. London: Routledge.

Grant, Robert M. 1981. "Charges of Immorality Against Religious Groups in Antiquity." Pages 161–70 in *Studies in Gnosticism and Hellenistic Religions: Presented to Gilles Quispel on the Occasion of His 65th birthday*. Edited by Roelof van den Broek and Maarten J. Vermaseren, Études preliminaries aux religions orientales dans l'Empire Romain 91. Leiden: Brill.

Grypeou, Emmanouela. 2005. *"Das vollkommene Pascha." Gnostische Bibelexegese und Ethik.* Orientalia Biblica et Christiana 15. Wiesbaden: Harrassowitz.

Herrero de Jáuregui, Miguel. 2010. *Orphism and Christianity in Late Antiquity.* Sozomena 7. Berlin: De Gruyter.

Holl, Karl. 1915. *Epiphanius Band 1: Ancoratus und Panarion (Haereses 1–33).* Die griechischen christlichen Schriftsteller der ersten [drei] Jahrhunderte 25. Leipzig: Hinrichs.

Iricinschi, Eduard. 2013. "*Interroga matricem mulieris*: The Secret Life of the Womb in Ezra and Sethian Cosmology." Pages 751–70 in *Envisioning Judaism: Studies in Honor of Peter Schäfer on the Occasion of his 70th Birthday.* Edited by Ra'anan Boustan, et al. 2 vols. Tübingen: Mohr Siebeck.

Knust, Jennifer. 2006. *Abandoned to Lust: Sexual Slander and Ancient Christianity*: New York: Columbia University Press.

Krause, Martin. 1977. "Die Paraphrase des Sêem und das Bericht Hippolyts." Pages 101–110 in *Proceedings of the International Colloquium on Gnosticism, Stockholm, 20–25 August 1975.* Edited by Geo Widengren. Stockholm.

Kugel, James L., ed. 1998. *Traditions of the Bible: A Guide to the Bible as it was at the Start of the Common Era.* Cambridge, MA: Harvard University Press.

Layton, Bentley. 1987. *The Gnostic Scriptures.* New York: Doubleday.

Lietaer-Peerbolte, Bert. 2004. "Sodom, Egypt, and the Two Witnesses of Revelation 11:8." Pages 63–82 in *Sodom's Sin: Genesis 18–19 and its Interpretations.* Edited by Ed Noort and Eibert Tigchelaar. Themes in Biblical Narrative 7. Leiden: Brill.

Mahé, Jean-Pierre and Paul-Hubert Poirier, eds. 2007. *Écrits gnostiques. La bibliothèque de Nag Hammadi.* Bibliothèque de la Pléiade. Paris: Gallimard.

Marcovich, Miroslav, ed. 1986. *Hippolytus. Refutatio Omnium Haeresium.* Berlin: Walter de Gruyter.

Niese, Benedictus. 1887–1890. *Flavii Iosephi Opera.* Vols. 1–4. Berlin: Weidmann.

Oort, Johannes van. 2016a. "'Human Semen Eucharist' among the Manichaeans? The Testimony of Augustine Reconsidered in Context." *Vigiliae Christianae* 70:2, 193–216.

Oort, Johannes van. 2016b. "Another Case of Human Semen Eucharist among the Manichaeans? Notes on the 'Ceremony of the Fig' in Cyril of Jerusalem's *Catechesis* VI." *Vigiliae Christianae.* Forthcoming.

Painchaud, Louis. 1995a. "Texte et traduction." Pages 144–218 in *L'écrit sans titre. Traité sur l'origine du monde (NH II, 5 et XIII, 2 et Brit. Lib. Or. 4926[1]).* Edited and translated by Louis Painchaud, Bibliothèque Copte de Nag Hammadi Section "Textes," 21. Québec: Les presses de l'université Laval; Leuven: Peeters.

Painchaud, Louis. 1995b. "Commentaire." Pages 219–526 in *L'écrit sans titre. Traité sur l'origine du monde (NH II, 5 et XIII, 2 et Brit. Lib. Or. 4926[1]).* Edited and translated by Louis Painchaud, Bibliothèque Copte de Nag Hammadi Section "Textes" 21. Québec: Les presses de l'Université Laval; Leuven: Peeters.

Pearson, Birger. 1990. "Cain and the Cainites." Pages 95–107 in *Gnosticism, Judaism, and Egyptian Christianity*. Minneapolis: Fortress Press.

Pearson, Birger. 2006a. "Cainites." Pages 227–29 in *Dictionary of Gnosis and Western Esotericism*. Edited by Wouter J. Hanegraaff, et al. Leiden: Brill.

Pearson, Birger. 2006b. "Nicolaitans." Pages 867–69 in *Dictionary of Gnosis and Western Esotericism*. Edited by Wouter J. Hanegraaff, et al. Leiden: Brill.

Pettipiece, Timothy. 2012. "Towards a Manichaean Reading of the Nag Hammadi Codices." *Journal of the Canadian Society for Coptic Studies* 3–4: 43–54.

Ramelli, Ilaria L. E. 2009. *Bardaisan of Edessa: A Reassessment of the Evidence and a New Interpretation*. Piscataway: Gorgias Press.

Rasimus, Tuomas. 2009. *Paradise Reconsidered in Gnostic Mythmaking: Rethinking Sethianism in Light of the Ophite Evidence*. Nag Hammadi and Manichaean Studies 68. Leiden: Brill.

Roberge, Michel. 1986. "Anthropogonie et anthropologie dans la *Paraphrase de Sem* (NH VII,1)." *Le Muséon* 99:229–48.

Roberge, Michel. 2000a. "Introduction." Pages 1–114 in *La Paraphrase de Sem* (NH VII,1). Edited by Michel Roberge. Bibliothèque Copte de Nag Hammadi Section "Textes" 25. Québec: Les presses de l'Université Laval; Louvain: Éditions Peeters.

Roberge, Michel. 2000b. "Texte et traduction." Pages 117–215 in *La Paraphrase de Sem (NH VII,1)*. Edited by Michel Roberge. Bibliothèque Copte de Nag Hammadi Section "Textes" 25. Québec: Les presses de l'Université Laval; Louvain: Éditions Peeters.

Roberge, Michel. 2006. "L'analogie sexuelle et embryologique dans la *Paraphrase de Sem* (NH VII, 1)." Pages 847–71 in *Coptica—Gnostica—Manichaica: Mélanges offerts à Wolf-Peter Funk*. Edited by Louis Painchaud and Paul-Hubert Poirier. Bibliothèque Copte de Nag Hammadi Section "Études" 7. Québec: Presses de l'Université Laval; Leuven: Peeters.

Roig Lanzillotta, Lautaro. 2010. "Orphic Cosmogonies in the Pseudo-Clementines? Textual Relationship, Character and Sources of Homilies 6.3–13 and Recognitions 10.17–19.30." Pages 115–41 in *The Pseudo-Clementines*. Edited by Jan N. Bremmer. Studies on Early Christian Apocrypha 10. Peeters: Leuven.

Rousseau, Adelin and Louis Doutreleau eds. 1979. *Irenaeus: Contre les hérésies I*. 2 vols. Sources Chrétiennes 263–264. Paris: Éditions du Cerf.

Rudolph, Kurt. 1987. *Gnosis: The Nature and History of Gnosticism*. Translated and edited by Robert McLachlan Wilson. San Francisco: HarperSanFrancisco.

Ruelle, Charles-Émile, ed. 1889. *Damascii successoris dubitationes et solutiones*. 2 vols. Paris: Klincksieck.

Schenke, Hans-Martin. 2003a. "Die Paraphrase des Sêem (NHC VII,1): Einleitung." Pages 543–50 in *Nag Hammadi Deutsch. 2. Band: NHC V,2–XIII,1, BG 1 und 4*. Edited by Hans-Martin Schenke, et al. Griechische Christliche Schriftsteller 12; Koptisch-Gnostische Schriften 3. Berlin: de Gruyter.

Schenke, Hans-Martin. 2003b. "Die Paraphrase des Sêem (NHC VII,1): Übersetzung." Pages 550–68 in *Nag Hammadi Deutsch. 2. Band: NHC V,2–XIII,1, BG 1 und 4*. Edited by Hans-Martin Schenke, et al. Griechische Christliche Schriftsteller 12; Koptisch-Gnostische Schriften 3. Berlin: de Gruyter.

Scher, Addai., ed. 1910–12. *Theodorus bar Kōnī. Liber Scholiorum. 2*. Corpus Scriptorum Christianorum Orientalium 66. Paris: Carolus Poussielgue.

Schmidt, Carl, ed. Violet MacDermot, trans. 1978a. *The Books of Jeu and the Untitled Text in the Bruce Codex*. Nag Hammadi Studies 13. Leiden: Brill.

Schmidt, Carl, ed. Violet MacDermot, trans. 1978b. *Pistis Sophia*. Nag Hammadi Studies 9. Leiden: Brill.

Sevrin, Jean-Marie. 1975. "A propos de la Paraphrase de Sem." *Le Muséon* 88: 69–96.

Stroumsa, Gedaliahu A.G. 1984. *Another Seed: Studies in Gnostic Mythology*. Nag Hammadi Studies 24. Leiden: Brill.

Sunderman, Werner. 1991. "Der Lebendige Geist als Verführer der Dämonen." Pages 339–42 in *Manichaica Selecta: Studies presented to Professor Julien Ries on the occasion of his seventieth birthday*. Edited by Alois van Tongerloo and Søren Giversen. Manichaean Studies 1. Louvain.

Tardieu, Michel. 1974. *Trois mythes gnostiques: Adam, Éros et les animaux d'Égypte dans un écrit de Nag Hammadi (II, 5)*. Paris: Études Augustiniennes.

Tardieu, Michel. 1987. "La naissance du ciel et de la terre selon la 'Paraphrase de Sem'." Pages 409–25 in *La Création dans l'orient ancien*. Edited by F. Blanquart. Lectio Divina 127. Paris: Éditions du Cerf.

Tigchelaar, Eibert. 2004. "Sodom and Gomorrah in the Dead Sea Scrolls." Pages 47–62 in *Sodom's Sin: Genesis 18–19 and its Interpretations*. Edited by Ed Noort and Eibert Tigchelaar. Themes in Biblical Narrative 7. Leiden: Brill.

Turner, John D. 2001. *Sethian Gnosticism and the Platonic Tradition*. Bibliothèque Copte de Nag Hammadi Section "Études" 6. Québec: Université Laval; Leuven: Peeters.

Wilberding, James, trans. 2011. *Porphyry: To Gaurus on How Embryos are Ensouled and On What is in Our Power*. London: Bristol Classical Press.

Williams, Frank, trans. 2009. *The 'Panarion' of Epiphanius of Salamis: Book I (Sects 1–46)*, 2nd ed. Nag Hammadi and Manichaean Studies 63. Leiden: Brill.

Williams, Michael A. 1996. *Rethinking "Gnosticism": An Argument for Dismantling a Dubious Category*. Princeton: Princeton University Press.

Wisse, Frederik. 1996a. "Introduction to VII, 1: The Paraphrase of Shem." Pages 15–23 in *Nag Hammadi Codex VII*. Edited by Birger Pearson. Nag Hammadi and Manichaean Studies 30. Leiden: Brill.

Wisse, Frederik. 1996b. "The Paraphrase of Shem: Text, Translation, and Notes." Pages 24–127 in *Nag Hammadi Codex VII*. Edited by Birger Pearson. Nag Hammadi and Manichaean Studies 30. Leiden: Brill.

# Gnostic Self-Deification: The Case of Simon of Samaria

*M. David Litwa*
Lecturer in Classics, College of William & Mary
*mdl2dj@virginia.edu*

In his lectures at the Collège de France (1981–82), Michel Foucault spoke of a (Mediterranean) culture of the self that developed in the first and second centuries CE.[1] He used the Platonic dialogue *Alcibiades I* as a point of entry. In this text, self-knowledge is the beginning of philosophy, and the self is identified with the soul. Self-knowledge, Foucault asserted, was the chief gnostic form of self-care. Such knowledge provided access to truth, in particular the realization of one's own divine nature and destiny.[2] Although Foucault did not use the term, this form of realization can be (re-)described as deification.

Typically, deification means that a human comes to possess a divine status by sharing in qualities that, in the ancient Mediterranean world, constituted a divine identity. These qualities typically included immortality and superhuman power, as well as vast knowledge and extraordinary virtue. Recent work on deification in gnostic sources has focused on angelification,[3] assimilation to God,[4] and ecstatic vision.[5]

What needs further attention, I think, is the self-empowered or self-engineered aspect of gnostic deification. Gnostic deification is extraordinarily focused on self-knowledge and self-realization. Gnostics assimilated themselves to God, to be sure, but God was not always viewed as different from the true self. Many Gnostics experienced God as a greater or higher self. Some gnostics also viewed themselves as consubstantial with this higher self, as having a divine element—a spark that belonged to a greater divine fire. This sense of inward divinity was not automatic. The gnostic had to cultivate his or her divinity through reflexive practices of self-knowledge. The gnostic's intense focus on the self is thus manifest in three ways: (1) the sense of inward

---

1  Foucault 2005, 120, 180.
2  Foucault 2005, 256–57, 419–21, 454–55.
3  Turner 2014; Burns 2014, 122–39.
4  Roig Lanzillotta 2013, 71–102.
5  DeConick 2010, 311–15.

divinity, (2) intensely reflexive practices of self-knowledge, and (3) the realization that a particular divinity (at some level) is a higher self.

In order to highlight this intense focus upon the self, in this essay I redescribe gnostic deification as "self-deification." Such a redescription will likely be controversial, and for good reason. Heresiologists used the language of self-deification as a cudgel: so-called gnostics deified themselves and were thus arrogant rebels against God. Nevertheless, using the language of gnostic self-deification need not replicate heresiological discourse. Just as scholars are now in the process of vigorously redescribing gnosticism, they have the freedom and the power to redefine and redescribe self-deification with a new meaning and framework.

I propose that gnostic self-deification is realized in three "moments." First, the subject discovers his or her own innate divine core (often called "the divine spark").[6] This core, to use Aristotelian terminology, serves as the "material cause" of deification. Whatever exactly it is, the divine spark shares the same substance as deity or some form of mediate divinity. The mediate form of divinity is the immanent pole of divinity, often spoken of as a child or emanation of the primal (unknown) deity.[7]

Second, gnostics engage in practices of reflexivity which enable them to realize their inner divinity. In other words, they engage in peculiar "technologies of the self" wherein the real self gradually realizes itself as the inner, divine Self through practices of self-knowing. These practices can be moral, ritual, intellectual, communal, or individual.

The third moment of self-deification is identification with (most often a mediate) deity. This deity can be thought of as the primary "efficient cause" of self-deification. The mediate deity awakens the self to its inward divinity and allows it to begin the process of self-knowledge and self-realization. But the mediate deity is also the "final cause" of deification. That is to say: the end of gnostic deification is often identification with a mediate deity who is the same nature as the self, albeit a higher and purer form.

In gnostic myths, the mediate deity is often represented as external to the self. But the mediate deity is in fact the higher self.[8] The externality of this higher self is only a necessity of the lower self's embodied, historical existence. Throughout their lives, gnostics labor to "make the inside like the outside and

---

[6] The divine spark is often described as a key Gnostic trait (e.g., Marjanen 2008, 211; van den Broek 2013, 2). In DeConick's cognitive model, the divine spark corresponds to what she calls "*Innate Spiritualness*.... The Gnostic is a person whose essential nature is believed to be uncreated, deriving directly from the divine," 2013, 300–301.
[7] On mediate and primal deity, see further Litwa 2013, 232–35.
[8] For a possible Jewish background of the higher self, see Orlov 2004, 2.66–71.

the outside like the inside."[9] They realize, in other words, that the mediate deity is the true self, and therefore not ultimately "other" at all.[10]

These three elements, then, make possible the language of gnostic self-deification: (1) the presence of divinity in the self, (2) ritual, moral, and contemplative practices of self-recognition, and (3) identification with a higher divine self. In what follows, I flesh out these three "moments" with the help of brief examples and then turn to a case study (Simon of Samaria) to see the process of self-deification at work.[11]

## 1 Innate Divinity

The foundation of gnostic self-deification is the presence of a dynamic divine element in the self, or (in shorthand) "the divine spark." In modern terms, the spark is the true or ideal self. It is different than a person's physical frame, and in most cases it is different from one's (lower) soul as well (that part of the self that focuses on the management of the physical body).

Inward divinity does not lie as a static lump within the self. It is progressively intensified through the transformation of consciousness.[12] Initially, the spark remains in a latent or a potential state—like a glowing ember needing to be fanned into flame.[13] Through cognitive, ethical, and ritual practices of self-cultivation, it is increasingly illuminated, enflamed, and finally released—as sparks fly upward (Job 5:7).

Ancient philosophers—Platonists in particular—conceived of the divine element in intellectualist terms. The divine core is *nous*—commonly translated as "mind" or "intellect." Other rational and cognitive metaphors were used to speak of the divine or most divine portion of humanity: διάνοια (thought), φρόνησις (wisdom), and λόγος (reason). These basic intellectual endowments make possible the richness of θεωρία, which means vision or contemplation.

---

9   Gos. Thom. NHC II,2 22 (Layton 1989, 62).
10  The "formal cause" of deification is both the soul and the Savior. The soul, or inner self, is the form of God. But this form requires purification. Plotinus writes that "the soul, when it is purified, becomes form and formative power (εἶδος καὶ λόγος), altogether bodiless and intellectual and entirely belonging to the divine" (*Enn.* 1.6.6.14–15, A. H. Armstrong 1989). But the form of God in the soul is also the form of the Savior. In Great Pow. NHC VI,4, the Savior says: "For all those in whom my form (μορφή) appears ... will be saved" (36.8–11, Parrott 1979, 294).
11  In what follows, all translations, unless otherwise noted, are mine.
12  Luttikhuizen 2006, 30–43, 64–65.
13  Roig Lanzillotta 2005, 448–49.

Through the discipline of θεωρία, said Aristotle (speaking Platonically), people can immortalize themselves.[14]

In his myth of creation, Plato (ca. 429–347 BCE) depicts the divine mind as an immortal seed sown within humans by the demiurge, or creator deity.[15] This immortal soul is the divinest part of the human being. It is also the most intimate.[16] In a famous passage, the most sovereign part of the soul is called the δαίμων, or divinity, which each person has—like Socrates of old—as a friendly guide and internal "roommate" (σύνοικον).[17]

Following Plato, the Stoic Chrysippus (third century BCE) called this internal god a *daimōn*, or guardian divinity.[18] The theory was developed by Posidonius (early first century BCE), who spoke of "the divinity (δαίμων) in oneself, which is akin and has a similar nature to the one which governs the whole universe."[19] In the first century CE, the Roman philosopher Seneca referred to a "holy spirit" (*sacer ... spiritus*) dwelling within as a "guardian" (*custos*).[20] A century later, the Stoic and former slave Epictetus announced that god presented to each person an unsleeping guardian daimon.[21]

Epictetus's contemporary Plutarch approvingly cited Menander's saying that "our mind (νοῦς) is god (ὁ θεός)."[22] In his *On the Genius of Socrates*, Plutarch tells the story of Timarchus who, buried in the sacred cave of the divinized Trophonius, spoke with his own divine mind.[23] It told him that part of the

---

14  Aristotle, *Eth. Nic.* 1177b. See further Sedley 1999; Annas 1999, 52–71; J. M. Armstrong 2004; Roig Lanzillotta 2013, 80–81; Long 2015, 162–97.

15  Plato, *Tim.* 41c8 (σπείρας); cf. 90a2–b1.

16  Plato, *Resp.* 589e (τὸ ἑαυτοῦ θειότατον); cf. *Tim.* 45a1–2 (the head is τὴν τοῦ θειοτάτου καὶ ἱερωτάτου ... οἴκησιν); 69d6 (τὸ θεῖον); 73a7–8 (τοῦ θειοτάτου τῶν παρ' ἡμῖν); 88b2 (τὸ θειότατον τῶν ἐν ἡμῖν φρονήσεως); *Leg.* 726a (ψυχὴ θειότατον, οἰκειότατον ὄν).

17  Plato, *Tim.* 90c. Plato may have depended on the saying of Heraclitus: "the character of a person is his divinity" (ἦθος ἀνθρώπου δαίμων) (B119 DK). Cf. also Plato, *Leg.* 897b1–2: νοῦν ... ἀεὶ θεὸν ὀρθῶς θεοῖς ("mind ... ever rightly a god among gods"). See further Kidd 1995, 221.

18  Diogenes Laertius, *Vitae phil.* 7.87–88 (τοῦ παρ' ἑκάστῳ δαίμονος). J. M. Rist (1969, 263–64) emphasized that for Chrysippus, the *daimōn* was "with" (παρά) not "in" the individual person. Cf. Long 2002, 163–64.

19  1.170, Frag. 187.6–8 (Edelstein and Kidd 1989): τῷ ἐν αὐτῷ δαίμονι, where αὐτῷ is a correction of the manuscript reading αὐτῶ.

20  Seneca, *Ep.* 41.2 in Gummere 1917, 1.272.

21  Epictetus, *Diatr.* 1.14.12 in Oldfather 1925, 104. See further Thom 2005, 63.

22  Plutarch, *Quaest. plat.* 999d–e: ὁ νοῦς γὰρ ἡμῶν ὁ θεός ("for our mind is god") in Babbit, and Cherniss, De Lacy and Einarson 1914–2004, 13:1:.20. See further Kidd 1995, 222.

23  We are told directly that his soul is released from his head (*Gen. Socr.* 590b). Timarchus then has a long conversation with his mind (which resists revealing its identity). Finally his divine mind returns the same way it came, causing a sharp pain as it reenters Timarchus's head (*Gen. Socr.* 592e) in Babbit, Cherniss, De Lacy and Einarson 1914–2004, 7:460–76.

mind is not dragged down in the varied concerns of the soul, but bobs like a buoy immediately above the head. This higher self is itself a divinity (δαίμων) that is released at death and soars above the moon.[24]

Historically, then, when gnostic writers spoke of inward divinity, they were participants in and contributors to a recognizable discourse. Like the philosophers, gnostics could refer to the divine element as mind (νοῦς). *The Teachings of Silvanus* refer directly to "the divine mind (νοῦς)" that human beings have from God.[25] The ancient matriarch Norea is given "the first mind (νοῦς)," later identified with "the mind (νοῦς) of the Father," and "the great mind ([νο]ῦς) of the Invisible One."[26]

Yet gnostics went beyond intellectualist understandings of the divine spark. In their poetic and narrative universes, they had an amazing array of metaphors to describe it: seed,[27] (drop of) light,[28] spark,[29] word,[30] power,[31] name,[32] pearl,[33] inner human,[34] breath,[35] and so on. Each metaphor expressed something distinctive about inward divinity: how it is integrated into the self, how it operates in human development, and how it attains fulfillment.

Many of the metaphors are biblical. The divine breath is breathed into the first human in Genesis 2:7. The seed, representing the word of God, is sown in a famous parable (Mark 4:3–9). The pearl is tossed among pigs (Matt 7:6). Paul often spoke of humans inhabited by divine Spirit (e.g., Rom 8:9).

Some of these same images have philosophical correlates. For Plato, the creator sows the seeds of intellect. The Platonic dialogue *Axiochus* speaks of a "divine spirit (θεῖον ... πνεῦμα) in the soul."[36] Stoics thought of the indwelling divinity as *pneuma*, a kind of rational, fiery breath.

---

24  Plutarch, *Gen. Socr.* 591e–f. Iamblichus speaks of a doctrine, sometimes supported by Porphyry, that "the soul differs in no way from intellect and the gods, and the superior classes of being, at least in respect to its substance in general" (νοῦ καὶ θεῶν καὶ τῶν κρειττόνων γενῶν οὐδὲν ἡ ψυχὴ διενήνοχε κατά γε τὴν ὅλην οὐσίαν) (*De anima* 6, trans. Dillon and Finamore).
25  Teach. Silv. NHC VII,4 92.25–27 (Pearson 1996, 300).
26  Norea NHC IX,2 28.4, 12, 18–19 (Pearson 1981, 94).
27  Dial. Sav. NHC III,5 135.16–23 (Létourneau 2003, 80).
28  Wis. Jesus Chr. NHC III,4 106.24–107.2; (Berlin Gnostic Codex 8502,3, 119.1–9; Parrott 1991, 129).
29  Saturninus in Irenaeus, *Haer.* 1.24.1 (Rousseau and Doutreleau 1979, 322).
30  Gos. Truth NHC I,3 26.5–6 (Attridge 1985, 94).
31  Disc. 8–9 NHC VI,6 52.25 (Parrott 1979, 346).
32  Disc. 8–9 NHC VI,6 61.9 (Parrott 1979, 366).
33  Naassenes in Hippolytus, *Haer.* 5.8.32 (Marcovich 1986, 161).
34  Corp. herm. 1.15 (οὐσιώδη ἄνθρωπον) (Festugière and Nock 1954, 11).
35  Tri. Tract. NHC I,5 105.22–27 (Attridge 1985, 282).
36  Pseudo-Plato, [*Ax.*] 370c (Hershbell 1981, 44).

## 2 Reflexivity

In gnostic sources, there is a constant dialectic between the divine spark and one's divine destiny. It resembles the dialectic in Platonism between the ideas of divine kinship (συγγένεια) and assimilation to god (ὁμοίωσις θεῷ).[37] Humans have a natural ("genetic") kinship with God. At the same time, they are called to be more like God in a long—often arduous—process of growth.

To be sure, one's innate likeness to God makes additional assimilation possible. If the eye were not sun-like, it could never see the sun.[38] Likewise, if the mind were not akin by nature to the Good, it could never intuit the Good and all that is perfect and eternal. In its power of recognizing the eternal, the soul bears within itself the surest proof that it is eternal, as well as the chance to realize that eternity.[39]

The road to realization is the road of reflexivity, or self-knowledge. "Know thyself," attributed to one of the Seven Sages, was one of the most famous sayings in the ancient world.[40] Carved on the ancient temple of Apollo at Delphi, its meaning was transformed by Platonists beginning in the fourth century BCE. In the Archaic and Classical periods, "Know thyself" was widely taken to mean "know your (social and ontological) place," "know that you are not immortal."[41] The aristocratic politicians and ambassadors who visited the oracle at Delphi were thus encouraged to "think soundly or soberly" (σωφρονεῖν) and not to seize undue power.[42] Plato was aware of this ancient meaning of the phrase, and employed it in his dialogue *Charmides* and elsewhere.[43]

Yet in the dialogue *Alcibiades I*, the maxim underwent a transformation.[44] In an epiphanic moment, Socrates takes "Know thyself" to mean: "know thy

---

37  Plato, *Leg.* 899d: συγγένειά τις θεία ("a divine kinship"). The classic study of ὁμοίωσις θεῷ is Merki 1952. Merki's study, though now dated, is still useful for presenting the texts on ὁμοίωσις. For a short list of texts, see Roig Lanzillotta 2013, 75 n.16.
38  Plato, *Resp.* 508b.
39  Plato, *Phaed.* 79d.
40  See the sayings of the Seven Sages in Diels and Kranz, 1954 62.8; Χίλων 63.25; Θαλῆς 64.6–7; Plato, *Prot.*, 343a–b; Pausanias, *Descr.* 10.24.1.
41  See, e.g., Aeschylus, *Prom.* 309; Xenophon, *Cyr.* 7.2.20–25.
42  The earliest association of self-knowledge and σωφροσύνη is Heraclitus (B 116 DK): ἀνθρώποισι πᾶσι μέτεστι γινώσκειν ἑωυτοὺς καὶ σωφρονεῖν ("It is given to all human beings to know themselves and to think soundly").
43  Plato, *Charm.* 164c–165b; *Tim.* 72a; *Phileb.* 48c-49a; *Leg.* 11.923a4; Pseudo-Plato, [*Alc. maj.*] 124b, 128d–129a, 131b4; 133c18; cf. Pseudo-Plato, [Amatores] 138a–b; Plutarch, *E Delph.* 394c; Clement of Alexandria, *Strom.* 5.4.23.1. On Socratic self-knowledge, see Foucault 2005, 3–4, 12–15, 51–60, 66–72, 169–85.
44  On the date and authenticity of *Alc. maj.*, see Denyer 2001, 11–26. Denyer argues for Platonic authorship, and opts for a date in the early 350s BCE.

true self—the soul." In the soul is a place where wisdom is born. This part of the soul—the seat of knowledge and thought—is divine and resembles God.[45] The one who gazes at this divine part, as if in a mirror, comes to grasp "all that is divine—mind and thinking."[46] God himself, in fact, is the best mirror for the soul, and he, as its archetype, reveals its true divinity.[47] The meaning of the Delphic maxim thus shifted from, "Know that you are human," to "Know that you are divine."[48]

In later antiquity, "Know that you are divine" became a kind of gnostic manifesto. In the Gospel of Thomas Jesus says, "When you know yourselves, then you will be known, and you will understand that you are children of the living Father."[49] Likewise: "When you produce that [which is] in you, what you have will save you.'"[50] In this model of soteriology, God is still the savior, but God is within. Salvation is the realization of what is already possessed; it is self-realization. The spark of remembrance is lit by the sayings of Jesus, but the glowing ember of the divine self is already embedded within, waiting to blaze forth. True spiritual investigation is *self*-investigation. It results in the realization of one's own divine identity.

In a similar fashion, the Testimony of Truth speaks of ideal gnostics:

> They asked [what they have been] bound with, [and how they] might properly [release themselves.] And [they came to know] themselves [(as to) who they are,] or rather, where they are [now,] and what is the [place in] which they will rest from their senselessness, [arriving] at knowledge. [These people] Christ will transfer to [the heights] since they have [renounced] foolishness, (and have) advanced to knowledge ... [he has come to] know [the Son of the Human,] that [is, he has come to] know

---

45  Pseudo-Plato, [*Alc. maj.*] 133c. "The" god here may be Apollo, the god of wisdom and the speaker of the Delphic maxim. Cf. Plato, *Phaedr.* 229e–230a.
46  Pseudo-Plato, [*Alc. maj.*] 133c (καί τις εἰς τοῦτο βλέπων καὶ πᾶντ τὸ θεῖον γνούς, θεόν τε καὶ φρόνησιν, οὕτω καὶ ἑαυτὸν ἂν γνοίη μάλιστα).
47  Whether or not we accept that *Alc. maj.* 133c8–17 was originally part of the dialogue, it remains an important part of its interpretation. The discovery of a Middle Platonic commentary on the Alcibiades (dated to the late second or early third century CE) indicates that 133c8–17 was not present (Lasserre 1991, 8). Johnson (1999, 10–13) reviews the debate and argues that god is present in the comparison whether or not the lines are removed.
48  See further Betz 1970, 471; Pépin 1971, 71–114.
49  Gos. Thom. NHC II,2 3 (Layton 1989, 54).
50  Gos. Thom. NHC II,2 70 (Layton 1989, 80).

himself. This is the perfect life: [that] a person know [himself] by means of the All.[51]

Once knowledge of the true self occurs, so does spiritual resurrection (the "transfer to the heights"). In short, arriving at self-knowledge means coming to know one's true nature. One's self is not separate from mediate divinity (in this case, the Son of the Human). One's self *is* the mediate deity in embryonic form.

### 2.1 *The Finalized Self*

The mediate deity may come to the self as "other," but this deity also comes as the fullest manifestation of the self. The Savior is the mediate god to whom one assimilates. But since the mediate deity is also the higher self, the gnostic assimilates not to something alien, but to his or her true self.

Assimilation to the mediate deity begins, in one case, with a sense of mutual indwelling. In the Valentinian tractate The Gospel of Truth, the saved "were joyful in this discovery, and he [the mediate deity] found them within himself and they found him within themselves."[52] When the mediate deity comes to earth, spiritual persons instantly recognize in him something of their own true self.

In some cases, the mediate deity is indistinguishable from the gnostic's own mind. Seth speaks to his divine Father Geradamas: "and you are my mind, O my Father."[53] The mediate deity is revealed as a second self. He (or She) does not need to be found without, but within. As the Savior says in the Second Discourse of Great Seth: "I am Christ, Son of Humanity, one from you who is within you."[54]

Yet the identity between self and Savior can be even more radical. Epiphanius quotes a visionary encounter found in the Gospel of Eve. It begins: "I stood upon a high mountain and saw a tall man and another short one. I heard as it were the sound of thunder and drew near to hear." A voice (of thunder?) addresses the narrator personally, declaring: "I am you and you are I, and wherever you are, there I am. I am sown in all people. Wherever you want to gather me, in gathering me, you gather yourself."[55]

---

[51] Testim. Truth NHC IX,3 35.26–36.28, following the reconstruction of Pearson (and Giverson) 1981, 135–37.

[52] Gos. Truth NHC I,3 18.28–31 (Attridge 1985, 84).

[53] Steles Seth NHC VII,5 118.31–119.2 (Pearson 1996, 388). In Corp. herm. 1, the narrator refers to the divine revealer Poimandres as "my mind" (νοῦς ἐμός, e.g., 1.21).

[54] Disc. Seth NHC VII,2 65.18–20 (Pearson 1996, 188).

[55] Epiphanius, *Pan.* 26.3.1 (Holl, Bergermann, and Collatz 2013, 278).

Unity with the mediate deity is also portrayed in a beautiful passage of Pistis Sophia. Here Christ promises that the saved are now, even while in the world, superior to angels, archangels, luminaries, and even gods. The saved person will be a ruler with Christ in his kingdom. In a rising crescendo of promises, the Savior solemnly announces: "And truly I say to you: that person is I and I am that person".[56] This promise is repeated in slightly different words three times. The last promise serves as a culmination: "Every person who will receive mysteries in the Ineffable will be on my left and my right [in the kingdom]. I am they and they are I."[57]

To sum up, these three elements make possible the language of gnostic self-deification: (1) the presence of divinity in the self, (2) reflexive practices of self-knowledge or self-recognition, and (3) integration into a higher self represented by a mediate deity. This deity can descend to earth, or the gnostic can ascend with divine aid. The gnostic typically ascends in ecstatic contemplation, while permanent ascent must await the separation of soul and body at death.

We turn now to a more in-depth examination of a gnostic text to illustrate how the three moments of self-deification play out.

## 3    Simon of Samaria

One of the more terrifying figures for early Christian heresiologists was the putative first head of the gnostic hydra, Simon of Samaria.[58] Importantly, this supposedly archetypal gnostic was made into a stereotypical self-deifier.[59] Regrettably, all Simonian sources have been lost, with the exception of one long report from a document called *The Great Declaration* (*Apophasis Megalē*).

---

56    Pist. Soph. AC 2.96 (Schmidt and MacDermot 1978, 231).
57    Pist. Soph. AC 2.96 (Schmidt and MacDermot 1978, 232).
58    It is actually not clear that Simon was a Samaritan, but this seems to be the assumption of early Christian writers (see further Fossum 1989, 361–64; Haar 2003, 160–66). Since Simon's common title "Magus" ("the magician") serves mostly as a heresiological slur, it is not foregrounded here (see further Heintz 1997, 45). For the hydra image, see Irenaeus, *Haer.* 1.30.14; Hippolytus, *Haer.* 5.11.1. In the twentieth century, Simon was a popular test-case for pre-Christian gnosticism—some affirming that he was gnostic, with others denying it. See the balanced position of Haar 2003, 306–7.
59    Foerster believed that Simon's self-deification was historical (1970, 194; cf. Klauck 2003, 15–19). Pétrement, however, argued that Simon's self-deification was a heresiological construct (1990, 245–46). The self-deification of Simon has not, to my knowledge, been a subject for independent investigation. See, however, the brief survey of Heintz 1997, 118–22.

Relatively long (though selective) quotations and summaries from this document are provided by an anonymous Roman churchman in the early third century. This author, who can no longer securely be called "Hippolytus," wrote his account of Simon in the *Refutation of All Heresies* (hereafter *Heresies*) around 222 CE.[60] Unlike other heresy hunters, the author of the *Heresies* directly quoted his (in this case, unique) source material because he believed that the very words of his opponents refuted them.[61]

According to the author of the *Heresies*, Simon himself composed *The Great Declaration*. This is not outside the range of possibility. Some historians have thought that the complexity and philosophical character of the *Heresies* disprove Simon's authorship.[62] Yet we have no reason to disbelieve that Simon (like Paul) was a complex thinker with a smattering of philosophical learning.

Nevertheless, the author of the *Heresies* seems to aim his criticisms at Simonians (whom he sarcastically calls Simon's "parrots")[63] and occasionally quotes the *Declaration* with the line: "they say" (φασί).[64] These two tendencies combined indicate that the *Declaration* was probably composed by Simon's followers.[65]

In terms of its literary representation, however, *The Great Declaration* is written in Simon's own voice. Indeed, Simon speaks in the voice of the divine revealer. In this respect, the Simonians who wrote the *Declaration* acted much like the authors of the Gospel of John. They put words into the mouth of their

---

60  A version of the two-author theory for the Hippolytan corpus is now widely held. That is, there is an eastern writer called Hippolytus who composes the biblical commentaries, and an anonymous western writer who composes the *Refutation* and a treatise *On the Nature of the Universe*. In Brent's reconstruction (1995), the author of the *Refutation* is an anonymous early third-century Roman bishop who dies, leaving the community to a member of the same school—in fact a Roman martyr called Hippolytus who reconciles with the catholic faction. Cerrato (2002) accepts the theory of an eastern Hippolytus, probably from Asia Minor who composed the exegetical commentaries. For him, all links are severed between this genuine Hippolytus and the author of the *Refutation*.

61  *Haer.* 9.16.2 (Marcovich 1986, 362).

62  Beyschlag 1974, 218–19.

63  *Haer.* 6.9.1 (Marcovich 1986, 213).

64  E.g., *Haer.* 6.15.3, 6.17.2 (Marcovich 1986, 220, 222). Note that Marcovich was prone to change φασί in the manuscript to φησί(ν).

65  Interpreters generally conclude that *The Great Declaration* was a late work (Yamauchi 1973, 62–64; Haar 2003, 97–99). According to Frickel, 1968, the author of *Haer.* did not quote from the *Great Declaration* but a paraphrase of it. This paraphrase was composed by a Gnostic exegete around 200 CE. Frickel's theory was refuted by Catherine Osborne (now Catherine Rowett), who points out that it is based on an overly selective source-critical analysis and a misunderstanding of how the author of *Haer.* uses φησίν. Osborne herself suggests that the *Declaration* was written, with commentary, by one of Simon's pupils (1987, 214–27).

deified founder that reflected the developed mythology of their community. In both cases, the mythology was not written down to provide a historical account of the founder's thought. It was written to foster and maintain a community. For both the Johannine and Simonian communities, empirical history was not the standard of truth. Both groups intuited the greater truth of their founder through the secret workings of his spirit.

Consequently, in our discussion of Simonian self-deification it is right to focus on *The Great Declaration*. Only this document gives us access to Simonian mythology in the language of the Simonians themselves.

## 4    The Great Declaration

The first teaching of *The Great Declaration* is that "the Great Power", or "Infinite Power," is the high God. This God is a kind of creative fire blazing throughout the universe and hidden in the human heart.[66] In fiery form, God exists as the divine core hidden within human beings.[67] Each part of the fire is intelligent.[68] When it finds its place in the human being, it constitutes human intelligence. The divine fire, in other words, is a form of consciousness. Human consciousness, in effect, is a kind of divine consciousness broken up into many bodies.

The fire, or Infinite Power, is identified with "the One Who Stood, Who Stands, and Who Will Stand."[69] The three designations, I suggest, represent three phases of God's evolution. To quote the *Declaration*: God "stood above in the Unborn Power. He stands below in the flow of waters, born in an image. He will stand above alongside the blessed Infinite Power, if made in the likeness."[70] In other words, God has a preexistent state, a state of becoming, and a state of restoration to perfected divinity.

Importantly, the Simonian author maps the two final states of God onto two states of the ideal human being. The human is made in God's image and will

---

66  *Haer.* 6.9.4–5 (Marcovich 1986, 214).
67  *Haer.* 6.17.1 (Marcovich 1986, 222); cf. 6.12.2 (Marcovich 1986, 217).
68  *Haer.* 6.11.1–12.1 (Marcovich 1986, 216).
69  The title "Standing One" (ὁ ἑστώς) is derived in part from God's statement to Moses in Deut 5:31: "But you, stand here by me" (LXX: στῆθι μετ' ἐμοῦ). With this verse in view, Philo says that Moses participates in the Standing One (ὁ Ἑστώς), i.e., God (*Post.* 28; *Conf.* 30). The philosopher Numenius also described the primal God (ὁ μὲν πρῶτος θεός) as the Standing One (Ἑστώς) (Frag. 15 [des Places] from Eusebius, *Praep. Ev.* 11.18, 20–21); cf. Corp. herm. 2.12 (Νοῦς ... ἐν ἑαυτῷ ἑστώς). See further Lüdemann 1975, 98–100; Williams 1985, 37–38, 57; Fossum 1989, 377–89; Haar 2003, 275–9, 286.
70  *Haer.* 6.17.1 (Marcovich 1986, 222).

eventually attain God's likeness.[71] In fact, God's state of becoming and restoration is worked out in human consciousness. In the end, there is no essential difference between the dynamic evolution of God and God's evolution in the human self. The story of God's evolution is the story of human deification.

The author of the *Declaration* calls the Infinite Power "the root of the universe."[72] This arboreal metaphor is expanded to describe the natural potential of God's growth within the human being. From the root will grow the trunk, the leaves, and finally the ripened fruit of divinity. The fruit is God when God reaches God's full potential in and through the human being.

Like the mustard seed, human consciousness begins extremely small. In a human infant, consciousness begins, as it were, as a single geometrical point with no extension or dimensions. But as it is written in the *Great Declaration*, "the small will become great, and the great will be in an unchanging and infinite eternity, no longer subject to generation."[73] Another metaphor for the divine potential in humanity is the spark. God within humanity begins "as from the tiniest spark," which "will be vastly enlarged and grow, and become an infinite and unchanging power in an infinite and unchanging eternity, no longer subject to generation."[74]

In short, the author of the *Great Declaration* understands deification as the vast growth of human consciousness.[75] The root of the universe within human beings branches into six roots, all of which develop in the human being. Divine consciousness grows from mind and thought, to voice and name, to reasoning and reflection.[76] The growth is intellectual, representing an evolution from mind to various forms of rational activity. Thought ('Επίνοιαν) and reflection ('Ενθύμησιν) ultimately circle back to mind in a blazing circle of divine intellect. The process is universal and cosmic, but is chiefly worked out in human beings. Individuals, by engaging in reflexive practices of self-knowing, understand their own divinity and unity with the divine fire.

The six stages of intellectual growth are likened to the six days of creation. Divine consciousness develops throughout the six days. The seventh (Sabbath) day is the day of God's own fulfillment, the day when God becomes the Seventh Power. The Seventh Power, we come to learn, is the mediate form of deity who

---

71   *Haer.* 6.14.5–6 (Marcovich 1986, 218–19).
72   *Haer.* 6.9.5 (Marcovich 1986, 214).
73   *Haer.* 6.14.6 (Marcovich 1986, 219).
74   *Haer.* 6.17.7 (Marcovich 1986, 223–24).
75   *Haer.* 6.9.810 (Marcovich 1986, 215).
76   *Haer.* 6.12.2 (Marcovich 1986, 217).

is both one and distinct from the Infinite Power.[77] The Seventh Power is God's likeness (the finished and completed image of God). By intellectually assimilating to the Seventh Power, the human being realizes his or her own deification, as well as the full growth of Godhood in the self.

The full formation of the God within is the attainment of God-likeness. But to be in God's likeness is not to be less than God; it is to be God. For Paul, the one who beholds Christ (God's Glory) is transformed into "the same image" (2 Cor 3:18). According to the *Great Declaration*: "Whoever attains the likeness ... will be in substance, in potential, in magnitude, in finished perfection *one and the same* as the Unborn and Infinite Power."[78]

The human assimilates to the mediate deity, or Seventh Power. When it is identified with the Seventh Power, human consciousness becomes equal, at least potentially, to the primal deity, or Infinite Power. The Seventh Power is the true self of the human being. Yet it is also the complete fruition of the human self that attains realization as an unborn divinity.

To sum up: there are two sides of God that correspond to two states of the human being. In Aristotelian terms, there is a God in actuality, and a God in potentiality. From one point of view, God has never left his state of perfect repose in pure being. This is "He Who Stood," or the Infinite Power. From another point of view, God is in a process of constant evolution. He starts in the human being as the Seventh Power, though in seed form. The Seventh Power eventually attains realization in human consciousness. These two sides of God—namely, the eternally completed as well as the maturing God—are ultimately one, such that one aspect of God can say to the other: "I and you are one. What is before me is you. What is after you is I."[79]

Importantly, since the Seventh Power attains its perfection in human consciousness, it is *also* the human who can say to God: "I and you are one. What is before me is you. What is after you is I." The God in potentiality is inside every human being. When God attains actuality, the human being is deified. God is developing in the human, and in the course of divine evolution, human consciousness attains a divine level. In this scheme, deification means transcending this world of generation, becoming pure, unborn Spirit in all respects equal to the Infinite Power.

---

77  *Haer.* 6.14.6 (Marcovich 1986, 219).
78  *Haer.* 6.12.3 (Marcovich 1986, 217).
79  *Haer.* 6.17.2 (Marcovich 1986, 222).

## Conclusion

In the *Great Declaration*, I argue, all three elements of self-deification are present: (1) innate divinity (i.e., the divine fire or root of the universe within the human self), (2) practices of reflexivity (i.e., human consciousness turning back on itself to reflect upon its own divinity), and (3) identification with the divine self (i.e., the Seventh, and ultimately the Infinite Power).

In short, Simonian deification can be called "self-deification" because it is the divine self who seeks itself by a practice of self-recognition and ever deeper self-knowledge. The practice of self-knowledge is worked out in the very reading of the *Great Declaration*. The message, in spite of the complex mythology, is comprehensible: Divinity is rooted in the human self; this self engages in reflexive practices to realize its own divinity; in the end, the self realizes its union with a higher divine self. Almost everything in this model is focused on or circles back to the self. What I am calling "self-deification" is (to borrow the language of Foucault) "the vigilant, continuous, and completed form of the relationship to self closed in on itself. One saves oneself for the self, one is saved by the self, one saves oneself in order to arrive at nothing other than oneself ... the self is the agent, object, instrument, and end of salvation."[80]

And yet—despite this focus upon the self—there is (*contra* the heresiologists) nothing openly selfish about Simonian deification. Those who practice it are not focused on themselves as *themselves*, but on realizing themselves as part of a higher, divine self. "Simon" himself is not a self-deifier in the sense of someone who hubristically claims to be god. Indeed, such a claim—if it is true—can only be made when hubris is left behind. That is to say, only when one realizes that one's self is not the true self, but the divine "Other," does one realize one's own divinity. This is "Simon's" goal in *The Great Declaration*: to help make his readers *other* than themselves so that they can realize their greater divine selfhood.

Self-deification in gnostic thought is in some sense a reverse imitation of God. God engages in an eternal act of self-reflexivity that results in self-limitation and eventual incarnation in human persons. The high God's archetypal self-reflexive act is a kind of self-creation, which makes possible the creation of everything else. All that exists is ultimately a multiply-refracted projection of God's self.

Human deification is a kind of reverse spiral of divine reflexivity. God knows himself. This self-knowledge constitutes the unfolding of the universe. In turn,

---

80   Foucault 2005, 184–85.

humanity's self-knowledge begins the process of refolding back into God. The consciousness of God, when embedded in human beings, has the potential to realize its identity and to return into the divine whole. This return results in the ultimate expansion of the self and the restoration of the higher divine self.

Nothing in this mythology suggests rebellion against the true God. To be sure, gnostics are rebels and transgressors insofar as they oppose an evil demiurge and his minions. Nonetheless, a myth of cosmic rebellion does not constitute the core story of gnostic deification. Like Jesus, the gnostic is not a rebel against God, but God's child. Temporarily, the gnostic has been separated from her royal family. She has been seized by robbers—even raped—and thrown into another kingdom. The ruler of this kingdom is a fool and a usurper. The dominant desire of the gnostic is not to do battle with this (already doomed) tyrant, but to bypass him and return to her true realm.

Gnostics engage in self-deification not because the immanent self by itself completes the work of transformation, but because reflexive knowing reveals that the self includes the divine Other. This divine Other is integrated into the self to the point of identity. The reflexive process of identification with the divine Other is *self*-deification because the Other is also the greater self. The mediate God comes as divine Other, but in the process of inward revelation, a gradual "de-othering" of God occurs. Realizing oneself means becoming an "other" to the world while simultaneously making the divine Other the S/self.

In the end, gnostic self-deification is a form of self-fashioning and self-creation. Clement of Alexandria wrote that the gnostic, when assimilated to God, "forms and creates himself" (ἑαυτὸν κτίζει καὶ δημιουργεῖ).[81] Clement was speaking of his own (early catholic model of the) "gnostic." Yet in this respect the early catholic and Simonian gnostic are alike: they are both self-creators; and they are destined to attain their true divine S/self.

As a prophet of postmodernism, Michel Foucault rejected the idea that a person had a "true self." Still, late in his career he was able to write: "From the idea that the self is not given to us, I think that there is only one practical consequence: we have to create ourselves as a work of art."[82] This process of self-creation—of self-beautification—is exactly what gnostic self-deification is all about.

---

81  Clement of Alexandria, *Strom.* 7.3.13.3 (Le Boulluec 1997, 70).
82  Foucault 1984, 351. See the comments of Nehamas 1998, 177.

## Bibliography

Armstrong, Arthur Hilary, ed. 1989. *Enneads*. Vol. 1. Loeb Classical Library. Cambridge, Mass: Harvard University Press

Armstrong, John M. 2004. "After the Ascent: Plato on Becoming Like God," *Oxford Studies in Ancient Philosophy* 26: 171–83.

Attridge, Harold W., ed. 1985. *Nag Hammadi Codex I (The Jung Codex)*. NHS 22. Leiden: Brill.

Annas, Julia. 1999. *Platonic Ethics, Old and New*. Ithaca: Cornell University Press.

Babbit, Frank Cole, Harold Cherniss, Phillip H. De Lacy and Benedict Einarson. 1914–2004. *Plutarch. Moralia.* 28 vols. Loeb Classical Library. Cambridge, Mass.: Harvard University Press.

Betz, Hans Dieter. 1970. "The Delphic Maxim ΓΝΩΘΙ ΣΑΥΤΟΝ in Hermetic Interpretation." *Harvard Theological Review* 63: 465–84.

Beyschlag, Karlmann. 1974. *Simon Magus und die christliche Gnosis*. Wissenschaftliche Untersuchungen zum Neuen Testament 16. Tübingen: Mohr Siebeck.

Brent, Allen. *Hippolytus and the Roman Church in the Third Century: Communities in Tension Before the Emergence of a Monarch-Bishop.* Vigiliae Christianae Supplements 31. Leiden: Brill 1995.

Burns, Dylan M. 2014. *Apocalypse of an Alien God: Platonism and the Exile of Sethian Gnosticism*. Philadelphia: University of Pennsylvania Press.

Cerrato, John A. 2002. *Hippolytus between East and West: The Commentaries and the Provenance of the Corpus*. Oxford: Oxford University Press.

DeConick, April D. 2010. "Jesus Revealed: The Dynamics of Early Christian Mysticism." Pages 299–324 in *With Letters of Light: Studies in the Dead Sea Scrolls, Early Jewish Apocalypticism, Magic, and Mysticism in Honor of Rachel Elior*, eds. Daphna V. Arbel, Daphna Andrei A. Orlav, Ekstasis: Religious Experience from Antiquity to the Middle Ages. Berlin: de Gruyter, 2010.

DeConick, April D. 2013. "Crafting Gnosis: Gnostic Spirituality in the Ancient New Age." Pages 287–305 in *Gnosticism, Platonism and the Late Ancient World: Essays in Honour of John D. Turner*. Edited by Kevin Corrigan and Tuomas Rasimus. Nag Hammadi and Manichaean Studies 82. Leiden: Brill.

Denyer, Nicholas, ed. 2001. *Plato: Alcibiades*. Cambridge: Cambridge University Press, 2001.

Diels, Hermann and Walther Kranz, eds. *Fragmente der Vorsokratiker, griechisch und deutsch, erster band*. 7th ed. Berlin: Weidmann, 1954.

Dillon, John M. and John F. Finamore, trans. 2002. *Iamblichus: De anima*. Philosophia Antiqua. Leiden: Brill.

Duke, E. A. et al. 1995. *Platonis Opera*. 5 vols. Oxford Classical Texts. Oxford: Clarendon.

Edelstein, L. and I. G. Kidd, eds. 1989. *Posidonius I: The Fragments*. 2nd ed. 2 vols. Cambridge University Press.

Festugière, A. J. and A. D. Nock, eds. 1954. *Corpus Hermeticum*. 4 vols. Budé. Paris: Belles Lettres.

Foerster, Werner. 1970. "Die 'ersten Gnostiker' Simon und Menander." Pages 190–96 in *Le origini dello Gnosticismo: Colloquio di Messina 13–18 Aprile 1966*. Edited by Ugo Bianchi. Leiden: Brill.

Fossum, Jarl. 1989. "Samaritan Sects and Movements." Pages 293–389 in *The Samaritans*. Edited by Alan D. Crown. Tübingen: Mohr Siebeck.

Foucault, Michel. 1984. "On the Genealogy of Ethics: An Overview of Work in Progress." Pages 340–72 in *The Foucault Reader*. Edited by Paul Rabinow. New York: Random House.

Foucault, Michel. *The Hermeneutics of the Subject: Lectures at the Collège de France, 1981–82*. 2005. Edited by Frédéric Gros. Translated by Graham Burchell. New York: Palgrave.

Frickel, Josef. 1968. *Die "Apophasis Megale" in Hippolyt's Refutatio (VI 9–18): Eine Paraphrase zur Apophasis Simons*. Rome: Pontifical Institute of Oriental Studies.

Gummere, Richard M. 1917–1925. *Seneca. Epistles*. 3 vols. Loeb Classical Library. Cambridge, MA: Harvard University Press.

Haar, Stephen. 2003. *Simon Magus: The First Gnostic?* Beihefte zur Zeitschrift für die neutestamentliche Wissenschaft 119. Berlin: de Gruyter.

Heintz Florent. 1997. *Simon "le magician": Actes 8,5–25 et l'accusation de magie*. Paris: Gabalda.

Hershbell, Jackson P. 1981. *Pseudo-Plato, Axiochus*. SBL Texts and Translations 21. Chico, CA: Scholars Press.

Holl, Karl, Marc Bergermann, and Christian-Friedrich Collatz, eds. 2013. *Epiphanius: Ancoratus und Panarion haer. 1–33*. 2nd ed. Griechischen Christlichen Schriftsteller 10/1. Berlin: de Gruyter.

Johnson David M. 1999. "God as the true Self: Plato's *Alcibiades I*," *Ancient Philosophy* 19(1): 1–19.

Kidd, Ian. 1995. "Some Philosophical Demons." *Bulletin of the Institute of Classical Studies*: 40(1): 217–224.

Klauck, Hans-Josef. 2003. *Magic and Paganism in Early Christianity: The World of the Acts of the Apostles*. Translated by Brian McNeil. Fortress: Minneapolis.

Lasserre, F. 1991. "Commentaire de *l'Alcibiade I* de Plato." Pages 7–23 in *Varia Papyrologica*. Edited by F. Decleva Caizzi. Firenze: Leo S. Olschki.

Layton, Bentley, ed. 1989. Nag Hammadi Codex II,2–7 together with XIII,2*, Brit. Lib. Or.4926(1) and P.Oxy. 1,654, 655. Nag Hammadi Studies 20. Volume 1. Leiden: Brill.

Létourneau, Pierre. 2003. *Le Dialogue du Sauveur (NH III,5)*. Bibliothèque Copte de Nag Hammadi. Textes 29. Louven: Peeters.

Le Boulluec, Alain. 1997. Clement of Alexandria. *Les Stromates VII*. Sources Chrétiennes 428. Paris: Cerf.

Litwa, M. David. 2013. *Becoming Divine: An Introduction to Deification in Western Culture*. Eugene, OR: Cascade.

Litwa, M. David. 2014. *Iesus Deus: The Early Christian Depiction of Jesus as a Mediterranean God*. Minneapolis: Fortress.

Long, Anthony A. 2002. *Epictetus: A Stoic and Socratic Guide to Life*. Oxford: Clarendon.

Long, Anthony A. 2015. *Greek Models of Mind and Self*. Cambridge: Harvard University Press.

Lüdemann, Gerd. 1975. *Untersuchungen zur simonianischen Gnosis*. Göttingen: Vandenhoeck & Ruprecht.

Lüdemann, Gerd. 1987. "The Acts of the Apostles and the Beginnings of Simonian Gnosis." *New Testament Studies* 33(3): 420–26.

Lüdemann, Gerd. 1999. "Die Apostelgeschichte und die Anfänge der simonianischen Gnosis." Pages 7–20 in *Studien zur Gnosis*. Edited by Gerd Lüdemann. Bern: Lang.

Luttikhuizen, Gerhard. 2006. *Gnostic Revisions of Genesis Stories and Early Jesus Traditions*. Leiden: Brill.

Marcovich, Miroslav, ed. 1999. *Diogenes Laertius: Vitae philosophorum*. Stuttgart: Teubner.

Marjanen, Antti. "Gnosticism." 2008. Pages 203–220 in *The Oxford Handbook of Early Christian Studies*. Edited by Susan Ashbrook Harvey and David G. Hunter. Oxford: Oxford University Press.

Merki, Hubert. 1952. *Homoiosis Theo: Von Der Platonischen Angleichung an Gott Zur Gottähnlichkeit bei Gregor von Nyssa*. Freiburg, Switzerland: Paulusverlag.

Nehamas, Alexander. 1998. *The Art of Living: Socratic Reflections from Plato to Foucault*. Berkeley: University of California Press.

Oldfather, W. A. 1925. *Epictetus: The Discourses as Reported by Arrian, and Manual and Fragments*. 2 vols. Loeb Classical Library. Cambridge, MA: Harvard University Press.

Orlov, Andrei A. 2004. "The Face as the Heavenly Counterpart of the Visionary in the Slavonic *Ladder of Jacob*." Pages 59–76 in volume 2 of *Early Jewish Interpretation and Transmission of Scripture*. Edited by Craig A. Evans. 2 vols. London: T&T Clark.

Osborne, Catherine. 1987. *Rethinking Early Greek Philosophy: Hippolytus of Rome and the Presocratics*. London: Duckworth.

Parrott, Douglas M., ed. 1979, *Nag Hammadi Codices V, 2–5 and VI*. Nag Hammadi Studies 11. Leiden: Brill.

Parrott, Douglas M., ed. 1991. *Nag Hammadi Codices III,3–4 and V,1: Eugnostos and the Sophia of Jesus Christ*. Nag Hammadi Studies 27. Leiden: Brill.

Pearson, Birger A., ed. 1981. *Nag Hammadi Codices IX and X*. NHS 15. Leiden: Brill.
Pearson, Birger A., ed. 1996. *Nag Hammadi Codex VII*. NHMS 30. Leiden: Brill.
Pépin, Jean. 1971. *Idées grecque sur l'homme et sur dieu*. Paris: Belles Lettres.
Pétrement, Simone. 1990. *A Separate God: The Christian Origins of Gnosticism*. Translated by Carol Harrison. San Francisco: Harper & Row.
Rist, J. M. 1969. *Stoic Philosophy*. Cambridge: Cambridge University Press.
Roig Lanzillotta, Lautaro. 2005. "Devolution and Recollection, Deficiency and Perfection: Human Degradation and the Recovery of the Primal Condition according to some Early Christian Texts." Pages 443–60 in *The Wisdom of Egypt: Jewish, Early Christian, and Gnostic Essays in Honour of Gerard P. Luttikhuizen*. Edited by Anthony Hilhorst and George H. van Kooten. Ancient Judaism and Early Christianity 59. Leiden: Brill, 2005.
Roig Lanzillotta, Lautaro. 2013. "A Way of Salvation: Becoming Like God in Nag Hammadi." *Numen* 60: 71–102.
Rousseau, Adelin and Louis Doutreleau. 1965–82. *Irénée de Lyon: Contre les hérésies livres I-V*. Sources Chrétiennes 100, 153, 211, 263–64, 294. Paris: Cerf.
Schmidt, Carl, ed. Violet MacDermot, trans. 1978b. *Pistis Sophia*. Nag Hammadi Studies 9. Leiden: Brill.
Sedley, David. 1999. "The Ideal of Godlikeness." Pages 309–28 in *Plato 2: Ethics, Politics, Religion, and the Soul*. Edited by Gail Fine. Oxford: Oxford University Press.
Thom, Johan C. 2005. *Cleanthes' Hymn to Zeus: Text, Translation, and Commentary*. Studien und Texte zu Antike und Christentum 33. Tübingen: Mohr Siebeck.
Turner John D. 2014. "Baptismal Vision, Angelification, and Mystical Union in Sethian Literature." Pages 204–16 in *Beyond the Gnostic Gospels: Studies Building on the Work of Elaine Pagels*. Edited by Eduard Iricinschi, Lance Jenott, Nicola Denzey Lewis and Philippa Townsend. STAC 82. Tübingen: Mohr Siebeck.
Van den Broek, Roelof. 2013. *Gnostic Religion in Antiquity*. Cambridge: Cambridge University Press.
Williams, Michael Allen. 1985. *The Immovable Race: A Gnostic Designation and the Theme of Stability in Late Antiquity*. Leiden: Brill.
Yamauchi, Edwin. 1973. *Pre-Christian Gnosticism: A Survey of the Proposed Evidences*. London: Tyndale Press.

# *Demon est Deus Inversus*:
# Honoring the Daemonic in Iamblichean Theurgy

*Gregory Shaw*
Stonehill College
gshaw@stonehill.edu

The later Platonists were "mystical existentialists." They recognized the value of embodied life and believed that only mortal existence allowed human souls to experience immortality. In my scholarship I have tried to make sense of this seemingly impossible vision. It may have been wiser to study the social or historical aspects of the Neoplatonists, but I have been drawn to this *kōan* at the heart of their metaphysics and believe it is the key to understanding their existential experience.[1]

I would like to begin, then, by inviting us to consider a living example of this *kōan* with an entirely mundane experience: sitting at a dinner table where one individual seems bent on gobbling up all the attention, hijacking every story, and filling every moment with yet another self-absorbed tale. We might ask what a fourth century Platonic philosopher could say about such a maddening situation; as it turns out, quite a bit. In the vision of Iamblichus, the entire cosmos is a theophany, a revelation of divine activity. But when a self-absorbed dinner guest is holding forth it may be hard to see him or her as a revelation of the divine. I wish to explore this iteration of the *kōan* of later Neoplatonism and see how Iamblichus's "mystical existentialism" might help us recognize the divinity revealed in self-absorbed dinner guests, even when that guest is us.

## 1      The Cosmos as Theophany

The imaginative frame for all forms of Platonism is outlined in the *Timaeus* of Plato. This Pythagorean description of the generation of the cosmos and its harmonious structure forms the basis for all Platonic metaphysics and psychology. The *Timaeus* describes the cosmos as the manifestation of a divine

---

[1]   In the Zen tradition a *kōan* is a paradox that cannot be solved by reason. It is designed to lead students to an intuitive awareness beyond discursive thought.

impulse, the generosity of the Demiurge that pervades all aspects of existence.[2] The structure of this cosmos is mathematical and exhibits arithmetic and geometric ratios revealed in the heavens and the rhythms of nature.

The Platonic cosmos is a living and breathing Intelligence. It is, as Plato calls it, a "blessed god."[3] It is also a great temple, an "*agalma* of the everlasting gods"[4] through which the generosity of the Demiurge is revealed. Human souls are woven into this temple, with each soul designed to be a participant in its harmony and generosity. We exhibit the same mathematic ratios as are present in the World Soul and, it was believed, through a philosophic life and visionary initiation, we can embody the generosity of the Demiurge even in our mortal lives.

But it was not quite so easy. Plato also explains that human souls undergo a radical trauma in embodiment. The divine ratios we share with the cosmos and the heavens are disturbed by the flood of sensations at birth. Our original geometry and harmony is lost and embodied souls become fundamentally disoriented, a condition that Plato portrays with the image of an upside-down man.[5] The embodied soul becomes *anatropē*, turned inside out and upside down, fundamentally disoriented.[6]

Ralph Waldo Emerson, with a profound grasp of this Platonic vision, says simply: "Man is a god in ruins."[7] The ruins may appear to us in the form of self-absorbed dinner guests, or—more painfully—this desperate self-absorption may be seen in oneself. *Man is a god in ruins*, so it was not easy for Platonists to reorient themselves, to recover their original harmony and cosmic generosity. We work in ruins. We *are* ruins.

Yet there is light in this somber vision. Again, according to Plato's creation story, our existence is rooted in the generosity of the Demiurge. He is imagined as a Divine Mind that orchestrates the powers of the One into a cosmos. His rhythmic weaving of the Forms and Matter in cosmogenesis is analogous, Iamblichus says, to the weaving of the Monad and Dyad in numbers.[8] Thus, the

---

2 Plato, *Tim.* 29e.
3 Plato, *Tim.* 34b.
4 Plato, *Tim.* 37c6.
5 Plato, *Tim.* 43b–e.
6 Plato, *Tim.* 43b–e. The image of the embodied soul as upside-down is also expressed in *Tim.* 90b where the soul is compared to an inverted tree with its roots in heaven. Further, Plato characterizes our inversion as sustained by the way we think, conceptually rather than noetically (see *Tim.*90c–d). The soul is enjoined to align its thinking with the "divine principle in us" seen in the revolutions of the cosmos. On the *anatropē* of the Platonic soul see Bebek 1992, 194.
7 Emerson 2000, 36.
8 Iamblichus, *In Nic.*, 78.22–28 (Pistelli 1994).

numerical ratios, the *logoi* that the Demiurge uses to bring the world and our souls into existence, are rooted in the arithmogonic powers of the One.

In this unfolding, the World Soul and individual souls play a crucial role. In mathematical terms Platonists understand that the soul is a living expression of demiurgic weaving. The soul is defined as the mathematical mean that connects the opposing threads of Monad and Dyad, spirit and matter. So, beneath the apparent dualism of the Forms and Matter is a living continuity initiated by the Demiurge and completed by souls in their role as mediators. According to Iamblichus the soul is "the mean (*meson*) between divisible and indivisible, corporeal and incorporeal beings; it is the totality (*plēroma*) of universal ratios (*logoi*), which, after the Forms, serve the work of creation; it is the Life that proceeds from the Divine Mind (*nous*), has life itself and is the procession of classes of Real Being as a whole to an inferior status."[9]

Following the *Timaeus*, Iamblichus maintains that the human soul, like the World Soul, is a mean between extremes. It contains divinely numbered proportions (*logoi*) and, with the Demiurge, projects these *logoi* outside itself as it becomes embodied.[10] The soul sews itself into the fabric of the material world, yet its collaboration with the Demiurge comes at a cost. Although immortal, the soul becomes mortal and is exiled from the circle of the gods. Iamblichus presents this in stark terms:

> The soul is a mean not only between the undivided and the divided, the remaining and the proceeding, the noetic and the irrational, but also between the uncreated and the created ... *Thus, that which is immortal in the soul is filled completely with mortality and no longer remains only immortal.*[11]

## 2    Plotinian and Iamblichean Metaphysics

This description of the soul may sound unfamiliar because we have long understood Neoplatonism according to the *Enneads* of Plotinus, not according to Iamblichus and the theurgical Platonists. It may be useful, then, to explain

---

9    Iamblichus, *De Anima* 30.19–23 (Finamore and Dillon 2002). Translation modified. This teaching, Iamblichus said, was shared by "Plato, Pythagoras, Aristotle, and all of the Ancients" (Finamore and Dillon 2002, 30.24–27).
10   As the soul descends, Iamblichus says it acquires appropriate bodies from the surrounding universe and creates proper organic forms in accordance with its *logoi*. See Simplicius, *Commentary on Aristotle's Categories* 374.36–375.1 (Gaskin 2000, 110–111).
11   Simplicius, *De Anima* 89.33–37,90.21–23 (Hayduck).

their differences. In almost all respects Iamblichus follows Plotinus's metaphysics: all things are rooted in an inexhaustible source that continually overflows, divides, and reveals itself in the phenomenal world with each creation mysteriously reflecting and revealing the hidden source. We exist in this continual emanation and bear its traces, but Plotinus and Iamblichus disagree on how the soul participates in this activity. For Plotinus, the soul never *fully* descends into a body.[12] As he puts it "there is always something of the soul that remains in the spiritual world."[13] The Plotinian soul does not become embodied; it merely *illuminates* a body.[14] We remain above, he says, with "our heads in heaven" and look down at our body-self as an "inferior companion."[15] Embodiment for Plotinus was almost an embarrassment. As Porphyry put it: "Plotinus, the philosopher, seemed ashamed to be in a body."[16]

Iamblichus's vision of the soul is radically different. He believes that to fulfill its role as cosmogonic mean, the soul *must* descend to animate a body even if this causes us to become mortal, "self-alienated," and estranged from divinity.[17] Individual souls, Iamblichus says, "are confined to a single form and are parceled out among bodies."[18] Plotinus and Iamblichus also differ on another metaphysical issue that is intrinsically related, the status of matter. Although Plotinus says that sensible matter is the last emanation of the One,[19] he nevertheless describes it as "primal and absolute evil" and encourages souls to escape from matter and withdraw to their unfallen essence.[20] Iamblichus acknowledges that our material embodiment is the context for the soul's alienation, but he believes this experience is essential, not only to the soul's creative mediating function, but to its deification as well. Matter, for Iamblichus, cannot be evil. It is the expression of the Divine Dyad. It reveals the powers of

---

12 Plotinus's view of the embodied soul is similar to Christian Docetism, the belief that Christ did not fully descend into human flesh but only "appeared" to be in a body.
13 Plotinus, *Enn.* IV.8.8.2–4 (Armstrong). Plotinus acknowledges that his view contradicts the Platonic tradition and later Platonists did not adopt his position.
14 Plotinus, *Enn.* I.1.12.25–29.
15 Plotinus, *Enn.* IV.3.12; see also *Enn.* 1.2.6.28.
16 Porphyry, *Vit. Plot.* 1 [Armstrong]. *aischunomenō hoti en sōmati eiē*; I should emphasize that this was *Porphyry's* assessment for nowhere does Plotinus express this sentiment explicitly.
17 Simplicius, *In de An.* 223.26 (Hayduck), *allotriōthen*; he also says that according to Iamblichus the embodied soul is also "made other to itself", *heteroiousthai pros heautēn* 223.31 (Hayduck).
18 Iamblichus, *De Anima*, 44.25–25 (Finamore and Dillon]). Cf. *De Myst.* 148.12–14, translated by E. Clarke, J. Dillon, and J. Hershbell 2003; references will follow the Parthey; all my translations of are based on Clarke, Dillon and Hershbell.
19 Plotinus, *Enn.* V.8.7.3.
20 Plotinus, *Enn.* I.8.3.38–40.

the One and facilitates the work of the Demiurge in creation. As recipient and revealer of divine *logoi*, matter is entirely good.[21]

The differences between Plotinus and Iamblichus on the descent of the soul and the status of matter establish two trajectories in Platonism. Following the Plotinian trajectory, since matter is evil, the soul's embodiment is a problem to be overcome by contemplative withdrawal from the world. As Plotinus put it, "we must close our eyes" to sensate reality and call upon "another vision;" we must escape from our bodies and return to our unfallen essence.[22] Although he opposed Gnostics for their dualism and disparagement of the cosmos, dualism remains evident in Plotinus, and since his *Enneads* helped shape Christian spirituality through the Augustinian tradition, this dualism influenced Christianity as well. Christian theologians today who criticize the denial of the body and matter as "anti-incarnational" blame this on Platonic dualism. Yet the leading teachers of the Platonic school from the third to the sixth centuries CE: Iamblichus, Syrianus, Proclus, and Damascius, all rejected Plotinus's doctrines of an unfallen soul and the evilness of matter *precisely* because they were dualist and *not* Platonic.[23]

The French scholar of Neoplatonism, Jean Trouillard, captures the essential difference in these two Platonic trajectories. Plotinus, he says, "returns to the One through a severe negation … He goes to divinity by night."[24] Iamblichus and the theurgical Platonists return by day. The physical world and the body

---

21  Iamblichus, *Comm. Math.*, 15.6–14 (Festa), speaks of the "principle of the Many" (*archē tou plethous*) which allows the One to acquire "being" and says it is like "a completely fluid and pliant matter" (*hugra tini pantapasi eupladei hulē*).
22  Plotinus, *Enn.* 1.6.8.
23  While Plotinus's doctrine of matter as evil remains a topic of significant scholarly debate, the fact is that Iamblichus, Proclus, and the later Platonists disagreed with Plotinus. For Plotinus the value of the cosmos is diminished in proportion to its degree of sensible expression. This is not the case for the theurgical Platonists. Proclus dedicated much of his treatise On the Existence of Evils to the refutation of Plotinus's position on matter. As he argues, if matter is evil it becomes an "alternative principle of beings, dissident from the cause of good things, and there will be 'two sources releasing their flow in opposite directions,' one the source of good things, the other of evil things" (Opsomer and Steel 2003, 84). For Iamblichus and Proclus matter is necessary for the universe; it is produced by the Good, and the Good cannot produce anything evil. "If, then, matter offers itself to be used in the fabrication of the whole world, and has been produced for the sake of being 'the receptacle of generation and, as it were, a wet-nurse' and 'mother' (Tim. 49a–50d), how can it be said to be evil, and even the primary evil?" (Opsomer and Steel, 81). I would suggest the dualism in Christianity is more likely rooted in its apocalyptic origins and belief in "two aeons." The dualist misreading of Plato and the literalizing of Plotinus's metaphors fit well with Christianity's dualist/apocalyptic origins.
24  Trouillard 1965, 23–25.

are affirmed. They become transfigured into symbols that reveal the One. Iamblichus maintained that in theurgic rites material objects can be perceived as activities of the One. Plotinus himself had described this kind of seeing as possessing the "eyes of Lynceus," the Argonaut who saw treasures beneath the earth,[25] yet it was Iamblichus who used these eyes to develop his theurgic school. The soul no longer must escape from matter to unite with the One because the One *is* the material cosmos and is present, Iamblichus says, even in "stones, plants, animals, and human beings."[26] The objects that were obstacles for Plotinus become icons that unite theurgists with divine activity. In the Iamblichean trajectory, the soul descends into a body and a world animated by the World Soul. Yet in its mediation of divine *logoi* the soul loses its global identity, and it becomes identified with a single mortal body. To deny this, as the doctrine of the undescended soul seems to do, would deny to the soul its demiurgic function.

Thus, for Iamblichus, our dividedness, mortality, and even our self-alienation are not errors to be erased by spiritual insight. They are expressions of the One itself orchestrated by the Demiurge and effected through souls. In the Iamblichean trajectory of Platonism, *mortality and self-alienation constitute the soul's very essence as human*—which leads us back to Iamblichus's *kōan*: our immortality is realized precisely by becoming mortal.

## 3 Theurgy, Demiurgy and Daemons

The trajectory of Iamblichean Neoplatonism is as much downward as upward. It does not try to escape from the body and material reality. Its goal, rather, is to bring divinities into the world through souls. As Iamblichus put it, "the purpose of the souls' descent is to reveal the divine life, for the will of the gods is to reveal themselves (*ekphainesthai*) through human souls."[27] The goal of theurgy is

---

25  Plotinus, *Enn.* v.8.4.25–27.
26  Iamblichus, *De Myst.* 233.9–13. It should be noted that in many respects the Iamblichean trajectory of Platonism was simply the extension of Plotinus's own thinking. Plotinus, *Enn.* IV.4.35.68–70, also spoke of the presence of divinity in the "nature of stones and herbs with wondrous results". Iamblichus was simply following Plotinus' lead and theurgy could be seen as extension of this trajectory of Plotinus's Platonism. However, in his effort to explain the problems of the soul Plotinus seems to have adopted the dualist language he disparaged in the Gnostics.
27  Iamblichus, *De Anima* 54.20–26 is citing with approval the view of Calvenus Taurus, a 2nd century Platonist, on the purpose for the soul's descent into a body. The rest of the quotation includes the following: "*For gods come forth into bodily appearance and reveal themselves in the pure and faultless lives of human souls.*" The translation of this passage is

"to establish the soul in the demiurgic god completely,"[28] which is to enter into the divine activity that continually creates the cosmos. The theurgist invites the Demiurge to take its seat in the soul. In Christian terms, it is to transform embodiment into Incarnation. It is not surprising, therefore, that Radical Orthodoxy's leading theologian, John Milbank, understands the significance of the Christian Incarnation through the lens of theurgical Neoplatonism. Iamblichus's emphasis on the penetration of the One throughout all material existence provides the metaphysical framework Milbank needs to support a more profound and expansive understanding of the Incarnation.[29] The crucial difference with Iamblichean theurgy, however, is that the Incarnation for Christians is a unique historical event, the singular paradox of Christ being "truly god and truly man." But for Platonic theurgists this paradox is universal, applicable to *every* human soul and fully realized, Iamblichus says, when the theurgist "takes the shape of the gods" while remaining human and mortal.[30]

Because Iamblichus is fully invested in embodied reality he gives a detailed account of how the soul recovers its continuity with the Demiurge. Consequently, he emphasizes the role of the *ochēma*, the astral body that serves as the vehicle that mediates our immortal and mortal identities. Significantly, Plotinus does not discuss the *ochēma*.[31] Why explore a vehicle that connects soul to body if the soul never truly enters a body? Since Iamblichus's Platonism was non-dual he maintained that a unified continuity extended from the One to the furthest reaches of matter. Because he was compelled to explain how the One proceeds into and returns from materiality he developed the triadic metaphysics of remaining, procession and return (*monē, prohodos and epistrophē*) that was adopted by later Platonists to understand *all* levels of reality.[32]

---

my own but I have consulted the translations by Finamore and Dillon 2002, as well as that by Dillon 1977, 245.

28  Iamblichus, *De Myst.* 292.1213.
29  Milbank and Riches, 2014, v–xvii. See also Milbank 2009, 45–86.
30  Iamblichus, *De Myst.*, 184.1–8.
31  Dillon 2013a, 487: "It is the purpose of this essay to enquire as to why, given that Plotinus was acquainted with the theory [of the soul's *ochēma*], he is not inclined to make any use of it."
32  Dodds 1963, xix–xx: "Not only can we trace to him [Iamblichus] many individual doctrines which have an important place in the later system, but the dialectical principles which throughout control its architecture, the law of means terms, the triadic scheme of *monē, prohodos* and *epistrophē*, and the mirroring at successive levels of identical structures ... appear to have received at his hands their first systematic application"; cf. Iamblichus, *In Tim.* Frag. 53, 331 (Dillon 1973).

Iamblichus also focused on intermediary beings, daemons and heroes that provide continuity between souls and gods.[33] Daemons have the specific function of unfolding divine *logoi* into material manifestation, not only in nature but also in souls. Plato had described daemons as entities that connect humans to gods through the arts of divination;[34] for Iamblichus they play an essential role in creation, including the embodiment of souls. He explains:

> Daemons are the generative and creative powers of the gods in the furthest extremity of their emanations and in its last stages of division.... Daemons finish and complete encosmic natures and exercise oversight on each thing that comes into existence.... They oversee nature and are the bond that unites souls to bodies.[35]

In terms of the metaphysics of *prohodos* and *epistrophē*, daemons exemplify *prohodos*; they reveal the divine procession into the corporeal world. As Iamblichus puts it:

> Daemons bring into manifest activity the invisible good of the Gods ... reveal what is ineffable in them, give form to what is formless, and render what is beyond all measure into visible ratios.[36]
> 
> "Daemons," Iamblichus says, "lead souls down into nature."[37]

Yet, despite being the agents of division and embodiment, daemons themselves are not subject to division. They are, Iamblichus says, "multiplied in unity" and thus remain rooted in the gods.[38] Daemons effect corporealization yet remain incorporeal. It is souls who become corporeal and souls who can become heroic by transforming their embodiment into fully realized theophanies. Heroic souls for Iamblichus exemplify *epistrophē*. They recover their divinity and return to the gods. And here we may begin to unravel the *kōan* of the later Platonists, for souls become heroic and transform embodiment into theophany precisely by cooperating with daemons. Theurgists do not escape

---

33   I note the fortuitous discovery of two fine papers while writing this essay, Layne 2015 and Butler 2014, 23–44. Both authors write with a fine sense of the non-dualism of the later Platonists. Layne in particular effortlessly weaves together the arithmogonic and mythological imagery that shaped later Platonic discourse.
34   Plato, *Symp.* 202e3–203a4.
35   Iamblichus, *De Myst.* 67.1–68.2.
36   Iamblichus, *De Myst.* 16.17–17.4.
37   Iamblichus, *De Myst.* 79.9–10.
38   Iamblichus, *De Myst.* 19.9–10.

the body but invite gods to descend into their bodies. They become organs of divinity, allowing gods to see through mortal eyes.[39]

This reception of the god makes souls into *sunthēmata*, symbols of the divine.[40] They become what the later Platonists called heroes whose *epistrophē* is achieved through their reception of *prohodos*. Theurgists ascend by descending. They remain human yet take the shape of the gods. In a dualist orientation taking the shape of the gods would be considered a *release* from the human condition, but in Iamblichus's Platonism remaining human and mortal is *precisely* how we take the shape of the gods, and this, I would argue, is what it meant to be a theurgist—a mortal human being through whom the god acts—a mortal god.

To achieve this state and experience the simultaneity of *prohodos* and *epistrophē* theurgists had to honor daemons as centrifugal agents of the Demiurge. Yet these same daemons bind souls to bodies. They effect our *anatropē*, our isolated sense of singularity and alienation from the divine. In his *Commentary on the Timaeus*, Iamblichus outlines the metaphysical framework of dividing and uniting, descending and ascending, a framework that produces the cosmos and was realized by theurgists.[41]

After commenting on the creation of souls in the "mixing bowl" (*Tim.* 41d), Iamblichus explains how souls enter their first vehicle (*ochēma*):[42] a universal

---

39  Iamblichus, *De Myst.* 115.4–5: "the god uses our bodies as its organs." Cf. Iamblichus, *De Myst.* 82.1, where he says that when the soul is possessed the noetic light, it *"reveals the incorporeal as corporeal to the eyes of the soul by means of the eyes of the body."*

40  Butler 2014, 37, puts it this way: "The entire body of the hero, in returning this way, has become a *sign* and heroes return because they have become signs: the *sēma* (sign) is the hero's body (*sōma*)." He then notes (37), the play on *sēma* as the tomb/body of the hero which becomes a pilgrimage site: "The *sēma* or tomb stands as the sign of this process in which the mortal has been metabolized into a fossil, a crystal in which a mortal's unique characteristics and the unrepeatable incidents of a mortal's life become *pure return.*" Layne (2) and Butler (30; f.n. 29) both explain that heroes are manifestations of our *erōs* for divinity. They cite Proclus's etymology of *hērōs* from *erōs*. Thus, the soul's *epistrophē* to the One, which is driven by *erōs*, makes the soul into a hero. As Proclus, *In Cratyl.* 71.8–10, puts it: "It is reasonable that heroes should be named after Eros, inasmuch as Eros is a 'great daemon' and the heroes are engendered through the cooperation of daemons;" Duvick 2007, 69–70.

41  The principle for this procession and return is described in arithmetic terms in *In Tim.* Frag. 53, Dillon 160–161; 331–334. Among noetic realities the dividing and uniting of procession and return occurs simultaneously and without disturbance, a condition that Iamblichus describes as *allēlouchia*, "indivisible mutuality" (*In Nicomachi Arithmeticam* 7.10–18). But among human souls *allēlouchia* is experienced "with suffering" (*meta pathous*; *De Myst.* 196.8–10). Theurgy transforms the soul's suffering by uniting it with the divine and universal *allēlouchia*.

42  Iamblichus, *In Tim.* Frags. 84, 85, 196–199 Dillon 1973.

etheric body that shares in creation, including the soul's animation of a body.[43] To animate a body the soul receives "numerous pegs" (*puknoi gomphoi*) that bind it to a single physical body (*Tim.* 43a4). Significantly, Iamblichus equates these "pegs" with the "reason principles of nature" (*hoi phusikoi logoi*), for being bound to the body with "pegs" is an accurate description of what happens to the soul in its bestowal of divine *logoi* into the world.[44]

In his *Commentary on the Sophist* Iamblichus says that souls are led into bodies by the Sublunary Demiurge, a sorcerer (*goēs*) who beguiles them with *phusikoi logoi* into the material world.[45] In theurgy, these *logoi*, discovered in nature and in one's natural habits, are ritually re-aligned with the eternal measures (*metra aidia*) of *prohodos*.[46] This allows theurgists to become united in mind (*homonoētikos*) with the Demiurge, which is their goal.[47] At this moment—united with the Demiurge—the soul re-enters its original *ochēma*.

This culmination of theurgy, the ascent to divine status and the recovery of one's luminous vehicle (*augoeides ochēma*), is experienced, Iamblichus says, as the soul's *first* birth (*protē genesis*).[48] In theurgy, therefore, the soul ascends to the gods by descending with them, *by descending as them*. *Epistrophē* is realized as *prohodos*. This apparent contradiction, Iamblichus explains, is the veil of a mystery:

> It is the case that from their first descent the Demiurge sent down souls for this purpose that they would return to him. There is no change of divine will in this ascent, nor is there any conflict between the descents

---

43  Iamblichus, *In Tim.* Frag. 84.4–5, 196–199 Dillon 1973.
44  Iamblichus, *In Tim.* Frag. 86.4–6, 198–199 Dillon 1973.
45  Iamblichus, *In Sophist.*, Frag. 1.9–11, 90–91. Dillon 2013b, 8–9 explains: "Basically, he [Iamblichus] sees the dialogue as portraying the activities of a trickster figure, who has woven a web of illusion in this realm, analogous to the Hindu concept of *maya*. He is 'a sorcerer, inasmuch as he charms the souls (on their descent into embodiment) with natural reason-principles (*physikoi logoi*), so that they it may be difficult for them to separate themselves from the realm of generation.' The Sophist is not, however, an evil being, as I understand the situation, but merely an entity set to test us, enabling those who can see through his blandishments to attain a higher state of consciousness, and realise the illusory nature of the physical world; he is thus an educational force."
46  Iamblichus refers to these *metra aidia* as having both cosmogonic and hieratic significance (*De Myst.*, 65.5–6). This is because the theurgist, as conduit for the activity of the Demiurge and gods of creation, experiences the culmination of hieratic worship as the exercise of demiurgy.
47  This state is the shared condition of the intermediary powers of cosmos, expressing the will of the Demiurge (*De Myst.* 23.1–6). It is also the condition of blessed souls united with the gods, Finamore and Dillon 2002, 70.21–22. Cf. *De Myst.* 292.12–13.
48  Iamblichus, *In Tim.* Frag. 85.3, 198–199 Dillon 1973.

and the ascents of souls. For just as the physical cosmos and realm of generation are, at the universal level, dependent on noetic reality, so also in the sphere of souls, their liberation from the physical world is in harmony with the care that they bestow upon it.[49]

While this outlines the metaphysical background of the soul's itinerary, we are still faced with the question: How is *anatropē* experienced? How is it that the soul experiences itself in a singular and mortal identity? I would suggest that the *centrifugal* activity of daemons on the macrocosmic level—binding each soul to a body—is complemented by the soul's reciprocal *contraction*. The simultaneity of demiurgic expansion—effected by daemons—and our psychological contraction are, in effect, one and the same activity as seen from universal and individual perspectives respectively. But it is the soul's contraction that is the specific cause of *anatropē*.[50] Plotinus spoke of it when he describes the embodied soul as feeling "battered by the totality of things in every way,"[51] and in response each of us *defends* our individual awareness. Each of us creates a "fortress of the self."[52] And once identified with the body-self, we become subject to the gods and daemons who, Iamblichus says, oversee the inevitable "divisions ... changes, growth and decay of all material bodies" including our own.[53] It is no wonder that the singular self, faced with such decay, would desire to reach the safe haven of immortality. Yet our very impulse to escape decay is an expression of the daemonic impulse to preserve the materialized self.

Theurgists, however, recognize that what is immortal in the soul needs no defense and needs no safe haven. What is immortal in the soul works with the daemons that bind souls to bodies. As Iamblichus had said, "there is no conflict between the descents and ascents of souls." Yet prior to realigning itself

---

49   Iamblichus, *De Myst.* 272.4–11.
50   "The self-contraction ... which 'creates' the fearful sense of separate mind" is described as "the unconscious logic of Narcissus" by the 20th century spiritual adept, Adi-Da Samraj 2004, 8; 96. To dissolve this self-contraction and the logic of Narcissus was the focus of his teaching.
51   Plotinus, *Enn.* IV.8.4.18.
52   I borrow this term from Carlos Castaneda 1998, 98, who refers to the "fortress of the self" as the mental and emotional condition that pre-occupies human beings and makes us incapable of becoming sorcerers; Castaneda also refers to this state as "the dominion of self-reflection" (210) which is analogous to Adi Da's "logic of Narcissus," *supra*, f.n. 51.
53   According to Iamblichus, these phenomena are under the jurisdiction of material gods (*De Myst.* 217.14–218.9). Without honoring the gods and daemons of the material realm "the ascent to the immaterial gods will not take place" (*De Myst.* 217.8–11).

with the eternal measures (*metra aidia*) of *prohodos*,[54] the soul experiences the daemon as similar to the demon/devil of Christian dualism: it alienates us from our divine totality; it fixes us in embodied mortality; it causes us to suffer and to die.

So what happens to the divinity of the soul after embodiment and how is it recovered? According to the *Chaldean Oracles* the Demiurge implants in each soul a deep *erōs* to return to our lost totality.[55] But this desire for totality, when directed by our "fortress self," becomes monstrous and self-delusional. The Platonists had a striking example of this in Alcibiades. Proclus explains that Alcibiades's desire to fill the world with his name is a perversion of our desire for totality and a misunderstanding of "the divine power which has entered into all men." Proclus says:

> The desire "to fill all mankind with one's name" bears a surprising resemblance to this. For the ineffable names (*arrheta onomata*) of the gods have filled the whole world, as the theurgists say....[56] The gods, then, have filled the world both with themselves and their own names, and, having contemplated these before their birth, and yearning to resemble the gods, *but not knowing the way (tropon) to achieve this*, souls become lovers of command and long for the mere representations of those realities and to fill the whole race of men with their name and power. The aspirations of such souls are grand and admirable but when put into practice they become petty (*smikra*), ignoble (*agennē*) and vaporous (*eidōlika*), because they are pursued without insight (*epistemē*).[57]

The later Platonists were acutely aware of what the contemporary Buddhist teacher, Chögyam Trungpa, called spiritual materialism—the ego's effort to acquire the spiritual credentials of enlightenment.[58] Alcibiades's grotesque desire to fill the world with his name was—as Proclus says—petty and vaporous, but his narcissism is not unique.[59] Platonists believed that all human beings are subject to this condition and refer to the Orphic myth of Dionysus and the Titans to understand why, like Alcibiades, we try to fill the world

---

54   Iamblichus, *De Myst.* 65.4–5.
55   *Orac. chald.* Frag. 43 (Majercik 1989).
56   Proclus refers to the *Orac. chald.* Frag. 108 that states: "For the Paternal Nous has sown symbols throughout the cosmos." see Majercik 1989.
57   Proclus, *In Alc.* 150.4–23 (Westerink and O'Neill), translation modified.
58   Trungpa 1973.
59   Proclus, *In Alc.* 150.20 (Westerink and O'Neill).

with our individual "names" rather than discover the *ineffable names already present in our souls.*

In the myth of Dionysus they saw the human condition dramatically portrayed. The elements of the myth are as follows: Zeus fathers a child, Dionysus/Zagreus, from Persephone and plans to make him the Lord of the physical cosmos. Hera is jealous and conspires with the Titans to have Dionysus killed. She gives him toys, a spinning top and a mirror, to distract him. While the child wanders off *gazing into the mirror,* the Titans seize him, tear him in pieces (in some versions "seven" pieces),[60] roast him in a fire and then devour all but his heart, which is somehow preserved still beating by Athena. Zeus is attracted to the aroma until he realizes what has happened and incinerates the Titans with a thunderbolt. From their ashes human beings are born, a mix of the devouring hunger of the Titans with the divine nobility of Dionysus. Human beings are both. Our psychology is dual. We are divine *and* we are titanic.[61]

Explaining this myth in terms of the soul's embodied itinerary, Damascius says:

> The soul must constitute an image of herself in the body (that is what animating the body means); secondly, she must be in sympathy with her image because of its likeness, since every form is drawn towards its replica as a result of its innate concentration on its likeness [i.e., Dionysius gazing at his *mirror image*]; thirdly, having entered the divided body, she must be torn asunder with it and end in complete disintegration until, through a life of purification, she gathers herself from her dispersed state, loosens the bonds of sympathy, and actualizes the primal life that exists within her....[62]

---

60   Proclus, *In Tim.* III.2 146.11–17, referring to the Orphic myth, says: "'They divided up all seven parts of the body' says the Theologist concerning the Titans, just as Timaeus divides the soul into seven portions (36d). Perhaps the fact that the soul is stretched through all the cosmos is meant to remind the Orphics of the Titanic dividing of parts because, not only does the soul envelop the universe, it is also stretched through all of it (34b)" Baltzly 2009, 109. As is evident, the Platonists read the myth of Dionysus and the Titans as an allegory of the soul sharing in the demiurgy of the sublunary world.

61   The basic elements of this myth can be found in Olympiodorus, *In Phaed.*, 1.3 Westerink 1979; 2009.

62   Damascius, *In Phaed.* 128.1–8 Westerink. Immediately following this, Damascius (129.1–4) explains how the soul's descent into a body is effected by the mirror of Dionysus and how souls (= Dionysus) recover their divinity: "The myth describes the same events as taking place in the prototype of the soul. When Dionysus projected his reflection into the mirror, he followed it and was thus scattered over the universe. *Apollo gathers him and brings him back to heaven,* for he is the purifying God and savior of Dionysus."

Damascius interprets the soul's identification with the "fortress of the self" by relating it to the myth of Dionysus. He says:

> The impulse to belong to oneself alone ... comes from the Titans; through this impulse we tear apart the Dionysus in ourselves and break up the continuity that ties the world above with the world below. In this divided condition we are Titans; *but when we recover our lost unity, we become Dionysus and attain perfect completeness.*[63]

## Summary

For the later Platonists the solution to our existential problem is to find the right way to express our desire for totality. It requires giving eyes to the daemons in their processional expansion and aligning our reciprocating *contraction* with the *metra aidia* of demiurgic creativity.[64] To find these limits requires a profound catharsis of the soul's embodied life, but this results, Iamblichus says, not in escaping from the world but in sharing its creation, "joining parts to wholes and bestowing power, life, and activity from the wholes to the parts."[65] In sum, the purified theurgic soul becomes an embodied Demiurge working not against but with the processional daemons. The mythical image for embodied demiurgy is Dionysus,[66] the god who undergoes division *and* reunification, and insofar as the soul is demiurgic it becomes Dionysus.

According to Iamblichus, the human soul is radically paradoxical. Like the sublunary Demiurge of the *Sophist* the soul, "embraces the falsity of matter yet fixes his gaze on reality."[67] As Iamblichus explains: "The soul remains in

---

63    Damascius, *In Phaed.* 9.3–8 (Westerink).
64    Iamblichus, *De Myst.* 249.11–250.4, says theurgic rites mirror the "demiurgic energy of the gods" and reveal the "invisible measures" through "visible images;" he, *De Myst.* 65.5–6, describes these invisible measures of demiurgy as the eternal measures (*metra aidia*) engaged in theurgic ritual.
65    Iamblichus, *De Anima* 70.1–5 (Finamore and Dillon) (my translation).
66    Damascius, *In Phaed.* 1.3 (Westerink), says that Dionysus rules over the "divided demiurgy" while Zeus rules over the "undivided demiurgy." Dionysus is also said to be the "cause of *individual* life (*merikē zoē*)" (10.2–3). For Olympiodorus, he is lord of the sublunary world: "Dionysus is ruler of this lower world, where extreme division prevails because of 'mine' and 'thine'" (Olympiodorus, *In Phaed.* 10.1–2; Westerink 1976). According to John Lydus (Dillon 1973, 246) the sublunary demiurge is identified by Iamblichus with *Ploutōn* / Hades, who is later transformed by Christians into the Devil.
67    Iamblichus, *In Sophist.* Frag. 1.6–7, 90–91 (Dillon 1973), modified translation.

itself and *simultaneously* (*hama*) proceeds out of itself[68].... It is *simultaneously* born and unborn, immortal and mortal, unified and divided."[69] This is a diminished view of the soul as compared to Plotinus who sees the soul as unfallen, but Plotinus elevates the soul at the cost of accepting the reality of embodiment. Iamblichus, on the other hand, accepts the reality of the embodied self. Yet the fall into division can never be total or the soul would completely dissolve.[70] The soul is simultaneously fallen *and* unfallen and the key, for Iamblichus, is to find ways to recover the soul's unfallen aspect even in its fragmentary experience. For theurgists the soul's divinity is found in the ruins of our embodied life.

This principle is a reflection of the paradox of Unity itself. The oppositions of the human soul express—at its level of reality—the oppositions of the One. Iamblichus maintained that the power of the One pervades all things undividedly and thus establishes the *continuity* of all existence, yet since the One defines each existence as "one" it also establishes *discontinuity*: "its power *simultaneously* remains and proceeds (*hama kai menei kai proeisin*)."[71] The power of the One, Iamblichus says, is the source of both continuity *and* discontinuity for it makes each entity "stand" as separate and yet *simultaneously* "flows" through all things to make a continuous whole.[72] This paradox of the One is the legacy of the Platonic *Parmenides* where the "one" simultaneously is *and* is not. And the One that "is"—in the argument of the *Parmenides*—must be *all* things: the One that *is*, is not "one," but many.[73] Reflecting this mystery, the embodiment of the soul and even the foolish excesses of our personal lives are revealed to be the way that each soul uniquely participates in the One. As Damascius puts it: "The soul possesses its unchanging essence *precisely* by changing it."[74] So, it is not by identifying with an undefiled "unity" that we recover our divinity, not by trying to find the "One" above the many—because there *is no such "one."*

The desire to grasp an unsullied unity is recognized by later Platonists as a delusion. It is the Titanic impulse to grasp and devour divinity. Rather, the way (*tropos*) for Platonists to "resemble the gods" is to enter Unity as *process*, as activity, as the *prohodos* flowing into the diversity of the world and the

---

68   Iamblichus quoted by Simplicius, *De Anima* 6.14.
69   Iamblichus quoted by Simplicius, *De Anima* 90.20–24.
70   Steel 1978, 65, on this point and for his articulation of Iamblichus's critique of Plotinus.
71   Simplicius, *In Cat.*, 135.24 (Kalbfleisch 1907); my translation. See discussion of this passage in Steel 1978, 65.
72   Steel 1978, 65.
73   Plato, *Parm.* 141e–143a.
74   Damascius, *In Parm.*, IV, 30.27–31.1–3 (Combès and Westerink); cf. Steel 1978, 110.

tortured drama of our lives. For theurgists, ultimately, *we* are the Demiurge turned inside out: *Demon est Deus Inversus*. We are the demonized and inverted divinity, god particularized and made mortal. We recover the god not by rejecting our particularity and mortality (effected by daemons) but by tracing the daemonic path from the Source. We become theophanic not by going up but by going down demiurgically, which is to say by becoming theurgic.

So, let us return to the dinner guest sitting across from you, gobbling up all the attention and expanding the boundaries of her fortress self. She is simply manifesting the blind activity of daemons (or Titans) that have not yet been recognized, honored, and given their limits. They mirror and remind us of our own self-alienation and desire to fill the world with our names. According to the Platonists, souls who have not yet become heroic companions of the gods are *blindly* demiurgic and enslaved to daemons that preserve their creations. In Orphic terms these souls are Titanic and—until we become Dionysus—we are all Titans.

I cannot help but think that the magicians and poets at the beginning of the twentieth century understood these matters better than we do. It is revealing that when W. B. Yeats was initiated to the Order of the Golden Dawn he took as his magical name *Demon est Deus Inversus*: A Demon is God Inverted,[75] for this was, as I have argued, the experience of later Platonists with respect to the manifesting daemons and their embodiment. In the magical practices of Yeats and in the theurgy of the later Platonists, the daemon that alienates us from the god is the vehicle through which we become the god.

---

75  Ellman 1948, 99. Yeats surely borrowed this phrase from his former teacher, Helena Blavatsky, the oft-maligned founder of the Theosophical Society. In her immensely influential treatise, *The Secret Doctrine*, Blavatsky has an entire chapter entitled "*Demon est Deus Inversus*," in which she contrasts the non-dualism of the ancient Greeks and Hindus with the dualism of Christianity. Espousing what seems to be a later Platonic understanding of the mystery of the Demiurge, Blavatsky 1964; 1888, I, 411–424, speaks of "the reflection of the first in the dark waters, showing the black reflection of the white light...." In the language of the Neoplatonists, *Demon est Deus Inversus*, points to the sublunary demiurge, Dionysus-Hades, as the inverted reflection of the super-celestial demiurge, Zeus. In the esoteric psychology of the Platonists these *demiurgoi* represent levels of *psychic* reality. According to Olympiodorus, *In Phaed.* (Westerink), 4.8–10 "these ... kingdoms of the Orphic tradition are not sometimes existent and sometimes non-existent, but they are *always* there and represent in mystical language the several degrees of virtues that our soul can practice."

## Bibliography

Armstrong, Arthur H. 1966–1988 *Plotinus Enneads*. Translation and commentary. Vols. I–VI. Cambridge: Harvard University Press.

Baltzly, Dirk. 2009. *Proclus Commentary on Plato's Timaeus*. Volume IV: Book 3 Part II: *Proclus on the World Soul*. Cambridge: Cambridge University Press.

Bebek, Borna. 1992. *The Third City*. London: Routledge & Kegan Paul.

Blavatsky, Helena P. 1964; 1988. *The Secret Doctrine* Vols. I and II. Los Angeles CA: The Theosophy Company.

Butler, Edward. 2014. "Time and the Heroes." Pages 23–44 in *Walking the Worlds: A Biannual Journal of Polytheism and Spiritwork*. Winter.

Castaneda, Carlos. 1998. *The Active Side of Infinity*. San Francisco: Harper Perennial.

Clarke, Emma C., Dillon, John M. and Hershbell, Jackson P. 2003. *Iamblichus. On the Mysteries*. Translation, introduction and notes. Atlanta: Society of Biblical Literature.

Combès, Joseph and Westerink, Leendert G. 2003. *Damascius Commentaire du Parmenide de Platon*. Vol. IV. Text and translation. Paris: Les Belles Lettres.

De Haas, Frans A. J. and Fleet, Barrie. 2001. *Simplicius On Aristotle's Categories 5–6*. Translation. Ithaca: Cornell University Press.

Dillon, John M. 1973. *Iamblichus Chalcidensis. In Platonis Dialogos Commentariorum Fragmenta*. Translation. and commentary. Leiden: Brill.

Dillon, John M. 1987. "Iamblichus of Chalcis," *Aufsteig und Niedergang der Römischen Welt*. Part II, 36.2 New York: de Gruyter.

Dillon, John M. 2013a. "Plotinus and the Vehicle of the Soul." Pages 485–496 in *Gnosticism, Platonism, and the Late Antique World: Essays in Honour of John D. Turner*. Editors K. Corrigan and Tuomas Rasimus. Leiden: Brill.

Dillon, John M. 2013b. "*Paidea Platonikē*: Does the Later Platonist Programme of Education Retain any Validity Today?" Hvar, Croatia. www.academia.edu/5117137/Paideia_Platonik%C3%A9_Does_the_Late_Platonist_Course_of_Education_Retain_any_Validity_Today.

Dodds, Eric R. 1963. *Proclus: The Elements of Theology*. Text with translation, introduction and commentary. Oxford: Clarendon Press.

Duvick, Brian. 2007. *Proclus On Plato's Cratylus*. Translation. Ithaca: Cornell University Press.

Ellman, Richard. 1948. *Yeats: The Man and the Masks*. New York: W.W. Norton & Company.

Emerson, Ralph Waldo. 2000. *The Essential Writings of Ralph Waldo Emerson*, edited by Brooks Atkinson. New York: Modern Library.

Festa, Nicola. 1891; 1975. *Iamblichus. De Communi Mathematica Scientia* additions and corrections by U. Klein, Stuttgart: Teubner.

Finamore, John and Dillon, John M. 2002. *Iamblichus: De anima*. Text, translation and commentary. Leiden: Brill.

Gaskin, Richard. 2000. *Simplicius On Aristotle's Categories 9–15*. Translation. Ithaca: Cornell University Press.

Hayduck, Michael. 1882. *Simplicius = Priscianus. De Anima [DA]*, ed. Berlin: B. Reimeri.

Kalbleisch, C. 1907. *Simplicius In Aristotelis Categorias Commentarium*. Berlin: G. Reimeri.

Layne, Danielle. 2014. "The Platonic Hero (Work in Progress)." unpublished https://www.academia.edu/10059821/The_Platonic_Hero_Work_in_Progress_

Majercik, Ruth. 1989. *Chaldean Oracles*. Text, translation and commentary. Leiden: Brill Publishing.

Milbank, John. 2009. "Sophiology and Theurgy: The New Theological Horizon." Pages 45–85 in *Encounter Between Eastern Orthodox and Radical Orthodoxy: Transfiguring the World Through the Word*. Edited by Adrian Pabst and Christoph Schneider. Farnham, UK: Ashgate.

Milbank, John and Riches, Aaron. 2014. "Neoplatonic Theurgy and Christian Incarnation." Pages v–xvi in Greg Shaw, *Theurgy and the Soul: the Neoplatonism of Iamblichus*. 2nd edition, Kettering, OH: Angelico Press.

Opsomer, Jan and Steel, Carlos. 2003. *Proclus: On the Existence of Evils*. Translation. Ithaca, NY: Cornell University Press.

Pistelli, Hermenegildus. 1894; 1975. *Iamblichus. In Nicomachi Arithmeticam Introductionem*. Stuttgart: Tuebner.

Pistelli, Hermangildus. 1994; 1975. *Iamblichus. In Nicomachi Arithmeticam Introductionem* Liber additions and corrections by U. Klein, Stuttgart: Teubner.Samraj, Adi Da. 2004; 1972. *The Knee of Listening*. Middletown, CA: Dawn Horse Press.

Shaw, Gregory. 2014; 1995. *Theurgy and the Soul: The Neoplatonism of Iamblichus*. Kettering, OH: Angelico Press.

Steel, Carlos. 1978. *The Changing Self: A Study on the Soul in Later Neoplatonism: Iamblichus, Damascius, and Priscianus*, tr. by E. Haasl, Brussels: Paleis der Academien.

Trouillard, Jean. 1965. *Proclos: Éléments de Théologie*. Paris: Aubier.

Trungpa, Chögyam. 1973. *Cutting Through Spiritual Materialism*. Berkeley: Shambhala.

Westerink, Leenedert G. and O'Neill, William. 2011; 1965. *Proclus Commentary on the First Alcibiades*. Text, translation and commentary. Dilton Marsh: The Prometheus Trust.

Westerink, Leenedert G. 2009; 1976. *Olympiodorus Commentary on Plato's Phaedo*. Text and translation. Dilton Marsh: The Prometheus Trust.

Westerink, Leenedert G. 2009; 1977. *Damascius Commentary on Plato's Phaedo*. Text and translation. Dilton Marsh: The Prometheus Trust.

# PART 2

*Modernity*

∴

# The Coming of the Star-Child: The Reception of the Revelation of the Magi in New Age Religious Thought and Ufology

*Brent Landau*
University of Texas at Austin
bclandau@utexas.edu

In the study of ancient Christian apocryphal writings, one aspect that continues to be particularly neglected is their reception history.[1] That is, how did readers a hundred, five hundred, or more years after a given text was written make sense of it? In a number of prominent cases, the afterlives of apocryphal texts have been amazingly rich, with texts finding their way into art, doctrine, music, and so forth—even while being excluded from the biblical canon.

One apocryphal Christian text that I have researched for more than a decade has had this kind of rich afterlife. Called the Revelation of the Magi, it purports to be the personal testimony of the Magi—perhaps better known as the Three Wise Men or the Three Kings from the Christmas story—on their experience of Christ's coming. It was a particularly important text in medieval and renaissance Europe. A summary of its narrative was preserved in a Latin commentary on the Gospel of Matthew, which was then utilized by Jacob of Voragine's *Legenda Aurea*, or *Golden Legend*. Its inclusion in this highly influential compendium of legends about biblical figures and saints facilitated its introduction into broader European culture. Thomas Aquinas mentions it in his *Summa*, a number of artistic representations of its narrative exist, and it even was cited by several explorers of the Americas, who thought that the peoples they encountered might have been the descendants of these Magi.[2]

Quite an impressive resume for an apocryphal text, especially one that, until approximately five years ago, was virtually unknown by specialists in apocryphal Christian literature and had never before been translated into English. But despite this rich reception in medieval Europe, I want instead to focus on

---

1 One significant exception is L. Roig Lanzillotta's 2007 study of the Apocryphal Acts of Andrew, which analyzes the text's transmission from the perspective of reception history. See also Jenkins 2015, which studies the afterlives of apocryphal gospels. Reception history studies of individual apocryphal writings remain very uncommon nevertheless.
2 See *Summa Theologica*, Question 36, Article 5. Artistic representations of the Revelation of the Magi can be found in Landau 2010. For discussion of the Revelation of the Magi's influence on early explorers of the Americas, see Trexler 1997.

its reception in the five years since I have published my English translation of it; its reception not in traditional academic circles (though it is slowly entering more discussions in the field of Christian Apocrypha[3]) but rather among New Age religious thinkers and among ufologists—that is, people who investigate unidentified flying objects or UFOs. It is worth pointing out that there is frequently some overlap between these two categories, and the most significant reception of the Revelation of the Magi I examine is representative of this overlap.

Why has the Revelation of the Magi attracted interest from such groups? To be sure, there is a general receptiveness to discoveries of new apocryphal writings, which are often presented by the media and/or read by these groups as offering a countercultural narrative of Christian origins.[4] But the salience of the Revelation of the Magi in particular for these groups is primarily because of two key features of its narrative. First, for the Revelation of the Magi it is not the case that the Magi's star helps them to find the Christ child. Instead, the Star of Bethlehem and Christ are the same entity. When the Magi's guiding star appears, it descends from the sky and transforms into a small, luminous humanoid figure who is none other than Christ himself. Second, this shape-shifting Christ tells the Magi that this is by no means the first time that he has appeared in the world, but that, in fact, he is actually the underpinning of all of humanity's religious revelations. Thus, the Revelation of the Magi presents us with a sentient ball of light who can take the form of a little humanoid and who tells his witnesses that he has appeared to many other individuals throughout human history. Such a presentation coheres extremely well with the perennialist interpretation of religious/mystical experience found in many New Age traditions, as well as with the sorts of entities reported in ufological literature (including the so-called "ancient astronaut" theory). As April DeConick observes elsewhere in this journal, this indicates an impressive level of similarity between the questions and approaches of ancient mystical texts like the Revelation of the Magi and New Age religious thought: "Put simply, I think it is valuable to view the gnostic and our modern descriptor gnosticism as identifying its own unique form of spirituality, one that emerged when some ancient religious seekers attempted to make meaning of their experiences of the world in a radically pluralistic environment much like ours today. When I try to imagine what this looked like on the ground, I consider modern New Agers as a

---

3   For a selection, see Reed 2009; Kaestli 2011; Touati and Clivaz 2015; Hannah 2015.
4   I have argued elsewhere that this typical approach to new discoveries of ancient Christian texts is due, at least in part, to the claims about such texts that have been made by the "Harvard School" of Christian Apocrypha studies. See Landau 2015.

parallel. These are religious seekers who, like the ancient gnostics, claim multiple religious affiliations, while questing for the God beyond convention."[5]

Before we discuss the specifics of this reception in more detail, some basic information about the text is warranted. In my previous publications on the Revelation of the Magi, I have devoted significant attention simply to clarifying basic questions about the text: what are the witnesses to it; when and where was it written; did the text suffer any interpolations; and so forth. While focusing on such fundamental issues has been helpful, given how poorly known this text is, in this article I will move through these basic considerations more succinctly so that I can concentrate on the specific issue of the Revelation of the Magi's representation of Jesus as a star-child and its recent religio-spiritual interpretation.

There are at least two sources I would mention briefly for those seeking further information about the text. First, my 2008 dissertation is available in PDF format on my academia.edu page,[6] which is currently being revised for publication in Brepols's *Corpus Christianorum Series Apocryphorum*, a series of critical editions of apocryphal Christian writings.[7] Second, in 2010 I published with HarperCollins an English translation of the Revelation of the Magi, with an introduction and conclusion designed for a general audience.[8] Although this book is not directly primarily at a scholarly audience, scholars will certainly benefit from the detailed notes to my translation, and from the annotated bibliography that provides information about the previous scholarly work that had been done on the Revelation of the Magi. As pertains to the subject matter of this article, it is almost entirely due to this book's publication by a major trade press and the publicity resulting therefrom that it became known by New Age enthusiasts. Put differently, I have been responsible almost singlehandedly (the publicity wing of HarperCollins notwithstanding) for this text's introduction into New Age religious communities. That is an odd position for a scholar; unfortunately, the implications of a scholar's research impacting contemporary religious groups is a question that cannot be addressed in this paper.

---

5 DeConick 2016.
6 Accessible at http://www.academia.edu/207910/The_Sages_and_the_Star-Child_An_Intro duction_to_the_Revelation_of_the_Magi_An_Ancient_Christian_Apocryphon.
7 See Bovon 2012 for an overview of this valuable series.
8 See Landau 2010. Apart from my dissertation and book, see Landau 2016 for a summary of the Revelation of the Magi's narrative and an overview of the main scholarly issues concerning it.

1    The Narrative of the Revelation of the Magi and its Ancient
     Christian Context

The Revelation of the Magi is by far the longest apocryphal writing devoted to the Magi, and almost the entire narrative is told from the perspective of the Magi themselves. Since its narrative is quite complex, I will first summarize it and then discuss my main scholarly arguments about the text. In the Revelation of the Magi, the Magi are descendants of Adam's son Seth, who live in the far-eastern land of Shir, a semi-mythical place that seems to have been roughly equivalent to China, based on comments about the land in other Greek, Latin, and Syriac authors (2:4–6).[9] They are called "Magi" in the language of their country because they pray in silence, an intriguing but puzzling etymology (1:2; 2:1).[10] The Magi have been entrusted with the guardianship of Seth's books of revelation, the first books written in the history of the world. In these books is found a prophecy of a coming star that will signal the birth of God in human form (4:1–10). The Magi have waited for the fulfillment of this prophecy for thousands of years, passing down the prophecy from generation to generation. In anticipation of the coming star, every month the Magi gather at their country's most sacred mountain, called the "Mountain of Victories." They immerse themselves in a spring at the mountain's foothills, and ascend over a period of several days to the summit of the mountain. They pray in silence, and then finally enter a cave atop the mountain's summit, the "Cave of Treasures of Hidden Mysteries," in which Seth's books of revelation are housed. Thus the Magi do throughout the years, throughout the generations (5:1–11).

At last, the star appears in the sky, so bright that the sun seems as faint as the daytime moon (11:5–7); yet it can only be seen by the Magi themselves and no one else. It descends to the Magi, enters their cave, and the impossibly bright light concentrates itself into "a small and humble human being" (13:1). This being, whom the text makes clear is Christ despite never actually naming him

---

9    See Reinink 1975.
10   The text of Revelation of the Magi 1:2 reads: "… who were called Magi (*mgoše'*) in the language of that land because in silence (*šelya'*), without a sound, they glorified (*mšabhin*) and they prayed (*mtsaleyn*)." As is evident, the Syriac word for "Magi" does not have a strong resemblance to the terms for "silence" or "pray." Nor does a wordplay between Magi (*magos*), silence (*sigē*), and pray (*proseuchomai*) seem to be plausible in Greek. It may be that a wordplay exists in another, less obvious language, but it is also possible that this is a fictitious etymology created by the author to develop the Magi as characters. Yet even in that case it is in no way obvious why the Magi would be linked with the practice of silent prayer, since Matt 2:1–12 never hints that the Magi practice this. In connection with this, it may be relevant that silent prayer was relatively uncommon in the ancient world, and was frequently viewed with suspicion. See Van der Horst 1994.

as such, tells the Magi to follow him to Bethlehem to witness his birth. This long and strenuous journey is accomplished in an impossibly short period of time, wherein the star's light relieves the Magi of their fatigue and causes the food brought by the Magi to multiply (16:1–7). At Bethlehem, the Magi witness their star transform into a luminous, talking infant, who commissions them to return to the land of Shir to proclaim his Gospel to their fellow countryfolk (18:1–21:12).

When the Magi return to their land under the guidance of their star, the people of Shir gather together to hear about their journey. The Magi's provisions of food are now overflowing from the power of the star, and they invite the people to eat of them. As soon as they do, the people of Shir immediately start seeing visions of the heavenly and earthly Jesus, and convert gladly to the faith that the Magi proclaim (27:1–28:6). Finally, presumably after many years have passed, the Apostle Judas Thomas arrives in the Magi's homeland and after being told of the revelation of Christ that they experienced, he baptizes them and commissions them to preach throughout the entire world (29:1–32:4).

The Revelation of the Magi is preserved in a single Syriac manuscript (Vaticanus Siriacus 162), housed today in the Vatican Library but copied at a monastery in southeastern Turkey at the end of the eighth century. In this manuscript, it has been incorporated into a world-chronicle, a history of the world supplemented by a number of previously independent literary documents, the Revelation of the Magi being among them; this manuscript and the world-chronicle it contains is known as the *Chronicle of Zuqnin* (or, less accurately, as the *Chronicle of Pseudo-Dionysius of Tell-Mahre*).[11] Since we can compare the texts of some of the *Chronicle*'s documents with other extant versions, it is probable that the compiler of the *Chronicle* has incorporated the Revelation of the Magi with few, if any, changes.[12]

In my dissertation, I expressed uncertainty about whether the original language of the Revelation of the Magi was Syriac or Greek, even though the text is only extant in Syriac. A number of early Syriac Christian texts (the Acts of Thomas, the Diatessaron, and the Odes of Solomon) are extant in both Greek and Syriac, and the summary of the text found in a Latin commentary on the Gospel of Matthew was most likely derived from a Greek form of the text housed in Constantinople.[13] In more recent publications, I have argued more

---

11   At present, the two scholarly editions of the *Chronicle of Zuqnin* are Tullberg 1850 and Chabot 1927. My forthcoming CCSA edition will also print the Syriac text, with improvements over previous editions that have been facilitated by the use of high-resolution digital photographs of the manuscript taken under ultraviolet light.
12   See Witakowski 1987, 124–136.
13   See Witakowski, 2008, 813.

strongly that Syriac is its original language.[14] While a number of arguments can be marshaled in favor of a Syriac original, the most persuasive of these include the presence of the Apostle Judas Thomas (a foundational figure for early Syriac-speaking Christianity) and several plays on words that make sense only in Syriac. However, L. Roig Lanzillotta has recently called into question the thesis that the Acts of Thomas was originally written in Syriac, holding that many of the arguments for a Syriac original are rather weak.[15] If the Syriac identity of the Acts of Thomas—one of the texts regarded as the most characteristic of Syriac Christianity—is in doubt, then the question of the Revelation of the Magi's original language will need to be examined more thoroughly.

Only the *Chronicle of Zuqnin* preserves the full form of the text; however, the aforementioned Latin commentary on Matt from the fifth century, known as the *Opus Imperfectum in Matthaeum*, summarizes its narrative.[16] The summary contained in the *Opus Imperfectum* proved to be far more influential for the reception history of the Revelation of the Magi than did the full Syriac text, since it was through the *Opus Imperfectum* that this story about the Magi found its way into the *Golden Legend* of Jacob of Voragine, a thirteenth-century compendium of hagiographical lore that became enormously popular in medieval Europe.[17] The *Opus Imperfectum* allows us to place the *terminus ad quem* of the Revelation of the Magi no later than the fifth century. But this Latin summary is the only other textual witness to the Revelation of the Magi; in order to determine the dating of this text more precisely, it is necessary to use internal criteria.

Regarding the integrity of the received Syriac text, the ending featuring the Apostle Judas Thomas is probably a secondary addition to the text, given the sudden shift from first person to third person narration and the sudden introduction of new terminology, including the name "Jesus Christ," never found in the first person portion of the text. Without Judas Thomas, the Magi receive no official ecclesiastical sanction, and instead receive a direct revelation from Christ without ever knowing him by this name. It is worth noting that these emphases of the original form of the Revelation of the Magi on the unmediated mystical experience of the Magi and on the cosmic and even anonymous

---

14  See Landau 2016.
15  See Roig Lanzillotta 2015.
16  At present, the Latin text of the *Opus Imperfectum in Matthaeum* is most accessible in Migne, PG 156, cols. 637–38. A prefatory volume to a new critical edition was published by van Banning 1988, but no volumes of the edition have thus far appeared. See Landau 2010, 97–98; Kellerman 2010, 1:32; and Toepel 2013 for English translations of the summary of the Revelation of the Magi's narrative.
17  See Jacobus de Voragine, 1995.

character of Christ's revelation make this text particularly amenable to New Age religious sensibilities.

The secondary ending of the Revelation of the Magi shows connections with the Acts of Thomas not only by the presence of the Apostle Judas Thomas, but also by the inclusion of a baptismal hymn (30:2–9) that has strong similarities to the ritual epicleses found in the Acts of Thomas.[18] Yet this ending shows no awareness of the tradition of Thomas traveling to India and being martyred there, so it may be that the Revelation of the Magi's secondary ending was produced in the same environment as the Acts of Thomas, but at a time—perhaps in the third or fourth century—when the tradition of Thomas evangelizing India had not yet become the dominant form of Thomas's missionary exploits.

When the redactional Judas Thomas ending is stripped away, we are left with a first-person plural pseudepigraphon ostensibly authored by the Magi themselves. Dating this section of the text precisely is difficult, though it has affinities with a number of second- and third-century Christian apocryphal texts. First and foremost, it is strongly invested in the idea of Christ's polymorphy, the shape-shifting ability attributed to Christ in the Acts of John, the Acts of Peter, the Apocryphon of John, and the Latin infancy gospel known as the J Compilation.[19] Also like the major Apocryphal Acts, it includes lengthy (one might say tedious) speeches by a number of characters. It can also be considered an example of "pagan pseudepigrapha"—Christian texts written as if by a sympathetic outsider to the Christian movement—akin to the Pilate correspondence, the Abgar correspondence, or the Epistles of Paul and Seneca. Finally, the Revelation of the Magi has very impressive parallels with the material about the Magi and the Christ Child found in the J Compilation infancy narrative, such as the emergence of the infant out of a ball of light, the Magi learning about the star from writings older than the Hebrew Scriptures, and the fact that only the Magi are able to see the star; it seems clear that some sort of literary relationship exists between these two texts, even if the direction of influence is not clear.[20]

---

18  See Brock 2006, who observed this independently of my own research.
19  The episodes of polymorphy appear in these texts at Acts of John 87–93, Acts of Peter 21, Apocryphon of John 2:1–8, and J Compilation 74, 84. The best overview of polymorphy and its development in early Christian thought is Foster 2007. The Latin text of the J Compilation was first published by James 1927; an improved edition of the Latin text appears alongside of related texts preserved in Old Irish was published by McNamara et al. 2001; Ehrman and Pleše 2011, 115–155, have produced an English translation with the revised Latin text on facing pages.
20  The parallels between the Revelation of the Magi and the J Compilation were first noticed by Kehl 1975. Landau 2008 and Landau 2010 expanded upon these, and Kaestli 2011 further discussed the relationship between the texts.

## 2     William Henry's Revelation of the Revelation of the Magi

I was very fortunate that, shortly after completing my dissertation on the Revelation of the Magi, the American trade press HarperCollins expressed interest in publishing my translation of the text with an introduction and conclusion designed for a general audience. The book was published in the fall of 2010, and the HarperCollins publicists were able to procure interviews with a significant number of media outlets.[21] This resulted in a great deal of interest paid to the Revelation of the Magi by nonscholarly readers, a number of whom took the time to write and tell me how they made meaning out of the text. Among these readers, one William Henry left a voicemail on my office phone. He had read my book, described it in superlative terms as a "revelation," and was calling to ask me if he could interview me on his radio show, which incidentally was called *Revelations*. A quick Google search turned up his website, williamhenry.net, which had, among a great deal of other information, pictures of him in front of the signs of the zodiac and symbols of Egyptian mythology. I chose not to return his phone call.

Nevertheless, Henry went on with his study of the Revelation of the Magi, and in preparing this paper, I had the opportunity to examine in greater detail his main beliefs and how the Revelation of the Magi is relevant to them. Most simply, Henry saw in the Revelation of the Magi evidence that the historical figure of Jesus was, in fact, a being of light who entered our universe through a rip in the fabric of space-time—a stargate or a wormhole. This thesis is in continuity with his longer-term research agenda: in an ongoing series of books and other media, Henry has argued that highly advanced beings—perhaps human, perhaps extraterrestrial—have appeared to humankind throughout its history, accessing our world through interdimensional stargates. These beings are attempting to explain to us that we too can be like them—beings of light that transcend the normal limitations of human existence. They have appeared to humanity in revelations that later become codified as organized religious traditions. In the process, the teachings of these beings inevitably become distorted away from their initial instructions about transformation into a higher stage of humanity. In sum, Henry is a proponent of the perennial philosophy with some accents provided by ufology and science mysticism.[22]

---

21    Links to nearly all of the print, audio, and video pieces on the Revelation of the Magi from the 2010 holiday season can be found at my (now almost completely inactive) blog, revelationofthemagi.blogspot.com.

22    For Henry's own words on his theory of stargates used by advanced beings, supplemented by a vast number of artistic representations from a variety of religious traditions that he

The idea of Jesus as a stargate-using interdimensional time traveler may, at first blush, appear highly anachronistic, owing far more to twenty-first century theoretical physics than to ancient Christian beliefs. However, as April DeConick has recently pointed out, a number of ancient religious organizations did indeed discuss something very similar. In her interpretation of the Ophite diagram, DeConick notes, "The ancients speculated about the soul's descent and ascent through various planetary routes, as well as through specific star gates within the Zodiacal belt or along star columns like the Milky Way. In fact, one of the attractions of initiatory guilds like the Ophian-Christian was their claim to the secret knowledge of the precise path the soul uses to enter and exit the world."[23] One should therefore not be so quick to dismiss any relationship between Henry's ideas about stargates and the ancient texts to which he has often looked for support.

Indeed, in my own recent correspondence with Henry, it is clear that the emergence of stargates in science-fiction films like *Stargate* and *Contact* was not, for him, his first encounter with this concept. His entry into this subject was through the descriptions of cosmic gates in the Sumerian form of the Gilgamesh epic and in the Egyptian Pyramid texts. Moreover, he regarded the motion-picture appropriations of stargates as overly materialistic (and militaristic) understandings of how such portals could be used. Henry has contended, based on a diverse range of religious texts (not all of which expressly contain the idea of a stargate) that one cannot traverse these gates with an ordinary human body, but must instead be transformed into a being of light. This, he believes, is what the being known as Jesus of Nazareth actually was, and Jesus came to teach humanity how to undergo this transformation.[24]

Although Henry published a book in late 2011, *The Secret of Sion: Jesus's Stargate, the Beaming Garment and the Galactic Core in Ascension Art*, that integrated the *Revelation of the Magi* into his previously developed theories, his first public discussion of the *Revelation of the Magi* occurred on the Wednesday, January 26, 2011 episode of his *Revelations* radio show.[25] On this episode, Henry was actually the guest, and was interviewed by guest host Whitley Strieber, author of the bestselling book *Communion*, which describes Strieber's alleged

---

sees as evidence of stargates, see: http://www.williamhenry.net/about.html. For the concept of "science mysticism," see Kripal 2010, 123–124.

23   DeConick 2013, 56. See also her discussion in DeConick 2012.
24   Personal correspondence, December 15, 2015.
25   Audio available (with paid subscription) at: http://www.unknowncountry.com/revelations/revelation-magi-and-winged-serpents. The transcription of the broadcast quoted in the paper is my own; it has been revised slightly in places to make its conversational style conform more closely to written prose.

encounters with non-human entities.[26] Because Henry's comments in this interview are more extensive than those in the later book, and because of the fascinating exchanges between Strieber and Henry, I will devote the majority of my analysis in this section to the interview.

Although Henry does most of the speaking in the interview, Strieber himself begins the radio show by referring to my book on the Revelation of the Magi as "absolutely astonishing," and goes even further in his comments just prior to interviewing Henry, describing it as "an incredible revelation that came out of the depths of the Vatican Library ... it is truly a revelation." Henry begins the interview by thanking Anne Strieber,[27] Whitley's wife, for bringing the book to his attention. She contacted him in December of 2010 and urged him to read it, saying that it could be very important for his ongoing work. He immediately purchased a copy, and his excitement over its contents was palpable: "I couldn't put it down: this is the hottest piece of literature, really not literature, but as you say, 'revelation' that I've encountered in a long time."

Thus, both Strieber and Henry use the terminology of religious experience to describe both the Revelation of the Magi itself and my translation of and introduction to it, most notably the word 'revelation.' Although it is possible to regard Strieber's comments about the book as praise—albeit very effusive praise—about the originality and creativity of the book's contents, it will become clear in the interview that, at least for Henry, this is truly a revelation in the most literal sense of a divine disclosure.

More specifically, for Henry, this was a valuable confirmation of his long-held theory of advanced beings entering our world through stargates or wormholes:

> [The text] simply and directly says that Jesus is a light being, he is a star child. And when the Magi go seeking him, they ultimate encounter him in a cave ... and he appears, he emerges through a gate! And so as I'm reading this, my jaw is dropping because it's basically saying in modern vernacular that Jesus is a light being, he's a star child, he's manifesting through what we today would identify as portal or a stargate.

It is worth noting here that while it is easy enough to understand how Henry connected the narrative of the Revelation of the Magi with the idea of beings

---

26  Strieber has resisted characterizing his experience as an "extraterrestrial abduction," despite it being frequently presented in popular culture as such. Although he has discussed his interpretations of these events in multiple publications, for his most recent comments see Strieber and Kripal, 2016.
27  Anne Strieber died, after a lengthy illness, on August 11, 2015.

of light visiting humanity, his argument that the Revelation of the Magi also contains evidence that Jesus arrived in our world via a wormhole or a stargate is not immediately obvious. It is, in fact, based on the Revelation of the Magi, but on a very minor detail in the narrative. In *The Secret of Sion*,[28] Henry underscores the Magi's description of the star's appearance, taken from Revelation of the Magi 12:3: "And again, we saw that heaven had been opened like a great gate and men of glory carrying the star of light upon their hands. And they descended and stood upon the pillar of light, and the entire mountain was filled by its light, which cannot be uttered by the mouth of humanity." In other words, the Revelation of the Magi depicts heaven opened in the manner of a gate or a door, through which angels carry the star and descend to the Magi's sacred mountain.

It is unclear whether the Revelation of the Magi has the sort of elaborate cosmology, with multiple mechanisms for both escape and entry of the universe, that appears in ancient gnostic traditions. The text does, however, begin with a statement about how the transcendent God is hidden "by his great brightness" (1:3) such that no one in "his upper worlds nor the lower ones" (1:5) can speak about him. Therefore, while Henry's marshaling of the Revelation of the Magi as evidence for his stargate theory is predicated on a seemingly minor mention of how the Magi's star descends from heaven through a gate, the fact is that from its inception the Revelation of the Magi speaks in cosmological terms and, furthermore, describes the supreme God as an unspeakably bright light. It is an opening to the text that clearly resonated with Henry, for good reason.

In addition to Henry's unexpected (but not necessarily anachronistic) reading of Jesus in the Revelation of the Magi as a stargate traveler, I was struck in the interview by the degree to which Henry considered my translation and publication of the Revelation of the Magi to be nothing short of a revelatory event taking place "in the fullness of time." When asked by Strieber why Jesus, according to this text, appeared "in one of the darkest periods of the human spirit that has ever been known," Henry replied, in essence, that the appearance of Jesus in the world as described in the Revelation of the Magi marked the beginning of a new age, one that may be reaching toward its crescendo with the publication of this text. He muses, "So maybe he was appearing at that time to bring us forward into this age of light and now, of all times, now we get the Revelation of the Magi suddenly published in English so that everybody can have access to it, and maybe now we're coming to a point where we can truly comprehend the original Christian message, that we can all transform in this way."

---

28   Henry 2011, loc. 277.

Similarly, using sentiments that I myself expressed in the book about the potential consonance between the Revelation of the Magi and twenty-first century religious thought, he asserts in *The Secret of Sion*, "In my view, the Revelation of the Magi is the most important apocryphal text ever discovered. As Brent Landau observes, it could only be fully appreciated today. I believe our understanding of the nature of time and space, and especially stargates, enable [*sic*] us to decode this remarkable book."[29]

The statement to which he alludes comes in the conclusion of my book, where I raise the question of why the Revelation of the Magi had remained largely unknown, both to scholars and to the general public. Although the reasons for scholarly neglect were quite obvious—a general lack of interest in apocryphal writings, an obscure language of transmission—I had attempted, if for only a moment, to speak (hypothetically) from the perspective of a theologian:

> But one might as willingly believe, if so inclined, that the introduction of the *Revelation of the Magi* to a wide audience at this precise moment in time is hardly a matter of chance .... [T]he *Revelation of the Magi* practically stands alone among early Christian writings in its positive appraisal of religious pluralism. So, another way of answering the question of why the *Revelation of the Magi* is now beginning to be studied more closely is that such a text could be fully appreciated *only* in a moment such as today. Now more than before, religious diversity is a fact of life in many parts of the world.[30]

In sum, whereas I was reflecting on the way in which the Revelation of the Magi remarkably reflected the pluralistic religious *Zeitgeist* of the twenty-first century, William Henry views the Revelation of the Magi as instead reflecting a twenty-first century understanding of theoretical physics.

One might choose to say that Henry has misread or misunderstood the point of this statement; indeed, as the author of this statement, I myself am tempted to do so. However, many practitioners of reception theory would hold that the concept of "original meaning" attempts to domesticate texts, which are inherently unstable and pluriform. Jonathan Roberts expresses this perspective well:

---

29   Henry 2011, loc. 312.
30   Landau 2010, 97.

Aside from textual meanings not being empirically verifiable in the way that, say, the DNA sequence of a kingfisher may be, the search for an 'original sense' implies that original senses are singular, not plural. But of course it may be the case that 'original meanings' are themselves intrinsically multivalent, and that the hermeneutical genius of painters such as Rembrandt and writers such as Kierkegaard lies in their ability to sense and explore those multifaceted meanings. Reception history also picks up this variety of meanings by showing us different individuals and groups seeing the same texts from different angles.[31]

When this perspective on reception history is kept in mind, we are better able to recognize that, in my statement, I indicated a certain degree of openness to seeing the publication of the Revelation of the Magi at this moment in time as something beyond coincidence, something closer to a synchronicity. William Henry most certainly recognized this dimension of my statement.

Not only did Henry regard my publication of the text as a sort of perfectly-timed cosmic dispensation that made clear Jesus' true nature as a stargate-traveling being of light; he also considered the text to be a veritable "how to" manual for the next stage in the evolution of humanity. In the interview, Henry expressed the hope that he could interview me soon—not to learn about my theories of the text's redaction and its date of composition, but to learn how I think this text might change humanity: "I'm hoping to actually interview Dr. Brent Landau on *Revelations* to really find out, what is this actually going to mean for us? I mean, if people get ahold of this idea that Jesus is a light being and that he is traveling through these gates, well ... it opens up just an amazing new dynamic about the Jesus story."

This new dynamic, as Henry goes on to make clear, is that Jesus is an exemplar for the rest of the human race to strive towards a transformation into beings of light. Strieber appeared to agree with this reading of the Revelation of the Magi as a "how to" manual, drawing a parallel with the "visitors" with which he has communicated:

> I worked with and meditated with for years a group of beings, if you will, or people who were in one form human beings, in another form they were beings of light, and they were able to change form at will apparently. But they were very much ordinary people, they felt like ordinary people; they certainly didn't live around here, let me put it that way, but there was an ordinariness to them and a real sense that I could be like

---

31   Roberts 2013, 4.

that, that this was not impossible for the average person, and I think that where the Church was wrong is that it distanced the immediate possibility of transformation by making Christ a kind of special, separate being, different from us. And in a way, the *Revelation of the Magi* continues that theme, but in a way also it doesn't. And I guess that's why it was hidden away in the Vatican Library for so long:[32] it's profoundly heretical in the sense that it gives, it opens the possibility that anyone could walk through that gate.

Near the end of the interview, both Henry and Strieber assert that Jesus "toggle[s] between the worlds" in the Revelation of the Magi, and that this is the destiny toward which he is calling humanity at large. Indeed, Henry even suggests that the very narrative structure of the Revelation of the Magi, with its close attention to the details of the Magi's semi-mythical land, is beckoning readers to journey to this new land: "You get the impression that this text, the *Revelation of the Magi*, is acting like an invitation. It's saying, 'Come along, you can come here too, just follow the story and you too can come to this land that borders the great ocean in the very east of the inhabited world.' So mysterious and enticing."

### 3  Beyond William Henry's Revelation of the Magi: Other Encounters with Beings of Light

In my above assessment of William Henry's reading of the Revelation of the Magi, there is one part of his interpretation I have not directly addressed, because it is by no means restricted to him alone. While William Henry's marshaling of the Revelation of the Magi as evidence for the existence of advanced extraterrestrial beings that have appeared to humans throughout is probably the most public example of this way of interpreting the Revelation of the Magi, it is by no means the only one. I mentioned earlier that I had received a number of emails from individuals who had read my book and felt compelled to write me.

---

32  This notion that religious bodies or scholars are suppressing explosive materials found in apocryphal Christian writings appears in many places, but has been popularized especially by Dan Brown's 2003 novel, *The Da Vinci Code*. Conspiracy theories have also affected public discourse about the Dead Sea Scrolls, as Ullmann-Margalit 2006 has described.

The most recent of these is from a man in Scotland whom I shall call "Ben" (although this is not his real name). Rather than attempting to summarize his email, I have reproduced (with permission) most of it here:

> I have just finished reading your book and your translation. I am only church religious in a "3 weddings and a funeral" way, and just an ordinary guy who works for a bank, living in an ordinary street and married with 2 children.
>
> I bought your book a few days ago because in the Kindle sample I read something familiar to me ... the "light like a star." I have seen that light too ... in my front room 3 years ago. A life changing moment. Sounds crazy doesn't it? But it's not. It actually happened.
>
> I believe these men of ancient times saw what has literally been written ... a small human coming out of the light. At that moment a connection was established between Earth and ... well, call it what you want ... some call it heaven. Whatever else is out there awaits to be truly discovered. A hidden mystery indeed.
>
> Something happened to me when I saw that light in our room. A door was opened in my mind through which pass innumerable questions ... what was it? Where did it come from? Where did it go to? How did it pass straight through the walls and glass door? What was inside the light? What would have happened if I had touched it? Wouldn't it be fantastic if it just appeared in, say, the middle of a church service somewhere one day in front of 'true' believers (some would have heart attacks I am sure due to the shock!) ... then wondering why it doesn't ... and many more.[33]

So, Ben, who is not very religious at all, saw some sort of sentient light in his house, and the impact on him was profound. It is quite intriguing that he describes the light as opening a door in his mind; this sounds very much like Henry's idea of a stargate, though here internalized. Not only did this light impart to him new information (or at least a new set of questions); furthermore, as Ben revealed to me in a follow-up message, it has also affected him physically: "Something else happens to me as well now since I saw what I saw. Something which never happened before ... I tingle from head to toe when I think about it. Imagine severe 'pins and needles' over your whole body ... it's just like that. I can turn it on and off at will with ease. I once did that

---

[33] Personal correspondence, November 30, 2015. See Fox 2008 for similar narratives about encounters with "lightforms."

every 30 seconds for 30 minutes just to see if it faded ... it didn't. What's that all about???"[34]

What, ultimately, are we to think of the connections that Henry and Ben make between the narrative of the Revelation of the Magi and encounters with beings of light who are perhaps not of this world and impart some sort of revelation or effect some kind of physical change? One might be tempted to say that such interpreters have ripped the Revelation of the Magi out of its ancient Christian context and ascribed to it meanings located in modern New Age or ufological thought. After all, it is often thought that a key reason for the production of Christian apocryphal texts was that the earlier canonical gospels did not say enough about certain moments in the life of Jesus to satisfy curious Christians. Thus, the Christian Apocrypha in general, and apocryphal infancy gospels like the Revelation of the Magi in particular, could be understood as a sort of ancient "fan fiction," wholly contrived narratives without any connection to external historical events. What evidence is there that the Revelation of the Magi might be more than ancient "fan fiction"?

It is true that the Revelation of the Magi purports to describe the actual experience of the biblical Magi, and that some of the text's depiction of the Magi is dependent upon earlier Christian and Jewish exegetical traditions. But I do not think that one should be so quick to dismiss the Revelation of the Magi as entirely fan fiction. My reason for this is twofold. First, the Revelation of the Magi goes into exquisite detail on the Magi's ritual system: how they pray in silence (even including a description of their posture), their practice of immersing in a sacred spring, and their ascension of a holy mountain over a period of several days (5:1–11). Although this could simply be the author of the Revelation of the Magi's attempt to craft a social context for the Magi with a high degree of verisimilitude, there is no obvious biblical antecedent for their practices, which one might expect an author of Magi fan fiction to utilize. Because of this unexpected level of detail, I have argued elsewhere[35] that the Revelation of the Magi may have been some early Christian group's self-description of their religious practice, which was presented by the community that produced it as the testimony of the biblical Magi—both to provide the text itself with authority and to provide themselves with a prestigious spiritual genealogy.

The second reason for my skepticism that the Revelation of the Magi is nothing more than elaborate fan fiction is the same element that drew Henry and Ben so strongly to the text: its depiction of an encounter between human beings and an otherworldly being of light. I believe that there are good reasons

---

34   Personal correspondence, December 17, 2015.
35   See Landau, forthcoming.

for regarding this to have been an actual experience of the people who produced the Revelation of the Magi. Let me be clear: I do not claim here that the being whom the Magi encounter is actually an alien life-form (though neither Henry nor Ben appear to do so, either).

In rejecting the extraterrestrial hypothesis for this incident, I am allying myself with one of the most thoughtful commentators on the UFO phenomenon, Jacques Vallee. In a series of studies, beginning with his seminal work, *Passport to Magonia: From Folklore to Flying Saucers*, Vallee has noted that strange encounters with small human-like beings have been reported throughout human history.[36] But the frequency of these encounters, the difficulties inherent with interstellar space travel, and the unlikelihood that alien life would be so humanoid have led Vallee to regard the extraterrestrial hypothesis as an implausible explanation for the UFO phenomenon.[37]

Vallee's theory about what these incidents might ultimately be if not extraterrestrials is not entirely clear, and an introduction to his thought would require a separate paper.[38] Nevertheless, such experiences are quite widespread throughout human culture, and their prevalence is even greater if we include encounters with what Mark Fox calls "lightforms," unusual light phenomena with which numerous individuals have reported spiritual experiences.[39] As one example, the anthropologist Diego Escolar described in a 2012 article strange balls of light that he witnessed while doing fieldwork among indigenous peoples in Argentina.[40] So, I think there is ample reason to suppose that the group that produced the Revelation of the Magi did in fact have some sort of experience with anomalous light phenomena—howsoever we may wish to explain that.

## Conclusion

In concluding this study, it may be helpful to highlight a couple of general observations that other researchers might find applicable to texts and contexts different from what I have addressed here. First, few specialists in ancient Christian texts would characterize the Revelation of the Magi as overtly gnostic, since it was not found at Nag Hammadi, nor does it have the

---

36 Vallee 1969. See also his cataloguing of unexplained aerial phenomena from the period before human flight in Vallee and Aubeck 2010.
37 See the arguments presented in Vallee 1990.
38 Though see the overview of his life and thought in Kripal 2010, 142–197.
39 See Fox 2008.
40 See Escolar 2012.

demiurgical interpretation of the Jewish God found therein. Nevertheless, it can be profitably situated as gnostic within ancient Christian literature based on DeConick's understanding of gnostic religious movements as countercultures that emphasize "non-intellective knowledge and personal visions of truth over cultural constructions of knowledge."[41] The Revelation of the Magi certainly privileges direct contact with the entity known as Christ and also seems to reject identifying its religious belief and practice with the institutional Church. Such an understanding of a non-demiurgical text as exhibiting gnostic/ countercultural characteristic may result in other texts, both apocryphal and canonical, being understood in the same way.

A second insight follows from the first. If the Revelation of the Magi is gnostic/countercultural, then its religious outlook has much in common with that of present-day New Age communities and individual thinkers like Henry. Both the Revelation of the Magi and many New Age practitioners had their origins in Christian religious communities, but, through a combination of personal transformative experiences and cross-cultural knowledge, they have put themselves in tension with organized Christianity. In the specific case of the Revelation of the Magi, those who produced it have imagined what a revelation of the transcendent Christ on the very periphery of the civilized world might have been like, quite possibly because they regarded themselves as being similarly alienated from traditional religious practice. Readers like Henry have become drawn to the Revelation of the Magi because it speaks in a register familiar to them, not because of a superficial fascination with "hidden" or "lost" scriptures. More points of contact between ancient religious texts and New Age religious thought are no doubt waiting to be found, as is the identification of New Age religious sensibilities in other cultural and historical contexts.

## Bibliography

Bovon, François, 2012. "The Corpus Christianorum Series Apocryphorum and the Association pour l'étude de la littérature apocryphe chrétienne." *Early Christianity* 3, 137–143.

Brock, Sebastian P., 2006. "An Archaic Syriac Prayer over Baptismal Oil." Pages 3–12 in *Studia Patristica: Papers Presented at the Fourteenth International Congress on Patristic Studies Held in Oxford 2003*. Edited by F. Yong, M. Edwards, and P. Parvis. Leuven: Peeters.

---

41  DeConick 2016, discussing Roszak's understanding of the "counter culture."

Chabot, Jean-Baptiste, 1927. *Chronicon anonymum Pseudo-Dionysianum vulgo dictum, I. CSCO SS 3.1.* Paris: E Typographeo Reipublicae.

DeConick, April D., 2012. "From the Bowels of Hell to Draco: The Mysteries of the Peratics." Pages 3–38 in *Mystery and Secrecy in the Nag Hammadi Collection and Other Ancient Literature: Ideas and Practices. Studies for Einar Thomassen at Sixty.* Edited by Christian Bull, Liv Ingebord Lied, and John D. Turner. Leiden: Brill.

DeConick, April D., 2013. "The Road for the Souls is through the Planets: The Mysteries of the Ophians Mapped." Pages 37–74 in *Practicing Gnosis: Ritual, Magic, Theurgy and Liturgy in Nag Hammadi, Manichean and Other Ancient Literature. Essays in Honor of Birger A. Pearson.* Edited by April D. DeConick, Gregory Shaw, and John D. Turner. Leiden: Brill.

DeConick, April D., 2016. "The Countercultural Gnostic: Turning the World Upside Down and Inside Out." *Gnosis* 1–2.

Ehrman, Bart D., and Zlatko Pleše, 2011. *The Apocryphal Gospels: Text and Translations.* New York: Oxford University Press.

Escolar, Diego, 2012. "Boundaries of Anthropology: Empirics and Ontological Relativism in a Field Experience with Anomalous Luminous Entities in Argentina." *Anthropology and Humanism* 37, 27–44.

Foster, Paul, 2007. "Polymorphic Christology: Its Origins and Development in Early Christianity." *Journal of Theological Studies* 58, 66–99.

Fox, Mark, 2008. *Spiritual Encounters with Unusual Light Phenomena: Lightforms.* Cardiff: University of Wales.

Hannah, Darrell D., 2015. "The Star of the Magi and the Prophecy of Balaam in Earliest Christianity, with Special Attention to the Lost Books of Balaam." Pages 433–462 in *The Star of Bethelehem and the Magi: Interdisciplinary Perspectives from Experts on the Ancient Near East, the Greco-Roman World, and Modern Astronomy.* Edited by Peter Barthel and George van Kooten. Leiden: Brill.

Henry, William, 2011. *The Secret of Sion: Jesus's Stargate, the Beaming Garment and the Galatic Core in Ascension Art.* Hendersonville, TN: Scala Dei. Kindle Edition.

Jacobus de Voragine, 1995. *The Golden Legend: Readings on the Saints.* Translated by William G. Ryan. 2 volumes. Princeton: Princeton University Press.

James, M.R., 1927. *Latin Infancy Gospels.* Cambridge: Cambridge University Press.

Jenkins, Philip, 2015. *The Many Faces of Jesus: The Thousand-Year Story of the Survival and Influence of the Lost Gospels.* New York: Basic.

Kaestli, Jean-Daniel, 2011. "Mapping an Unexplored Second Century Apocryphal Gospel: the Liber de Nativitate Salvatoris (CANT 53)." Pages 506–533 in *Infancy Gospels: Stories and Identities.* Edited by Claire Clivaz et al. Tübingen: Mohr Siebeck.

Kehl, Alois, 1975. "Der Stern der Magier: Zu §94 des lateinischen Kindheitsevangeliums der Arundel-Handschrift." *Jahrbuch für Antike und Christentum* 18, 69–80.

Kellerman, James A. (trans.), 2010. *Incomplete Commentary on* Matthew (Opus Imperfectum). Edited by Thomas C. Oden. 2 volumes. Downers Grove, Ill.: Intervarsity Press.

Kripal, Jeffrey, 2010. *Authors of the Impossible: The Paranormal and the Sacred.* Chicago: University of Chicago.

Landau, Brent, 2008. "The Sages and the Star-Child: An Introduction to the Revelation of the Magi, An Ancient Christian Apocryphon." ThD diss., Harvard Divinity School.

Landau, Brent, 2010. *Revelation of the Magi: The Lost Tale of the Wise Men's Journey to Bethlehem.* San Francisco, CA: HarperOne.

Landau, Brent, 2015. "The 'Harvard School' of the Christian Apocrypha." Pages 58–77 in *Forbidden Texts on the Western Frontier: The Christian Apocrypha from North American Perspectives.* Edited by Tony Burke. Eugene, OR: Cascade.

Landau, Brent, 2016. "The Revelation of the Magi: A New Summary and Introduction." In *New Testament Apocrypha: More Noncanonical Scriptures.* Edited by Tony Burke and Brent Landau. Grand Rapids, MI: Eerdmans.

Landau, Brent, forthcoming. "Under the Influence (of the Magi): Did Hallucinogens Play a Role in the Inspired Composition of the Pseudepigraphic Revelation of the Magi?" In *Fakes, Forgeries, and Fictions: Writing Ancient and Modern Christian Apocrypha.* Edited by Tony Burke. Eugene, OR: Cascade.

McNamara, Martin, et al. (eds.), 2001. *Apocrypha Hiberniae 1: Evangelia Infantiae.* 2 volumes. CCSA 13–14. Turnhout: Brepols.

Reed, Annette Yoshiko, 2009. "Beyond the Land of Nod: Syriac Images of Asian and the Historiography of the West." *History of Religions* 49, 48–87.

Reinink, G.J., 1975. "Das Land "Seiris" [Shir] und das Volk der Serer in jüdischen und christlichen Traditionen." *Journal for the Study of Judaism* 6, 72–85.

Roberts, Jonathan, 2013. "Introduction." Pages 1–8 in *The Oxford Handbook of the Reception History of the Bible.* Edited by Michael Lieb, Emma Mason, and Jonathan Roberts. New York: Oxford University Press.

Roig Lanzillotta, Lautaro, 2007. *Acta Andreae Apocrypha: A New Perspective on the Nature, Intention and Significance of the Primitive Text.* Geneva: Patrick Cramer.

Roig Lanzillotta, Lautaro, 2015. "A Syriac Original for the Acts of Thomas? The Hypothesis of Syriac Priority Revisited." Pages 105–33 in *Early Jewish and Christian Narrative: The Role of Religion in Shaping Narrative Forms.* Edited by Ilaria Ramelli and Judith Perkins. Tübingen: Mohr Siebeck.

Strieber, Whitley, and Jeffrey Kripal, 2016. *The Super Natural: A New Vision of the Unexplained.* New York: Tarcher/Penguin.

Toepel, Alexander, 2013. "The Apocryphon of Seth." Pages 33–39 in *Old Testament Pseudepigrapha: More Non-Canonical Scriptures.* Edited by Richard Bauckham, James R. Davila, and Alexander Panayotov. Grand Rapids, MI: Eerdmans.

Touati, Charlotte, and Claire Clivaz, 2015. "Apocryphal Texts about Other Characters in the Canonical Gospels." Pages 48–64 in *The Oxford Handbook of Early Christian Apocrypha*. Edited by Andrew Gregory and Christopher Tuckett. New York: Oxford University Press.

Trexler, Richard, 1997. *The Journey of the Magi: Meanings in History of a Christian Story*. Princeton, NJ: Princeton University.

Tullberg, Otto F., 1850. *Dionysii Telmahharensis Chronici liber primus. Textum e codice ms. Syriaco Bibliothecae Vaticanae*. Uppsala: Regiae Academiae Typographi.

Ullmann-Margalit, Edna, 2006. *Out of the Cave: A Philosophical Inquiry into the Dead Sea Scrolls Research*. Cambridge, MA: Harvard University Press.

Vallee, Jacques, 1969. *Passport to Magonia: From Folkore to Flying Saucers*. Chicago: Regnery.

Valle, Jacques, 1990. "Five Arguments Against the Extraterrestrial Origin of Unidentified Flying Objects." *Journal of Scientific Exploration* 4, 105–117.

Valle, Jacques and Chris Aubeck, 2010. *Wonders in the Sky: Unexplained Aerial Objects from Antiquity to Modern Time*s. New York: Tarcher/Penguin.

Van Banning, Joop, 1988. *Opus Imperfectum in Matthaeum. Praefatio. CCSL 87b*. Turnhout: Brepols.

Van der Horst, Pieter W., 1994. "Silent Prayer in Antiquity." *Numen* 41, 1–25.

Witakowski, Witold, 1987. *The Syriac Chronicle of Pseudo-Dionysius of Tel-Mahre: A Study in the History of Historiography*. Uppsala: Uppsala University Press.

Witakowski, Witold, 2008. "The Magi in Syriac Tradition." Pages 809–843 in *Malphono w-Rabo d-Malphone: Studies in Honor of Sebastian P. Brock*. Edited by George Kiraz. Piscataway, NJ: Gorgias.

# The Great God Pan

*Sarah Iles Johnston*
Arts and Humanities Distinguished Professor of Religion and Professor of Classics, The Ohio State University
*johnston.2@osu.edu*

What if you had a gnostic experience and it turned out to mean nothing at all? Or at least, nothing that you could make any use of? Or what if it *did* mean something, but that something was so contrary to everything else you thought you knew about the goodness of God and the universe that the experience offered you no way forward? What if it was a sort of gnostic experience from Hell?[1]

In this essay, I want to think about those questions. I'll do so first through the lens of a horror story published at the *fin de siècle: The Great God Pan*, by Arthur Machen. But although I will contextualize that story a little within its historical period, it's important to realize that stories like it didn't stop appearing when the *fin* was finished. The reputation of the *fin de siècle* as a time of degeneration and decadence cannot fully 'explain' the story, therefore, even if the story does fit the spirit of its time. In later parts of this essay, I'll look at two subsequent authors whose works were inspired by *The Great God Pan* and think about how *Pan*'s gnostic elements were handled by them.

Historical context alone, in any case, cannot help us understand what such stories tell us (in ways that only *stories* can tell us) about how humans grapple with the vast gulf that lies between the puny knowledge that we have accrued over the millennia and the potentialities of the other world that we strive to understand. Gnostic means 'to know,' and sometimes when we, as scholars, read about gnostic systems and the thinkers who developed them, we slip into assuming that it's actually possible to construct a neat and tidy picture of the cosmos and the rules by which it runs. Perhaps we can't be sure how many archons are dancing on the head of a particular gnostic pin, but we lapse into assuming that whoever composed the ancient text we're reading would have had a ready answer to that question. We assume that it's only the lacunose state of our ancient sources or our inability to accurately situate those sources within their intellectual *milieux* that prevents us from getting a complete picture of

---

[1] I offer this essay to Philippe Borgeaud, in celebration of his 70th birthday. This is not the Pan he knows so well, and has enabled us to know so well (Borgeaud 1979), but it is a Pan nonetheless, and I have thought of Borgeaud's work often as I wrote this.

the system, and that if a complete picture *were* to be provided to us, it would be satisfyingly elegant, logical, instructive and coherent.

Horror stories, of course, are not gnostic treatises, but horror stories often focus on what can broadly be called gnostic experiences. Another way of saying this is that characters in horror fiction often experience a darker version of the same thing as the gnostics, theurgists and other mystics of that ilk experienced, namely a more intimate knowledge of and closer contact with entities who normally lie beyond human reach. Sometimes, as in the cases I will discuss below, the characters in horror stories even *court* these experiences, just as gnostics and other mystics court theirs. The most obvious difference between the two genres (gnostic treatises and horror fiction) is that whereas the gnostic seeker ideally makes contact, eventually, with angels, archangels and gods who enhance his soul, the protagonist in a horror story (often to his or her surprise) meets ghosts, demons and other entities who threaten to steal his very life and soul away. This is not to imply that mystics themselves never encounter dangerous entities. Iamblichus spent part of his treatise *On the Mysteries* explaining how to differentiate amongst various types of suprahuman entities who might appear to the theurgist as he called upon higher powers, and warned his readers that if they mistook one for another they would be opening themselves up to spiritual peril. Iamblichus knew whereof he spoke: he had once unmasked the ghost of a dead gladiator who was pretending to be the god Apollo.[2] Closer to us in time, but still in a neoplatonic spirit, the 17th century mystic Emmanuel Swedenborg, in his *Arcana Coelestia* and other writings, warned that opening the inner eye of the spirit in an improper manner left one at the mercy of evil 'correspondences,' demonic entities that fed upon their victims' particular corporeal weaknesses. Gnostics and other mystics also had to beware of demonic entities when their souls undertook journeys to the other world, whether after death, as they traveled to the particular realms where they would spend eternity, or before death, during their initiation into mysteries that were meant to protect them after death.[3]

Horror stories, then, could be said to elaborate upon what gnostic traditions concede to be a problem: there are things out there in the cosmos, lying in wait for amateur dabblers in the occult, that are best avoided. Horror stories, indeed, thrive upon this problem—thrive so vigorously and unabashedly upon its sensational aspects that we may miss some of the work that they do. Yet

---

[2] Iamblichus, *De Myst.* 2.3–11.
[3] See DeConick 2012 and 2013 for examples of this amongst early Christians who are grouped under the term "gnostic." More generally on this challenge to the traveling soul as confronted by mystics in late antiquity: Johnston 1997.

precisely because they are flagrantly fictional, horror stories are able to lure us into contemplating scenarios that we would never tolerate in what we took to be a sober work of philosophy or theology; in the name of being entertained, we let down our guards. Precisely because they are fictional, horror stories can be engrossingly vivid in their imagery and language, pulling us along into their worldviews without our even realizing that we are being pulled. And finally, because they are fictional, horror stories can get away with merely sketching an idea that a more systematic enquiry would be unable to sustain; fiction can convincingly hint at possibilities that fail the test of the structured sorts of arguments that theologians and philosophers (and there is an inclination towards both theology and philosophy within many mystics) tend to admire.

Victoria Nelson has suggested that horror fiction flourishes at moments when a culture has rejected, for whatever reasons, open discourse about God. The repressed thoughts bubble to the surface, disguising themselves as discussions about the negative side of the transcendent.[4] Nelson is certainly right, but I would add that horror fiction also flourishes (whatever the cultural moment may be) as a venue through which to explore possibilities that mainstream religion and philosophy simply will not countenance, even when God is discussed openly—because those ideas contradict mainstream theology, because they fail to follow traditional patterns of logic, or because (and this is the thread that I will follow in the rest of this essay) they disempower God or call into question the very idea of God's existence.

1

*The Great God Pan* was published by Arthur Machen first in 1890, in a periodical called *The Whirlwind*, and then again in a revised and longer version in 1894, bound together with a second short novel, *The Inmost Light*. We meet three of *Pan's* main characters at the very beginning of the tale. Mr. Clarke, who narrates part of the story, is a man of leisure, fascinated with the occult and intent on compiling his 'Memoirs to prove the Existence of the Devil.' His friend Dr. Raymond is a surgeon who describes himself as 'devoted to transcendental medicine.' Mary is an orphan whom Dr. Raymond has raised to young womanhood.

---

4  Nelson 2001. The specific reference is to page viii, but the topic forms one of the foci of the book as a whole.

The story opens with Clarke's arrival at Raymond's house, following an urgent summons. Raymond is ready to try out a surgical experiment that he has been perfecting for years. He will operate on Mary making

> a slight lesion in the grey matter, that is all; a trifling rearrangement of certain cells, a microscopical alteration

In making this lesion, he will stimulate a certain nerve center in the brain whose function no other doctor has fully understood before. Against Clarke's protests about the possible dangers to Mary, Raymond thunders:

> I am perfectly instructed as to the possible functions of those nerve-centers in the scheme of things. With a touch I can bring them into play, with a touch, I can set free the current, with a touch I can complete the communication between this world of sense and—we shall be able to finish the sentence later on. Yes, the knife is necessary; but think what that knife will effect. It will level utterly the solid wall of sense, and probably, for the first time since man was made, a spirit will gaze on a spirit-world. Clarke, Mary will see the god Pan!

The surgery is performed, and when Mary awoke:

> [Her eyes] shone with an awful light, looking far away, and a great wonder fell upon her face, and her hands stretched out as if to touch what was invisible; but in an instant the wonder faded, and gave place to the most awful terror. The muscles of her face were hideously convulsed, she shook from head to foot; the soul seemed struggling and shuddering within the house of flesh. It was a horrible sight, and Clarke rushed forward, as she fell shrieking to the floor.

Three days later Raymond took Clarke to Mary's bedside. She was lying wide-awake, rolling her head from side to side, and grinning vacantly.

> "Yes," said the doctor, "it is a great pity; she is a hopeless idiot. However, it could not be helped; and, after all, she has seen the Great God Pan."[5]

This was, then, no friendly Pan of the forests and meadows, idly whistling to a blackbird as he lounged on a riverbank, a positive figure familiar in popular art

---

5   This and the preceding excerpts are taken from Chapter I of *The Great God Pan*.

and literature during the period immediately preceding Machen's story.[6] This was instead a horrifying creature—a god who could send one into madness and perversity and from there into permanent imbecility and emptiness.

In encountering Pan, Mary has lost everything that made her Mary. But, she has come away from the encounter with something new: a pregnancy that leads to the birth of Helen, on whom the rest of the story focuses; Mary herself dies days after this child is born.

From birth, Helen has a corrupted soul and a determination to corrupt others. Once grown, she is, as another character says, 'the most beautiful woman' he has ever seen, and yet 'the most repulsive.' A man whom she has married and ruined later tells us that:

> The night of the wedding I listened to her as she spoke in her beautiful voice of things which even now I would not dare whisper in the blackest night. ... You may think you know life, but I tell you, you can have no conception of what I know, not in your most fantastic, hideous dreams can you have imaged forth the faintest shadow of what I have heard—and seen.... In a year I was a ruined man, in body and soul—in body and soul (*Pan* III).

Helen continues her career of destruction, changing her name as needed, easily cutting her way through both the lowest and highest ranks of English society—until finally, Clarke and another man track her down and compel her to hang herself. Her body instantly transmogrifies first into that of a man, then into that of a beast, then 'from beast to worse than beast,' then into a 'substance as jelly' and finally

> a Form, shaped in dimness before me, which I will not farther describe. But the symbol of this form may be seen in ancient sculptures, and in paintings which survived beneath the lava, too foul to be spoken of ... a horrible and unspeakable shape, neither man nor beast (*Pan* VIII).

As Dr. Raymond later concedes,

> What I said Mary would see, she saw, but I forgot that no human eyes can look on such a sight with impunity. And I forgot that when the house of

---

6 See in general Merivale 1969, especially chapters 3 and 4, although I think specifically here of a painting done by Arnold Böcklin in 1864 or 1865, entitled "Faun, einer Amsel zupfeidend," now in the Neuen Pinakothek in Munich.

life is thus thrown open, there may enter in that for which we have no name, and human flesh may become the veil of a horror one dare not express (*Pan* VIII).

In this story we have one instantiation of a paradigm that also drives a number of other horror stories of the time, such as Joseph Sheridan Le Fanu's 'Green Tea' (1872) and Algernon Blackwood's 'A Psychical Invasion' (1908): the search to open the inner eye can leave one vulnerable to incursions of evil.[7] But here, there are even worse results. For it is not only Mary who suffers, but potentially all of humanity. Thinking back on all that has happened, Clarke writes in his Memoirs: ET DIABOLUS INCARNATUS EST. ET HOMO FACTUS EST. Helen was an Antichrist, born of a Mary whose inner eye was opened by a foolish man in his misguided attempt at easy gnosis.

2

Let us ponder the form taken by that madness and evil: Pan. Before the Victorian period, Pan appears in literature and art either as a benevolent symbol for nature, expressing a nostalgia for a time when humans lived more in accord with it; or as what some scholars have called 'the Orphic Pan'—a Pan who reflects the Greek word that they heard in his name: 'All.' This Pan is the soul of all things, a cosmic force that unifies all.[8]

It was Machen who first introduced the god's sinister side, with a look backwards at the Romantic longing for union with Pan-the-soul-of-all-things. In Machen's story this longing injects into the world a force not of unity but of degeneration—degeneration in both the moral sense (I refer here to certain disgusting practices into which Helen introduces her victims) and in an evolutionary sense (I refer here to the puddle of slime into which Helen herself decomposes). Adrian Eckersley was surely right when he suggested that

---

[7] As Sheridan Le Fanu presents it, the paradigm is openly indebted to Swedenborg's ideas— most explicitly in 'Green Tea' but also in his stories "Mr. Justice Harbottle" and "The Familiar," all of which were published in the same volume, *In a Glass Darkly*, in 1872. See the comments on Swedenborg's theory of correspondences in Tracy 1993, xi–xiv, as well as remarks in Tracy's explanatory notes to 'Green Tea' in the same volume. Notably, however, Machen claims not have been influenced by Swedenborg (nor did he fully recognize the Swedenborgian theme of 'Green Tea'): see Machen 1943 in response to Rowland 1943. Of course, as a reader of Sheridan Le Fanu, Machen could have become acquainted with Swedenborg's idea of the inner eye indirectly.

[8] Further on this, and more generally on the use of Pan in literature: Merivale 1969, especially chapter 2.

Darwin lurks in the background (the logic being that if there is evolution then there is also the possibility of devolution), and there also lurks, as Aaron Worth suggests, the fear of what Daniel Lord Smail would later dub 'deep history'—that is, the new awareness, after Darwin had sunk into the popular consciousness, that history went much further back than the Bible would have led one to think.[9] This would have been a very disquieting thought for many people, although I will suggest that Machen brings another thought to bear that is just as disquieting, or perhaps even more so.

Machen seems to have been quite taken with the idea of devolution. We see it again in his story *The Novel of the White Powder* (1895) in which a young man who is accidentally given the wrong homeopathic elixir turns into

> ... a dark and putrid mass, seething with corruption and hideous rottenness, neither liquid nor solid but melting and changing right before our eyes ... and out of the midst of it shone two burning points like eyes, and I saw a writhing and a stirring as of limbs, and something moved and lifted up what might have been an arm.

And again in his *Novel of the Black Seal* (1895), in which decipherment of the cryptic, cuneiform-like language on an artifact found at the site of Babylon, leads an 'authority on ethnology whose one thought was for knowledge' to encounter his own puddle of slime one night, a puddle from which emerges a wavering tentacle—a tentacle that three decades later extends its reach all the way to a certain house on Angell Street in Providence, Rhode Island.

But before we go there, let us consider the vehicles through which Machen chooses to introduce this horror into the world. Pan himself, however much Machen has shifted him to the dark side, simultaneously retains his identity as the classical god. About midway through the story, a little boy is stricken with hysteria after foundations for a new building turn up a curiously sculpted head dating to the Roman period, which archaeologists pronounce to be that of a faun or satyr. At another point, the narrator lingers near the mouldering remains of Roman walls, where a young girl has recently died in a terrible way—and where once had stood the temple of Nodens, a Celtic deity who was sometimes equated with the Roman god Silvanus, a god of the woods whom ancient authors associated with Pan. The ruins of the temple had been covered over by a house where Helen once lived.

So also does the ethnologist of *The Black Seal* end in trouble—if not through Classics in the strict sense of Greek and Roman languages and cultures, then

---

9  Eckersley 1992. Worth 2012. Worth draws on Smail 2008.

in the sense of what has long lay at the heart of Classics: a dedication to deciphering ancient languages and a familiarity with even the most abstruse of ancient texts, such as Solinus' fourth-century treatise on the 'Wonders of the World.' which Machen represents as describing the *foeda mysteria* (the 'disgusting mysteries') of the Libyans. That we are here meant to remember *The Great God Pan* (first published five years earlier and in a revised form only a year earlier) seems clear, not only because of the degenerate slime, but also because the frame tale within which *The Black Seal* and *The White Powder* are narrated, along with other stories, signals that. The frame is a short novel called *The Three Imposters*, which concerns the theft of a coin called the Gold Tiberius. The coin shows the face of a faun, a face that is 'both lovely and yet terrible.' Later, the hero of the novel is shanghaied into joining a debauched mystery cult after having drunk the 'wine of the fauns.'

M.R. James, a contemporary of Machen's, repeatedly plays on this theme as well—we might call it the 'evil released through classical philology' theme. Over and over, it is the discovery of an ancient text or an object with a Greek, Latin or Hebrew tag written or engraved upon it that leads James' protagonists (who are often clerics, academics or amateur antiquarians, i.e., the very people with the most highly developed philological skills) into trouble.[10] James was also, of course, the 20th century's greatest scholar of Biblical apocrypha; he made his name by excelling in the knowledge of ancient texts containing ideas that had never won the approval of the church: apocalyptic visions of the torments of Hell, tales of a young Jesus killing his playmates, etc.

And it is important to note how Machen's Helen ended up at last: *not* as a puddle of slime, but rather, after the slime had disappeared, as this:

> a Form, shaped in dimness before me, which I will not farther describe. But the *symbol* of this form may be seen in ancient sculptures, and in paintings which survived beneath the lava, too foul to be spoken of … a horrible and unspeakable shape, neither man nor beast (*Pan* VIII).

Machen intimates that before the slime, before what Darwin had made everyone all too well familiar with as the puddle from which humans had crawled forth, there was something even more horrifying, with which the ancients were well acquainted, even if they chose to express it only symbolically through

---

10 E.g., "An Episode of Cathedral History," "Canon Alberic's Scrapbook," "Casting the Runes," and "O Whistle and I'll Come to You My Lad;" cf. "Lost Hearts," which alludes to a variety of knowledge concerning the Eleusinian and Mithraic Mysteries, the Orphic poems, neoplatonic mysticism and Hermetic texts.

the form of Pan—who himself was neither god nor beast, an imperfectly evolved creature.

The grimness of this idea, especially when it was expressed by Machen, cannot be overemphasized. As a young man of 17, nineteen years before he published *The Great God Pan*, Machen had composed a poem called *Eleusinia*, which exultantly describes what an initiate into Demeter's mysteries would have done and experienced (so far as we know it, anyway), culminating in the line 'The glory of the goddess was revealed.' The epigram that Machen attached to this poem was OUDEIS MUOMENOS ODURETAI: 'No one laments being initiated.' The Greek gods and their mysteries were *desiderata* towards which his young intellect and spirit strove. By the time he wrote *The Great God Pan*, however, he could imagine that a close encounter with an ancient god might be far from glorious, and lamentable indeed.

This idea was beginning to show itself in classical scholarship of the time, as well, particularly in the work of Jane Ellen Harrison, who spent the bulk of her career tearing away the bright glory of the Olympian gods to reveal the dark and dreadful truths of what she argued was 'real' Greek religion. A chapter of Harrison's ground-breaking *Prolegomena to the Study of Greek Religion*, for example, was entitled 'The Demonology of Ghosts, Sprites and Bogeys,' and she famously pronounced in her autobiography that:

> Great things in literature, Greek plays for example, I most enjoy when behind their splendours I see moving darker and older shapes.[11]

The past upon which they all had depended, once, to save them from savagery and lift them into civilization ('they' and 'them' being not just the average citizens of Britain in the 1890s, who could be counted on to have had a rote admiration of 'the glory that was Greece and the grandeur that was Rome' drummed into their heads; but even more markedly, the scholars who had tried to pry open the esoteric mysteries of these civilizations) is presented as more degenerate than anything that even the most determined evolutionist could have imagined. Gnosis of its mysteries could bring only horror. If these gods had once existed, they and what they stood for certainly had not been good. The early Christian fathers had been right after all, then, to call these gods demons.[12]

---

11   Harrison 1965, 344.
12   Starting already with Paul, 1 Cor. 10:20.

## 3

In the first two decades of the twentieth century, quite a few authors picked up on Machen's theme of the threatening Pan. Some of them are famous, even if their stories about Pan are not: E. M. Forster, Saki, E.F Benson and Algernon Blackwood, for example.[13] All of these stories are about people who spurn what Pan stands for, which is always some version of the majesty of nature and freedom from social constraints. The form that Pan's vengeance takes in some of these stories is chilling, but none involves the element of *gnostic* horror that Machen's does.

Until we get to H.P. Lovecraft's 'The Dunwich Horror' (1929), that is. Here we encounter another slimy creature with tentacles that is called into menacing action when someone applies well-honed philological skills to deciphering an obscure language. The similarity is not coincidental: we know that Lovecraft had Machen in mind when he wrote the story.[14]

There are important differences, however. In *Pan*, and for that matter in James' stories, the people who release gnostic horrors upon the world do so mistakenly, out of hubristic curiosity or occasionally out of ignorant greed, but nothing more calculating or evil-intentioned than that. Lovecraft's story, in contrast, begins with witchcraft that is explicitly directed towards inviting evil into the world so that it may impregnate a human woman with a ghastly, destructive creature. This event is followed, years later, by another character's search through dusty university libraries to acquire arcane knowledge that lies hidden behind an unknown language, which he decodes in order to sustain that evil. *Gnosis*, once again, leads to horror by way of philology—'The Horror that Lurks in the Stacks,' we might call it—but purposely so. This deliberate application of philology in the pursuit of evil sets 'The Dunwich Horror' apart from Machen's and James' stories, where philology and other antiquarian pursuits become tools in the hands of people who misguidedly, yet without bad intentions, use them to pry into things that they shouldn't.

---

[13] For example, Forster 1904; Saki 1911; Benson 1912; Blackwood 1917; Machen's Pan also influenced music of the time; see Richards 2015.

[14] Towards the end of Part V of the story, the character Dr. Armitage refers to "Machen's Great God Pan." See also Price 1996, ix–x.

4

The child of *The Great God Pan* that interests me most is Peter Straub's *Ghost Story* (1979). Straub is on record as having been inspired by *Pan*,[15] and he signals this to the observant reader in a number of ways. For example, there is a beautiful woman who seduces and ruins men, like Machen's Helen. She takes on many aliases in the course of the novel, but her initials are always 'A.M.' which, I presume, is an *homage* to Arthur Machen. Eventually, there is a Machen-like scene of devolution, although it doesn't end in slime or mysterious symbols:

> For an instant only, as if [the] corpse were a film, a photographic transparency over another substance, the three of them saw a writhing life through the dead woman's skin—no simple stag or owl, no human or animal body, but a mouth opened beneath [her] mouth and a body constrained within [her] bloody clothing moved with ferocious life: it was as swirling and varied as an oil slick, and it angrily flashed out at them for the moment it was visible; then it blackened and faded, and only the dead woman lay on the floor.
>
> In the next second, the color of her face died to a chalky white and her limbs curled inward, forced by a wind the others could not feel. The dead woman drew up like a sheet of paper tossed on a fire, drawing in, her entire body curling inward like her arms and legs. She fluttered and shrank before them, becoming half her size then a quarter her size, no longer anything human, merely a piece of tortured flesh ... (*Ghost Story* III.19).

The scene evokes Helen's death in *The Great God Pan*, but Straub has taken his own path to get there, for there is nothing esoteric about the way that the protagonists of this novel get into trouble. They are not seeking to open their inner eyes to arcane knowledge. Indeed, most of those who end up literally seeing the truth, such as it is, are looking for nothing more mysterious than the faces of their loved ones.

There is, however, another gnostic experience taking place in *Ghost Story*, which I suggest is already implicit in *The Great God Pan*. Namely, the discovery that greater knowledge of what lies beyond the curtain 'means' nothing at all by any standard of knowledge that a gnostic (or indeed, the average person) would embrace. Straub's novel moves towards the revelation that evil merely *toys* with us, aimlessly, for its own pleasure. There may be *proximate* causes for some of its incursions into the human world—evil entities pursue a particular

---

15   Bosky 1988, 8. See also the interview with Straub at Cruz 2008.

man because he dared to rebuff them once, when they tried to seduce him into degeneracy, for example,—but the main desire of these creatures is simply to amuse themselves. As one of Straub's characters says:

> They have wit. They love jokes, and they make long-term plans, and ... they love to flaunt themselves (*Ghost Story* 11.14).

The devolution that comes upon Machen's Helen has a logical order to it (it's logical if you have been reading Darwin, that is): she regresses to beast, then to 'worse than beast,' then into a 'substance as jelly' before her final, shocking transmogrification into the Form glimpsed in ancient sculptures that was too foul to be spoken of. The Dunwich Horror, dreadful though it be, has been brought into existence through a weird splicing together of witchcraft and philology, each of which also has its own order and rules, perverse though some of them are. Straub, in contrast, insists upon an evil that has no dependable order or rules at all. The only 'gnostic' revelation that Straub's glimpse at evil offers to his readers is that there can be no revelation in the true sense of that word, because there is nothing useful to reveal.[16]

## 5

Straub offers two epigrams to his novel. One, from folklorist R.D. Jameson, is 'Ghosts are always hungry.' But what are they hungry *for*? The disquieting answer seems to be 'just laughs, at the expense of the living.'

The other epigram is from Nathaniel Hawthorne's novel *The Marble Faun*—this is surely also meant as an *homage* to *The Great God Pan*.[17] But the epigram is not only an *homage*. It's also a thematic prelude to the story itself. It reads 'The chasm was merely one of the orifices of the pit of blackness that lies beneath us, everywhere.' I assume that Straub means it to hint at the multiplicity and ubiquity of the metamorphic demons who will terrorize his characters.

---

16   It is significant (although natural, given that he is an American) that Straub has moved the setting of what is otherwise a tale much like that of Machen or M.R. James into pronouncedly American settings—a small town in upstate New York, primarily, and secondarily the Bay Area. The "deep background" of his evil, correspondingly, is not classical, as in the case of Machen or M.R. James, but Native American: in the course of the novel, characters speculate that it is a *manitou*, a shape-shifting entity that the Algonquins believed in.

17   Although it is surely also meant as an *homage* to Hawthorne himself, who is another of the authors whose horror stories underlie the novel, according to Straub. Yet another is Henry James. Two of *Ghost Story*'s main characters are, in fact, named Hawthorne and James.

They follow their victims across continents and decades, emerging at times from what seem to be the most reassuringly banal of settings and situations, shifting shapes as needed.

But I also understand this second epigram (although perhaps it is only I who do so; I can offer no proof that Straub intended this)[18] to be in dialogue with the epigram to 'The Dunwich Horror,' which Lovecraft took from Charles Lamb's 1823 essay 'Witches and Other Night Fears' (Lovecraft's italics):

> Gorgons, and Hydras, and Chimaeras—dire stories of Celaeno and the Harpies—may reproduce themselves in the brain of superstition—*but they were there before.* They are transcripts, types—the archetypes are in us, and eternal.[19]

Lamb argues, in this essay, that each of us is born with terror deeply lodged in our infant minds, which goes on to manifest itself in whatever forms are suggested by the stories we are told in childhood. Stories, by this reading, are themselves orifices of the pit of blackness that lies beneath us.

Four of Straub's main characters, who are men in their waning years, have taken to telling one another ghost stories, apparently in hopes of purging a terrible experience that they shared as young men, which seems to have returned to haunt the ends of their lives. This doesn't work, in part because (as we have learned) the evil that is dogging them has no rules, no predictable behavior, no structure to be grasped and conquered; it is purposely vague and elusive. In the end, the evil is at least partially defeated by Don, the visiting nephew of one of its victims, an unemployed professor of literature who has had his own encounter with it elsewhere but who has survived and has, indeed, managed to turn that encounter into a novel that he published.

---

18  Straub is on record as having reread, 'The Dunwich Horror' repeatedly since his boyhood (see Langan 2012), and he edited a collection of Lovecraft's stories in 2005 for the Library of America, which included 'The Dunwich Horror.' The story directly inspired Straub's novel *Mr. X.* (1999). None of this, of course, proves that Straub intended the epigrammatic allusion that I discuss here.

19  The epigram continues (still quoting Lamb): "How else should the recital of that which we know in a waking sense to be false come to affect us at all? Is it that we naturally conceive terror from such objects, considered in their capacity of being able to inflict upon us bodily injury? O, least of all! *These terrors are of older standing. They date beyond body*—or without the body, they would have been the same. ... That the kind of fear here treated is purely spiritual—that it is strong in proportion as it is objectless on earth, that it predominates in the period of our sinless infancy—are difficulties the solution of which might afford some probable insight into our ante-mundane condition, and a peep at least into the shadowland of pre-existence."

Yet when I say that Don defeats the evil, I am not referring to the scene of devolution that I quoted in the last section of this essay (which is orchestrated by the other hero of the novel, a teenaged boy). In contrast to Machen's Helen, Straub's evil survives its devolution—teasing us and frightening us with its pertinacity. Don, the wielder of words that create (story) worlds, finally succeeds against the evil in the same way as have the heroes of many a folktale: he drives it to take on the form of a creature that is compelled to play by the rules of our own, physical world—rules that give humans an advantage. When that creature finally is defeated, it is defeated not as primeval slime, or even as some representation of evil inherited from a classical past—no Pan, no Gorgon, no Hydra, Chimaera, or Harpy—but as a zoologically discrete animal, a product of our familiar, evolved world.

I have suggested that the most important 'gnostic revelation' to be obtained from *Ghost Story* is that the Other World and its creatures have nothing beneficial to reveal to us because they play by no rules. But we also learn this: that in the final analysis, the resources of our own corporeal existence are our best defenses, and that what the careful person learns from a lifetime of reading stories can provide roads out of the pit of blackness as well, as into it.[20]

## Bibliography

Benson, E.F. 1912. "The Man Who Went Too Far." Pages 1–21 in *The Room in the Tower and Other Stories* (London, Mills & Boon, 1912).

Blackwood, Algernon, 1917. "A Touch of Pan." Pages 16–40, in *Day and Night Stories*. New York, E. P. Dutton.

Borgeaud, Philippe, 1979. *Recherches sur le dieu Pan*. Geneva: Institut Suisse de Rome. Translated by Kathleen Atlass and James Redfield as *The Cult of Pan in Ancient Greece*. 1988 Chicago: University of Chicago Press.

Bosky, Bernadette, 1988. "Peter Straub: From Academe to Shadowland." Pages 3–17 in *Discovering Modern Horror Fiction II*. Edited by Darrell Schweizer. San Bernardino CA: Borgo Press.

Cruz, Gilbert, 2008. "Horror Writer Peter Straub." *Time* Tues. Oct. 14 (http://content.time.com/time/arts/article/0,8599,1850412,00.html). Last accessed January 16, 2016.

---

20 Some readers may wonder why I have not followed through into the work of Stephen King, which has engaged with Machen's *Pan* (and Straub's *Ghost Story*) several times in recent years, most notably in his novel *Revival* (2014). The primary reason is that of space; it would take more words than I am here allotted. A second reason is that King's treatment departs more markedly from *Pan* and the themes I have discussed here than do the treatments of Lovecraft and Straub. But certainly, if one is looking for a gnostic experience from Hell, *Revival* is one place to find it.

DeConick, April D., 2013. "The Road for the Soul is Through the Planets: The Mysteries of the Ophians Mapped." Pages 37–74 in *Practicing Gnosis. Ritual, Magic, Theurgy and Liturgy in Nag Hammadi, Manichaean and Other Ancient Literature. Essays in Honor of Birger A. Pearson*. Edited by April D. DeConick, Gregory Shaw and John D. Turner. Leiden: Brill.

DeConick, April D., 2012. "From the Bowels of Hell to Draco: The Mysteries of the Peratics." Pages 3–38 in *Mystery and Secrecy in the Nag Hammadi Collection and Other Ancient Literature: Ideas and Practices. Studies for Einar Thomassen at Sixty*. Edited by Christian H. Bull, Liv Ingeborg Lied and John D. Turner. Leiden: Brill.

Eckersley, Adrian, 1992. "A Theme in the Early Work of Arthur Machen: Degeneration." Pages 277–87 in *English Literature in Transition, 1880–1920* (1992) 35.3.

Forster, E.M., 1904. "The Story of a Panic." *The Independent Review*. Later collected in E.M. Forster. 1912, *The Celestial Omnibus and Other Stories*. London, Sidgwick & Jackson.

Harrison, Jane Ellen, 1965. "Reminiscences of a Student Life." *Arion* 4.2: 312–46. Originally published 1925. London: The Hogarth Press.

Johnston, Sarah Iles, 1997. "Rising to the Occasion: Theurgic Ascent in its Cultural Milieu." Pages 165–94 in *Envisioning Magic: A Princeton Seminar and Symposium*. Edited by P. Schäfer and H. Kippenberg. Leiden: Brill.

Langan, John, 2012. "Interview: Peter Straub (Part 2)." *Nightmare: Horror and Dark Fantasy* 2 (http://www.nightmare-magazine.com/nonfiction/interview-peter-straub-part-2/). Last accessed January 16, 2016.

Machen, Arthur, 1943. "Letter to John Rowland," personal correspondence of July 23. Reprinted in 2015. *Faunus, The Journal of the Friends of Arthur Machen* 32: 42–3.

Nelson, Victoria, 2001. *The Secret Life of Puppets*. Cambridge MA: Harvard University Press.

Price, Robert M., 1996. *The Dunwich Cycle: Where the Old Gods Wait*. Hayward, CA: Chaosium.

Richards, Fiona, 2015. "Strange Territories: Arthur Machen and John Ireland." Reprinted in 1992. *Faunus. The Journal of the Friends of Arthur Machen* 32: 29–41.

Rowland, John, 1943. "The Mysticism of Arthur Machen." *The New Church Herald* July 17. Reprinted in 2015. *The Journal of the Friends of Arthur Machen* 32: 44–6.

Saki [Hector H. Munro]. 1911. "The Music on the Hill," 149–159 in *The Chronicles of Clovis*. Edited by Saki.

Smail, Daniel Lord, 2008. *On Deep History and the Brain*. Berkeley: University of California Press.

Tracy, Robert, ed. 1993. *Joseph Sheridan Le Fanu: In a Glass Darkly*. Oxford: Oxford University Press.

Worth, Aaron, 2012. "Arthur Machen and the Horrors of Deep History." *Victorian Literature and* Culture 40: 215–27.

# Alan Moore's *Promethea*: Countercultural Gnosis and the End of the World

*Wouter J. Hanegraaff*
University of Amsterdam
*w.j.hanegraaff@uva.nl*

In his monograph *Mutants & Mystics*, published in 2011,[1] Jeffrey J. Kripal has demonstrated how deeply the extremely popular genre of superhero comics depends on gnostic, esoteric, and occultist references and traditions. On the pages that follow, I hope to make a modest contribution to the field of research that Kripal's work has opened up, by analyzing a particularly representative series of "gnostic comics" created the famous British writer Alan Moore in collaboration with penciling artist J.H. Williams III and inker Mick Gray. Their *Promethea* series was published from 1999 to 2005 and has received wide recognition as a virtuoso performance in the art of comics writing and drawing.[2] Specialists in media studies have understandably focused on its formal aspects, but clearly feel out of their depth in discussing its religious or spiritual contents, which usually receive short shrift or are treated with bland incomprehension. On the following pages I will try to fill this hiatus by discussing *Promethea* as a significant example of the search for gnosis in contemporary popular culture.

Kripal himself selected *Promethea* for special discussion in the Introduction of *Mutants & Mystics* (next to Grant Morrison's *The Invisibles*, published from 1994–2000),[3] and his analysis left no doubt about its explicit gnostic message:

> By *gnostic*, Moore means a particular kind of direct and immediate experiential knowledge of one's own divinity that cannot be reduced to reason or faith and stands very much opposed to the consensus reality of society and religion: "Faith is for sissies who daren't go and look for themselves. That's my basic position. Magic is based upon gnosis. Direct knowledge."[4]

---

1  Kripal 2011.
2  E.g. Di Liddo 2009; Hoff Kraemer and Winslade 2010.
3  Kripal 2011, 8–16.
4  Kripal 2011, 15–16; with reference to Moore and Babcock 2007, 131.

In spite of the attention it receives in the Introduction to *Mutants & Mystics*, however, *Promethea* plays no further role in the rest of Kripal's book: except for one passing reference, it is never mentioned again. This might seem a surprising omission at first sight; but in fact, it provides us with some indirect clues to *Promethea*'s specificity in the wider context of superhero comics. One aspect of *Promethea* that makes it special is its explicit feminist agenda.[5] Whereas Kripal's *Mutants & Mystics* focuses on the dominant genre of masculine superheroes or "He-Men," with much attention to male erotic trauma as a source of creative energy, Promethea is the rare example of a female superhero whose superpowers must clearly come from somewhere else. As such, she simply does not seem to fit Kripal's analysis of the comics genre and its underlying erotics. A second factor is more immediately relevant to my concerns in this article: although *Promethea* does contain some secrets hidden beneath the surface, it differs from other superhero comics in requiring no hermeneutics to demonstrate its "esoteric" content. In this particular case, readers do not need Kripal's exegetical skills to unveil its hidden message for them, because that message is stated openly and spelled out in detail. Indeed, as will be seen, *Promethea* is perhaps the most explicitly "occultist" comics ever published. It is a work with thoroughly didactic intent, a crash course in occult philosophy as Moore understands it. In this regard one might perhaps call it "exoteric" rather than "esoteric."

## 1 Alan Moore's Encounter with Asclepius

Born in Northampton in 1953, Alan Moore has received accolades as possibly "the best writer in the history of comic books."[6] His highly innovative *Watchmen* series (1987) is known for its deconstruction of superhero conventions in the context of a grim analysis of Thatcher's England, and propelled its writer to fame in the later 1980s. Several of his other works, notably *From Hell* and *The League of Extraordinary Gentlemen*, have become the basis for mainstream movie adaptations. Describing himself as an atheist in his earlier years, Moore made his coming-out as an occultist magician in the wake of an impressive religious experience on 7 January 1994. On this day, he claims, he encountered a Roman snake god named Glycon who turned out to be none else than the ancient god of healing Asclepius:

---

5 Cf. Green 2011.
6 Khoury 2008.

> Starting with January 1994, all of a sudden, [the occult] suddenly got a little less of a remote academic topic for me. I found myself in the middle of what seemed to be a full-blown magical experience that I could not really account for.
>
> When you've found that you've spent at least part of an evening talking to an entity that tells you that it is a specific Goetic demon that was first mentioned in the Apocrypha, there's only so many ways that you can take that. The most obvious way is that you had some sort of hallucination, or that you had some sort of mental breakdown. Something like that. Which is fine, unless there have been other people there with you who had similar experiences at the time, or something similar. Then, when you say, Alright this was some sort of real experience, you then have to think Well, was it therefore something that was *purely* internal? Was this some part of myself that I've given a name and face to, or projected in some way? That's possible. Or, was this what it said it was? Was this some entirely *external* entity that *actually was* what it claimed to be and was talking to me. That's possible. I tend to try and not rule out any of those. The thing that actually feels most satisfying is the idea that actually it might be both of them.[7]

Moore is here describing a classic dilemma for occultists. Whether such entities must be understood psychologically or metaphysically was a core question already for the 20th century's most influential occultist author, Aleister Crowley,[8] who happens to make some prominent appearances in *Promethea*. Describing his experiences with the snake god Glycon, Moore is quick to emphasize that according to our chief ancient source on the matter (Lucian of Samosata's satire of Alexander of Abonoteichus, who presented himself as a priest of "the new Asclepius"),[9] Glycon was a simple hoax.[10] But this fact does not worry him. On the contrary, it leads him to his chief point:

> To me, the IDEA of the god IS the god.... THAT was what I believe that visited me and my friend upon this first occasion, and [with] which I've had contact on subsequent occasions."[11]

---

7   Moore and Babcock 2007, 125.
8   Pasi 2011, 143–160.
9   Robert 1981.
10  Moore and Babcock 2007, 126.
11  Moore and Babcock 2007, 126.

A few years later, Moore was thrilled to discover that the famous science fiction writer Philip K. Dick had claimed to be in contact with Asclepius as well,[12] thus strengthening Moore's assumption that whatever this "entity" might be, it could not be limited to his personal psyche alone.

What should we make of this experience? Moore is perfectly open about his use of psilocybin mushrooms and other psychoactive substances as spiritual and magical agents,[13] and this makes him representative of an important but under-investigated phenomenon or current in contemporary spirituality that I have elsewhere proposed to refer to as "Entheogenic Esotericism." In its strictest understanding, this term refers to the religious use of psychoactive substances to induce unusual states of consciousness in which practitioners believe they are "filled," "possessed," or "inspired" by some kind of divine entity, presence, or force.[14] Presumably, psychedelic agents facilitated Moore's encounter with Glycon *alias* Asclepius in 1994 as well. Given the intrinsic nature of psychedelic visuals,[15] this perhaps makes it easier to understand his description of how one of the entities he encountered revealed its true nature to him:

> when I actually was allowed to see what the creature looked like, or what it was prepared to show me, it was this latticework ... that was turning itself inside out as I spoke to it, and I was talking to my partner at the time and sort of saying, This thing's showing us it's got an extra dimension I haven't got, and it's trying to tell me that it's good at mathematics.[16]

With this, we are led straight into the heart of a contemporary esoteric worldview based upon the post-Kantian notion that our phenomenal three-dimensional

---

12  Moore and Babcock 2007, 127.
13  Moore and Babcock 2007, 128–129.
14  Hanegraaff 2013b. In this article I draw a distinction between Entheogenic Religion in a strict sense (defined by the use of psychoactive substances) and in a wider sense (referring to the use of other techniques for altering consciousness, such as specific breathing techniques, rhythmic drumming, ritual prayer and incantations, and so on). For a short systematic overview of these different types of trance induction and their relevance to religion, cf. Hanegraaff 2015. Entheogenic Religion becomes Entheogenic *Esotericism* if these entheogenic experiences are interpreted in terms of previous traditions currently classed under the "esotericism" rubric (for a short overview, see Hanegraaff 2013a, 18–44).
15  For the phenomenology of psychedelic experience (induced by a specific class of psychoactive agents including e.g. Psilocybine, LSD-25, and Dimethyltryptamine) see the excellent visual representations in Grey 2012. As one can see there, a seemingly infinite "latticework" (in Moore's formulation, see text) of geometrical patterns in bright colours is highly characteristic of closed-eyes visions induced by such agents.
16  Moore and Babcock 2007, 127.

world is merely the reflection in our minds of a deeper reality of noumenal mystery. True reality is believed to be ultimately beyond our comprehension; but following a broadly Platonic and Pythagorean line of speculation, it may at least be approached through mathematical abstractions (traditionally thought to be perceivable by the Intellect, a mental faculty superior to Reason). While we are capable of experiencing the "energies" of ultimate or noumenal reality, its essence or true nature just cannot be understood in terms of our common Cartesian distinctions between mind and nature or spirit and matter.

This perspective allows Moore to rely on *correspondences* and *analogies* rather than historical connections or causal mechanisms in his efforts to make sense of his spiritual experiences. For instance, it now becomes deeply meaningful, rather than just coincidental, that Glycon is associated with the god of healing Asclepius; that the same name appears in the Hermetic literature; that Asclepius' magical caduceus is circled by two serpents; that the messenger of *gnosis* appeared as a serpent coiled around a tree according to Gnostic interpretations of the Genesis narrative; and that this symbolism recalls the DNA double helix, so that the symbolism of a "cosmic serpent," which also appears in Ayahuasca visions, might be seen as the molecular key to the mystery of life.[17]

By means of such analogical reasoning, Moore leads us straight into the heart of a radical spiritual vision that perceives meaningful correspondences between advanced theories in the natural sciences, elements of transpersonal psychology, psychedelics, and the study of religious symbolism, all in the service of a systematic assault on Cartesian dualism and materialist philosophy.[18] Like all such responses to "the problem of disenchantment,"[19] the ultimate motivation is a search for meaningful and inspiring values that must be grounded in the true nature of reality. Let us now take a closer look at *Promethea* to see what those values are like.

## 2   Fiction as Reality

First and foremost, *Promethea* is an exuberant celebration of the creative imagination.[20] The narrative is based consistently on one single Master Thesis:

---

17   Moore and Babcock 2007, 128, with reference to Narby 1998. Ayahuasca is a famous entheogenic agent from the Amazon region (see e.g. Shanon 2002; Labate and Cavnar 2014).
18   For general overviews of such attempts to synthesize religion, science, and psychology, see Hanegraaff 1996/1998 or Partridge 2004.
19   Asprem 2014.
20   Di Liddo 2009, 99.

*There is no difference between fiction and reality.*

This central focus makes Alan Moore's work extremely relevant to a currently emerging subfield in the study of contemporary religion and esotericism that is sometimes referred to as "fiction-based religions,"[21] sometimes as "hyper-real religions,"[22] and sometimes as "invented religions."[23] The terminology is still very much in a state of flux, but scholars seem to agree that in much of contemporary popular culture (whether online or offline), the question of whether gods, demons, angels, or other spiritual entities or realities are "real" or "imaginary" is becoming ever less relevant to practitioners. As a result, the distinction between "belief" and "non-belief" is becoming a non-issue for them as well.

If the centrality of belief is declining in contemporary religion, its place seems to be taken by the all-important dimensions of *personal experience* and *meaningful practice*. What matters most to practitioners is that it *works* for them to invoke or otherwise interact with spiritual entities, through prayer, ritual, meditation, visualization, and so on. In other words, what counts is that the experiences and practices are powerful and rewarding to them.[24] From such a perspective, theoretical and intellectual questions such as "in what exact sense" can these entities be considered to be real, or what theoretical concept of "reality" is entailed in calling them real, seem a somewhat stuffy legacy of Protestant obsessions quite alien to most practitioners. They are usually happy to leave such questions for philosophers to figure out.

Alan Moore can be seen as such a philosopher, and *Promethea* should be considered his chief theoretical statement. The series is preceded by an essay written in scholarly prose, titled "The Promethea Puzzle: An Adventure in Folklore," in which Moore discusses the historical emergence of the figure of "Promethea."[25] It all began, he tells us, with *A Faerie Romance*: an epic sentimental fantasy written around 1780 by the New England poet Charlton Sennet (1751–1803), in which the nymph Promethea appeared as one of the four handmaidens of the Faerie Queen Titania. Her next appearance was in a comic strip drawn by Margaret Taylor Case, published in Randolph Hearst's *New York Clarion* from 1901 onwards and titled "Little Margie in Misty Magic Land." Next, during World War I, popular rumors began floating around about a warrior

---

21  Davidsen 2014.
22  Possamai 2012.
23  Cusack 2010.
24  Cf. Hanegraaff 2007.
25  Moore et al. 1999–2000.

angel "Promethea" who sometimes appeared to soldiers in the trenches. In 1924, the pulp magazine *Astonishing Stories* began featuring a series called "Promethea, Warrior Queen of Hy Brasil," illustrated by Grace Brannagh. When the magazine was taken over by a new publisher in 1938, *Astonishing Stories*' successor *Smashing Comics* continued the tradition with a new Promethea series drawn by William Woolcott until his death in 1970. Finally, Steven Shelley continued the series until his death in 1991. Alan Moore now picks up the Promethea tradition with his new comics series, starting in 1999.

On the face of it, Moore's introductory prose essay looks like a perfectly convincing piece of historical writing, but in fact it turns out to be his first *theoretical* statement. Similar to Jean Baudrillard's famous treatise *Simulacra and Simulation*, which begins provocatively with a wholly invented quotation from the biblical book of Ecclesiastes,[26] the point is that none of Moore's historical references "really" exist anywhere else than in his own fictional universe. It just so happens that Moore has invented all of them. It is here that we see the beginning of a complex game that he is playing with his readers and their ideas about reality.

## 3   The Story of Promethea

At the very beginning of the *Promethea* cycle, the main protagonist, a college student named Sophie Banks, is busy researching the Promethea myth for her term paper. In other words, she is doing precisely what the average reader is most likely *not* doing: checking the literary sources mentioned in Moore's introductory essay and tracing them back to their historical origins. These investigations lead her to visit Barbara Shelley, the widow of the last Promethea author Steven Shelley.

Through the following series of events, we learn that the fictional figure of Promethea is capable of incarnating in the real world as a demi-goddess with incredible superpowers. Her origins go back to early fifth century Alexandria, where the last pagans are being persecuted by the Christians. A Hermetic philosopher sends his young daughter into the desert to save her from the killers who are coming for him, and it is there that she meets Thoth-Hermes. But the god/s cannot keep her safe in this world: "our influence here is waning, our priests slain by those of the new god. A dark age is coming."[27] However, they can take her to their own world, the "Immateria" or realm of ideas, where she

---

26   Baudrillard 1994, 1.
27   Promethea #1.

will no longer be a little girl but will live eternally *as a story*. Will she ever be able to return to this world, she asks? Well..., they answer, "sometimes, if a story is *very* special, it can quite take people *over*. We'll see."[28]

This process of being taken over by a story in fact happened to the poet Charlton Sennet in 1779.[29] In a dream he saw the faerie Queen Titania with her four helpmaidens, one of whom inspired him to write a long poem:

> About their Queen, four nymphs in waiting stood,
> Girded in armor, each of beauty rare
> Courslip and Flax and Jenny-in-the-Wood
> And sweet Promethea with her plaited hair
>
> Promethea, the shepherd understood,
> Had with her glamours captivated him;
> With lips, with skin like polished betel-wood,
> With ocean eyes, wherein a man might swim.
>
> Her smile ethereal, magnificent,
> Her lyric movements, her fragility,
> Her gentleness, her orchidaceous scent
> Enraptured him, enslaved him utterly.[30]

Charlton Sennet's story ends badly. While he is reciting his poem to his housemaid Anna, she is magically transformed into the faery Promethea, and he can no longer tell the difference between dream and reality. His passionate love affair with the faerie ends in disaster: his wife divorces him, his housemaid Anna dies while giving birth to a monstrous child, and Charlton spends the rest of his days in utter loneliness—although surrounded by elemental beings that he cannot see.

From now on, Promethea keeps incarnating from time to time, and it is always through the medium of art or poetry that she is invited into this world. This reflects Moore's conviction that art and magic are "almost completely interchangeable.[31] We are told that the 20th-century artists who wrote Promethea comics were in fact channeling her into their own bodies or those of their partners. This makes them into Sophie Bank's predecessors, and these

---

28   Promethea # 1.
29   Promethea # 4.
30   Promethea # 4.
31   Martin 2014; Moore 2011, 189.

previous Prometheas or vehicles of the faerie goddess are now watching her adventures with great curiosity from the realm of Immateria.

The last of the artists was Steven Shelley, and his wife Barbara was the last of the Prometheas. After his death she has put on weight and turned into an embittered and lonely woman, so when Sophie starts questioning her about Promethea, she shrugs her off and sends her on her way. In the meantime, however, the forces of darkness have learned of Sophie's inquiries. They want to prevent her from learning too much, lest she might become a new vessel for their mortal enemy Promethea. She gets attacked on the street by a shadow demon (a Smee), but is saved by a superheroine who suddenly turns up out of nowhere. This appears to be no one else than Barbara herself transformed into Promethea. It is the beginning of an apprenticeship and a friendship through which Sophie learns that she, too, has the power of transforming herself into Promethea by means of writing poetry:

> I am Promethea, God-adopted one,
> Reared in their immaterial hills and vales.
> My tale is in the world of substance spun,
> Yet is my substance in the world of tales
> ....
> I am Promethea, art's fiercest spark
> I am all inspiration, all desire,
> Imagination's blaze in mankind's dark
> I am Promethea, I bring you fire![32]

Sophie alias Promethea finds herself transformed into a "science heroine" (not a science *fiction* heroine, for what could that possibly mean in a fictional universe?), and enters into collegial competition with the other superheroes who are active protecting the population of Moore's alternative New York, notably the "Five Swell Boys" who are battling a sinister killer known as The Painted Doll. Most spectacularly, she has to fight an army of demons who appear disguised as gangsters but reveal their real shapes to those who have the vision to see them. Behind them are sinister forces, notably a black magician named Benny Solomon and an organization that calls itself The Temple. Eventually, we learn that this is a group of naïve but determined Evangelicals who are convinced that Promethea is a demon. Here Moore is making the excellent point that contemporary Evangelicals and Christian Fundamentalists are among the most serious believers in the reality of the occult today. They

---

32   Promethea # 1.

*really* believe in demons and occult powers, arguably more so than many occultist practitioners, who tend to have a more complex, ironic, or distanced attitude towards questions of reality/unreality or existence/non-existence.

## 4  Tarot Initiation and Tarot History

Moore then takes his reader through Sophie's first forays into the world of Immateria[33] and her meeting with the previous Prometheas (first introduced in *Promethea* # 4), who eventually join her in battling the forces of darkness. Meanwhile Sophie's friend Stacia Vanderveer, the prototype of a shallow teenage bimbo, is having a hard time catching up with what is happening; but eventually, she too embarks upon a parallel path of magical exploration that will bring her into conflict with Sophie.

Crucial to Sophie's own story is her step-by-step initiation into the mysteries of magic by means of the four Tarot suits: Cups, Swords, Coins or Pentacles, and Wands. In *Promethea* # 5, Sophie's guide is the former Promethea Margaret—no one else than Margaret Taylor Case, the author (as we have seen) of the original series "Little Margie in Mystic Magic Land." It is she who, transformed into Promethea, had made those appearances as an angel of mercy to soldiers in the trenches of World War I. Taking Sophie on a visionary tour through the 20th-century horrors of war, Margaret initiates her into the mysteries of the Cup: *Compassion* for suffering humanity.

In *Promethea* # 6, the former Promethea Grace (Grace Brannagh) initiates her into the Tarot mysteries of Swords, which stand for the power of *reason and discrimination* that slices through illusion ("frankly, dear, they cut through bullshit"). Sophie meets Grace in the threatening landscape of the comics she created while alive, "Hy Brasil," full of "torture, chambers, demon altars, hunchbacks and skeletons." As it turns out, Grace's work has been usurped by a writers' collective that goes by the name Marto Neptura, whose face appears in the sky like an all-seeing creator God. But Sophie appears to be learning fast: she breaks Marto Neptura's power by using the "Sword" of reductionist logic to destroy his appearance of divine omnipotence.

In *Promethea* # 7, Sophie is initiated into the mystery of Coins or Pentacles by yet another former Promethea: a fun-loving girl who goes by the incongruous name of Bill (because that is how she was imagined by her creator William Woolcott, who was gay). Coins/Pentacles stands for the world of *the senses*: Bill is utterly in love with "all the things we have a taste for," such as food, comfort,

---

33  Promethea # 3.

love, wealth, fame, or happiness. The message is that such pursuits are not necessarily bad, as would be suggested by more ascetic or otherworldly interpretations of the search for *gnosis*: the things of this world are there for us to be enjoyed to the fullest, as long as we do not fall prey to the delusion that there is nothing else.

Finally, in *Promethea* # 10, Sophie is initiated into the mysteries of the Wand, "symbol of god considered as male ... The symbol of the magician, of the will, of that which penetrates the mystery." It happens through tantric sex with Jack Faust, a shady occultist in the Crowley tradition. Contrary to the view of some critics, whose politically correct reflexes seem to blind them to what is going on in this sequence,[34] I consider it to be one of the highlights of the *Promethea* cycle. Sure enough, it seems to begin as a rather sordid story, with the beautiful young heroine performing a striptease and consenting to intercourse with a horrible old man on a dirty mattress, in exchange for his magical knowledge. However, it culminates in an orgasmic experience of supreme love and divine union, when the two lovers succeed in leading the "serpent power" of *kundalini* all the way up from the lowest to the highest *chakra* and both find themselves transformed into their higher and better selves. The symbolism is clear, or should be: even the sordid realities of this dark and horrible world (symbolized by Jack Faust's dirty room in a New York City basement) are not ultimately real, but can become a world of heavenly bliss through the magical power of our consciousness in union with our creative imagination. In basic Platonic terms, this transformation of the human passions is ultimately driven by erotic desire for ultimate beauty,[35] and thus we see how what begins with physical sex culminates in a transcendent experience of universal love.

Next we are presented to Moore's vision of world history and the evolution of consciousness, explained in *Promethea* #12 through a dazzling tour-de-force of multilevel multimedia instruction.[36] The two snakes of Promethea's caduceus delightfully introduce themselves as Mike and Mack (for "microcosm" and "macrocosm"!), and recite a long metric poem that takes Sophie from the period before the Big Bang all the way up to the present time. The poem is a running commentary on the twenty-two lower Arcana cards of the Tarot, and while those cards are presented one by one, Aleister Crowley is telling a story that explains the nature of the imagination in the form of a joke. Both Crowley and the universe (standing, again, for the parallel realities of microcosm and macrocosm) are moving simultaneously from the fetal state through

---

34  E.g. Fischer 2004, 124, with reference to Linda Santiman.
35  Hanegraaff 2011.
36  Cf. Locke 2012, 391–394.

the various stages of maturity towards old age, death, and ultimately rebirth. There is a bonus for readers who delight in puzzles: the name "Promethea" appears on Scrabble stones in a series of frankly amazing permutations (e.g. "Metaphore," "Mater Hope," "Ape Mother," "Me Atop Her," "O Mere Path," "A Pro Theme," "Hear Tempo," "O Harem Pet," "O Reap Them," "The Mop Era," "Metro Heap," "Meet Harpo," and "Heart Poem").

As for Moore's vision of world history, it starts at the physical level, from the initial quantum vacuum through the Big Bang to the emergence of Planet Earth and animal life; then it moves from physical to cultural history, beginning with primitive and shamanic hunter/gatherer societies and leading up to classical civilization, "where history as we know it commences."[37] Finally, we are taken from the Roman Empire to the Age of Reason, the emergence of industrial society, and the horrors of the World Wars. After World War II, the psychedelic age marks the beginning of a process of ever-quickening spiritual evolution, finally leading up to "the end of the world" (as we will see below). It should be noted that Moore's evolutionist narrative, like most occultist views of world history, is unapologetically Whiggish and ethnocentric: the whole of world history converges upon the modern West, with no significant role for the Orient or any other culture of the world.

## 5 The Sefirotic Tree

For many readers, the most puzzling part of *Promethea* is the middle section, where Sophie and Barbara travel from the Immateria through the ten Sefirotic spheres of the kabbalistic tree of life in search of Barbara's deceased husband Steven Shelley. It is here that the conventional superhero format most clearly takes a back seat in favour of thoroughly didactic instruction about the true nature of reality and ultimate values.

Alan Moore's 1999 City of New York is located, of course, at the bottom: in Malkuth ("Kingdom"), the material world. From here, Sophie takes route 32, at the end of which Charon takes her over the Styx to Yesod ("Foundation"). This is the lunar realm of the unconscious, the dream world or world of the dead. Here she finds Barbara, who seems to be talking with her deceased husband Steven but has just discovered that instead of the real Steven it is just his shadow. Sophie and Barbara take off over route 30 to Hod ("Splendour"). This is the sun-drenched world of the intellect, language, magic, thought, ideas, time, and communication.

---

37  *Promethea* # 12.

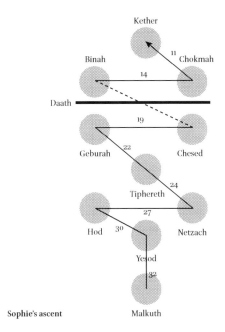

Predictably, given those attributes, it is here that they meet Hermes Trismegistus. But they also meet Aleister Crowley, who is playing chess with another famous occultist, Austin Osman Spare. Sophie and Barbara are directed towards route 27, over which they reach Netzach ("Victory"), the Venusian realm, where they find themselves literally drowning in a sea of love and deep emotions. Having climbed ashore, on route 24 they meet the figure of Death, who attacks and seems to kill them, but in fact kills only their earthly attachments, worldly ideas, and petty emotions. They make it to Tiphereth ("beauty, harmony"), the realm of the Self, where Barbara meets her own Higher Self or "Holy Guardian Angel," in the shape of her own 15-year old persona.

Through route 22, the three travel on to Geburah ("Strength, Stern Judgment"), a fiery red landscape that functions like a kind of purgatory. Here they get trapped in the demonic Qlippoth or world of the Shells, from which they escape only by learning to treat the presiding demon Asmodeus with respect instead of anger and hatred. Over route 19 they reach Chesed ("Mercy"), a cloudy blue world that smells like cedar incense and is described as "the Fatherland." Here Sophie is reunited with the father of the entire myth, the Hermetic magus of Alexandria who had sent his daughter into the desert, where she was saved by Thoth-Hermes and became the "living story" Promethea. But Sophie is also reunited with her physical father, who had left her mother when she was pregnant. Sophie is now divested of her Promethea persona and has to continue the journey as no one but herself.

The lower seven sephiroth are separated from the upper three by an abyss, known as the "invisible" eleventh sphere of Daath: no route leads from the fourth sphere of Chesed to the third sphere of Binah. Sophie and Barbara therefore have to literally jump into the abyss. It is in the dreadful sphere of Daath that, among other things, they witness Crowley and Victor Neuberg in the midst of their infamous "Choronzon working," through which Crowley allegedly "sacrificed himself" through ritual sodomy with his partner Victor Neuberg.[38] They finally reach Binah ("Understanding"), a place filled with holiness, where Sophie dons a new and more splendid set of "Promethea" garments.

They meet the "benevolent adepts" headed by none else than the Elizabethan magus John Dee. He leads them towards the awesome figure of the Eternal Feminine, who encompasses the entire spectrum of female energies from the biblical Whore of Babylon to the Madonna or virginal Mother Mary. Over route 14 they reach Chokmah ("Wisdom"), dominated by her counterpart, the masculine divine energy. This visit culminates in a vision of the primal sexual act as the origin of creation, in the form of the god Pan having sex with the goddess Selene. This mythological scene culminates in a cosmic orgasm that signifies the Big Bang, with Barbara exclaiming in amazement "I just came. *Everything just came.*"[39]

Finally, they ascend route 11, a spiraling "stairway to heaven" that leads into the ineffable sphere of Keter ("Crown"). In this sphere of ultimate unity, all words and concepts become meaningless, and we see Sophie and Barbara shifting in and out of existence and conscious experience. In this place of ultimate unification, Barbara is reunited at last with her deceased husband Steven, and the two are transformed into a kind of mythical Adam and Eve. In other words: once having reached the end of their quest, they have gone back to The Beginning.

So what next? The only way forward leads into the world of matter once again. As Steven explains,

> When we climb up the tree winding from sphere to sphere, then we're *serpents*. The serpent is the will to climb, and rise. The will to *live*. But when we choose to descend from this sacred purity, back into the turmoil and suffering of the world, then we're *doves*. The dove is the will to sacrifice, to descend. The will to *die*. The will to die to this glorious world

---

38  See Owen 2004, 198.
39  *Promethea* # 22.

of *spirit*, and live again in *matter*. The will to take a little more *light* back down into the world, where it *needs* it.[40]

We should note the reversal of common assumptions that is implied here: in line with basic Platonic mythology, leaving the material world behind is a movement towards *life*, while moving back into the world of matter, out of compassion for suffering humanity, means a sacrificial *death*. In short: pure spirit is true life, pure matter is death. Sophie and her companions decide to take the plunge downwards and descend back into the world as spiritual light-bringers.

## 6   The End of the World

With this incarnational plunge downwards, we enter the third and final, apocalyptic part of the cycle. To understand it, we need to move back for a moment to *Promethea* # 5, where Sophie is in conversation with Margaret, her initiator into the mysteries of Compassion. Margaret explained why their enemies are afraid of Sophie: it is because she represents the fact that *anyone* can travel from the material world into the world of Immateria.

> Promethea makes people more *aware* of this vast immaterial realm. Maybe tempts them to *explore* it. Imagine if too many people followed where she led? It would be like the great *Devonian* leap, from *sea* to *land*. Humanity slithering up the beach, from *one* element into *another*. From *matter* to *mind*. We have many names for this event. We call it "the *rapture*." We call it "the opening of the 32nd path." We call it the *Awakening*, or the *Revelation*, or the *Apocalypse*. But "End of the World" will do.[41]

When Sophie responds "Uhh, but … the end of the *world*. That's a *bad* thing, right?," we are given a quick view of the horrors of the 20th century. Margaret responds to Sophie's question:

> Is it? "The world" isn't the *planet*, or the life and people *on* it. The world is our systems, our politics, our economies … our ideas of the world. It's our

---

40   *Promethea* # 23.
41   *Promethea* # 5.

flags and our banknotes and our border wars. I was at *Ypres*. I was at the *Somme*. I say end this filthy mess *now*.[42]

And that is what happens in the third and final part of the *Promethea* cycle. Alan Moore picks up the thread a few years after Sophie's travel through the *Sefirotic* spheres and her plunge back into earth. It is 2003, world news is dominated by the war in Iraq, and Sophie seems to have forgotten everything that happened to her. Once having returned to earth, she had barely managed to escape arrest by the FBI. As Margaret had pointed out to her earlier, the powers of this world

> have a vested interest in keeping the world as it is, because that's the world they have power over. You see, in the Immateria, there's no rent, no tax, no property. There's no real estate, no boundary fences, no limits.[43]

Promethea had been framed in the popular media as a dangerous terrorist, and all her friends have been imprisoned. Sophie barely managed to escape arrest herself, and is now living incognito with her boyfriend. But when the authorities finally discover her identity, she has no choice but to become Promethea once more, and this time she sets out to actually "end the world." Having traveled through all the Sefirotic spheres up to divine unity, she is now in full command of all her powers. For instance, when the cops try to shoot her, the bullets turn into butterfly moths—an explicit reference to the Promethea moth, symbol of transformation, and to Frederick Myers on the *imago* or "perfect insect."[44]

With Promethea flying above New York like a radiant angel, the consciousness of its inhabitants begins to be altered in strange and unpredictable ways. Time no longer seems to flow in a linear direction; solid things become fluid; reality shifts into hyper-reality; three-dimensional figures or objects turn into two-dimensional comic strips; people are swept away by radical psychedelic visions and no longer know where they are; and so on. Interspersed with these radical events are blocks of lyric prose commentary that further heightens the alienating sense of imagination encroaching upon reality:

> Suddenly we were all exactly who we were, for better or worse, and then the President announced more troops were needed in Iraq and we kept catching ourselves in the mirror, recognizing something, something

---

42   *Promethea* # 5.
43   *Promethea* # 5.
44   Myers 1903, xviii; and cf *Promethea* # 32 about the Promethea moth, *Callosamia promethea*.

shining under the familiar crease and contour of our faces, this unique light of our mythical, our holy personalities, each of us singular, each unrepeatable in the immensity of Spacetime and right there we all remembered we were real, were lovers, gods or friends in our own burning sagas so we cried "What are those dreary yards that we have built? What lives are these that drape us gray like shrouds?" and understood we were all heroes in our souls.[45]

This final section of *Promethea* is all about Alan Moore's personal vision of the apocalyptic "end of time" that, in countercultural esotericism, has been referred to by such terms as Omega Point, Timewave Zero, the Rapture, or the Singularity: a radical shift of global consciousness that many representatives of the contemporary spiritual counterculture expected would occur on the 21st of December 2012.[46]

These forms of contemporary millenarianism are the direct reflection of a radical countercultural critique directed against what is sometimes referred to as "the Society of the Spectacle" and its alienating effects on the human mind. The term was coined by Guy Debord originally in 1967[47] and has been widely adopted in anarchist and radical counter-cultural spiritual milieus. It refers precisely to the kind of life-world pictured as "New York" in Alan Moore's work: a society dominated entirely by "interlocking communications technology, mass media, and corporate control," in which "the simulacra of mass communications and advertising fill all available social space."[48] When Promethea "brings the world to its end," Moore does not mean that she is putting an end to the planet, but to this artificial world of global Capitalist consumerism.

So how is it done? Towards the end of the cycle, we find Promethea sitting in a room next to a cozy fireside, addressing the reader directly:

> Yes, Promethea's a fiction. Nobody ever claimed otherwise. I never lied. I'm at least an honest fiction. A true fiction. A fiction that can enter your dreams, possess her creators, talk through them to you. I'm an idea. But I'm a *real* idea. I'm the idea of the human *imagination* ... which, when you think about it, is the only thing we can really be certain *isn't* imaginary.[49]

---

45  *Promethea* # 28.
46  Braden et al. 2007; cf Hanegraaff 2010.
47  Debord 2000.
48  Sellars 2010, 85.
49  *Promethea* # 31.

Ultimately, she points out, nothing exists except "a funny little twist of aminoacids, playing a marvelous game of pretend."[50] The entire story of the universe is just a story told by the fireside. In the end, nothing really exists except the Reader and Promethea—or in other words, *Mind* and *Imagination*. These two have been together "since this room was a cave," and together they have created our world:

> Do you remember? When you first thought you saw things in the flames, in the dancing shadows ... and you needed me to tell you a tale. A story grand and glorious.[51]

So this is what the whole of reality is: a story told by the fireside, an infinite play of the imagination experienced by the human mind. The room slowly gets dark, and we read Promethea's final words: "stay awake."

## 7    Hermetic Gnosis

While the story of Promethea begins and ends there, the comics strip does not. In a first epilogue, we discover that life just goes on after the Apocalypse, only a little different. This is because "Everybody had the revelation, but not everybody understood it, or took any notice of it".[52] What seems to be implied here is very similar to how the "coming of the New Age" was understood already by some pioneering New Age authors in the 1970s, notably David Spangler.[53] Here the "end of time" stood for a global spiritual transformation that would, however, be perceived only by those with the right "attunement," those who were ready for it. As for all the others—those who had not yet been able to transcend their old, inherited, limited and limiting patterns of imagining reality—, they would remain trapped in the same world they had always known, because it was the only world they were capable of perceiving and understanding.

In a second epilogue, finally, our three-dimensional world has been left behind entirely. A naked goddess Promethea is addressing her readers not from the perspective of any particular world created by human consciousness, but from the perspective of consciousness itself. What Moore seems to have in

---

50   *Promethea* # 31.
51   *Promethea* # 31.
52   *Promethea* # 31.
53   See Hanegraaff 1996/1998, 354–355.

mind here is very similar to the "Devachanic Plane" of modern Theosophy.[54] We see Promethea freely flying or swimming through multiple dimensions and energies, depicted in swirling colours, while she gives the reader a final overview of the underlying philosophy, full of references to quantum physics and neuroscience and to favorite authors of the spiritual counterculture such as Aldous Huxley, Julian Jaynes, Carl Gustav Jung, Robert Anton Wilson, Robert Graves, Harold Morowitz, Douglas Hofstadter, and so on. Since the universal "cosmic memory" is supposed to be located on the Devachanic Plane, it is perhaps fitting that this final issue of Promethea amounts to a glimpse of Moore's bibliography or list of basic references for anybody who wants to continue exploring his ideas.[55]

Finally, *Promethea* # 32 is the ultimate example of a secret concealed behind the surface. If one pulls the pages apart they can be reconfigured into a double-sided poster with two large images of Promethea; and the spherical captions on each page turn out to be linked through trails of stars or ankh symbols, resulting in "a network of hypertextual rhizomes that bound around the picture plane unfettered by either page-by-page reading order or the visual rhetoric of the Promethea portraits".[56]

Alan Moore's myth of Promethea is clearly focused on the attainment of *gnosis*; but to be more specific about what this means to him, it may be useful to compare his work to another influential work of popular Gnostic fiction produced in the same year 1999. The central concept of the movie *The Matrix* by the Wachowsky brothers is that we are imprisoned in a computer-generated illusion called the Matrix, and need to "wake up" to reality as it really is. As many commentators have noted, this message is formulated explicitly as an update of "classic" gnostic dualism.[57] In the words of the super-hacker Morpheus, during his first meeting with the main protagonist Neo, the matrix is "the world

---

54   Leadbeater 1896.
55   Moore mentions (here in alphabetical order) Dead Sea Scrolls specialist and mushroom mythographer John Allegro (*The Sacred Mushroom and the Cross*); writer John Kendrick Bangs; Feminist writer Helene Cixous (*Le livre de Promethea*); Occultist Aleister Crowley; physicist Albert Einstein; physicist Murray Gell-Man ("Information Gathering and Utilizing Systems", or IGUS's); writer Robert Graves; physicist Werner Heisenberg; cognitive scientist Douglas Hofstadter (*Gödel, Escher, Bach*); writer Aldous Huxley (*The Doors of Perception*); psychologist Julian Jaynes (*The Origin of Consciousness in the Breakdown of the Bicameral Mind*); writer James Joyce (*Finnegan's Wake*); psychologist Carl Gustav Jung; composer Claudio Monteverdi; biophysicist Harold Morowitz; ethnobotanist Jeremy Narby (*The Cosmic Serpent*); occultist and artist Austin Osman Spare; visionary theosopher Emanuel Swedenborg; and discordian writer Robert Anton Wilson.
56   Fischer 2005, 126.
57   See Flannery-Dailey & Wagner 2001; and the chapter on *The Matrix* in DeConick 2016.

that has been pulled over your eyes to blind you from the truth." It was made by demonic powers (the demiurge and the archons, represented in the movie as "the Architect" and hosts of "Men in Black") who are trying to keep us enslaved through cultivating ignorance—absence of *gnosis*—about our true condition.

Interestingly, Moore's final message is different in a subtle but important sense. Whereas *The Matrix* begins significantly with the call to "Wake Up," *Promethea* ends (no less significantly) with the words "Stay Awake." Ultimately, Moore's work is not so much about waking up from the illusion of the world but about staying awake to what really exists and who we really are. In other words, Moore's story is not about escaping from the prison of the world but, rather, about realizing that there is no prison except the one that we create for ourselves through our own imagination. Sure enough, similar interpretations of "imprisonment" or "delusion" can be found in *The Matrix* as well (most obviously in the famous "there is no spoon" scene); and yet, although it might be possible to reconcile the underlying philosophies, the emphases are different. In a structural and typological sense, I would suggest, the *Promethea* cycle can be seen as a *Hermetic* panentheist or cosmotheist[58] alternative to classic understandings of "Gnostic" dualism. The difference lies precisely in the role of the imagination. Although Moore does not call attention to it, *Corpus Hermeticum* XI contains a doctrine that would seem to be tailor-made for him:

> All is within God; but not as if lying in a place.... Within God everything lies in bodiless imagination. Reflect on God in this way as having all within Himself as ideas: the cosmos, Himself, the whole. If you do not make yourself equal to God you cannot understand Him. Like is understood by like. Grow to immeasurable size. Be free from every body, transcend all time. Become eternity and thus you will understand God. Suppose nothing to be impossible for yourself. Consider yourself immortal and able to understand everything: all arts, sciences and the nature of every living creature. Become higher than all heights and lower than all depths.... Conceive yourself to be in all places at the same time: in earth, in the sea, in heaven; that you are not yet born, that you're within the womb, that you are young, old, dead; that you are beyond death.

---

58   Whereas "pantheism" means that God and the world are identical, "panentheism" means rather that they are inseparably interwoven (Hanegraaff 2013a, 71, 78, 115–116). The closely equivalent term "cosmotheism" was coined by Lamoignon de Malesherbes in 1782 and popularized by Jan Assmann (see Hanegraaff 2012, 371–373, 376–378).

> Conceive all things at once: times, places, actions, qualities and quantities; then you can understand God.[59]

According to this Hermetic perspective, the world does not stand over against God but, on the contrary, exists in (or as) God's imagination (*fantasia* according to the Greek original). Therefore, it is only through the imagination that human beings can become godlike and actually participate in the mind of God, thereby achieving divine *gnosis* in the most literal and radical sense.

Accordingly, it is not the world that must be rejected or from which human beings need to escape—"ending the world" does not mean destroying the matrix. Moore's message is more positive. It is about staying awake to the true nature of our own selves as omnipotent divine creators who have the power to create our own world as beautifully as we wish. From that perspective, "ending the world" means unmasking the Spectacle as the negative counterpart of what the imagination could and should be—an empty and soulless world of mere simulacra, sentimental and mechanical mass-produced images that belittle and limit the divine powers of the mind, impoverished surrogates of what creativity really means.

Alan Moore's *Promethea* is significant for several reasons. First, it is one of the most impressive and philosophically consistent manifestoes of a new kind of esotericism that is rapidly developing and spreading in popular culture at present, especially among younger people, both online and offline. Second, it is an excellent example of "fiction-based religion" that both reflects *and* theorizes the rapidly dissolving boundary between "fiction" and "reality" in popular media culture. Third, it exemplifies the subversive potential of popular comics, as its ultimate objective is to break the spell of corporate control and capitalist consumerism on which the genre nevertheless depends for reaching its audience. Fourth, it presents a "Hermetic" alternative to Hans Jonas' classic reading of "Gnosticism" as both a product of and a revolt against alienation and nihilist despair. Fifth and last, it provides its readers with some serious food for thought concerning the nature and the role of the imagination in shaping our culture, our society, and our everyday life.

## Bibliography

Asprem, Egil. 2014. *The Problem of Disenchantment: Scientific Naturalism and Esoteric Discourse, 1900–1939*. Leiden / Boston: Brill.

---

59   Corp. herm. 11.18–20 (trans. Salaman et al. 1999, 57–58).

Baudrillard, Jean. 1994. *Simulacra and Simulation*. University of Michigan Press.

Braden, Gregg et alii. 2007. *The Mystery of 2012: Predictions, Prophecies & Possibilities*. Boulder: Sounds True.

Cusack, Carole. 2010. *Invented Religions: Imagination, Fiction and Faith*. Farnham / Burlington: Ashgate.

Davidsen, Markus Altena. 2014. *The Spiritual Tolkien Milieu: A Study of Fiction-Based Religion*. Ph.D. Dissertation, University of Leiden.

Debord, Guy. 2000. French Orig. 1967. *The Society of the Spectacle*. Detroit: Black & Red.

DeConick, April D. 2016. *The Gnostic New Age: How a Countercultural Spirituality Revolutionized Religion from Antiquity to Today*. New York: Columbia University Press.

Fischer, Craig. 2005. "Review Essay: Charmageddon! Or the Day Aleister Crowley Wrote Wonder Woman." *Iowa Journal of Cultural Studies* 6: 122–127.

Flannery-Dailey, Frances & Rachel Wagner. 2001. "Wake Up! Gnosticism and Buddhism in The Matrix." *Journal of Religion and Film* 5:2 https://www.unomaha.edu/jrf/gnostic.htm (no pagination).

Green, Matthew J.A. 2011. "'She Brings Apocalypse': Sex, Imagination and Redemptive Transgression in William Blake and the Graphic Novels of Alan Moore." *Literature Compass* 8: 739–756.

Grey, Alex. 2012. *Net of Being*. Rochester: Inner Traditions.

Hanegraaff, Wouter J. 1996/1998. *New Age Religion and Western Culture: Esotericism in the Mirror of Secular Thought*. Leiden: Brill and Albany: State University of New York Press.

Hanegraaff, Wouter J. 2007. "Fiction in the Desert of the Real: Lovecraft's Cthulhu Mythos." *Aries* 7: 85–109.

Hanegraaff, Wouter J. 2010. "'And End History. And go to the Stars': Terence McKenna and 2012." Pages 291–312 in *Religion and Retributive Logic: Essays in Honour of Professor Garry W. Trompf*. Edited by Carole M. Cusack and Christopher Hartney. Leiden: Brill.

Hanegraaff, Wouter J. 2011. "Under the Mantle of Love: The Mystical Eroticisms of Marsilio Ficino and Giordano Bruno." Pages 175–207 in *Hidden Intercourse: Eros and Sexuality in the History of Western Esotericism*. Edited by Wouter J. Hanegraaff and Jeffrey J. Kripal. New York: Fordham University Press.

Hanegraaff, Wouter J. 2012. *Esotericism and the Academy: Rejected Knowledge in Western Culture*. Cambridge: Cambridge University Press.

Hanegraaff, Wouter J. 2013a. *Western Esotericism: A Guide for the Perplexed*. London: Bloomsbury.

Hanegraaff, Wouter J. 2013b. "Entheogenic Esotericism." Pages 392–408 in *Contemporary Esotericism*. Edited by Egil Asprem and Kennet Granholm. Sheffield: Equinox.

Hanegraaff, Wouter J. 2015. "Trance." Pages 511–513 in *Vocabulary for the Study of Religion*. Edited by Robert A. Segal and Kocku von Stuckrad. Leiden: Brill.

Hoff Kraemer, Christine and J. Lawton Winslade. 2010. "'The Magic Circus of the Mind': Alan Moore's Promethea and the Transformation of Consciousness through Comics." Pages 274–291 in *Graven Images: Religion in Comic Books and Graphic Novels*. Edited by A. David Lewis and Christine Hoff Kraemer. London: Continuum.

Khoury, George. 2008. *The Extraordinary Works of Alan Moore: Indispensable Edition*. Raleigh: TwoMorrows.

Kripal, Jeff. 2011. *Mutants & Mystics: Science Fiction, Superhero Comics, and the Paranormal*. Chicago: The University of Chicago Press.

Labate, Beatriz Caiuby. 2014. *Ayahuasca Shamanism in the Amazon and Beyond*. Oxford: Oxford University Press.

Leadbeater, Charles Webster. 1896. *The Devachanic Plane: Its Characteristics and Inhabitants*. London: Theosophical Publishing Society.

Liddo, Annalisa di. 2009. *Alan Moore: Comics as Performance, Fiction as Scalpel*. Jackson: University Press of Mississippi.

Locke, Simon. 2012. "Spirit(ualitie)s of Science in Words and Pictures: Syncretising Science and Religion in the Cosmologies of Two Comic Books." *Journal of Contemporary Religion* 27: 383–401.

Martin, Tim, "Everything and Moore." *Aeon*, 17 October 2014 (Aeon.co/magazine/culture/alan-moore-i-am-in-charge-of-this-universe/) (online publication: no pagination).

Moore, Alan, J.H. Williams and Mick Gray. 1999–2000. *Promethea*. Book 1 (# 1–6). La Jolla: DC Comics.

Moore, Alan, J.H. Williams and Mick Gray. 2000–2001. *Promethea*. Book 2 (# 7–12). La Jolla: DC Comics.

Moore, Alan, J.H. Williams and Mick Gray. 2001–2002. *Promethea*. Book 3 (# 13–18). La Jolla: DC Comics.

Moore, Alan, J.H. Williams and Mick Gray. 2003. *Promethea*. Book 4 (# 19–25). La Jolla: DC Comics.

Moore, Alan, J.H. Williams and Mick Gray. 2005. *Promethea.*Book 5 (# 26–32). La Jolla: DC Comics.

Moore, Alan. 2011. "Fossil Angels." *Abraxas* 2: 182–195.

Moore, Alan and Jay Babcock. 2007. "Magic is Afoot." Pages 117–137 in *Alan Moore's Yuggoth Cultures and Other Growths*. Edited by William Christensen. Rantoul: Avatar.

Myers, Frederic William Henry. 1903/2011 reprint. *Human Personality and Its Survival of Bodily Death*. Volume 1. Cambridge: Cambridge University Press.

Narby, Jeremy. 1998. *The Cosmic Serpent: DNA and the Origins of Knowledge*. New York: Jeremy P. Tarcher/ Putnam.

Owen, Alex. 2004. *The Place of Enchantment: British Occultism and the Culture of the Modern*. Chicago: The University of Chicago Press.

Partridge, Christopher. 2004. *The Re-Enchantment of the West: Alternative Spiritualities, Sacralization, Popular Culture and Occulture*. London: T & T Clark.

Pasi, Marco. 2011. "Varieties of Magical Experience: Aleister Crowley's Views on Occult Practice." *Magic, Ritual, and Witchcraft* 6: 123–162.

Possamai, Adam, ed. 2012. *Handbook of Hyper-Real Religions*. Leiden: Brill.

Robert, Louis. 1981. "Le serpent Glycon d'Abônouteichos à Athènes et Artémis d'Éphèse à Rome." *Comptes rendus des séances de l'Académie des Inscriptions et Belles-Lettres* 125: 513–535.

Salaman, Clement, Dorine van Oyen and William D. Wharton, eds. 1999. *The Way of Hermes: The Corpus Hermeticum*. London: Duckworth.

Sellars, Simon. 2010. "Hakim Bey: Repopulating the Temporary Autonomous Zon." *Journal for the Study of Radicalism* 4: 83–108.

Shanon, Benny. 2002. *The Antipodes of the Mind: Charting the Phenomenology of the Ayahuasca Experience*. Oxford: Oxford University Press.

# Children of the Light:
# Gnostic Fiction and Gnostic Practice in Vladimir Sorokin's *Ice Trilogy*

*Victoria Nelson*
Goddard College
*victoria.nelson@goddard.edu*

Gnostic thinking has never been monolithic, but as a tradition it has long carried the all-purpose label "world hating." In most gnostic systems, the more physical something is, the less "being" or ultimate reality it possesses; perfection is found only in the transcendent realm, from which the soul descends to incarnate on earth and to which it ascends when its earthly sentence is over. Some gnostic adepts over the ages have forsworn sex and eating meat on the principle that any substance generated by sexual intercourse is more deeply tainted by the inherent corruptibility of matter than plant life.

For most early gnostics of late antiquity (who often called themselves "children of the Light"), the material world was an accidental creation not of God but of a clumsy intermediary. The Apocryphon of John and other gnostic texts of the third and fourth centuries CE tell the story, in various complicated versions, of the first human created as a reflection of God on the watery matter of this world. Then the ignorant lower god Ialdabaoth (in some systems equivalent to YHWH), offspring of Sophia (Wisdom), who is herself the daughter of God, tries to go one better by forming a fleshly man out of this divine reflection. The demiurge's creation doesn't come to life, however, until Sophia breathes her own essence into it. Thus humans, paradoxically, have more of the divine in them than the false creator who made them, inspiring his envy and leading to endless repercussions.[1]

## 1   Heavenly Ice and the Tunguska Event

These repercussions play out in fascinating ways both in the ancient texts and in the contemporary trio of novellas I want to examine by the Russian writer Vladimir Sorokin. Author of a number of novels and screenplays, he is more famous in Russia than in the West. His *Ice* trilogy, written between 2002 and

---

[1] King 2006, 3–5.

2005), creates the sensation in a reader is of working her way through layers of literary history, a sensation that can be attributed to Sorokin's skills as a gifted mimic who parrots the literary language of each era through which his characters pass. The eponymous narrator of *Bro* in the first novel enjoys an idyllic childhood of privilege in the twilight of czarist Russia as the son of a wealthy merchant.[2] This life, beautifully evoked by Sorokin in full Nabokovian mode, is quickly obliterated, along with his immediate family, by the Bolshevik revolution. Orphaned and traumatized, Sasha Snegirev (this character's birth name) is drifting through university in the new Soviet world when a classmate recruits him on a scientific expedition to Siberia. Its mission: to locate the remains of the meteorite whose explosion in Earth's atmosphere allegedly caused the great fireball that appeared over the Tunguska region in 1908, flattening more than 800 square miles of forest.

Known in UFO circles as the "Russian Roswell," the real-life Tunguska event has long been a magnet for esoteric speculation, in large part because no fragments of the giant meteor, nor even its impact crater, have ever been found. In his 1946 story "The Explosion," the Russian writer Alexander Kazantsev famously styled the Tunguska event as the massive nuclear explosion of a Martian spaceship.[3] In what will prove to be no coincidence, Sorokin's fictional hero is born the same day as this catastrophic historical event. He has been haunted through his young life by a vision of "Light" at the top of a great mountain and finds his only deep pleasure in astronomy classes that allow him to *hang* (in the distinctive style of typographic emphasis Sorokin favors) "amid the planets and the stars."

Selected by the charismatic Leonid Kulik (the scientist who led the real-life expedition on which this story draws) mainly because of the "good omen" of his birth, Sasha embarks on a fateful journey to Siberia that offers further echoes of Nabokov (the lepidoptery expedition to Central Asia in *The Gift*, a novel dismissed by a character in the third novel of Sorokin's series as "boring").[4] But in Siberia, Nabokov and modernity get kicked off the wagon for good as the story takes a completely different turn to—what? That is the great aesthetic and moral question of these novels and the answer, I would argue, is not to be found in postmodern irony, a label often stuck on Sorokin's work, or alternatively, in political allegory.

---

2  Sorokin actually wrote and published *Ice*, the second novel in the series, in 2002, followed by *Bro* (original title *Put' Bro* or "Bro's Way") in 2004 and *23,000* in 2005.

3  Not available in English translation. Current scientific speculation suggests that Lake Cheko in that region may represent the actual impact area. In 2002, another substantial meteor landed in the Irkutsk region.

4  Sorokin 2011b, 36.

CHILDREN OF THE LIGHT 251

Here's what happens: Approaching the impact zone, the young man feels strange intimations. His childhood dream of the Light recurs; he quits talking and eating. Finally he abandons the group in search of what he calls the *huge and intimate*, the mysterious energy that is calling to him. Striking out alone across the empty taiga, he plunges into a bog and swims wildly until he reaches the tip of the meteorite. Against all reason, it is not made of stone or iron but Ice with a capital "I": "an ideal Cosmic substance generated by the Primordial Light"[5] now safely preserved in the Siberian permafrost. In his excitement he slips and falls, hitting his chest hard and thereby unlocking a mystic connection with the Ice, which gives him his true name, Bro. "In this moment," says the transformed Bro, "the entire earthly world paled and became transparent for me ... The Ice and I hung alone in the universe."[6] Feeling the "vile vulgarity of this world,"[7] he realizes his personal past is over for good: "My happy childhood, the tornado of the Revolution, the loss of my family, the wanderings, studies, loneliness and orphanhood—it had all hardened under glass *forever.*"[8]

Singing the "Music of Eternal Harmony," the Ice reveals to Bro the secret cosmogony of the universe. In the beginning, outside space and time, there was only the Primordial Light. This Light consisted of exactly 23,000 rays, one of which was Bro. The function of these rays was to create worlds, which they did: stars and planets beyond number, all radiating Eternal Harmony. Then they made Earth, a creation that became their great mistake because they made it out of water. This unstable medium mirrored the rays back to themselves with the catastrophic result that they became trapped in their own reflections and incarnated as mortal creatures on Earth—first as simple amoebas, then evolving over billions of years into humans, soul-less carnivores who engage in mindless repetitive acts of "killing, birthing, killing, birthing" and exploiting the natural world around them.

Trapped in these sordid bodies, the 23,000 rays of Light (who, echoing the gnostics of late antiquity, call themselves the "children of the Light") have continued reincarnating, their hearts asleep like those of humans, until that pivotal moment in 1908 when the "huge piece of Heavenly ice," encased in a protective hard shell of cosmic dust, dropped to earth on a mission: to recover the rays so that they in turn may save the "perishing universe." Bro's mission is to find and awaken the other 22,999 rays hidden in their fleshly prisons. Once these blonde-haired, blue-eyed children of the Light are able to gather in one

---

5 Sorokin 2011b, 400.
6 Sorokin 2011b, 77.
7 Sorokin 2011b, 73.
8 Sorokin 2011b, 62.

place and join hands, Earth will dissolve. The liberated rays will regain their identity in the essential world and will go on to create a "New Universe—Sublime and Eternal."

As a reader who had settled comfortably into adventure-on-the-tundra reading mode, I found this sudden left turn into gnostic fantasy a bit startling. My reaction put me in mind, at first, of the shock I felt seeing my first painting by the dissident émigré Russian artists Komar and Melemid, reproduced in the *Village Voice* circa 1980, a lovingly Socialist Realist rendering of World War II partisans in greatcoats and rifles discovering, to their wonder, a tiny dinosaur cavorting at their feet. Resetting my reading dials for that distinctive K&M brand of subversive irony, I readied myself for postmodern satire and a parable of the authoritarian political system that ruled Russia for seventy years, a system often compared (by the political philosopher Eric Voegelin and others) to a gnostic elite who claimed that special knowledge would bring about apocalyptic changes in humanity's condition.

Once again my expectations were confounded. As visitors from the world of Light accidentally trapped in the watery prison of matter, Bro and his cohort of celibate vegetarians are clearly modeled on the teachings of these early sects from late antiquity as well as a rich mélange of Russian and Western esoteric sources. Sorokin's gnostic cosmogony, however, offers some interesting new features. Most notably, he presents his children of the Light not as human believers but as the incompetent demiurges themselves, sucked down to earth by the narcissistic pull of their reflected images and imprisoned in human bodies. In keeping with the older tradition, however, these clumsy creators ultimately reveal themselves to be false, unreliable, and faithless, both to the higher God they serve and the spirit of the Light they embody. In the end it will fall to the humans, the so-called "meat machines" they despise, to take up the search for the true God.

## 2   Sifting the Wheat from the Chaff: Rays of Light and Meat Machines

To return to our story: Handed his marching orders by the Ice, Bro sets off at once to locate his sisters and brothers around the world and reawaken their hearts to the Light. When Bro initiates his first sister, a runaway peasant, with a blow of the Ice to the chest, they have an ecstatic nonsexual experience of transcendental union: "Our hearts *spoke* in unknown words, words only they understood. The strength of the Light sang in each word. The joy of Eternity sounded in them."⁹ Their rapture quickly converts into the burning desire to find all the others. Devising an "Ice hammer" with a chunk of the meteorite Ice lashed to a wooden handle with straps of animal skin, they locate their brethren in the unlikeliest stations of life, from a bandit captain to the head of the Cheka secret police for the Far East. Deeply and painfully aware of the cruelty of humans toward each other, the children of the Light soon reveal an equal ruthlessness achieving their goal. When he kills his first man (in self-defense, fighting bandits), Bro realizes, "We would NEVER be able to REACH AN AGREEMENT with people."¹⁰ Instead, he decides, they must begin "a long, persistent war against humankind."¹¹

This marks the first of many progressively darker moral turning points for Bro and his fellows. As they move out in the world with their Ice hammers, power, not love, becomes the brethren's first priority. "In order to sift through the human race, searching for the golden grain of our Brotherhood," Bro declares, "we had to control this race."¹² In 1920s Russia, this means aligning 100 percent with the state:

> In order to achieve success ... we would have to become part of the state machine, take cover under it, and, wearing the uniforms of officialdom, go about achieving our goal.... We couldn't allow ourselves to become underground members of a secret order, hiding in the dark corners under the hierarchical ladder of power. That road led only to the torture chambers of the OGPU [Cheka] and the Stalinist camps. We had to clamber up this ladder and stand solidly on it.¹³

The head of the Cheka, therefore, once awakened to his cosmic identity, therefore, does not throw over his blood-soaked duties to become an ascetic meditating in the forest. Rather, the newly christened Ig, formerly Comrade Deribas, continues on his merry path of torture and execution and so is able to provide invaluable protection to his cosmic Brotherhood.

The reuniting of the children of the Light will take the next eighty years and all three novels to accomplish, an epic quest that devolves from idealism to fanaticism to base and cynical brutality—as the alphabet soup of secret police bureaus they parasitically attach themselves to morphs from OGPU to NKVD to

---

9   Sorokin 2011b, 85.
10  Sorokin 2011b, 113.
11  Sorokin 2011b, 135.
12  Sorokin 2011b, 136.
13  Sorokin 2011b, 136.

KGB to SVR. Over the decades the feeling tone of the great mission has altered from mildly compromised exaltation, with only the odd chauffeur or army colonel executed to preserve secrecy, to horrific. With the search slowed by the lack of an all-seeing male-female pair who can pick out their fellows instantly, the brothers and sisters wield their Ice hammers brutally and carelessly in a ritual that becomes cruel, unexplained, and frequently lethal. Still boasting of their love "as large as the sky, and as sublime as the Primordial Light,"[14] they now so despise the "meat machines" or "empties" (as they call humans) that potential recruits are often simply killed should they not prove to be part of the chosen 23,000. In their quest for the Great Transformation, the new female seer Khram admits, "We were merciless to the living dead."[15]

*Ice*, the second novel, picks up the story in the 1990s, with flashbacks to the postwar Soviet era. After the fall of communism, the children of the Light have all too successfully transitioned into the Wild West era of post-Soviet capitalism. Under Boris Yeltsin they are able to establish "mighty financial structures"[16] within the new oligarchy operating under the same conditions of corrupted absolute power as previous regimes. They drive the same fancy cars as the thugs, pimps, and thieves who deliver the dwindling stores of their precious Ice, now mined by convict labor in the Tunguska region, where imprisoned scientists also craft Ice hammers for mass distribution in a home kit called the "ICE Health Improvement System." Touting the benefits of being struck on the chest with the Ice hammer, the kit is a covert form of recruitment that becomes a global commercial success. This second novel ends with their website's array of testimonials from customers around the world (nicely mimicking the thumbs-up, thumbs-down cluelessness of the average Amazon.com product review section) along with the discovery of a little boy with Down syndrome who is the long-sought male seer to be paired with Khram after Bro's death.

## 3  Last Call: Ascension and Its Discontents

The final installment, *23,000*, begins and ends in the year 2008, exactly one century after the Tunguska meteorite event. The story is channeled first through the breathless rhetoric of Khram and then through the more matter-of-fact third-person voice of a Russian "empty" named Olga. By now the children of

---

14  Sorokin 2011b, 395.
15  Sorokin 2011b, 432.
16  Sorokin 2011b, 451.

the Light have corporatized into a multinational conglomerate. After exhausting the original cosmic substance, they have managed to synthesize the Ice and now market a globally successful Ice computer game. Olga finds herself enslaved, along with 174 other blonde, blue-eyed failed human recruits, in an outsourced Chinese factory grotesquely consecrated to skinning the dead dogs whose hides are used for the handles of the Ice hammers included in the health improvement kits.

Meanwhile the day of reckoning has finally come. As the last rays are located, the entire group gathers on an island off the coast of China for their long-awaited ascension. As "part hammered" humans who begin to share their mounting "longing for the light," Olga and her Swedish coworker Bjorn are pressed into service to hold awakened babies unable to stand unaided. The rays gather, naked, in the Prime Circle. The 23 Words are recited. The earth "shudders." But Olga and Bjorn open their eyes to discover the human bodies of all the 23,000 lying dead around them, faces frozen in grimaces of suffering and bewilderment. The ascension, if that is what happened, was apparently not a pleasant one, and Earth itself remains intact.

This is a death scene that irresistibly recalls real-life contemporary gnostic cults such as the Order of the Solar Temple and Heaven's Gate, whose apocalyptic millennial quest to reach the "Next Level" moved many of their followers to hasten the process with mass suicide. But it is also a scene whose intensity and exuberance does not suggest that the 23,000 were merely mortal humans who labored under the delusion they were beings from outer space. The story asks us to accept the 23,000 rays not as a deranged human cult, but as exactly who they say they are—nonhuman energies from somewhere other than Earth.

So what happened to these incarnated cosmic rays after they abandoned their fleshly prisons? They "crashed against" what they created, Bjorn tells Olga.[17] As in the ancient gnostic stories, the 23,000 rays, aware only of their own cosmic identity, labor under the delusion that they alone have created the universe. Beyond the reach of these clumsy cosmic demiurges, who further compromised themselves with vile deeds while incarnated, lies a true, or higher, transcendence. It is known by the word that is never uttered until the last page of the third novel and only, significantly, by human "empties." Humans alone have the ability to apprehend this true creator because humans possess a greater share of divinity than their immediate overlords.

---

17  Sorokin 2011b, 693.

So the unhappy demise of the children of the Light was done "for us," Bjorn cries. "And this was all done by God!" His declaration triggers the following remarkable exchange:

> "By God?" Olga asked cautiously.
> "By God," he declared.
> "By God," Olga answered.
> "By God!" he said with certainty.
> "By God," Olga exhaled, shaking.
> "By God!" he said in a loud voice.
> "By God!" Olga gave a nod.
> "By God!" he said even louder.
> "By God!" Olga nodded again.
> "By God!" he shouted out.
> "By God," she whispered.[18]

Both agree their next step must be to talk to God themselves. To find out how to do this, they must return to the "World of People" and ask other humans. And off they go, "their bare feet stepping across the sun-warmed marble."[19] End of story.

## 4   The *Ice* Trilogy: Antecedent and Parallels

Sorokin's parting message—that the new Adam and Eve, expelled from the dreadful underbelly of the children's Paradise, are tasked to go forth in the world and discover the ways of accessing the transcendence known as God— is unlikely to sit well with either Western secular humanist intelligentsia or traditional believers. Works of serious literature with mystical import, whether heterodox or orthodox, are rare in the contemporary West. In popular culture, however, the story is different, especially in American Christian fiction. Most notable are the apocalyptic *Left Behind* series[20] and William P. Young's *The Shack*,[21] which occupy a substantial niche in that special category of "never-reviewed bestseller." Gnostic fantasy abounds in English-language

---

18   Sorokin 2011b, 693.
19   Sorokin 2011b, 694.
20   LaHaye and Jenkins 1995–2006.
21   Young 2007.

science fiction and fantasy, including Theodore Roszak's *Flicker*[22]—an ingenious Gothic romance about a two thousand year old gnostic cult responsible, among other things, for German Expressionist film—and Thomas Pynchon's exuberant conspiratorial historical fantasy *V.*[23] Some close parallels to Sorokin's story are found in Alexander Key's *Escape to Witch Mountain*,[24] a tale of children from another galaxy cast away on earth better known in its substantially different 1975 Disney movie version (followed by various sequels and remakes). Here Robert M. Young's screenplay reframes the story as a group of brother-sister twins, exiled and scattered on Earth, who reunite on a mountain and happily ascend two by two in a column of purple iridescence back to their home in the world of Light.

The story Sorokin himself singles out, however, is F. Scott Fitzgerald's strange 1920s fantasia, "The Diamond as Big as the Ritz."[25] With its uneasy worship/critique of the condition of limitless wealth, this capitalist fable of a man who owns a mountain made of a gigantic diamond could have served equally well as a popular classroom text in Soviet times or as a cautionary tale for the new Russia. Reading this story of a "stingy, powerful man" whose fantastic treasure turns him into a monster, Olga reflects on her own fate serving the Ice elite: "Diamonds look like ice … But diamonds don't melt … the ice mountain. And we live under it."[26]

Beyond these echoes in Western popular culture, however, Sorokin's children of the Light are deeply embedded in the very different circumstances of Russia's cultural and political history. The *Ice* trilogy has its deepest roots in a rich cultural soil that encompasses pre-Soviet, Soviet, and post-Soviet Russian literature, philosophy, natural sciences, popular culture, and spiritual practices, especially the spirituality that sprang up after the Soviet era. "The media success of occult and new-religious movements in post-Soviet Russia can be only partially explained as a simple adaptation of western entertainment culture and zeitgeist trends," Matthias Schwartz emphasizes. "To a greater extent, these movements can be traced back to a deeply seated occult interest: namely, the decades-long engagement with this topic in Soviet SF texts and popular scientific journals."[27]

Even before the Soviet era, late nineteenth-century czarist Russia had experienced an occult renaissance across the arts and sciences that laid the

---

22   Roszak 1991.
23   Pynchon 1963.
24   Key 1968.
25   Fitzgerald 1962.
26   Sorokin 2011b, 610.
27   Schwartz 2011, 238.

foundation for the new century.[28] The Silver Age produced the apocalyptic mysticism of Symbolists such as Andrei Bely and Alexandr Blok as well as syncretic Christian philosophers such as Vladimir Soloviev, who, after having visions of the gnostic goddess Sophia or Divine Wisdom, attempted to unite mystic theology, philosophy and social action in his thinking. The Christian futurist philosopher Nicolai Fedorov attempted an analogous synthesis of science and mysticism in advocating colonization of space, immortality and resurrection of the dead by scientific means.[29] Out of this same cultural matrix came Helena Blavatsky, the founder of Theosophy, and the spiritual teacher and practitioner George Gurdjieff.

Even though the advent of Soviet rule electively cut off three to four generations from formal religious traditions during the twentieth century, Russian readers remained immersed in occult and esoteric material in the form of a rich harvest of science fiction and fantasy sanctioned by the state because it was considered popular or children's literature. A current of German Romantic *Naturphilosophie*, based on a belief in vitalist holistic universal knowledge, had been prominent in Russian science since the nineteenth century, and this framework of "cosmism," along with the fact that the Soviets formally classified the humanities as a category of science, resulted in a considerable esoteric seepage into the natural sciences in a manner completely foreign to the mainstream Western scientific perspective.[30] The 1950s saw officially sanctioned investigations of alien intelligence, UFOs, and yetis; nuclear submarines were commissioned to find the so-called "'blue continent' Atlantis on the bottom of the sea."[31]

These investigations were bolstered by serious research, including a lengthy tome by a respected scientist, Nicolas Zhirov, who argued that Atlantis had been located on a mid-Atlantic ridge.[32] On the heels of Kazantsev's 1946 science fiction story "The Explosion" mentioned earlier, the Tunguska event was factually described as the explosion of a spaceship in a 1950 popular science journal article.[33] The long-standing esoteric orientation of Russian science—what one scholar has called its "Gnostic strain"[34]—also supported the effulgence of Soviet research on the paranormal during the 1970s and 1980s.

28   Mannherz 2012.
29   Laruealle 2011b, 245, 248.
30   Laruelle 2011b, 238.
31   Menzel 2011, 152.
32   Godwyn 2011, 6.
33   Schwartz 2011, 228.
34   Rosenthal 1997, 13.

After the Stalin era, an esoteric revival in the 1960s and 1970s resurrected the teachings of Blavatsky and Gurdjieff along with eastern religions and Sufism.

With the final collapse of the Soviet regime in the early 1990s came a flood of pent-up religiosity, old and new, in Russia. For many scholars, this decade represented a replaying of the century-old Silver Age.[35] There was a resurgence of long-outlawed shamanism in the eastern regions of the old empire. Along with the relegitimization of the Orthodox Christian church came revivals of pre-Christian pagan spiritual practices that had long survived underground.[36] Unlike the goddess culture that permeates the Western New Age, some Russian ethnic faith movements such as Rodnoverie emphasize masculine values and nationalism and carry a heavy tinge of racism, anti-Semitism, and far-right political views.[37] Leonid Heller comments: "Mystical wanderings became entwined with Russian nationalism, became equal to an obtrusive obsession with identity—it seems that this evolution is what nowadays separates many Russian esotericists from the world of New Age, which is based on the principles of tolerance and universalism."[38] It is the "Aryan" bias of these groups Sorokin is satirizing in his blonde-haired, blue-eyed children of the Light.

Building on the renaissance of science fiction and fantasy in the 1990s, the *Ice* trilogy shares some resonances with the popular *Nightwatch* novels[39] by Russian science fiction writer Sergei Lukianenko (made into two global hit films by the director Timur Bekmambetov), about a supernatural horde divided in two groups, Light Ones and Dark Ones, locked in eternal combat on Earth. The demiurgic fashioning of the watery planet Earth breathlessly recounted to Bro in the first novel of the *Ice* trilogy also has some earlier echoes in Polish writer Stanislaw Lem's 1961 novel *Solaris*[40] made into a splendid 1972 film by the Russian director Andrei Tarkovsky,[41] about an oceanic world-consciousness that tunes into the deep obsessions of the scientists who study it and reflects them back in the form of human simulacra.

Sorokin's original screenplay for Alexander Zeldovich's 2011 film *The Target* (*Mishen*)[42] tells a futuristic tale of four wealthy Russians, an oligarch, his wife, her brother, and a corrupt customs official, who journey to the "Target," an abandoned Soviet astrophysical facility located in a remote region of Central

---

35    Rosenthal 1997, 1.
36    Kungurtseve and Louchakova 1994, 21–27.
37    Laruelle 2011a, 293–310.
38    Heller 2011, 210.
39    Lukianenko 1998–2012.
40    Lem 1970.
41    Tarkovsky 1972.
42    Zeldovich 2011.

Asia. Seeking space particles rumored to give eternal youth, they spend the night basking in radioactive emissions in a chamber suspended below a huge metal bulls-eye. Returning to Moscow with their aging process forever suspended, all are beset by destructive outbursts of passion and impulsivity. There are echoes here of Tarkovsky's 1979 postapocalyptic *Stalker*[43] (based on *The Roadside Picnic*, a novel by Arkady and Boris Strugatsky)[44] in which those trademark radioactive rays also "wield magical power over intellectuals from the capital city and promise the fulfillment of their secret wishes."[45]

Along with its other resonances with the *Ice* trilogy (supernatural transformation in the Asian wilderness), *The Target* like *Stalker* may have drawn inspiration from the Soviet sci fi writer Ivan Efremov's 1944 novel *The Observatory at Nur-i-Desht*,[46] featuring an ancient observatory in the desert "built of radioactive material the rays of which cause both healing and euphoric effects on people."[47] *The Target*'s structurally similar story of characters irresistibly drawn to a transformative substance or crucible in the Asian wilderness, and then somehow ruined as a result, feels more like social commentary than transcendental exegesis, though the final lingering image of the Target itself glistening in preternatural Light might suggest otherwise. What is important to note is the common thread of cosmism running through twentieth-century Russian science fiction: characters seeking ways of connecting to universal energies via "encounters with hitherto unknown 'fantastic' secrets of nature that enable humans to experience spiritual cleansing and inner enlightenment."[48]

It is far easier, though—especially because of the dense and dark Russian sociopolitical matrix in which the *Ice* trilogy is embedded—to abandon cosmic and esoteric considerations entirely and simply read these novels as a social metaphor. Sorokin himself has called them a "metaphor more than anything else," a "discussion of the twentieth century ... a kind of monument to it."[49] The mass market culture of the twentieth century, he says, has helped turn us into "meat machines," but adds, significantly: "Multiply this by the total atheism advancing upon us, and human beings become a cog in this machine and lose their cosmism and divine image."[50]

---

43   Tarkovsky 1979.
44   Stugatsky 1971.
45   Schwartz 2011, 234.
46   Not yet translated in English. I am drawing from the summary in Schwartz 2011, 12–13.
47   Schwartz 2011, 12–13.
48   Schwartz 2011, 226.
49   Llunggren and Totkirch 2008, 147–149.
50   Llunggren and Totkirch 2008, 147–149.

His two other novels available in English also feature dubious group entities as their main character: an elite force of despicable thugs in a futuristic Russia who enforce the will of a new absolute czar bearing more than a passing resemblance to Vladimir Putin in *Day of the Oprichnik*[51] and a slightly more benign multivoiced entity in his first novel, *The Queue*.[52] In the afterword to a new edition of *The Queue*, Sorokin proposes that the "collective body" formed by the endless lines of people waiting for goods and services in the old Soviet society represents a "new type of object or metaphorical subject."[53] The queue itself, he suggests playfully, neatly replaced the services of the Russian Orthodox church (during which the congregation traditionally remains standing), dispensing cabbage and American jeans instead of the Eucharist.

*The Queue* and *Day of the Oprichnik* are indeed metaphors, parables, fables, of a Russian society separated by thirty years but unchanged in certain grim fundamentals. Both works, however, differ strikingly in tone from the *Ice* trilogy and from each other. In the over-the-top, heavily satiric *Day of the Oprichnik*—which Sorokin says he composed in a single month "like an uninterrupted stream of bile" after five years of writing the *Ice* trilogy, as part of a conscious decision to become more politicized in his writing[54]—the elite cadre experiences a profane sacramental ecstasy as a consequence of group bonding even as they extol their own purity in the wake of unspeakable crimes. Where Bro and his brethren are entirely chaste ("No earthly love that I had ever experienced before could possibly be compared with this feeling," he cries. "I ceased to be a two-legged grain of sand. I became *we*! And this was OUR HAPPINESS!"),[55] the *oprichniki* indulge in a ritual sexual orgy of male bonding. Here the (relatively) innocent image of the "many-headed caterpillar" of collectivity invoked in *The Queue* gets played out in the form of a sodomizing caterpillar copulating and climaxing in their secret bath. It is a damning emblem of the consequences of absolutism in Russian society past, present, and future.

But does that mean that the 23,000 rays of Light are also simply a *metaphorical subject* (those italics are contagious)—yet another incarnation of the doomed Russian collectivity—or are they the *real thing*? Is Sorokin passing judgment here on the perils of human absolutism, or (more fancifully, for most highbrow readers inside and outside Russia) on the perceived failings of the gnostic archons themselves, the intermediate gods who created our world?

---

51  Sorokin 2006.
52  Sorokin 1975.
53  Sorokin 2008, 256.
54  Barry 30 April 2011.
55  Sorokin 2011b, 84.

The answer, I think, is both. The children of the Light are metaphorical subjects and "real" at the same time, but the deeper subtext is the transcendental one. In the *Ice* trilogy Sorokin is using the outer manifestations of Russian society to critique inner and transpersonal experience, not the other way around. The *Ice* trilogy is more than just a clever allegory of communist idealism gone wrong or a parody of right-wing Russian New Age pagans who celebrate Aryan *Übermenschen*. Even though the genetic exclusivity of the children of the Light is a tipoff that something's not quite kosher about them, Sorokin is not being ironic about them. He is, to channel Bro's voice, *dead serious*: not that 23,000 cosmic rays incarnated as humans exist anywhere outside his own imagination, of course, but rather that experiential mysticism is a real phenomenon whose personal, social, and spiritual implications deserve to be examined and critiqued. (Let it be noted that presenting transcendental experience as real is a far more subversive and unsettling proposition than any of the conveniently shifting positions taken inside the boundaries of late twentieth-century postmodernism.)

In 2008 Sorokin told an interviewer:

> I believe that humanity is not yet perfect, but that it will be perfected, that contemporary humans are thus far imperfect beings, that we still do not know ourselves or our potential, that we have not understood that we are cosmic beings. We are created by a higher intelligence, and we have cosmic goals, not just comfort and reproduction. We are not "meat machines."[56]

But this astonishing (to some) declaration only raises more questions. Does evil arise automatically from the energies of the collective, regardless of whether it is human or cosmic? For that matter, which part of the incarnated rays, their human bodies or their cosmic nature, brings evil to the table? Khram is scathing on the subject of humanity's capacity for evil, declaring, "There could be no brotherhood between meat machines," she declares. "Each meat machine wanted happiness for his own body above all. ... And they constantly killed each other to achieve the body's happiness."[57]

Does this mean that the children's originally pure cosmic essence has been corrupted by their human, all too human, incarnated nature? The humans in the *Ice* trilogy believe the opposite—that the cruelty of the Brotherhood stems

---

[56] Llunggren and Totkirch 2008, 145.
[57] Sorokin 2011b, 530.

precisely from their nonhuman nature. Beyond any critique of New Age groups or the larger arena of Russian society, Sorokin himself splits the difference, and this is what I think his "metaphor" amounts to: the children of the Light are us. We humans, all of us, are part meat machine, part cosmic ray. The quest that Olga and Bjorn embark on in the World of People is no final ironic twist, initiating another spiral into deluded religious fanaticism. Nor is it an adjuration to turn away from the evils of fanaticism for the joy and comfort of secular humanism. Olga and Bjorn have a serious task before them that is anything but postmodern. It is to understand their natures as "cosmic beings," and it means finding God.

But where to find God? In the World of People, as Bjorn says, but most certainly not in any of the usual places, including the Russian Orthodox Church. A priest who has sampled the "ICE home improvement kit" screeches about it as an implement of the devil. Though in one sense he is weirdly right about the children of the Light, he hates them for the wrong reason: that is, simply because they don't follow the Church's precepts. (In *Day of the Oprichnik* the Orthodox Church is presented, as in olden days, as an utterly corrupt lackey of the state.)

But if traditional religious institutions are no good, does such a conclusion imply that Olga and Bjorn, following the example of Bro and Russian history, must form a new ruthless elite in service to their cosmic nature? Is the *Ice* story merely starting all over again? Or can there be another way? That other way, if there is one, might lie in forswearing missions that elevate cosmic ends over human means. The trilogy reveals itself ultimately as an anti-gnostic manifesto. The Light is not to be accessed by escaping the prison of flesh; literal ascension is not the answer. The children of the Light, all of us, belong on corrupt, compromised Earth because half of our nature—the better half, or the worse?—belongs to it. Given the world they are walking back into, we tremble for Olga and Bjorn, but the hope and energy they exude is unmistakable. Sorokin leaves the future wide open and, as yet, untainted. One final question: Is this God they are looking for another *metaphorical subject*, or is he/she/it the *real thing*? To answer this question in any way other than with the reflexive biases of the secular humanist or traditional believer, Sorokin suggests, we must make that journey ourselves.

Portions of this paper appeared previously in *The Believer* (October 2011).

## Bibliography

Barry, Ellen. 30 April 2011. "From a Novelist, Shock Treatment for Mother Russia." *New York Times*, E1.

*Escape to Witch Mountain*. 1975. Dir. John Hough. Disney.

Fitzgerald, F. Scott. 1931. "The Diamond as Big as the Ritz." Pages 5–38 in Malcolm Cowley, ed. *The Stories of F. Scott Fitzgerald.* New York: Scribners.

Godwin, Joscelyn. 2011. *Atlantic and the Cycles of Time: Prophecies, Traditions, and Occult Revelations.* Rochester, VT: Inner Traditions.

Heller, Leonid. 2011. "Away from the Globe. Occultism, Esotericism and Literature in Russia during the 1960s–1980s." Pages 186–210 in *The New Age of Russia: Occult and Esoteric Dimensions.* Edited by Birgit Menzel, Michael Hagemeister, and Bernice Glatzer Rosenthal. Munich and Berlin: Verlag Otto Sagner. Key, Alexander. 1968. *Escape to Witch Mountain.* Philadelphia: Westminster Press.

King, Karen L., ed. 2006. *The Secret Revelation of John.* Cambridge, MA: Harvard University Press.

Kungurtsev, Igor and Olga Louchakova. Spring 1994. "The Unknown Russian Mysticism." *Gnosis*: 21–27.

LaHaye, Tim F., and Jerry Jenkins. 1995–2006. *Left Behind: A Novel of the Earth's Last Days* [and fifteen sequels]. Wheaton, IL: Tyndale House. Laruelle, Marlène. 2011a. "The *Rodnoverie* Movement: The Search for Pre-Christian Ancestry and the Occult." Pages 293–310 in *The New Age of Russia: Occult and Esoteric Dimensions.* Edited by Birgit Menzel, Michael Hagemeister, and Bernice Glatzer Rosenthal. Munich and Berlin: Verlag Otto Sagner.

Laruelle, Marlène. 2011b. "Totalitarian Utopia, the Occult, and Technological Modernity in Russia: The Intellectual Experience of Cosmism." Pages 238–258 in *The New Age of Russia: Occult and Esoteric Dimensions.* Edited by Birgit Menzel, Michael Hagemeister, and Bernice Glatzer Rosenthal. Munich and Berlin: Verlag Otto Sagner.

Lem, Stanisław. 1970. *Solaris.* Translated from the French by Joanna Kilmartin and Steve Cox. New York: Walker.

Llunggren, Anna and Kristina Totkirch, eds. 2008. *Contemporary Russian Fiction: Interviews.* Moscow: Glas.

Lukianenko, Sergei. 2006. *The Night Watch.* Translated by Andrew Bromfield. London: William Heineman.

Mannherz, Julia. 2012. *Modern Occultism in Late Imperial Russia.* DeKalb, IL: Northern Illinois Press.

Menzel, Birgit. 2011. "Occult and Esoteric Movements in Russia from the 1960s to the 1980s." Pages 151–160 in *The New Age of Russia: Occult and Esoteric Dimensions.* Edited by Birgit Menzel, Michael Hagemeister, and Bernice Glatzer Rosenthal. Munich and Berlin: Verlag Otto Sagner.

Menzel, Birgit, Hagemeister, Michael, and Bernice Glatzer Rosenthal, eds. 2011. *The New Age of Russia: Occult and Esoteric Dimensions.* Munich and Berlin: Verlag Otto Sagner.

Pynchon, Thomas. 1963. *V., a novel.* Philadelphia: Lippincott.

Rosenthal, Bernice Glatzer. 1997. *The Occult in Russian and Soviet Culture.* Ithaca and London: Cornell University Press.

Roszak, Theodore. 1991. *Flicker.* New York: Summit.

Schwartz, Matthias. 2011. "Guests from Outer Space: Occult Aspects of Soviet Science Fiction." Pages 211–237 in *The New Age of Russia: Occult and Esoteric Dimensions.* Edited by Birgit Menzel, Michael Hagemeister, and Bernice Glatzer Rosenthal. Munich and Berlin: Verlag Otto Sagner.

Sorokin, Vladimir. *The Queue.* 2008. Translated by Sally Laird. Afterword translated by Jamey Gambrell. New York: New York Review Books.

Sorokin, Vladimir. *Day of the Oprichnik.* 2011a. Translated by Jamey Gambrell. New York: Farrar, Straus and Giroux.

Sorokin, Vladimir. 2011b. *The Ice Trilogy.* New York: New York Review Books. Translated by Jamey Gambrell.

*Solaris.* 1972. Dir. Andrei Tarkovsky. Mosfilm.

*Stalker.* 1979. Dir. Andrei Tarkovsky. Mosfilm.

Strugatsky, Arkady and Boris. 1971. *Roadside Picnic.* Gollancz.

*The Target (Mishen).* 2011. Dir. Alexander Zeldovich. Renfilm.

Young, William P. 2007. *The Shack.* Los Angeles: Windblown Media.

# Symbolic Loss, Memory, and Modernization in the Reception of Gnosticism

*Matthew J. Dillon*
Rice University
mjdillon@rice.edu

As Karen King has demonstrated, the category "gnosticism" was discursively constructed in a way that helped establish the borders of normative Christianity in the twentieth century.[1] Forms of ancient Christianity outside what became "orthodoxy" were classified as "gnostic." As a number of ancient Christian texts were discovered, translated, or published for the larger reading public (e.g., Bruce, Askew, Nag Hammadi, and Tchachos codices), initial popular reception inevitably characterized the texts as gnostic. Gnosticism thus became at once Christian and non-Christian, outside but of the tradition.

This article demonstrates that the category of gnosticism offered a countermemory of the Christian past used by individuals to respond to what Peter Homans identified as "symbolic loss."[2] Homans's socio-psychological theory of symbolic loss argues that the processes of modernization (i.e., disenchantment, rationalization, and pluralization) destroyed the self-evident nature of the Christian symbolic order in the West.[3] Western culture lacks a meaningful and publically shared relationship to the Christian past.[4] Certain individuals experience this transition from participation in the Christian symbolic order to de-idealization in a single lifetime, leading to symbolic loss.[5] This article argues that individuals experiencing symbolic loss of Christianity use the counter-memory opened by gnosticism to achieve rapprochement with the Christian tradition and re-idealize its past. The process in which individuals

---

[1] King 2001, 2003, and 2005.
[2] On symbolic loss, see Homans 2000a, 2000b and 2008. In earlier writings, Homans used the term mourning to refer to the loss of a tradition or ideal as well as the process by which one overcomes symbolic loss through reinterpretation and rapprochement with it. See: Homans 1984 and 1989. Later theorists use the term mourning to encapsulate both the loss and the process. See Parsons 2008a, 2008b, and 2013; Carlin 2014. In this article, I used the term symbolic loss to refer explicitly to the loss of a religious tradition due to the effects of modernization. I use "mourning" to encapsulate the *process* in which individuals respond to symbolic loss with reinterpretation and achieve rapprochement.
[3] Homans 1989, 26–27; Homans 2008, 16–20 & 40–41.
[4] Homans 1989, 297–312.
[5] Homans 1989, 115–120, 145–150; Homans 2000a, 22–40; Homans 2008, 20–42.

experiencing symbolic loss reinterpret and achieve rapprochement with the tradition is referred to as religious "mourning." Significantly, such individuals often misread the ancient gnostic texts themselves, but do so in ways that respond directly to the conditions of modernization that had destroyed the self-evident nature of the Christian symbolic order.

After an explanation of Homans's theory of symbolic loss and the process of mourning, this article demonstrates its argument through case studies of three individuals: Swiss psychologist Carl Jung (1875–1961), Canadian-Austrian visionary artist Laurence Caruana (1962–), and American public speaker Jonathan Talat Phillips (1975–). As we shall see, each individual experiences a process of mourning for the Christian tradition and utilizes the gnostic texts to offer creative reinterpretations of these symbols and achieve rapprochement with the tradition.

## 1 Symbolic Loss and the Process of Mourning

Peter Homans's theory of symbolic loss elucidates the psychological impact of modernization. On his reading, before the advent of modernity, Western culture shared a "sacred canopy" of symbolic meanings: a symbolic order.[6] Religious meanings and interpretations of the world were publically shared and accepted. Psychoanalytically speaking, religion here marks a set of idealizations of shared symbols and values (e.g. Jesus, the Catholic Church, the Bible) that speak to the narcissistic sector of the personality.[7] Participating in a world of shared symbolic meanings—what Talcott Parsons refers to as the "common culture"—ensured individuals' unconscious needs for idealization, identity, and attachment would be satisfied.[8] This common culture was oriented towards a particular cultural memory of the Christian past.[9]

With the advent of scientific explanations of the external world, pluralization, and rationalization, the self-evident nature of these publically shared meanings was lost.[10] Traditional meanings of religious symbols became unstable and Christianity had to compete with alternative interpretations of the world. The religious past could no longer be used as an unquestioned source

---

6  Berger 1967.
7  Homans 1989, 19; Parsons 2008a, 63–64.
8  Homans 1989, 119 & 126; Parsons 1964, 21.
9  Homans 1989, 4–5 and 297–312; Homans 2008, 16–18. I use cultural memory in the sense designated by Jan and Aleida Assmann in a number of works. See J. Assmann 1997, 2011; J. Assmann and Livingstone 2006; A. Assmann 2011.
10 Homans 1989, 26; Homans 2000, 231–233; Homans 2008, 18–20.

of orientation. For some, the impact of these consequences of modernity is acutely felt. Raised with a sense that the Christian symbolic order is completely real, individuals experience these processes in a single lifetime, leading to de-idealization and symbolic loss.[11]

In psychoanalytic terms, symbolic loss is the sudden deprivation of a symbol—a person or place, but also a cultural symbol, ideal, or value—that had been attached to and reinforces the structure of a person's identity.[12] A sense of anxiety, instability, and identity-confusion arises from symbolic loss.[13] The unconscious needs met through idealizations and identifications with the common culture in an experience-distant manner are left unmet.[14] Divorced from the common culture, individuals may experience a drastic psychological regression.[15] In this phase, what Homans calls "analytic access," or the capacity to introspect oneself *outside* the common culture, becomes pivotal.[16] Introspection of anomic activity such as dreams is commonplace, and it is not uncommon for the loosed unconscious contents to erupt into hallucinations, visions, or "unchurched" mystical experiences.[17] Crucially, the symbolic loss of a religion may be compensated for by another, smaller subculture, such as a professional association.[18] When no such compensation arises an individual may feel alienated and withdraw from the culture to focus on their inner world.[19]

The mourning process encapsulates early attachment, de-idealization, symbolic loss, and the outcome of symbolic loss.[20] Mourning may lead only to resignation and moving on from the tradition.[21] However, in a successful mourning process, the individual achieves a new sense of self that heals

---

11   Homans 2008, 13–41.
12   Homans 2008, 18–20. See also Homans 2000a, 20: "symbolic loss refers to the loss of an attachment to a political ideology or religious creed ... and to the inner work of coming to terms with this kind of loss. In this sense it resembles mourning. However, in the case of symbolic loss the object that is lost is, ordinarily, sociohistorical, cognitive, and collective."
13   Homans 1989, 126. Identity-confusion refers to a state in which the ego becomes incapable of synthesizing self-understanding with the variety of roles played in the social environment. Reciprocity between self-identity and social identity/identities is lost. See Erikson 1968, 211–221.
14   Parsons 2008b, 102; Parsons 2013, 143–146.
15   Parsons 2013, 143; Homans 1989, 122–128.
16   Homans 1989, 5, 126–127.
17   Parsons 2008b, 102.
18   Homans 1989, 115–128, 139–142, and 336–338.
19   Homans 1989, 112, 126, and 150; Parsons 2013, 142–146.
20   Homans 1989, 306–307; Homans 2008, 18.
21   Homans 2000a, 20; Homans 2008, 18.

trauma from personal history in addition to rapprochement with the religion.[22] Rapprochement is accomplished through the "re-creation of meaning."[23] In the recreation of meaning, individuals produce reinterpretations of the "lost" symbol that are meaningful to their new self-understanding achieved with analytic access. The individual is then able to re-idealize and re-attach to the symbols of religion and its past *without* accepting the commonplace meanings of them.[24] Significantly, the reinterpretations adapt Christian symbols to the forces of modernization—pluralization, rationalization, and disenchantment—that led to symbolic loss of the Christian tradition in the West.[25] In sum:

> The Process of Mourning: Attachment → De-idealization → Symbolic Loss and Analytic Access → Reinterpretation → Recreation of Meaning and Rapprochement.

Jung, Caruana, and Phillips offer "extreme cases" of this phenomenon.[26] Each of them experience the full process of mourning for the Christian tradition, and in doing so, they show the role gnosticism plays in responding to a symbolic loss of the Christian tradition in the West. In the case studies below, the process of mourning will be divided into three stages: (1) early attachment and subsequent de-idealization; (2) symbolic loss and reinterpretations of Jesus; and (3) the recreation of meaning that responds to the forces of modernization.

## 2    Carl Jung

Swiss psychologist Carl Jung is the paradigmatic case of religious mourning. Homans and William Parsons have each analyzed his life and thought in terms of mourning for the religious past.[27] In light of the newly published *The Red Book* these analyses can be extended.[28] Specifically, Jung's mourning for the

---

22   The literature on the link between childhood relationships to parents and ones' concept of and capacity to relate to God is extensive. See especially: Freud 1964; Kakar 1978 and 1991; Obeyesekere 1981; Kripal 1995; Parsons 2013, 102–132. A useful overview can be found in Merkur 2014, 81–114. On how introspective activity can heal early relational trauma and the impact this has on personal concepts of God, see Erikson 1962; Rizzuto 1979; Obeyesekere 1990, 1–28; Jones 1991, 68–110; Merkur 2014, 155–179.
23   Homans 2008, 14–20.
24   Homans 1984, 142–154; Homans 1989, 150–152, 326–343; Homans 2000b; Homans 2008.
25   Homans 1989, 326–343; Homans 2008, 38–41; Parsons 2013, 143–146.
26   James 2002, 26.
27   Homas 1979; Homans 1989, 141–152; Parsons 2008b, 105–107.
28   Jung 2009.

Christian tradition is essential to understanding *The Red Book*, and his reinterpretations of Christ during what he called his "confrontation with the unconscious" are through gnostic texts. Jung's later theoretical writings recreate meaning by showing how a gnostic approach to Christ can revivify the symbol for modernity.

### 2.1 Early Attachment and De-idealization

As the son of a village parson, Jung was raised amidst theological conversations and formal Christianity.[29] The symbols of God and Jesus play a central role in his inner world as a child and adolescent. Jung was obsessed with the theology of God, the Trinity, and grace from a precocious age. The emotional dimension of this attachment is apparent in experiences such as his feeling comforted by his nightly prayer to Jesus and his sense of enchantment in the presence of a Cathedral.[30]

By the time he was a teenager he began to de-idealize the tradition due to a series of dreams, fantasies, readings of Nietzsche, and his father's own vagueness in religious matters. Paradigmatic here are the "cathedral fantasy" and his experience of confirmation. In the cathedral fantasy, after Jung experienced an emotional buildup of internal pressure, God himself suddenly defecated on the cathedral of Jung's inner vision.[31] Jung interpreted this as a signal that God could be approached outside of the vessel of the church. Similarly, during Jung's confirmation his father confessed that he did not understand the Trinity. When he took his first communion, Jung was astonished to feel absolutely nothing—much less an experience of participation with the divine.[32] Without a connection to the Christian symbolic order, his narcissistic needs for idealization, identity, and attachment were met first through his work as a medical student and psychologist, then later as Freud's appointed heir in the psychoanalytic association.[33]

Jung's narcissistic idealization and merger with Freud was lost, however, after publication of his *Wandlungen und Symbole der Libido*.[34] In this book, Jung gave the first major psychoanalytic interpretation of religion, concluding that all religious myths (including especially Jesus's death and resurrection) were at their core symbolic representations of a psychoanalytic process.

---

29  Jung 1989; There are an enormous number of biographies on Jung. The best include: Shamdasani 2005, Wehr 1987, and Bair 2003.
30  Jung 1989, 10 and 36.
31  Jung 1989, 39.
32  Homans 1979, 148–151; Parsons 2008b, 105–107; Jung 1989, 52–55.
33  Jung 1989, 146–169; Wehr 1987, 96–160.
34  Homans 1979, 29–56 and 111–114.

Specifically, he concluded all religions and myths at their base represent when an individual regresses through introversion into a pre-oedipal phase in order to release libido cathected in the early mother-son relationship.[35] Jung refers to this as the "hero's journey."[36] Symbolically, this is the hero's descent into the underworld, defeat of the dragon, and return to the social world for moral action. Freud was dismayed at Jung's distortion of his own libido theory and desire to turn psychoanalysis into a religion.[37] It is essential to note that the central symbols under analysis in *Wandlungen* were Mithras and Christ. Jung's desire to revivify the symbol of Christ through psychology shows he had begun to seek rapprochement with the religion.

## 2.2  Symbolic Loss and Reinterpretations of Christ

When Jung's relationship to Freud ended, his needs for idealization, attachment, and identification went unmet. He greatly reduced the number of patients he saw, resigned from the psychoanalytic association, stepped down as editor of the *Jahrbuch,* and abandoned his post as *Privatdozent* at the University of Zurich.[38] Unconscious contents erupted. Jung was plagued with anxiety and beset with rage. He experienced disturbing symbolic dreams (such as the "sarcophagi" dream) and recurring visions (the countryside coated in blood).[39] In terms of this article, these anomic activities—dreams, visions, and uncontrollable emotions—are precisely what would be expected as a consequence of symbolic loss.[40] These anomic activities inspire a period of intense analytic access. Jung himself makes this clear by calling the 1912–1916 period of his life a "confrontation with the unconscious."[41]

---

35  Jung and Hinkle 1916.
36  Jung and Hinkle 1916. Note that although Joseph Campbell would later utilize Jung to construct his own theory of the "hero's journey" monomyth, he and Jung depart on a number of points. Most notably, Campbell's approach only tangentially touched on issues of unconscious mentation, symbolization, and psychodynamic healing, which for Jung are paramount. Campbell does attempt to read a mythic dimension into the development of self, but this is not psychoanalytic in any technical sense. See Campbell 1972.
37  Freud and Jung 1974, 293–296; Jung 1916.
38  See: Jung 1989, 167–168 and 193; Jung 2009, 333; Freud and Jung 1974, 550 and 551. On analytic access leading to a general withdrawal from the common culture to focus on introspection, see: Homans 1989, 112, 126, 150; Parsons 2013, 142–146.
39  Jung and McGuire 1989, 172–173, 175–176.
40  Homans 1989, 24; Parson 2008b, 102.
41  Jung 1963, 174, "Die Auseinandersetzung mit dem Unbewußten." It should be noted Homans's own theorizing about mourning and individuation found first expression in his celebrated book on Jung. See Homans 1979, 115–132.

In order to understand these eruptions of unconscious content, Jung developed a technique he called "active imagination."[42] He would sit in a chair, eyes closed, and let his mind produce fantasies without interference. His experiments and dreams were recorded in narrative form in *The Black Books* and later transferred in handsome calligraphy and paintings into *The Red Book*. Each dream or vision is first presented in bare narrative form and followed by Jung's own interpretation of its meaning. *The Red Book* is divided into three sections: *Liber Primus*, *Liber Secundus*, and *Scrutinies*. At the beginning of these experiments Jung began to question his relationship to Christianity.[43] "In what myth does man live nowadays? In the Christian myth, the answer might be, "Do *you* live in it?" I asked myself. To be honest, the answer was no."[44] Jesus would become the primary figure of *The Red Book*.[45]

In *Liber Primus*, Jung symbolically experiences the dying-rising myth of the hero he outlined in *Wandlungen und Symbole der Libido*. Jung descends into the underworld, murders the false hero, conquers the snake, and becomes deified. It is here Jung is transformed into the Mithraic Chronos and identified as "Christ" by Salome.[46] Immediately Jung sees Elijah transformed in light, an apparent reference to the transfiguration.[47] Jung has clearly begun to identify with Christ.

*Liber Secundus* and *Scrutinies* are where Jung's new psychological theory of individuation, his reinterpretation of Christ, and his readings of gnostic texts first appear.[48] All three points are related. In book two, Jung encounters his "Devil," pines for and finally reconnects with his "soul" or "Eros," is taught by Philemon, and experiences the birth of his new god-image, Helios.[49] These images would translate directly into his psychological typology of the Shadow, Anima, Wise Old Man and the Self archetypes.[50] For instance, Jung's "Devil" persuades him that evil and the desire for joy are a fundamental part of the

---

42  Jung 1997.
43  Jung 1989, 171.
44  Jung 1989, 171.
45  Sonu Shamdasani, "Jung After the Red Book." Symposium given at The Jung Center, Houston, TX, April 20–21, 2011.
46  Jung 2009, 251–252. This imagination was not published in Jung 1989. It was published in Jung and McGuire 1989, 94–97.
47  Matthew 17:1–13.
48  Jung began researches into gnostic texts in 1914 with Dieterich 1891 and the writings of G.R.S. Mead (Mead 1896; Mead 1900; Mead 1987), with whom he started a correspondence that would last until Mead's death in 1933. See Jung 2009, 264 n. 29.
49  For the "Devil": Jung 2009, 259–261, 277–279, and 317–320; For "Eros": 298–299, 323–328; For Philemon: 327–331, 333–359; For Helios and the Self: 327–330.
50  Jung 1956, 182–254; Jung 1978, 1–35.

human psyche that cannot be repressed without imbalance.[51] His "Devil" informs him appetites and instincts have to be integrated into the personality so that they do not overpower the ego.[52] Similarly, Jung wants Philemon to teach him "magic." Philemon chides him that magic cannot be learned—only rational, discursive, logical formulations can be passed on. Magic is an opening to the irrational.[53] These ideas would be theorized in Jung's doctrine of individuation as integration of inferior functions.[54]

As Jung developed his theory of individuation he began a radical reinterpretation of Christ. In one imagination he stumbles upon a library to read *The Imitation of Christ*. The librarian chides him for his superstitions. Jung responds: "You know that I value science extraordinarily highly. But there are actually moments in life where science also leaves us empty and sick … We haven't come to an end with Christianity by simply putting it aside. It seems to me that there's more to it than we see."[55] In this quote, Jung expresses symbolic loss wrought by rationalization. Science leaves one "empty and sick," void the objects that had previously given values and meaning.

Theodicy presented a stumbling block towards reinterpreting the symbol of Christ. Christ denied the animal nature Jung met in his Devil. At this point, Jung has a fantasy:

> I saw the black serpent, as it wound itself upward around the wood of the cross. It crept into the body of the crucified and emerged again transformed from his mouth. It had become white. It wound itself around the head of the dead one like a diadem, and a light gleamed above his ahead, and the sun rose shining in the east.[56]

This imagination expresses symbolic loss and reinterpretation. Jesus, dead on the cross, is literally a lifeless god. He is entered through the mouth by the black snake. The snake symbolizes evil and rebirth throughout *The Red Book*.[57]

---

51 Jung 2009, 259–261.
52 Jung 2009, 322–323. Jung would theorize this idea in Jung 1957 and 1978.
53 Jung 2009, 314.
54 Jung and McGuire, 1989, 67–91.
55 Jung 2009, 292.
56 Jung 2009, 309–310.
57 "The Devil is the sum of the darkness of human nature. He who lives in the light strives toward being the image of God; he who lives in the dark strives toward the image of the Devil. Because I wanted to live in the light, the sun went out for me when I touched the depths. It was dark and serpentlike. I united myself with it and did not overpower it … If I had no become like the serpent, the Devil, the quintessence of everything serpentlike, would have held this bit of power over me." Jung 2009, 322.

Theophagy itself is a recurring theme as well, a means of sacrificing a god and ingesting its power.[58] Christ's ingestion of the snake is thus the incorporation of evil and the unconscious that leads to renewal. This is the first depiction of the integration of evil and darkness into the symbol of Christ in Jung's writings.

Jung began to read accounts of the gnostics in late 1914, first through Albrecht Dieterich's study of *Abraxas*, and soon thereafter through the writings of G.R.S. Mead, with whom Jung developed a correspondence that would last until Mead's death in 1933.[59] Jung creatively interpreted the writings of the ancient gnostics to produce a new conception of Christ that fit Jung's own developing psychology of individuation. He portrays this through what he calls "the dead." The dead personify two things in *The Red Book*: (1) aspects of the unconscious that were incapable of being integrated into the personality due to the Christian emphasis on light, and (2) the literal dead of the past whose belief in orthodox Christianity had left them in limbo. These dead are represented as ghosts wandering the afterlife seeking knowledge that will provide their salvation.[60]

In "Seven Sermons to the Dead," found in the *Scrutinies*, Jung presents a gnostic doctrine of God.[61] Delivered by Philemon and written under the pseudonym Basilides, the sermon preaches a new God: Abraxas.[62] For Jung, Abraxas is the personification of the Pleroma. He is the generator of Helios and Satan, the Summum Bonum and Infinium Malum, or the principles of light and darkness.[63] All that is light he compensates with darkness, and all that is darkness he injects with light. The Pleroma itself more closely resembles an idea from Hippolytus's version of Basilides, particularly the "non-existent, many formed, all empowering seed of the world."[64] It is the "Ground" as a dialectical monism: simultaneously fullness and emptiness, everything and nothingness, motion and stillness, life and death.[65] God-as-Pleroma here is reinterpreted as the matrix of all psychological potentials in dynamic balance. The Self is the

---

58   Jung 2009, 290–1 and 342.
59   Jung's researches into gnostic texts began with Dieterich 1891 and writings of Mead, with whom he started a correspondence that would last until Mead's death in 1933. In *Wandlungen und Symbole der Libido* Jung cites teachings of Hermes from Corp. herm. 4, but no references to Christian gnostics can be found. See Jung 2009, 264 n. 29. On Mead and Jung, see Goodrick-Clarke 2005, 27–31.
60   The dead are a common theme. See Jung 2009, 342.
61   Jung 2009, 346–356. Previously in Jung and Segal 1992, 182–193; Hoeller 1982, 44–59.
62   Jung's encounter with Abraxas was through Dieterich 1891. See Jung 2009, 264 n. 29.
63   Jung 2009, 350.
64   Hippolytus, *Haer.* 7.22.16 Appears in Greek in Jung 1978, 66: "οὐκ ὂν σπέρμα τοῦ κόσμου πολύμορφον ὁμοῦ καί πολυούσιον." Translation mine.
65   Jung 2009, 347.

personification of the Pleroma that integrates light and dark, good and evil into its horizon of consciousness. At the conclusion of the sermon, the dead recognize they have heard knowledge granting salvation. They then "ascended like smoke."[66]

Jung attributes the first recognition that Christ had to be counterbalanced and integrated with the Devil to the gnostics. In the final passage of *The Red Book* Christ enters the garden of Simon Magus and Helen. Simon tells Christ that "Men have changed. They are no longer the slaves and no longer the swindlers of the Gods and no longer mourn in your name."[67] That is to say, the individualism and humanism brought by modernity challenged traditional modes of relating to Christ. In order to become an object for them once again, Jesus must recognize his oneness with the Devil. "[Satan] came before you, whom you recognize as your brother … recognize, Oh master and beloved, that your nature is also of the serpent. Were you not raised on the tree like the serpent?[68] Have you laid aside your body, like the serpent its skin? … [D]id you not go to Hell before your ascent? And did you not see your brother there, who was shut away in the abyss?"[69] In other words, Simon convinces Christ that he needs the Devil/Antichrist in order to function as a symbol of wholeness for the men of this age. In Jung's interpretation, the gnostic Christ becomes meaningful for modernity as a paradigm of the process of descent into suffering, the incorporation of evil, and ultimate apotheosis as a symbol of the Self.

### 2.3 Recreation of Meaning and Rapprochement with Christianity

*The Red Book* was not published until 2009. As such, these fresh interpretations of Christ and God were initially consolidated into Jung's *Collected Works*.[70] As noted above, the interpretations of the Devil, Salome/Eros, and Philemon would be rationalized in his psychological theory of the archetypes.[71] The figure of Christ and Jung's theory that psychological wholeness was achieved through integration of the unconscious would be theorized directly in the archetype of the Self and his theory of individuation. He detailed his practice of achieving

---

66  Jung 2009, 347.
67  Jung 2009, 359.
68  An apparent reference to John 3:14.
69  Jung 2009, 359.
70  Homans 1979, 161–192.
71  See especially: Jung 1978, 1–35; Jung 1956, 70–99 and 182–253; and Jung 1957. Several scholars have analyzed how the "confrontation of the unconscious" became theorized in Jung's psychology. See Homans 1979; Hannah 1991; Shamdasani 2009; Hillman and Shamdasani 2013.

individuation through fantasy and art in "The Transcendent Function," the first writing he produced after his confrontation with the unconscious.[72]

Late in his life, however, he published two essays—"Christ as a Symbol of the Self" and "Gnostic Symbols of the Self"—that reproduced interpretations of Christ and his relationship to the psyche in *The Red Book* for the culture at large. He avers that Western culture has to reconnect to the symbol of Christ: "[Christ] is still the living myth of our culture ... He is in us and we in him."[73] Yet individuals have lost the capacity to be transformed by the symbol. Jung argues that this inability is due to orthodox Christian theology having denied existence to evil with the doctrine of *privatio boni*. Jung thus makes a *historical* argument to support his *psychological* theory.

Jung thought the ancient gnostic writings, including the by then discovered Nag Hammadi Library, exhibit how the symbol of Christ is experienced by the unconscious as a drive towards individuation. After reading *The Jung Codex* in 1955, Jung became enamored with the Gospel of Truth.[74] For Jung, the Gospel of Truth shows Christ descends as a revealer to awaken the unconscious individual from their stupor as a symbol of the Self.[75] This spontaneous experience of this symbol of the Self reorients the psyche teleologically towards achievement of psychic wholeness, as depicted in imagery of magnetic attraction in the Naasenes and Peratae.[76] The gnostic Christ already contained both poles: light and dark, good and evil.[77] Moreover, once confronted by a symbol of the Self in Christ, the unconscious naturally assimilates comparable symbols within the culture, just as in the Naasene sermon (e.g., Attis, Adonis, Osiris, Adam, Korybas) or today in symbols like *Atman* or the *tao*.[78] Like Basilides's Christ, the Self arising into consciousness would differentiate the previously unconscious contents in order to integrate them into awareness.[79] Finally, as in the Naasene sermon, after Christ awakens the inner, spiritual man, he

---

72   Jung and McGuire 1991, 67–91.
73   Jung 1978, 36.
74   See Jung and Segal 1992, 97–100. A multi-lingual translation of the Gospel of Truth, then entitled *Evangelium Veritatis*, was produced by Jung's dear friend Gilles Quispel, as well as H.C. Peuch and Michael Malinine. It is this edition Jung was familiar with. See Mainline, Puech, Quispel 1956.
75   Jung and Segal 1992, 98–99. Jung was presented with a translation of the Jung Codex in advance of the commemoration held for him in 1956.
76   Jung 1979, 185–186, quoting Hippolytus, *Haer.* 7.9 and 5.17 Jung refers to *Haer.* by its alternate title, *Elenchus*.
77   Jung 1959, 64–66. See Hippolytus *Haer.* 7.20–27.
78   Jung 1959, 199.
79   Jung 1978, 64; Hippolytus *Haer.* 7.27.

opens the door through which that man is transformed into their own integrated Self: the Anthropos.[80]

## 3 Laurence Caruana

Visionary artist and author Laurence Caruana is one of the most productive contemporary gnostics. He has written extensively on the Nag Hammadi Codices, producing two major works: *Enter through the Image*, a philosophical study of ancient epistemology as he sees it; and *The Hidden Passion: A Novel of the Gnostic Christ Based on the Nag Hammadi Texts*.[81] He founded and runs the Vienna Academy of Visionary Art.[82] Recently, he has begun work on a series of paintings that depict paradigmatic scenes from gnostic mythologoumena (e.g. the Anointing of the Christos, the Five Seals, and the Bridal Chamber) planned for a gnostic chapel in the southwest of France. Like Jung, his interest in gnostic texts is prompted by the de-idealization and symbolic loss of the Christianity of his upbringing. His encounter with ancient gnostic texts allowed him to reinterpret the Christian symbolic by embracing pluralism, sacralizing the psyche, re-enchanting the cosmos, and incorporating the divine feminine.

### 3.1 *Early Attachment and De-idealization*

Born in Toronto, Caruana was raised by Catholic parents who had immigrated from Malta.[83] As he describes it, the symbolic universe of Catholicism—Jesus's bodily dying and rising, the Trinity, Heaven and Hell—was self-evidently true to him. The Bible recounted sacred history, and the statues and rituals of the mass had genuine power. Even as he took a degree in Philosophy at the University of Toronto, he never brought his faith under critical analysis.

Unfortunately, both in his published materials and in interview, Caruana is silent about what precisely caused his de-idealization and loss of attachment.[84] It is inarguable, however, that this occurred. After graduating from college

---

80 Jung 1978, 212; Hippolytus *Haer.* 5.8.
81 Caruana 2007 and 2009.
82 http://academyofvisionaryart.com/.
83 Unless otherwise indicated, all details on Caruana's biography are from Caruana, e-mail message to author, Sept. 14, 2015 and skype interview, Oct. 1, 2015.
84 Interviews include: Caruana, e-mail interview with author, Sept. 18, 2015, and skype interview with author, Oct. 1, 2015. Aeon Byte Gnostic Radio Shows "What Would the Ministry of a Gnostic Jesus Look Like?" and "Secret Rituals in Gnostic Myths"; and Mental Contagion Interview 2002.

what he calls a "dark period" set in. As he remembers it, "beginning in my mid-twenties, I entered a period of instability on all levels: financially, professionally, and in personal relationships. *My former worldview collapsed and I basically became an atheist.* This dark period last for about seven years, with each new conflict plunging me deeper into the world of dreams, memories, and the unconscious (emphasis mine)."[85] In my interviews with him, Caruana expressed that during this period "the Catholic framework of faith which I'd inherited through my upbringing had been abandoned, and I was rationally an atheist."[86] Even today, self-identifying as a gnostic-Christian, he tries to avoid use of the name Jesus, which in his estimation has become "disgusting" due to the terrible associations it has gained as part of "traditional religion."[87] In such quotes, Caruana describes the shift from idealization to de-idealization and symbolic loss: a sense of alienation from the common culture (professional, personal, and religious), a loss of identity and psychological stability, the incapacity to idealize religious symbols, and the advent of "analytic access" with his interest in dreams and released unconscious contents.[88]

### 3.2 Symbolic Loss and Reinterpretations of Christ

During his "dark period," Caruana lived a peripatetic life in Vienna (1989–1990), Malta (1992–1994), and Munich (1994–1997), before settling in Paris. Given that Caruana is unfamiliar with Homans's theory of mourning, it is remarkable how the "dark period" he describes conforms to a period of symbolic loss and analytic access. The seven-year period plunged Caruana deeper and "deeper into the world of dreams, memories, and the unconscious." While in Malta, Caruana notes he "experienced a complete breakdown which allowed me to finally remember buried childhood memories and heal them."[89] In terms of symbolic loss, the location of this breakthrough is important. Malta is his ancestral homeland. Living and working in Malta, he experienced a reconnection with his cultural roots and was daily confronted by its Catholic imagery.

Early on in his "dark period," Caruana began to dream of Christ. In his words:

> In my dreams, the figure of Christ re-emerged, but significantly different from the one acquired through my Catholic upbringing. This was the symbol, archetype or eternal image of Christ, which had no physical

---

85   Caruana, e-mail interview with author, Sept. 18, 2015.
86   Caruana, e-mail Interview with author Sept. 18, 2015.
87   Aeon Byte Gnostic Radio Show, "What Would a Ministry of the Gnostic Jesus Look Like?"
88   See note 19.
89   Caruana, e-mail interview with author, Sept. 18, 2015.

or bodily existence. Through my reading, I interpreted this image of Christ as a mythic figure, the Christian version of the "ever-dying and rising savior."[90]

Soon thereafter, reading Kazantzaki's *The Last Temptation of Christ* inspired Caruana to consider Jesus as a man struggling with the appetites and fears of the flesh in order to recognize divinity within.[91] It was then, wrestling with the nature of Christ, that Caruana encountered gnostic texts. He read the first edition of *The Nag Hammadi Library in English*, Hans Jonas's *The Gnostic Religion*, Irenaeus's *Adversus Haercses*, and Hippolytus's *Refutatio* in 1989.[92] Caruana was drawn to the gnostics as Christian heretics whose belief and practice responded to a lack in Catholicism: visionary gnosis, the creation of new gospels in light of gnosis, the sacred feminine, and rites and sacraments that produced genuine transformation. "All in all, the Gnostic texts revitalized my interest in Christianity and blew a breath of fresh air into my spiritual outlook."[93] For example, Caruana found a parallel for the two states of Christ he had found in dreams and literature needing to be reconciled in the pre-existent image of the anointed and earthly Jesus in texts such as the Tripartite Tractate.[94] In theoretical terms, the combination of dreams, literature, and the Nag Hammadi codices provided a means for Caruana to begin to re-idealize the symbol of Jesus again.

During his period of intense symbolic loss, Caruana had a series of mystical experiences.[95] One of these in particular he identifies as *gnosis*. One afternoon, after having smoked hashish and sitting in his painting studio, he suddenly felt as though

> For the first time, I felt a genuine religious or mystical awakening with profound and life-altering consequences. I had a direct experience of Divinity beyond any categories or points of reference given to me in my life thus far. It came as a revelation, of the sudden remembrance of who

---

90 Caruana, e-mail interview with author, Sept. 18, 2015.
91 Kazantzakis 1960.
92 Robinson 1981, Jonas 1963. In our interview, Caruana states he made copies of Irenaeus and Hippolytus at the local library, though it is unclear what edition he consulted.
93 Caruana, e-mail interview with author, Sept. 18, 2015.
94 Tri. Trac. NHC I,5 86.23–87.17 and 114.32–115.30.
95 On mystical experiences as not uncommon in periods of analytic access, see Parsons 2008b, 102; Parsons 2013, 143. Significantly, but as would be expected after completing the process of mourning, Caruana notes that these experiences essentially stopped at the end of his "dark period." Caruana, e-mail interview with author, Sept. 18, 2015.

I was, where I came from, and where I would return after death. I experienced the Divine Presence as a unity, as the unified and ever-present source of all things, and I too was now a knowing particle of that Oneness, though that knowledge and experience had remained unknown and inaccessible to me for most of my life.[96]

After this experience, the *Nag Hammadi Library* became the centerpiece of Caruana's religious quest: "It was [after this experience] that many texts from the Nag Hammadi Library acquired a new level of meaning, a whole new series of resonances with known and lived experience."[97] The consolidation of these reinterpretations in a new system of meanings is found in his *The Hidden Passion*.

### 3.3 Recreation of Meaning and Rapprochement with Christianity

Immediately after the above-quoted experience, Caruana began work on *Enter through the Image*, titled after a passage in The Gospel of Philip.[98] Essentially, Caruana's new epistemology is as follows: the divine source, "the One," emanates itself first in archetypes (such as the Self archetype), then cultural symbols (such as Jesus), and last in human minds and lives.[99] Humans can come to reconnect with the divine source of all through forms of symbolic thinking, such as meditating on a cultural symbol, reflecting on one's life as an expression of mythic prototypes, and through interpretation of dreams. This language of images Caruana dubs "iconologic." By understanding iconologic, individuals can "enter through the image" to realize identity with the One.[100] Crucially, these symbols can be borrowed, displaced, or combined from different cultures to achieve *gnosis* since all of them are ultimately expressions of the One. In Caruana's view, this ancient image language was lost when modernity became excessively logocentric.

In his novel *The Hidden Passion* Caruana creates a new vision of Jesus that would simultaneously allow him to *identify* with a gnostic Christ while also *idealizing* him as a superior being. This novel features what Caruana felt Catholicism lacked: gnosis, transformative rites and sacraments, and a goddess. Moreover, his Jesus functions as a mythic paradigm for each

---

96  Caruana, e-mail interview with author, Sept. 18, 2015.
97  Caruana, e-mail interview with author, Sept. 18, 2015.
98  Gos. Phil. NHC II,3 67.17.
99  Caruana 2009. See especially 1–40.
100 Caruana 2009, 36, 291–293.

individual's own process of reconciling the two dimensions of humanity, the body and the divine.

Before composing the novel, Caruana began what he calls the "Gnostic Q" project. This morphological project identified themes and symbols common in gnostic texts, such as baptism, revealer, and light, and collected them into an index.[101] The novel enacts Caruana's iconologic by arranging these symbols along the mythic path of Jesus's "hero's journey" that the individual reader can identify with.[102] Furthermore, Caruana collected all theological statements from revealer figures in gnostic texts, including Zostrianos, Allogenes, and Seth and places them in the mouth of Jesus in the novel.

Beginning with Jesus's "separation" from his mother Mary by edict of Joseph, the novel follows Jesus in his "call" when the monastery he is being trained in identifies him as Messiah, followed by his "dark night of the soul" as he fails to incite a political rebellion on Yaltabaoth's orders. With a broken arm and in despair verging on madness, he describes feeling the 360 demons moving his body and sees the archons controlling all of time and space.[103] With his best friend Judas and his love interest Mary Magdalene, Jesus encounters John the Baptist at the river Jordan. John baptizes him three times. In the first, Jesus is healed and the demons are dispelled from his body. In the second, he is rendered luminous. In the third, he is granted his secret name, "Yesseus Mazareus Yessedekus."[104]

Caruana's depictions of the baptisms operate on two levels. The baptisms are an enactment in time of the initial moments of the Barbelo theogony, where the Son is born from the Father and Barbelo, light is poured upon him, and he turns towards the father as his image in the watery light.[105] Jesus here is a paradigm of the realization of the divine image within. On the second level, Jesus is a unique object for idealization. To wit, at the third baptism the "Jordan, his beloved river, began to flow backwards."[106] Everyone present was momentarily

---

101  http://www.gnosticq.com/.
102  Caruana follows Joseph Campbell's monomyth of the hero's journey and not Jung's version above. See Campbell 1972. Campbell was obviously influenced by Jung in his approach to symbol, myth, and the hero's journey. However, their theories of the "hero's journey" are quite different. Cf. note 36 above. Caruana utilizes many of the mythemes of Campbell's monomyth to structure the account of Jesus, for example "the call to adventure," "refusal of the call," "tests, allies, and enemies," "the ordeal," "the reward," and "the return with the elixir."
103  Caruana 2007, 120–121. The reference is to Ap. John NHC II,1 15.1–19.3.
104  Caruana 2007, 140–44, 170–171.
105  Ap. John NHC II,1 6.15–31.
106  Caruana 2007, 143. Source text Testim. Truth NHC XI, 3 30.20.

blinded by the release of light. John designates Jesus "the Messiah of the Five Seals!"[107]

The remainder of the novel depicts Jesus leading his disciples through spiritual transformation in the rite of the Five Seals. The Five Seals is a ceremony mentioned only in the Three Forms of First Thought, Gospel of the Egyptians, and long recensions of Apocryphon of John.[108] These references are sufficiently vague as to have led to diverse reconstructions from respected scholars.[109] John Turner has posited that the Five Seals is a visionary form of baptism, an interpretation that Caruana follows.[110]

Utilizing iconologic, Caruana maps these five seals onto the sacraments mentioned in the Valentinian text, the Gospel of Philip: "The lord did everything in a mystery: a baptism and a chrism and a eucharist and a redemption and a bridal chamber."[111] In order to maintain the hero's journey narrative, Caruana moves the eucharist to the fourth "seal" and replaces it with the resurrection. Two of these "seals" in particular—the resurrection and the bridal chamber—are necessary to understanding Caruana's recreation of meaning in Jesus.

Resurrection (ἀνάστασις), the third seal, consists of Jesus and his cousin Arsinoe leading the twelve disciples on a visionary pathworking through the cosmos of the Apocryphon of John: the five sub-lunar realms to discard the body and the seven planetary spheres to discard the passions of the soul. After ascending into the ogdoad, Arsinoe shrieks Yaltabaoth's name and he explodes. The disciples ascend into the Ennead and are gifted with visions of the Monad as "a foundation of clear, glowing light" and "a mosaic comprised of flawless crystals and glittering gems."[112] Each of the disciples enters into eternity, becoming an aeon in the mind of God.[113] In knowing their own divine Self and entering through the image, each disciple becomes part of the self-consciousness of God. In *Enter through the Image*, Caruana reads the theogony

---

107  Caruana 2007, 143.
108  See Three Forms NHC XIII,1 50.9–15; Ap. John NHC II,1 30.11–33; Gos. Eg. NHC III,2 62.24–63.4.
109  For Five Seaals as visionary baptism see Turner 1994, 137–149; Layton 1995, 18–19; Burns 2014, 134. For Five Seals as related to chrismation and sealing of the five senses see Logan 1997, 190; Brakke 2010, 73–75. For Five Seals as water baptism, see Sevrin 1986, 37–38.
110  Turner 1994, 137–149. Caruana is aware of and has read Turner's essay "Ritual in Gnosticism." Caruana, Skype interview with author, Oct. 1, 2015.
11   ⲁⲡϫⲟⲉⲓⲥ ⲣ̅ϩⲱⲃ ⲛⲓⲙ ϩⲛ̅ⲟⲩⲙⲩⲥⲧⲏⲣⲓⲟⲛ ⲟⲩⲃⲁ[ⲡ]ⲧⲓⲥⲙⲁ ⲙⲛ̅ ⲟⲩⲭⲣⲓⲥⲙⲁ ⲙⲛ̅ⲛⲟⲩⲉⲩⲭⲁⲣ[ⲓⲥⲧ]ⲓⲁ ⲙⲛ̅ⲛⲟⲩⲥⲱⲧⲉ ⲙⲛ̅ⲛⲟⲩⲛⲩⲙⲫⲱⲛ, Gos. Phil. NHC II,3 67.27–30. Translation by Isenberg 1989, 177, with slight modification.
112  Caruana 2009, 283–4.
113  Caruana 2009, 284.

of the Apocryphon of John as parallel to a mental event in which the consciousness of God (embodied in the aeons) is occluded by the passions of the soul and the appetites of the body.[114] Gnosis is the transcendence of these passions and appetites to recognize the consciousness of God within the self. As such, this is the fictional depiction of Caruana's experience of *gnosis*.

Significantly, Christ remains set apart. In their moment of gnosis the disciples see: "the blinding face of God, whose countenance bore the lineaments of the Son. The smile on the Savior's face was full of compassion; his eyes were closed in half-contemplative bliss. But the Son, they now recognized, bore their own features. They stared at themselves while staring, inexplicably, into the face of God."[115] Jesus is therefore the paradigm who each disciples sees themselves in (identification), but as the image of the full countenance of God each disciple is an aeon in *his* mind (idealization).

The bridal chamber, the fifth seal, occurs after the crucifixion. It is the "Hidden Passion" of the title. For Caruana the crucifixion remains central to Christian belief. The Nazarene, "through love and sacrifice ... found the path to a higher state of existence, a timeless state 'at one' with the Divine, which transcends our physical and temporal existence."[116] Physical and temporal existence is symbolically overcome in the crucifixion. However, neither embodiment nor sexuality is evil for Caruana. This is represented by Jesus's relationship to Mary Magdalene. Mary's journey mirrors Jesus's in the novel. A childhood friend of Jesus, Mary is cast out by her mother. She loses her virginity in Babylon performing the *hieros gamos* rite between Astante and Baal.[117] Within the sex-rite she feels "ecstatic"—is set loose from her body—only to "fall" back into herself. When it is over, she is labeled a "whore." She is plagued by visions where she identifies as Helen or Sophia. She is the Christian Goddess.

The reconciliation of the Goddess and the Christ is accomplished in the bridal chamber. After Jesus's crucifixion, Mary is distraught. Then, in a vision, she experiences the resurrected Christ. They kiss, and as they do they ascend through the archonic spheres, light swallows up the abyss, the disciples ascend to marry their holy angel consorts, and the Pleroma is made whole again.[118] Caruana depicts here the "restoration" (ἀποκατάτασις), a doctrine found in certain Valentinian texts where the fallen aspect of Sophia, Sophia-Achamoth, returns to the Pleroma and thereby ends the need for a separate material world.[119]

---

114  Caruana 2009, 95–109.
115  Caruana 2007, 285.
116  Caruana, e-mail interview with author, Oct. 1, 2015.
117  Caruana 2007, 105.
118  Caruana 2007, 408–409.
119  Irenaeus, *Haer.* 1.1.7.

In some texts, Sophia can only return by receiving her consort Jesus.[120] In terms of Caruana's own reinterpretation of Christianity, the syzygy with Mary/Sophia-Achamoth is the unification of the flesh with the spirit or primordial image of the Christ. The seeming end of the evil, hylic world is psychologically the end of the distracting, demonic, tempting aspects of embodiment. The body and spirit are each transformed and reconciled in one another as the image of eternity.

## 4  Jonathan Talat Philips

Jonathan Talat Philips is a major figure in "consciousness culture," a counterculture associated with Burning Man and concerned with integrating eco-consciousness, sustainability, technology, and spirituality. Along with author Daniel Pinchbeck, he launched the website Reality Sandwich.[121] He has written and spoken about his return to Christianity through a sequence of religious experiences and readings of the Nag Hammadi codices. In his memoir *The Electric Jesus: The Healing Journey of a Contemporary Gnostic*, Phillips recounts his youth in a Methodist church, his suffering from depression in his teens and twenties, and his healing through an encounter with psychedelics and "the Electric Jesus." Phillips's autobiography as narrated precisely fits the process of mourning.

### 4.1  Early Attachment and De-idealization

Raised Methodist in a small mining town in Colorado, Phillips recalls "hating" church as a child. Nevertheless, Phillips was evidently attached to Christian symbolism and interpreted the world through it.[122] After watching a violent depiction of the Rapture in film at ten years old, for example, Phillips was plagued with nightmares of Jesus standing "on a mountain of broken, tortured bodies, victoriously holding a sword above his head while surveying the bombed gray landscape around him. Every morning I feared the coming slaughter of the Tribulation."[123] His attachment to Christianity was inflected by parental dynamics.[124] Phillips could not idealize his father and was therefore prone to grandiosity. Though his mother would fan Phillips's

---

120  Val. Exp. NHC XI, 2 2.39.28–39.
121  http://realitysandwich.com/u/talat-jonathan-phillips/.
122  Phillips 2011, 53.
123  Phillips 2011, 55.
124  See note 24.

narcissistic grandiosity by praising his accomplishments to neighbors—school president, valedictorian, prom king—she rarely displayed affection at home. Instead, she was prone to fits of anger, openly wishing Phillips and his siblings "had never been born."[125] It is no surprise he would suffer depression through much of his life. Phillips describes his depression symbolically as the "black bowling ball" in his stomach.[126] The interrelationship between narcissistic injury from his mother and attachment to Christianity is central to the healing journey of Phillips's memoir.

In his college years and twenties Phillips became utterly disillusioned with Christianity, becoming a self-described "cynical secular materialist."[127] The break from the common culture was attenuated by a sense of belonging to subcultures that provided venues for idealizations, narcissistic mirroring and attachment.[128] He became enthralled by Beat Generation, frequenting the same bars as Kerouac and Neal Cassady, writing until dawn, and indulging in alcohol and sex as much as his literary heroes.[129] He spent a few years as an expat author in Prague but returned to the United States after 9/11 and became an anti-war demonstrator. Nicknaming himself "General Johnny America" and wearing a George Washington overcoat, sky blue pants and vest, and sliver stars from his ankles to his shoulders, Phillips was the leader of the street-media team "Green Dragon." But when George W. Bush was re-elected in 2004 Phillips's hopes for a revolution were crushed. In theoretical terms, his attempts to connect to American symbols of the common culture were thwarted, leading to a period of intense depression.[130]

### 4.2 Symbolic Loss and Reinterpretations of Christ

It was during this period, divorced from any common culture and in the midst of a depression, that Phillips discovered the Nag Hammadi codices and began to reinterpret the symbols of Christianity through them. His interpretations attempt to make sense of a sequence of psychedelic experiences while also connecting the Christian symbolic order to Eastern religious traditions, an "enlightenment of the body," and a re-enchantment of the world that adapt the symbol of Jesus to a modernized world.[131]

---

125  Phillips 2011, 53–61.
126  Phillips 2011, 12.
127  Phillips 2011, 1.
128  See note 20.
129  Phillips 2011, 61.
130  Phillips 2011, 1–11, 61–71.
131  On re-enchantment as a response to disenchantment and modernization, see Partridge 2004.

Phillips interprets his own journey towards healing under the paradigm of mythicist Christianity as presented by Timothy Freke and Peter Gandy. In a trio of popular histories, Freke and Gandy used the Nag Hammadi codices to argue that the historical Jesus of Nazareth never existed.[132] He was an invention of a small group of Jewish mystics who wanted to adapt the dying-and-rising godman archetype of the mystery religions to a Jewish context. On their interpretation, Jesus is a symbol of the psychological death of the ego-self and mystical awakening to a deeper sense of identity with an impersonal divine consciousness, known as "the Christ within."[133] The "Literalists" of the Catholic Church misinterpreted this myth as a series of historical events, while the gnostics continued to accept the allegorical reading.[134]

Phillips is influenced by these ideas in three ways.[135] First, he structures his memoir to fit the dying-rising godman myth, identifying with the symbol of Christ as a paradigm of self-transformation. Second, the ample parallels Freke and Gandy cite between Jesus and figures like Osiris draws the Christian symbolic order into a universal frame of reference that legitimizes Phillips's own connections between the gnostics and Tantra. Third, for Freke and Gandy canonical and noncanonical gospels are gnostic in the sense of being allegories that encode the mystery religion of Christianity.[136] Phillips in turn reads the New Testament with the same eyes as the Nag Hammadi codices.[137]

Phillips's reinterpretation of Jesus presumes that a doctrine of an underlying metaphysical body is found cross-culturally. With what Jeff Kripal calls an "enlightenment of the body," such metaphysical body doctrines (usually Tantric) undergird embodied practices that catalyze and cultivate altered states of consciousness and energy.[138] For Phillips, the alternative memory opened up by the gnostics and their texts allows him to reinterpret Christianity in terms of a Tantric enlightenment of the body. He reads Logion 106 of the Gospel of

---

132   Freke and Gandy 1999, 2001, and 2006. Mythicism in its hard form (i.e., Jesus is not a historical personage) is typically traced to Bruno Bauer, 1850. Arthur Drews 1909 is the first to blend this notion of Mythicism with invention by a mystically oriented group of Jewish persons. Freke and Gandy go further in utilizing the Nag Hammadi codices to portray the original form of Christianity as a gnostic mystery religion.
133   Freke and Gandy 2001, 88.
134   Freke and Gandy 1999, 191–250; Freke and Gandy 2001, 7–38.
135   For Phillips's adoption of these ideas, see: http://www.huffingtonpost.com/jonathan-talat-phillips/gnosis-mystical-history-of-jesus_b_1199493.html.
136   Freke and Gandy 1999, 89–132.
137   Phillips, Skype interview with author, Sept. 11, 2015.
138   For Kripal's "enlightenment of the body," see Kripal 2007, 22. This Tantric notion is dependent upon both the body and consciousness being understood as expressions of divine energy that can be awakened, harnessed, and channeled

Thomas, "When you make the two one, you will become children of Adam, and when you say 'Mountain, move away from here!' it will move" as a recognition of the Tantric concept of the *ida* and *pingala* channels which rise up from the lowest chakra, encircling one another through the remaining seven until rising up and through the crown chakra at the top of the skull.[139] Significantly, in his rendering of this passage Phillips substitutes "children of Adam" for "sons of man" (ⲚϢⲎⲢⲈ ⲘⲠⲢⲰⲘⲈ) in an effort to read this state of non-duality as a return to Eden, for him as much an ecological ideal of conservation, tribalism, and sustainability as a spiritual state.[140] Realization of non-duality is accomplished by release of the kundalini energy that shoots up the *sushumna*, a central channel through the chakras that evaporates the polarity of the *ida* and *pingala* in its tremendous rush of force.[141] For Phillips, the gnostic Tree of Life in the Garden of Eden symbolizes the Tantric "enlightened body." In the ecstasy of rising kundalini, "spiritual adepts pass through the veil of ego death and find themselves in communion with the "ineffable," "eternal," and "immeasurable light"" surrounding the Invisible Spirit in the Apocryphon of John.[142]

Phillips further interprets gnostics and the Jesus of history as "healers" who recognized this underlying spiritual energy base to the body. Informed by Freke and Gandy, Phillips believes *soter* (σωτήρ) did not initially mean "Savior," but was a means to signify the healing miracles of mythic godmen such as Asclepius.[143] Jesus's healing miracles were energetic acts that shifted the auras of the ill back into alignment.[144] Gnostics ("pneumatics") encode energetic healing in their language of *pneuma*, a Greek synonym for *ruah, qi, prana*, and *mana*.[145] Baptism is a matter of transmitting this spiritual energy from master to disciple, as when the living Jesus intoxicates a disciple with "the bubbling spring that [he] has tended."[146] Baptism in "rushing water" is meant to convey

---

139 Phillips 2011, 104. See Gos. Thom. NHC II,2 50.18–22.
140 Phillips 2011, 21.
141 Phillips 2011, 105.
142 Phillips 2011, 105. See Ap. John NHC II,1 6.11–12.
143 Phillips 2011, 78. Freke and Gandy 1999, 37–42.
144 Phillips 2011, 116.
145 Phillips 2011, 116. Phillips apparently accepts the equation between the Paul's language of *pneumatikos* (1 Cor 15), Valentinian *pneumatikoi* and the more general category of Gnostic made between Freke and Gandy throughout their work. See Freke and Gandy 1999, 168–170 and 2001, 68–78. *Ruah* is Hebrew for "spirit." *Qi* is Mandarin for "air, breath" and is most commonly associated in an American context with the practice of Tai Chi. *Prana* is Sanskrit for "breath" and is associated with practices in *prana yoga*. *Mana* is Maori for "pervasive supernatural power." Phillips equates all of these as spirit power that can be used for healing and to cultivate altered states of consciousness and energy.
146 Gos. Thom. NHC II,2 35.4–8.

this underlying energetic conception.[147] Jesus and the gnostics are therefore practitioners of energy healing that secularized medicine has not caught up to. The underlying conception of the (metaphysical) body brings Christianity into a cross-cultural frame of reference.

In both content and interpretation, Phillips's psychedelic experiences utilize gnostic-Christian symbolism to show his reattachment to the tradition through psychological healing. During an Ayahuasca ceremony Phillips finds himself visited by his spirit guides. He suddenly feels "a blinding light open[ed] up above me, descending into my crown chakra, filling my entire body with energy. *It was what I had imagined early Christian baptisms to be like* ... white energy gushed through my meridians, pumping pleasant sensations through my body. I was charged to the point of being overwhelmed."[148] His guides inform him he had become like Christ, Buddha, or Krishna, an enlightened being returned to the Edenic state.[149] Although Phillips does not draw attention to this, his own visionary experience recapitulates his own interpretations of the anointing of the Son with the Light of the Father to become Christ in the Apocryphon of John.[150] Phillips's religious vision is encoded and interpreted in manner that reconnects him to the Christian symbolic order.

The psychological healing Phillips sought is also accomplished through re-attachment to the Christian symbolic order. Phillips became a public speaker after Reality Sandwich went live. In one of these talks, he spontaneously began speaking about the role of Christ and the gnostics in his healing journey. Later that evening, Phillips's guides informed him they had a message from Jesus. As Philips tells it, a "sermon" came down as a holographic image the size of a volleyball that downloaded into his heart chakra. The guides informed him that the message encoded "healing vectors" that he could transmit when talking about Jesus. The hologram descended down his chakras until:

> the black bowling ball in my stomach lurched upward. It rotated clockwise and then pulsated rapidly, until a pool of dark energies broke through my pelvis and rushed down my legs and out the soles of my feet ... I felt purified. Thank you Jesus, I found myself saying.[151]

---

147  Phillips, Skype interview with author, Sept. 11, 2015.
148  Phillips 2011, 124–125; emphasis mine.
149  Phillips 2011, 125.
150  Phillips 2011, 80; Ap. John NHC II,1 6.15–31. See parallels in Ap. John NHC III,1 9.2–11 and BG8502,2 30.2–11.
151  Phillips 2011, 184.

In that moment two things happened that completed Phillip's process of mourning. First, the healing of the bowling ball of depression can be understood as his own symbolism of narcissistic injury. When downloading the sermon he sees an image of his mother and realizes that her abuse was necessary for him to transmute his own ills into love and compassion for all, including her.[152] In essence, overcoming his depression and reconciling with his mother are representative of the new, integrated, healthy sense of self Phillips achieved with introspection during the process of mourning.[153] A second meaning is found in a new Christology. He concluded from this experience that Jesus was not merely a mythic prototype, but "a vast and complex cosmic plane, an overarching energy structure that stretched across realms of the divine pleroma."[154] In other words, Jesus is both a symbol of the healer (identification) *and* a conscious field of energy (idealization) that operates as an agent of healing.

### 4.3   *Recreation of Meaning and Rapprochement with Christianity*

Unlike Jung and Caruana, Phillips's recreation of meaning is not in theoretical products, but in his memoir. His narrative follows Freke and Gandy's depiction of Jesus as the dying and rising God, from Phillips's captivation by the world of appetites, to disillusionment, through the process of ego-death and healing into identification with the "Christ consciousness" within. His own autobiography is presented as a prototype of the recreation of meaning and potential for rapprochement with Christianity.

In many public talks since, Phillips has found that his yearning to reconnect with Christian symbols is hardly unique. Many attendees of his talks thank him for allowing them to feel like a Christian again.[155] As part of his "recreation of meaning," Phillips hopes to revivify Christian practice from within the churches themselves. In his estimation the orthodox churches are "imitation churches" that have become the "dry canals" spoken of in the Revelation of Peter.[156] Phillips sees, however, that a new religion is beside the point insofar as it fails to integrate the Christian tradition that undergirds Western culture. What is needed is for the established churches to enhance "their services with meditation, prayer, breath work, energy healing, body movement, possibly even late-night dancing, and among the more radicalized, the dispensing of psychoactive sacraments."[157]

---

152   Phillips 2011, 184.
153   See note 22.
154   Phillips 2011, 184.
155   Phillips, Skype interview with author, Sept. 11, 2015.
156   Apoc. Pet. NHC VII,3 30.1.
157   Phillips 2011, 82.

In theoretical terms, Phillips vision after his process of mourning is to revivify the Christian symbolic for others in America. With experiential technologies that overcome disenchantment, the integration of non-Western practices that encompass pluralism, and a new historical vision of Jesus, Phillips believes the Christian symbolic can once again be a resource for idealization, attachment, and meaning in America.

## Conclusion

As Homans made clear, symbolic loss, cultural memory, and modernization are tightly intertwined. In his words:

> It is mourning that puts loss and history together. Mourning is a part of both loss and memory. In fact, loss, mourning, and memory are inseparable from each other ... this continuity makes it possible to explore the dark side of modernization: its failure to recognize that a dimension of loss—at times personal, at other times collective and historical—always accompanies progress.[158]

The "dark side" of the progress of modernization is symbolic loss, specifically the loss of the self-evident facticity of the Christian symbolic order and a culturally shared relationship to the past. In order to complete the process of mourning, individuals need to revise the cultural memory of their tradition to reinterpret it for a modernized age. Gnosticism as a category opened a new interpretive possibility in early Christian memory that individuals use for revision of and rapprochement with the tradition. Gnosticism, then, fits hand-in-glove with the revision of memory necessary for individuals to resolve religious mourning.

Clearly, Western individuals *en masse* are not experiencing symbolic loss and the process of mourning with the intensity of these "extreme cases."[159] But the cases of Jung, Caruana, and Phillips show in high relief the ways in which modernization, symbolic loss, and gnosticism are closely related. Each writer experienced symbolic loss in a single lifetime. In midlife, this loss manifested itself as a compelling need to introspect their unconscious contents and reinterpret Christ. The lack of attachment to and idealization of the Christian

---

158  Homans 2008, 16.
159  William James famously asserted the methodology of the "extreme case" in *Varieties of Religious Experience*. See James 2002, 48.

tradition set loose unconscious contents. Unchurched mystical experiences erupted.

In the midst of this symbolic loss, each of these authors became obsessed with the Christian gnostics. Crucially, all turn to the gnostics in order to reinterpret Christian symbols, such as Jesus, not simply to understand the gnostics themselves. In fact, in the cases of Jung and Phillips their interpretations, though creative, are historically quite wrong. Caruana is more interested in fidelity to historical scholarship, but even he admits to taking license when he places all statements from revealer figures into the Nazarene's mouth.

The disconnect between the historical gnostics and contemporary religious interpretation necessitates analysis of what these interpretations have in common. This article has shown the new interpretations of Jesus are acute responses to modernization. Jung reframed Jesus as a psychological symbol of the Self that individuals may use as a paradigm to guide their own awakening to psychological wholeness. In so doing, he makes Jesus a universal symbol, located in the brain, that befits a rationalized and pluralized West. Caruana creatively reinterprets Jesus as a perennial manifestation of the dying and rising God, consort of the divine feminine, and a paradigm for life as a journey into gnosis. This *gnosis* re-enchants his world while commenting on the logocentrism wrought by secularization. Phillips's reinterpretations of Jesus made of him a healer and Tantric guru pointing to the hidden metaphysics of embodiment that attempts to embrace America's unprecedented pluralism. His Jesus even speaks in favor of a prelapsarian, neotribal share economy, and in so doing offers a critique of the excesses of capitalism and industrialization.

In closing, if one accepts the principle that individual case studies are representative of sociological dynamics, then this article suggests an as yet unacknowledged factor in the reception and construction of gnosticism in the West.[160] The unprecedented mainstream popularity of the gnostics and their texts in the last century—evident in everything from best-selling novels such as *The Da Vinci Code* and National Geographic's documentary *The Gospel of Judas* to the popularity of Elaine Pagels's scholarship—may be a response to the symbolic loss of the Christian tradition in the West.[161] This approach makes

---

160   The relationship between the individual and collective processes is fundamental to Homans's contextual approach. See Homans 1979, 14–22 and 155–158. Parsons explores this relationship in the development of unchurched, psychological mysticism in Parsons 2008b, 101–116 and Parsons 2013, 142–155.

161   Barret et al., "The Gospel of Judas," 2006. Pagels' *Beyond Belief* achieved New York Times best-seller status in 2003. See "New York Times—Best-Seller List for June 22, 2003." Dan Brown's *The Da Vinci Code* spent over two years on the New York Times best-seller list,

sense of characteristics that popular works on the gnostics highlight, to wit: proto-feminism, psychological and individual approaches to the divine, openness to sexuality as a spiritual technology, and resonances with non-Christian (Kabalistic, Buddhist, Yogic) religions.[162] These characteristics key the gnostics into the modernized West at the turn of the 21st century. The relationship between mourning, memory, and modernization that Homans illuminated suggests that the popular reception and construction of gnosticism is more than a category for what Christianity is not. It has become an imaginative space through which individuals in the West reimagine what Christianity can be by re-envisioning its origins.

## Bibliography

Aeon Byte. *Aeon Byte Gnostic Radio Show.* 2013. "Secret Rituals in Gnostic Myths with Laurence Caruana," https://www.youtube.com/watch?v=dj9yhWqH8fc.

Aeon Byte. *Aeon Byte Gnostic Radio Show.* "Aeon Byte Gnostic Radio Show 'What Would the Ministry of a Gnostic Jesus Look Like?'" https://itunes.apple.com/us/podcast/l.-caruana-on-ministry-gnostic/id347832278?i=322323383&mt=2.

Assmann, Aleida. 2011. *Cultural Memory and Western Civilization: Functions, Media, Archives.* Cambridge: Cambridge University Press.

Assmann, Jan. 2011. *Cultural Memory and Early Civilization: Writing, Remembrance, and Political Imagination.* Cambridge: Cambridge University Press, 2011.

Assmann, Jan. 1997. *Moses the Egyptian the Memory of Egypt in Western Monotheism.* Cambridge, Mass.: Harvard University Press.

Assmann, Jan and Rodney Livingstone. 2006. *Religion and Cultural Memory: Ten Studies.* Stanford: Stanford University Press.

Bair, Deirdre. 2003. *Jung: A Biography.* Boston: Little, Brown and Company.

Barrat, James, John B. Bredar, Michael Rosenfeld, Herbert Krosney, Peter Coyote, Bart D. Ehrman, Marvin W. Meyer, et al. 2006. *The Gospel of Judas.* National Geographic: Burbank: Warner Home Video.

Bauer, Bruno. 1850. *Kritik der Evangelien und Geschichte ihres Ursprungs.* Berlin: Hempel.

---

over one year of those at number 1. See "New York Times—Best-Seller List for April 23, 2006."

162  The literature on each of these characteristics is extensive. For proto-feminism see especially: Pagels 1979a, 66–69; 1979b; 2011, 86–89; Houston 2006. For psychological and individualistic approaches to the divine, see especially: Hoeller 1982, 1989, and 2002; Quispel 1995; Caruana 2009; Singer 1990. For sexuality as a spiritual technology, see: Osho 1984, 191–193; Brown 2003; Churton 2015. On the Kabbalistic Jesus, see Keizer 2009. On Buddhism and Jesus, see Borg and Reigert 1997. On Hinduism and Jesus, see Newman 2011.

Berger, Peter L. 1967. *The Sacred Canopy; Elements of a Sociological Theory of Religion.* Garden City: Doubleday.

Borg, Marcus J and Ray Riegert. 1997. *Jesus and Buddha: The Parallel Sayings.* Berkeley. Calif.: Ulysses Press. Distributed in the U.S. by Publishers Group West.

Brakke, David. 2010. *The Gnostics: Myth, Ritual, and Diversity in Early Christianity.* Cambridge: Harvard University Press.

Brown, Dan. 2003. *The Da Vinci Code: A Novel.* New York: Doubleday.

Burns, Dylan M. 2014. *Apocalypse of the Alien God Platonism and the Exile of Sethian Gnosticism.* Philadelphia: University of Pennsylvania Press.

Campbell, Joseph. 1972. *The Hero with a Thousand Faces.* 2nd edition. Princeton: Princeton University Press.

Carlin, Nathan. 2014. *Religious Mourning: Reversals and Restorations in Psychological Portraits of Religious Leaders.* Eugene: Wipf and Stock.

Caruana, L. 2009. *Enter Through the Image: The Ancient Image Language of Myth, Art and Dreams.* Toronto: Recluse Publishing.

Caruana, L. 2007. *The Hidden Passion: A Novel of the Gnostic Christ Based on the Nag Hammadi Texts.* Toronto: Recluse Publishing.

Caruana, L. "Welcome to The Gnostic Q." http://www.gnosticq.com/.

Churton, Tobias. 2015. *Gnostic Mysteries of Sex: Sophia the Wild One and Erotic Christianity.* Rochester, VT: Inner Traditions.

Dart, John. "Gnostics Held Adam and Eve Superior to Their Creater." The Washington Post, Times Herald, February 6, 1971, sec. STYLE People/The Arts/Religion.

Dieterich, Albrecht. 1891. *Abraxas Studien zur Religionsgeschichte des spätern Altertums.* Leipzig: B.G. Teubner.

Doresse, Jean, Philip Mairet, and Leonard Johnston. 1960. *The Secret Books of the Egyptian Gnostics: An Introduction to the Gnostic Coptic Manuscripts Discovered at Chenoboskion, with an English Translation and Critical Evaluation of the Gospel according to Thomas.* New York: Viking Press.

Doresse, Jean. 1949/50. "Images de dieux gnostiques." *Bulletin de l'Institut d'Egypte* 32:364–365.

Doresse, Jean. 1957. "Un ritual magique des gnostiques d'Egypte." *La Tour Saint Jacques* 11–12:65–75.

Drews, Arthur. 2010. *Die Christusmythe.* Kessinger Publishing, LLC.

Erikson, Erik H. 1962. *Young Man Luther: A Study in Psychoanalysis and History.* New York: Norton.

Erikson, Erik H. 1968. *Identity, Youth, and Crisis.* New York: W.W. Norton.

Freke, Timothy and Peter Gandy. 2001. *Jesus and the Goddess: The Secret Teachings of the Original Christians.* London: Thorsons Publishing Group.

Freke, Timothy and Peter Gandy. 1999. *The Jesus Mysteries.* London: Thorsons Publishing Group.

Freke, Timothy and Peter Gandy. 2006. *The Laughing Jesus: Religious Lies and Gnostic Wisdom*. New York: Harmony.

Freud, Sigmund. 1964. *The Future of an Illusion; Civilization and Its Discontents: And Other Works: (1927–1931)*. Trans. James Stratchey. London: Hogarth Press: Institute of psycho-analysis.

Freud, Sigmund and Carl Jung. 1974. *The Freud/Jung Letters*. Trans. William McGuire. Princeton: Princeton University Press.

Goodrick-Clarke, Nicholas and Clare Goodrick-Clarke. 2005. *G.R.S. Mead and the Gnostic Quest*. Berkeley: North Atlantic Books.

Hannah, Barbara. 1991. *Jung: His Life and Work*. Reprint edition. Boston: Shambhala.

Hillman, James and Sonu Shamdasani. 2013. *Lament of the Dead: Psychology after Jung's Red Book*. New York: W. W. Norton & Company.

Hoeller, Stephan A. 1982. *The Gnostic Jung and The Seven Sermons to the Dead*. Wheaton: Theosophical Publishing House.

Hoeller, Stephan A. 2002. *Gnosticism: New Light on the Ancient Tradition of Inner Knowing*. Wheaton: Quest Books.

Hoeller, Stephan A. 1989. *Jung and the Lost Gospels: Insights into the Dead Sea Scrolls and the Nag Hammadi Library*. Wheaton: Theosophical Publishing House.

Homans, Peter. 1979. *Jung in Context Modernity and the Making of a Psychology*. Chicago: University of Chicago Press.

Homans, Peter. 1984. "Once Again, Psychoanalysis, East and West." *History of Religions* 24.2: 133–154.

Homans, Peter. 1989. *The Ability to Mourn: Disillusionment and the Social Origins of Psychoanalysis*. Chicago: University of Chicago Press.

Homans, Peter. 2000a. "Introduction." Pages 1–40 in *Symbolic Loss: The Ambiguity of Mourning and Memory at Century's End*. Edited by Peter Homans. Charlottesville: University of Virginia Press.

Homans, Peter. 2000b. "Loss and Mourning in the Life and Thought of Max Weber: Toward a Theory of Symbolic Loss." Pages 225–237 in *Symbolic Loss: The Ambiguity of Mourning and Memory at Century's End*. Edited by Peter Homans. Charlottesville: University of Virginia Press.

Homans, Peter. 2008. "Symbolic Loss and the Recreation of Meaning: Freud and Eliade as Culture-Makers." Pages 12–43 in *Mourning Religion*. Edited by William Parsons. Charlottesville: University of Virginia Press.

Houston, Siobhan. 2006. *Invoking Mary Magdalene Accessing the Wisdom of the Divine Feminine*. Boulder: Sounds True.

Isenberg, Wesley W. 1989. "The Gospel According to Philip." Pages 143–215 in *Nag Hammadi Codex II,2–7*. Edited by Bentley Layton. Volume 1. Nag Hammadi Studies 20. Leiden: Brill.

James, William. 2002. *Varieties of Religious Experience: A Study in Human Nature.* London and New York: Routledge.

Jonas, Hans. 1963. *The Gnostic Religion: The Message of the Alien God and the Beginnings of Christianity.* Boston: Beacon Press.

Jones, James William. 1991. *Contemporary Psychoanalysis and Religion: Transference and Transcendence.* New Haven: Yale University Press.

Jung, C. G. 1997. *Jung on Active Imagination.* Edited by Joan Chodorow. Princeton: Princeton University Press.

Jung, C. G. 1989. *Memories, Dreams, Reflections.* Edited by Aniela Jaffe. Translated by Clara Winston and Richard Winston. Reissue edition. New York: Vintage.

Jung, C. G. 1957. *The Transcendent Function (1916).* Zurich: Edited and published by the Students Association, C.G. Jung Institute.

Jung, C. G. 1956. *Two Essays on Analytical Psychology.* New York: Meridian Books.

Jung, C. G. 2009. *The Red Book.* Edited by Sonu Shamdasani. Translated by Sonu Shamdasani, Mark Kyburz, and John Peck. New York: W.W. Northon & Company.

Jung, C. G. 1978. *Aion: Researches into the Phenomenology of the Self.* Princeton: Princeton University Press.

Jung, C. G. 1963. *Erinnerungen, Träume, Gedanken von C.G. Jung.* Zürich: Rascher Verl.

Jung, C. G. and William McGuire. 1989. *Analytical Psychology: Notes of the Seminar given in 1925.* Princeton: Princeton University Press.

Jung, C. G. and Mrs. Beatrice Moses Hinkle. 1916. *Psychology of the Unconscious; a Study of the Transformations and Symbolisms of the Libido, a Contribution to the History of the Evolution of Thought.* New York: Moffat, Yard and Company.

Jung, C. G., and Robert A. Segal. 1992. *The Gnostic Jung.* Princeton, N.J.: Princeton University Press.

Kakar, Sudhir. 1991. *The Analyst and the Mystic: Psychoanalytic Reflections on Religion and Mysticism.* Chicago: University of Chicago Press.

Kakar, Sudhir. 1978. *The Inner World: A Psycho-Analytic Study of Childhood and Society in India.* Delhi: Oxford University Press.

Kazantzakis, Nikos and Peter Bien. 1960. *The Last Temptation of Christ.* New York: Simon & Schuster.

Keizer, Lewis. 2009. *The Kabbalistic Words of Jesus in the Gospel of Thomas: Recovering the Inner-Circle Teachings of Yeshua.* 2nd edition. Self published by Lewis Keizer.

King, Karen. 2001. "The Politics of Syncretism and the Problem of Defining Gnosticism." *Historical Reflections/Réflexions Historiques* 27.3: 461–479.

King, Karen. 2003. *What Is Gnosticism?* Cambridge: Belknap Press of Harvard University Press.

King, Karen. 2005. "The Origins of Gnosticism and the Identity of Christianity." Pages 103–120 in *Was There a Gnostic Religion?* Edited by Antti Marjanen. Helsinki: The Finnish Exegetical Society and Göttingen: Vandenhoeck & Ruprecht.

Komroff, Manuel. "UNKNOWN SAYINGS: The Truth about the Lost 'Fifth Gospel' OF JESUS." *The Washington Post and Times Herald* (1954–1959). April 7, 1957, sec. AMERICAN WEEKLY.

Kripal, Jeffrey J. 1995. *Kālī's Child: The Mystical and the Erotic in the Life and Teachings of Ramakrishna*. Chicago: University of Chicago Press.

Kripal, Jeffrey J. 2007. *Esalen: America and the Religion of No Religion*. Chicago: University of Chicago Press.

Layton, Bentley. 1995. *The Gnostic Scriptures: A New Translation with Annotations and Introductions*. New York: Doubleday.

Logan, A. H. B. 1997. "The Mystery of the Five Seals: Gnostic Initiation Reconsidered." *Vigiliae Christianae* 51.2: 188–206. doi:10.2307/1584025.

Malinine, Michel, Henri-Charles Puech, and Gilles Quispel. 1956. *Evangelium veritatis*. 1, 1. Zürich: Rascher.

Mead, G. R. S. 1900. *Sketches among the Gnostics, Mainly of the First Two Centuries. A Contribution to the Study of Christian Origins Based on the Most Recently Recovered Materials*. London and Banares: Theosophical Publishing Society.

Mead, G. R. S, E. Amélineau, and M. G. Schwartze. 1896. *Pistis Sophia; a Gnostic Gospel (with Extracts from the Books of the Saviour Appended) Originally Tr. from Greek into Coptic and Now for the First Time Englished from Schwartze's Latin Version of the Only Known Coptic Ms. and Checked by Amélineau's French Version with an Introduction by G.R.S. Mead* London and New York: Theosophical Publishing Society.

Mead, G. R. S. and Stephen Ronan. 1987. *The Complete Echoes from the Gnosis*. Hastings and East Sussex: Chthonios Books.

Mental Contagion. 2002. "An Interview with L. Caruana." http://www.lcaruana.com/webtext/interview.html.

Merkur, Daniel. 2014. *Relating to God: Clinical Psychoanalysis, Spirituality, and Theism*. New York: Jason Aronson, Inc.

Newman, John M. 2011. *Quest for the Kingdom: The Secret Teachings of Jesus in the Light of Yogic Mysticism*. CreateSpace Independent Publishing Platform.

"New York Times—Best-Seller List for June 22, 2003." Accessed November 8, 2015. http://www.hawes.com/2003/2003-06-22.pdf.

"New York Times—Best-Seller List for April 23, 2006." Accessed November 8, 2015. http://www.hawes.com/2006/2006-04-23.pdf.

Obeyesekere, Gananath. 1981. *Medusa's Hair: An Essay on Personal Symbols and Religious Experience*. Chicago: University of Chicago Press.

Obeyesekere, Gananath. 1990. *The Work of Culture: Symbolic Transformation in Psychoanalysis and Anthropology*. Chicago: University of Chicago Press.

Osho. 1984. *The Mustard Seed: Discourses on the Sayings of Jesus Taken from the Gospel according to Thomas*. Rajneeshpuram: Rajneesh Foundation International.

Pagels, Elaine. 1979a. *The Gnostic Gospels*. New York: Random House.

Pagels, Elaine. 1979b. "The Suppressed Gnostic Feminism," in The New York Review of Books, November 22, 1979.

Pagels, Elaine. 2003. *Beyond Belief: The Secret Gospel of Thomas*. New York: Random House.

Pagels, Elaine. 2011. *Adam, Eve, and the Serpent: Sex and Politics in Early Christianity*. Vintage Books. Vintage.

Parsons, Talcott. 1964. *Social Structure and Personality*. New York: Free Press of Glencoe.

Parsons, William B. 2008a. "Mourning and Method in Recent Psychoanalytic Studies of Indian Religions." Pages 62–80 in *Mourning Religion*. Edited by William Parsons. Charlottesville: University of Virginia Press.

Parsons, William B. 2008b. "Psychologia Perennis and the Study of Mysticism." Pages 97–121 in *Mourning Religion*. Edited by William Parsons. Charlottesville: University of Virginia Press.

Parsons, William B. 2013. *Freud and Augustine in Dialogue: Psychoanalysis, Mysticism, and the Culture of Modern Spirituality*. Charlottesville: University of Virginia Press.

Partridge, Christopher H. 2004. *The Re-Enchantment of the West: Alternative Spiritualities, Sacralization, Popular Culture, and Occulture*. London and New York: T & T Clark International.

Phillips, Jonathan Talat. 2011. *The Electric Jesus*. Berkeley: Evolver Editions.

Phillips, Jonathan Talat. 2015. "Gnosis: The Not-So-Secret History Of Jesus." *The Huffington Post*. http://www.huffingtonpost.com/jonathan-talat-phillips/gnosis-mystical-history-of-jesus_b_1199493.html.

Quispel, Gilles. 1995. "Gnosis and Psychology." Pages 10–25 in *The Allure of Gnosticism*. Edited by Robert Segal. Chicago: Open Court Publishers.

Realitysandwich.com. "Jonathan Talat Phillips | Reality Sandwich." http://realitysandwich.com/u/talat-jonathan-phillips/.

Robinson, James, ed. 1981. *The Nag Hammadi Library in English*. San Francisco: Harper & Row.

Rizzuto, Ana-Maria. 1979. *The Birth of the Living God: A Psychoanalytic Study*. Chicago: University of Chicago Press.

Sevrin, Jean-Marie. 1986. *Le dossier baptismal séthien: études sur la sacramentaire gnostique*. Québec: Presses de l'Université Laval.

Shamdasani, Sonu. 2005. *Jung Stripped Bare by His Biographers, Even*. New York: Karnac.

Shamdasani, Sonu. 2009. "Liber Novus: The "Red Book" of C.G. Jung." Pages 193–221 in *The Red Book*. New York: W.W. Northon & Company.

Singer, June. 1990. *Seeing through the Visible World: Jung, Gnosis, and Chaos*. San Francisco: Harper & Row.

Turner, John. 1994. "Ritual in Gnosticism." Pages 136–181 in *SBL 1994 Book of Seminar Papers*. Edited by Eugene Lovering. Atlanta: Society of Biblical Literature, 1994.

"The Vienna Academy of Visionary Art | Ad Sacrum—Toward the Sacred." http://academyofvisionary art.com/.

Wehr, Gerhard. 1987. *Jung*. Boston: New York: Shambhala.

# Gnostic and Countercultural Elements in Zora Neale Hurston's "Hoodoo in America"

*Margarita Simon Guillory*
University of Rochester
*mguillor@ur.rochester.edu*

"A Genius of the South" is the inscription etched on the gravestone of novelist, folklorist, and anthropologist Zora Neale Hurston. As a literary figure, Hurston published over fifty short stories and seven novels, which include *Mules and Men, Tell My Horse,* and *Moses, Man of the Mountain*.[1] These works solidify Hurston as a novelist. More importantly though, they serve as markers used to designate her as a folklorist of African Diaspora culture, primarily because her novels contain rich folklorist content drawn from Southern regions of the United States, Jamaica, and Haiti.

While Hurston's literary works are essential to consider, her academic publications are also equally as important when examining her multi-dimensional professional life. Hurston's first journal article, "Hoodoo in America," is a one-hundred page culmination of extensive anthropological fieldwork conducted in Alabama, Florida, and Louisiana. In this work, Hurston provides a comprehensive study of hoodoo. Specifically, she defines hoodoo as a system of transplanted African rituals and practices transmitted through esoteric knowledge.[2]

While some scholars have given attention to the overall religious significance of "Hoodoo in America," they have paid little attention to the use of esoteric knowledge in hoodoo.[3] This current article serves as a corrective in that it focuses on the central role that gnosis plays in the transmission of hoodoo.[4] Specifically, I argue that Hurston's ethnographic study of New Orleans hoodoo captures a system of African-derived ritual practices that is characterized by gnostic and countercultural elements. These practices, which are presented in the form of ritual prescriptions, possess a gnostic quality because they represent secret forms of knowledge used by the hoodooist (i.e. practitioner of

---

1 Hurston 1935; Hurston 1938; Hurston 1939.
2 Hurston 1931, 319–320.
3 Estes 1998, 66–82; Turner 2002, 112.
4 It is important to note that gnosis here is a secret knowledge that can be transmitted through human agents like individual hoodooist. However, because some hoodooists acknowledge a divine origin is responsible for their knowledge, gnosis also then represents a direct knowledge that comes from divine sources: God, Spirit, Moccasin. See Hurston 1931, 328, 360, 362.

hoodoo) to transform the everyday life realities of their clients. These ritual prescriptions, particularly in the eyes of hoodooists, represent hidden truths that have been transmitted by means of heredity, apprenticeship, or the "call."[5]

Beyond this gnostic element, I seek to show how Hurston's work illustrates at least two ways in which New Orleans hoodoo is counterculture. First, it, on one hand, is publicly seen in direct opposition to Catholicism, the dominant religious tradition in New Orleans. On the other hand, however, hoodoo culturally aligns itself with Catholicism through the incorporation of material culture into its ritual practices. Secondly, New Orleans hoodoo acts as counterculture because its practitioners deliberately integrate Catholicism into their ritual performances. For instance, initiation rituals are conducted on Catholic feast days; Catholic devotion candles are used to secure financial success; and images of saints like St. Benedict and St. Roque are employed to ascertain tranquility and real estate. While this form of ritual blending is publicly deemed as unacceptable, it is acceptable to many leading New Orleans hoodooists who unapologetically blend Catholicism and hoodoo in many of their ritual practices.[6] Taken together, these gnostic and countercultural elements of New Orleans hoodoo correspond to rituals, prescriptions, and practices that, upon examination, reveal an intimate interaction between gnosis, human agency, and material culture usage.

The three sections of this article examine this relationship. The first section explores how Hurston acknowledges and attempts to resolve an antithetical relationship between Catholicism and hoodoo by looking at the ways that both traditions manipulate material culture to ascertain desired outcomes. It is this very relationship between these two religious traditions that I maintain results in the creation of a complex system of rituals, which is transmitted in the form of secret knowledge. The second section looks at how these rituals employ principles of opposition and attraction to mimic the countercultural relationship between New Orleans hoodoo and Catholicism. The concluding section provides a case study analysis of four ritual prescriptions drawn from "Hoodoo in America" to further highlight the instrumental role that gnosis plays in New Orleans hoodoo. This detailed analysis is meant to provide an intimate view of how hoodooists employ transmitted secret knowledge of material manipulation (specifically the altering of sand and magnets) to attract favorable results by countering undesirable conditions.

---

5 Hurston 1931, 320. The call is defined as a direct summoning of the individual by a divine entity. See note 4 for examples of authorities of divinity in the hoodoo pantheon.
6 Hurston 1931, 326, 357, 362, and 368.

## 1 Gnosis, Counterculture, and New Orleans Hoodoo

In a 1928 letter written to fellow Harlem Renaissance artist Langston Hughes, Hurston writes, "I have landed here in the kingdom of Marie Laveau and expect to wear her crown someday—Conjure Queen as you suggested."[7] As the letter implies, Hurston's arrival in New Orleans signals the beginning of her ethnographic research on hoodoo, or as she calls it conjure. What she encounters is a city whose religious identity can best be described as a hybrid of Catholic dominance and multi-faith diversity. By 1928, Catholicism had been a part of the city's ecclesiastical landscape for well over two centuries and continued to secure its dominance through the establishment of a multitude of parishes (including fifteen African American parishes), seminaries, convents, and colleges (e.g. Xavier University).

This Catholic preeminence, however, did not preclude religious diversification. For example, enslaved Africans who helped erect the city's infrastructure in the early 1720s brought with them their own religious belief systems and practices. The second and third articles of the *Code Noir*, a royal edict issued in 1724, which prohibits the observance of any other religion outside of Catholicism, act as a means to regulate enslaved populations in general and non-Catholic religions in particular that were operative in these same communities.[8] Despite these legal attempts, religious diversification takes place primarily in the following forms: (1) the influx of Protestants after the Louisiana purchase, (2) the increased presence of Haitian Vodou with the rising population of immigrants from Saint-Domingue, and (3) the immigration of Europeans with diverse spiritual practices such as mesmerism, spiritism, and other folk forms of Catholicism.[9]

Despite the presence of this religious diversity, Hurston notes that Catholicism remained the "dominant religion" in New Orleans. Again, the city uses the law to ensure the continuation of this dominance. For example, Hurston discusses how the forbiddance of fortunetellers outlined in Ordinance 13347 impacted her research on hoodoo. She states, "I could see distrust in his eyes, [and because] the City of New Orleans has a law against fortune tellers, hoodoo doctors and the like, he all but threw me out."[10] Here, Hurston describes an ethos of distrust that she had to overcome in order to work with

---

[7] Kaplan 2002, 124.
[8] Rodriguez 2007, 541–543.
[9] For a general history of religions in Louisiana, see Nolan 2004, 1–774. The following sources provide historical accounts for various religions in New Orleans: Tomlinson and Perrett 1974, 1402–1404; Roberts 2015, 1–256; Cox 2003, 162–188.
[10] Hurston 1931, 357.

renowned hoodooists in the city. More importantly, she highlights how the complexities of hoodoo are flattened and equated to that of fortunetelling—a form of divination that centers on making predictions about an individual's life. New Orleans hoodooists, in response to this type of judicial marginalization, began to practice their faith in private, residential spaces. Accordingly, hoodoo becomes, as Hurston states, "a suppressed religion [with] thousands of secret adherents [whose] worship is bound in secrecy [because] it is not an *accepted* theology."[11] [emphasis added] According to Hurston, this suppression is, on the one hand, the direct result of discriminatory laws like Ordinance 13347. However, on the other hand, she maintains that hoodooists practice in secrecy because their practices are categorized as unacceptable in relationship to the normative Catholic orientation that dominates the New Orleans' religious identity. Hurston, in a letter written to Langston Hughes during her research trip in New Orleans, takes this oppositional conceptualization of hoodoo to task:

> I am convinced that Christianity as practiced is an attenuated form of nature-worship. Let me explain. The essentials are a belief in the Trinity, baptism, sacrament. Baptism is nothing more than water worship as has been done in one form or the other down thru the ages.... I [also] find fire-worship in Christianity too. What was the original purpose of the altar in all churches? For sacred fire and sacrifices BY FIRE. The burnt offering is no longer made, but we keep the symbol in the candles, the alter and the term sacrifice. Symbols my opponents are going to say. But they cannot deny that both water and fire are purely material things and that they symbolize man's tendency to worship those things which benefit him to a great extent ... Sympathetic magic pure and simple. They have a nerve to laugh at conjure.[12]

For Hurston, Christianity's foundational tenets are based on human recognition of nature's power. Water possesses the ability to both cleanse the individual and initiate a process of spiritual re-birth. Fire consumes sacrifices that are offered to God. Both fire and water usage, according to Hurston, reveals the significant role of materiality in the everyday realities of Christians. It is this interconnection between divine access, material culture, and human agency that the Catholic authoritative structure in New Orleans uses to posit hoodoo as a counter religion but that Hurston maintains connects Catholicism to

---

11 Hurston 1990, 183;185.
12 Kaplan 2002, 139.

religions like hoodoo. In this way, Hurston raises the following question: Why do Christians (read: Catholics in New Orleans) laugh at hoodoo when at the root of both religions is the human manipulation of material realities in order to ascertain a beneficial outcome?

What Hurston ultimately identifies in the above question is a connective thread between Catholicism and hoodoo, which allows her to see a cultural alignment between the two religious traditions. Conjoined with the previously described oppositional view, hoodoo can be truly presented as a *countercultural* religion. Hoodoo, in relationship to the publicly accepted religious identity of New Orleans, is in opposition to Catholicism, but hoodoo is also culturally aligned with the dominant religion due to its doctrinal emphasis on divine/human agency and material manipulation.

This countercultural orientation is further complicated when Hurston introduces the important function of secret knowledge (i.e. gnosis) in hoodoo. In the New Orleans section of "Hoodoo in America," Hurston describes in detail several initiation rituals that she had to complete in order to ascertain secret ritual prescriptions. For example, Hurston terminates a detailed description of her initiation with hoodooist Albert Frechard with the following words: "I was told to burn the marked candle every day for two hours—from eleven till one, in the northeast corner of the room. While it is burning I must go into the silence and talk to the spirit through the candle. On the fifth day Albert called again and I resumed my studies, but now as an advanced pupil."[13] As a student, Hurston receives instructions from Frechard on how to tap into the spiritual dimension to apprehend esoteric knowledge from one of the many spirits in the hoodoo pantheon. Thus, Hurston gains access to a secret knowledge that can only be learned through experiential means.

In addition to highlighting the instrumentality of secret knowledge in the propagation of hoodoo, the above excerpt captures another, even more important role that gnosis plays in hoodoo. Hurston recognizes that a divine source is the origin of the secret knowledge that she learns but maintains that it is through the lit candle that this form of gnosis is transmitted to her. Gnosis in this way functions as a mediating medium between agency (whether human or divine) and the use of materiality to achieve desired outcomes. In other words, the hoodooist possesses the knowledge to manipulate objects and get results. It is here at this juncture between gnosis, human agency, and materiality that New Orleans hoodoo can be characterized by its gnostic and countercultural elements, for it is a religious system propagated by esoteric knowledge, publicly conceived of as oppositional to Catholicism, and, as argued by Hurston,

---

13   Hurston 1931, 363.

doctrinally aligned with Catholicism by way of human manipulation of material culture to gain desired outcomes.

The relationship between Catholicism and New Orleans hoodoo is vital to consider because it highlights gnostic and countercultural aspects of hoodoo. Equally as important though is a consideration of a specialized system of hoodoo rituals that results from this countercultural interaction between Catholicism and hoodoo. These rituals of attraction involve the use of specific material or objects to draw a favorable outcome by countering unfavorable conditions. Attraction here is a form of alignment between the client's desire and perceived ritual outcome. Unlike cultural alignment, a notion presented earlier, this form of alignment is not premised on similarity, instead it involves the lining up of desire and outcome that results from the ritual space of attraction created by the hoodooist's manipulation of material culture. Thus, whether located in private, residential spaces or public places like a courthouse or a church, these spaces are meant to attract desired outcomes by aligning them with the actual desires of the client. The drawing of these favorable outcomes results from the repulsion of tangible or spiritual forces. In this way, rituals of attraction are oppositional in that they counter undesirable conditions in order to attract what the client desires.

For instance, this use of materiality to attract by means of repulsion can be found in a ritual prescription that a New Orleans hoodooist shares with Hurston on how to win a court case. He instructs her to chew a plant known as Wish Beans (also known as St. Joseph beans) and scatter the hulls on the courtroom floor. This action, the hoodooist maintains, draws pleasurable words from testifying witnesses, which results in the judge deciding in favor of the client.[14] In this way, the manipulation of a certain plant transforms the courtroom into a space of attraction because it draws favor to the petitioning client through the repulsion of potentially negative testimonies.

Here and throughout many other detailed transcriptions of these rituals of attraction, Hurston highlights the variety of ways that materiality acts as an agent of attraction (via alignment between client's desires and actual outcomes) and opposition. She explores how the hoodooist uses secret knowledge about material manipulation to *attract* desirable results and *oppose* undesirable forces. What Hurston ultimately captures is a system of ritual practices that counter normative ways of achieving the same results. For instance, an individual uses Wish Beans to win a court case, instead of depending on solid legal representation. These hoodoo rituals of attraction in this way possess a countercultural function that mimics the relationship between

---

14   Hurston 1931, 332.

New Orleans hoodoo and Catholicism, which is premised on cultural alignment with and opposition to the normative religious culture (read Catholicism) in the Crescent City. This countercultural orientation is further made evident in Hurston's transcriptions of rituals of attraction that employ fundamental principles of magnetism to draw the desires of clients by *countering* undesirable conditions.

## 2   Magnetism and the Countercultural Function of New Orleans Hoodoo Rituals

Hurston's definition of hoodoo is worth repeating here for it highlights constitutive elements of material magnetism, as it is used in New Orleans hoodoo. For Hurston, hoodoo is a blended system of African-derived rituals that utilizes organic elements like herbs and inorganic objects such as candles, metal coins, oils, and water to draw desired results for individual clients. This definition focuses on the *how* or processual aspects of New Orleans hoodoo. Specifically, it focuses on material manipulation and the drawing of desired results. Hurston illustrates the inseparability of these two processes in a ritual description taught to her by hoodooist Ruth Mason, which is worth quoting at length:

> To rule a man head and feet: Get his sock. Take one silver dime, some hair from his head or his hatband. Lay the sock out on a table, bottom up. Write his name three times and put it on the sock. Place the dime on the name and the hair or hatband on the dime. Put a piece of "he" Lodestone on top of the hair and sprinkle it with steel dust. As you do this, say, "Feed the he, feed the she." That is what you calling feeding the Lodestone. Then fold the sock heel on the toe and roll it all up together tight. Pin the bundle by crossing two needles. Then wet it with whiskey and set it up over the door.[15]

What this ritual prescription captures is the satisfaction of human desire by means of material manipulation. The petitioning woman desires to have authority over her man's mental and physical faculties. So, in order to accomplish this task, the hoodooist gives the woman a list of specific objects—a sock, dime, lodestone, steel dust, and of course, strands of her partner's hair—needed to perform the ritual. The hoodooist, then, provides step-by-step instructions on

---

15   Hurston 1931, 372.

how to manipulate these objects. For instance, the woman is instructed to create a compact stack of objects arranged in the following order: a piece of paper with the man's name, a dime, a sample of his hair, a lodestone, and steel dust. This stack is enclosed in the sock, soaked with liquor, secured with pins, and strategically placed above the front door, where the man is sure to pass.

The physical alteration of these objects is quite obvious in the above description. The variety of ways in which a hoodooist like Mason uses an object's composition to get a particular result is less obvious, however. Specifically, Mason's ritual prescription calls for the inclusion of objects with certain magnetic properties. These objects are instrumental in that they are the driving force behind a particular process in hoodoo known as magnetic drawing—a process that draws the desire of the petitioner through the creation of a field of attraction. The lodestone, for instance, is a magnetite (black iron oxide) that attracts an iron alloy like steel dust. Mason's ritual stack utilizes these two objects in conjunction with a metal dime and the man's hair to draw a specific desired result. Taken together, these objects, once rolled in the sock and soaked in whiskey (agent used to further awaken the lodestone), act as a magnet, for it attracts the man's energy so that the petitioning woman can easily control his mind and body. The selection and manipulation of objects with magnetic properties illustrate that Mason not only possesses a working knowledge of basic magnetism, but that she also knows how to integrate these scientific principles into a ritual scheme to secure actual desired outcomes. This ability in and of itself is a form of gnosis or, according to Hurston, secret knowledge that is transmitted "in one of three ways: by heredity, by serving an apprenticeship under an established practitioner, or by the call."[16] Regardless of the path, the importance here lies in the instrumental role that magnetism as a form of esoteric knowledge plays in New Orleans hoodoo.

While Hurston highlights the variety of ways that New Orleans hoodooists use other substances like Essence of Attraction and Powder of Attraction to create ritual spaces of magnetism, she commits a considerable amount of space in "Hoodoo in America" examining how sand functions in this same capacity. Sand is generally described as "loose material consisting of small but easily distinguishable grains resulting from the disintegration of rocks."[17] New Orleans hoodooists indeed use this form of sand in many of their rituals. They, however, also employ the term as a descriptor in that sand for them represents fine grains of magnetic material (e.g. powered gold gilt and silver gilt). Sand of this

---

16   Hurston 1931, 320.
17   Moore 2012, 146.

sort possesses the ability to attract desired conditions, objects, and/or subjects. This latter understanding of sand incorporates general aspects of magnetism. Acting as magnetic material, sand has the ability to produce a magnetic field. Representing the immediate area surrounding the magnet, this field produces magnetic forces of both attraction and repulsion. For New Orleans hoodooists, then, sand is used to create a magnetized environment of attraction, which is the necessary condition needed to draw what the client desires. These desires, as discussed in Hurston's essay, includes but are not limited to:

1. Bringing spouses that have gone astray back home.
2. Attracting potential intimate partners and/or friends.
3. Gaining financial success.
4. Drawing death to specific named individuals.

New Orleans hoodooists in this way employ sand to generate magnetic forces that are capable of "influencing the action of others" and to create specific conditions in order to enhance the client's "own personal well-being." In other words, sand creates magnetism, establishes an alignment between the client and her desires (by way of attraction/repulsion), and actualizes said desires to enhance the everyday life realities of the petitioner.

## 3  The 'Secret' is in the Sand: Case Study Analysis of Hoodoo Rituals of Attraction

In this section, a smaller sample of New Orleans hoodoo rituals is treated as case study material. Such an approach affords a closer look at the variety of ways that *Catholic* hoodooists like Marie Laveau, Albert Frechard, and Father Simms use sand to create ritual spaces of magnetism to draw love, companionship, and death. It is important to note here that Hurston highlights the religious orientation of these hoodooists to further advance a notion of cultural alignment and opposition between Catholicism and hoodoo. These Catholic hoodooists are authoritative human agents who possess esoteric knowledge of how to manipulate material objects like sand to attract what the client desires. They use revelatory forms of esoteric knowledge to provide their clients with ritual prescriptions that involves the manipulation of materiality to attract what a client desires. The actualization of such an attraction is obtained by eliminating oppositional forces that have initially blocked these desires. Overall, this in-depth analysis offers a compelling view of the working relationship between human agency, gnosis, materiality, and magnetism in New Orleans hoodooism.

### 3.1 Ritual "Works" of Marie Laveau

Marie Laveau, while quite often associated with Louisianan Voodoo, was also a member of St. Louis Cathedral, the oldest Catholic parish in New Orleans. She was indeed, in the words of anthropologist Martha Ward, "a Catholic in the morning and Voodoo[ist] by night."[18] Hurston bestows Laveau with yet another title. She refers to Laveau as "the greatest hoodoo queen in America."[19] This designation explains why Hurston commits a considerable amount of time outlining hoodoo rituals that have been credited to Laveau. It is important to know that these Laveau rituals have been passed down solely through a genealogical form of oral transmission. Thus, Hurston's primary task was to find a hoodooist in Laveau's lineage. Samuel Thompson, a devout Catholic and allegedly the grandnephew of Laveau, became a primary source for Hurston. He shared with Hurston a body of ritual formulas that were passed down to him from his mother and grandmother, who were both hoodooists in New Orleans. These rituals are known as the "traditional works of Marie Leveau [Hurston's spelling]."[20]

Each of these works consists of three parts. The first part is known as the petition. Here, the client gives reverence to Laveau, describes in great detail her condition, and asks for guidance in attending to this particular matter. "Answering directions from the God" follows the petition.[21] This answer is of divine origin but utilizes the hoodooist as a conduit. In this role, the hoodooist conveys specific instructions that the petitioning client must follow in order to resolve the condition presented in the supplication. Each of Laveau's ritual prescriptions ends with the following affirmation: So Be It. This verbal proclamation from the hoodooist assures the client that her issue is resolved, as long as she carries out the prescribed ritual given to her by the God. What follows are two abbreviated examples of Laveau rituals, which vividly illustrates the use of sand to create magnetic ritual spaces:

Ritual 1: The Lady Whose Husband Left Home

Supplicant: O, good mother, I come unto you in deep distress and tears have coursed my face in the dark hours of the night, for him who was

---

18    Ward 2004, 21.
19    Hurston 1931, 326. It is important to note that Hurston establishes a direct correlation between Haitian Vodou and hoodoo as practiced in New Orleans.
20    Hurston 1931, 327.
21    Hurston 1931, 327.

flesh of my flesh, the blood of my heart and the companion of my soul, my dear husband, has left home and gone from my side.

The God: O, my good daughter, do not lose hope and faith, for the stars say that there is a way to make your loved one's spirit commune with you and to have him come back to your side, there to remain and to comfort you and protect you. In order to bring this about ... you will into your house bring a magnetic horse shoe, that which is red in the circle and bright on the ends, and you will get of the Gold Magnetic Sand and Silver Magnetic Sand, of each one drachma. These you will pour of each on the bright end of the magnetic horse shoe so that some will remain on it. This you will do to *attract* his love again, and so that his gold, his silver, his worldly goods shall remain with you. [emphasis added]

Affirmation: So Be It.[22]

Ritual 2: The Lady Who Cannot Keep Lady Friends

Supplicant: O, good mother, the evil spirit seems to completely envelope me. I have no *attraction*, no sympathy from my kind. My lady friends look at me with indifference. Their friendship is only lukewarm. Their indifference is great. Their sympathy for me has fled. I ask them and they promise, but they do not do as I ask. I invite them and they say yes, but they do not come .... So I seem to have lost the power to hold my friendships. [emphasis added]

The God: Oh, my daughter ... you have lost your magnetism, so your actions do not attract others to you. Look well to yourself first. Take heed that you try to value your friends. For the spirits have said that she who wishes to get back her power to attract must put around her neck a small bag made of the skin of the chamois who lives in the mountain. And she must make the bag round so that there shall be no beginning and no end to her friendship. And, into this bag she shall put a drachma of the silver magic sand and a drachma of the powder of the violet root made of the

---

[22] Hurston 1931, 336.

heart of root, so that she shall receive of the heart of the earth, and the magic of the stars.

Affirmation: So Be It[23]

An analysis of these two ritual formulas reveals at least three commonalities. First, both rituals begin with a petition made on behalf of each client to restore a broken relationship. The first client wants her husband back and the other one seeks female companionship. Secondly, the God (who is Laveau) identifies a loss of attraction as the cause behind the fractural states described in each petition. The first woman's home has experienced a loss of attraction, which has lead to her husband leaving the home. However, the second woman is herself the reason behind her lack of friends, for according to the God, she has lost her magnetism.

Lastly, and more importantly, both rituals illustrate the ways in which hoodooists like Laveau employ sand to create ritual spaces of attraction in order to recover that which was lost. For instance, the first ritual prescription calls for two types of magnetic sand: silver magnetic sand and gold magnetic sand. Silver magnetic sand is composed of minute particles of iron, while gold magnetic sand is finely ground lodestone, an iron oxide mineral that naturally attracts iron. The God instructs the client to use these sands in conjunction with a magnetic horseshoe. Pouring these magnetic sands unto the ends of this horseshoe creates two forces of attraction: one between the gold and silver particles of sand and the second between the sand and the polar ends of the magnet. These forces act as a strong magnetic field that draws the client husband's spirit. It is important to note that hoodooists like Laveau are interested in attracting the spirit, for the God states that the overall goal is to re-establish a communion between the woman and her husband's spirit. In addition to attracting the essence of a person, the conjoined use of gold and silver magnetic dust draws worldly goods.

The second ritual prescription utilizes sand to magnetize the person not the residence. The client is instructed to place a small bag around her neck that contains silver magnetic sand and powder of violet root. The violet root is a strong attractant usually prescribed to women. The powdered form of this root combined with the magnetized sand is meant to draw female friends to the female client. Because these attractants are worn on the body, the client becomes an embodied form of magnetism exerting magnetic influence over potential lady friends. What these two rituals ultimately illustrate are the ways in

---

23   Hurston 1931, 341–342.

which New Orleans hoodooists like Laveau employ magnetized forms of sand (i.e. fine grains of iron) to create attraction field lines meant to draw people.

3.2  *Death Rituals of Albert Frechard and Father Simms*

Albert Frechard, like Samuel Thompson, is Catholic and also claims to be the grandnephew of Marie Laveau. Frechard is an instrumental hoodooist to consider because he initiated Hurston during her fieldwork in New Orleans. As a result of this initiation, Frechard elevated Hurston to the status of advance student and for four months taught her the intricate details of his complex system of rituals. While she learned how to hold a man true, fix a landlord, remove neighbors, and win lawsuits, most of her time was committed to learning about and conducting death rituals. Frechard's command of ritualistic death and the ways in which he used sand to achieve this desired result is intricately captured in Hurston's "Hoodoo in America." What follows is only one of the three rituals that Hurston describes:

> Wash candles in whiskey. Then take the candles to hydrant and let water run on them upside down. Bring them inside and before you light them, say: "Dobinus, Bobinus, Spiritus! Kind spirit, I want you to dress the candle. I call on the king of the spirits, which is Moccasin."
>
> Now take sand and throw on the floor. Write on paper the names of the people concerned, and throw it on the floor. Rub the paper back and forth with your foot (like cleaning a needle). Pick up all the sand along with the particles of paper. Take a large bottle of iodine. Make a box and mix the sand with iodine. Put two black candles in the sand—one on each side. That starts your work. It drown the enemies of the person for whom you work.[24]

Before analyzing this ritual prescription, it is important to note that Hurston recognized the complex role that sand plays in Frechard's ritual system and as a result of this recognition dedicates a sub-section in "Hoodoo in America" to his particular usage of sand. This section primarily discussed how Frechard prepares and painstakingly stores ritual sand. The sand that appears in the above death ritual is taken from a divided trough that Hurston discusses in this section on sand.

The first step of the ritual involves throwing a selected portion of this sand on the floor. From a practical standpoint, the floor provides a significant amount of surface area needed to conduct the ritual. But, the floor also aids

---

24   Hurston 1931, 364.

the sand. Sand, with the floor providing the necessary support, acts as an abrasive, grinding the paper with the written "names of the people concerned" into smaller pieces. In this grinding process, the name, which hoodooists maintain is equivalent to one's spirit, is magnetized. This magnetization is different than that presented in the ritual works of Laveau where an actual magnetic field is constructed by way of magnets and ferromagnetic metals like silver and gold gilted iron. Instead, Frechard creates a symbolic form of magnetism premised on his conceptualization of sand, in the form of finely granulated rocks, as a possessor of magnetic property. For Frechard, sand in this way converts the spirit of the individual into a type of ferromagnetic material that can now be attracted. Sand, then, possesses a dual function in that it both magnetizes and attracts the desired spirit(s). Transference of the sand into the box equates to the movement of drawn magnetized spirits. Now that these spirits are contained Frechard can start the work of the next phase, which is to "drown the enemies" of the petitioning client.

The last case study, which highlights hoodooist Father Simms, can be distinguished from the previously discussed ritual works of Laveau and Frechard in two ways. First, Father Simms is a Protestant with "Catholic leanings." He publicly proclaims Protestantism but incorporates titles, vestments, and paraphernalia associated with Catholicism into his hoodoo practice. Secondly, Father Simms, despite discriminatory laws, openly practices hoodoo. He held "meetings" every week in Myrtle Wreath Hall.[25] During these meetings, he proclaimed his power to curse people, undo hoodoo curses, and read people lives (past, present, and future). It is at the end of one of these public gatherings that Hurston introduces herself to Father Simms. He schedules a private session with her, and, as a result of this one-on-one consultation, he invites Hurston to become his student. Hurston provides great details concerning her initiation process. Specifically, she points out the essential role of candles and sand in this process. She discussed, for instance, the sacred sand pail. Situated in the middle of Father Simms' primary working altar, this bucket contains holy sand to be used throughout the ceremony. It also provides support for the primary light (large cream candle) used to evoke specific spirits. The holy sand furthermore represents a symbolic confirmation, and Hurston attests to this function when she states, "I was then seated on a stool before the altar, sprinkled lightly with holy sand and confirmed as Boss of Candles [one who can work spirits via the lighting of candles]."[26] Now that she is fully initiated, Father Simms begins to share with Hurston esoteric practices associated with New Orleans hoodoo.

---

25   Hurston 1931, 380.
26   Hurston 1931, 382.

Under the tutelage of Father Simms, Hurston learns how to punish individuals, make husbands stay home, break-up relationships, keep a person on the job, move an enemy from one's neighborhood, win court cases, "run" a person crazy, and make herself invisible. Each of these rituals centers on the manipulation of objects and substances like metal keys, holy water, rubber bands, honey, apples, silk thread, feathers, and cooking pots. However, Father Simms teaches Hurston only one ritual that centers on sand usage. The bad work or death ritual uses sand in conjunction with other organic objects:

> Take a coconut that has three eyes. Take the name of the person you want to get rid of and write it on the paper like a coffin. (Put the name all over the coffin.) Put this down in the nut. (Pour out water.) Put beef gall and vinegar in the nut and the person's name all around the coconut. Stand nut up in the sand and set one black candle on top of it. Number the days from one to fifteen days. Every day mark that coconut at twelve o'clock A. M. or P. M., and by the fifteenth day they will be gone.[27]

In order to understand the way in which Father Simms employs sand as a means to draw death, the role of the coconut must be subjected to analysis. The ritual prescription calls for a three-eyed coconut—a mature fruit covered with a dark outer shell. These "eyes" are access points that when pierced allows one to access the liquid portion of the fruit. Father Simms instructs the client to discard of this liquid. He then tells his client to stuff into the coconut's hollow space a coffined shaped piece of paper with the name of the person she wants to get rid of, a beef gall, and vinegar. The cow's bile is meant to devour the spirit of the named person, while the vinegar (liquid form of impure acetic acid) serves as the very source of impurities to be used in this consumption. The name of the potential victim is written all around this stuffed coconut. The coconut functions to bring about death. But, now it is important to take into account *how* the spirit of the individual will be drawn to this symbolic death trap. Duel forces produced by sand and the black candles are responsible for drawing the spirit. The sand is a mixture of finely granulated rocks and magnetic sand. Once placed in a metal container, Father Simms maintains that this interaction between the metallic properties of both the sand and pail creates an initial drawing force. This particular force is compounded with the placement of a black candle on top of the coconut. The black candle, in the words of Hurston, "always draws evil or death."[28] Therefore, the sand pail, black candle,

---

27  Hurston 1931, 387.
28  Hurston 1931, 414.

and dressed coconut work together to draw, capture, and devour the spirit of an individual, which leads to the physiological death of this same person.

Taken together, these rituals illustrate how ritualized forms of material magnetism can be utilized to formulate New Orleans hoodoo as an Africanized religious tradition that possesses both gnostic and countercultural qualities. The ritual use of magnetism to create conditions of attraction and opposition also mimics the countercultural relationship that Hurston establishes between New Orleans hoodoo and Catholicism. Specifically, she utilizes materiality to align the two religions, and in this way she counters a publically oppositional relationship between hoodoo and Catholicism that is based on doctrinal difference. Whether through doctrinal understandings or esoterically transmitted knowledge about material magnetism, Hurston's capturing of this element of alignment and opposition in New Orleans hoodoo allows one to again conceive of this religion as both *gnostic* and *countercultural*.

### Summary

In conclusion, by utilizing Hurston's "Hoodoo in America" to advance an understanding of New Orleans hoodoo based on gnosis and counterculture, this article offers a few core contributions to African American religious studies in general and gnostic studies in particular. "Hoodoo in America" is a comprehensive resource that transcribes hoodoo rituals of material manipulation that are usually transmitted orally. Hurston's anthropological work, then, is invaluable because it serves as valuable source material to be considered in the study of African American religion. More importantly, it provides the field a more expansive view of hoodoo, which includes the variety of ways that hoodooists use esoteric teachings on how to manipulate material realities to ascertain desired results by creating ritual spaces of alignment. Additionally, this particular contribution has an implication in the field of gnostic studies. While hoodoo is not considered a traditional religious current of gnosticism, the ritual prescriptions offered in Hurston's work is a modern interpretation of gnosis. The ritual prescriptions on material manipulation represent secret knowledge with divine origination. However, because hoodooists are embodied conduits of gnosis and responsible for the transmission of this secret knowledge to both clients and initiates, this secret knowledge, which is divinely originated, at times is directly associated with human agents in the system of New Orleans hoodoo. These hoodoo rituals offer a new of way of examining the intersectionality between gnosis, human agency, and materiality. New Orleans hoodoo in this way provides a space in which scholars of gnostic studies can have rich cross-cultural conversations about the significant role that gnosis plays in African American religion.

## Bibliography

Cox, Robert S. 2004. *Body and Soul: A Sympathetic History of American Spiritualism.* Charlottesville: University of Virginia Press.

Estes, David. 1998. "The Neo-African Vatican: Zora Neale Hurston's New Orleans." Pages 66–82 in *Literary New Orleans in the Modern World.* Edited by Richard Kennedy. Baton Rouge: Louisiana State University Press.

Hurston, Zora Neale. 1931. "Hoodoo in America." *The Journal of American Folklore* 44: 317–417.

Hurston, Zora Neale. 1935. *Mules and Men.* Philadelphia: J. B. Lippincott. Repr. 1990. New York: Harper and Row.

Hurston, Zora Neale. 1938. *Tell My Horse.* Philadelphia: J. B. Lippincott.

Hurston, Zora Neale. 1939. *Moses, Man of the Mountain.* Philadelphia: J. B. Lippincott.

Kaplan, Carla, ed. *Zora Neale Hurston: A Life in Letters.* New York: Anchor Books.

Moore, John E. 2012. *Field Hydrology: A Guide for Site Investigations and Report Preparations.* Boca Raton: CRC Press.

Nolan, Charles E., ed. 2004. *Religion in Louisiana.* Vol. 19 of *The Louisiana Purchase Bicentennial Series in Louisiana History.* Edited by Charles E. Nolan. Lafayette: Center for Louisiana Studies.

Roberts, Kodi A. 2015. *Voodoo and Power: The Politics of Religion in New Orleans, 1881–1940.* Baton Rogue: Louisiana State University Press.

Rodriguez, Junius P., ed. 2007. "Code Noir of Louisiana (1724)." Pages 541–543 in *Slavery in the United States: A Social, Political, and Historical Encyclopedia.* Santa Barbara: ABC CLIO.

Tomlinson, W. K. and J. J. Perrett. 1974. "Mesmerism in New Orleans, 1845–1861." *American Journal of Psychiatry* 131: 1402–1404.

Turner, Richard Brent. 2002. "The Haiti-New Orleans Vodou Connection: Zora Neale Hurston as Initiate Observer." *Journal of Haitian Studies* 8:112–133.

Ward, Martha. 2004. *Voodoo Queen: The Spirited Lives of Marie Laveau.* Jackson: University Press of Mississippi.

# Index of Modern Authors

Abramowski, L.   62n31, 89n35
Adamson, G.   32n1, 40n27, 41n32
Ahbel-Rappe, S.   132n37
Allberry, C. R. C.   133n38
Anderson, G. A.   37n20
Annas, J.   152n14
Armstrong, A. H.   43n38–n41, 55n9, 57n16–n17, 58n18, n20, 60n25, 61n30, 64n38, 65n42, n44, 66n47, 71n66, 151n10, 171n13, n16, 171n13, n16
Armstrong, J. M.   152n14
Asprem, E.   229n19
Assmann, A.   267n9
Assmann, J.   267n9, 244n58
Attridge, H. W.   153n30, n35, 156n52
Aubeck, C.   205n36

Babbit, F. C.   152n22–n23
Babcock, J.   225n4, 227n7, n10–n11, 228n12–1n3, n16, 229n17
Bair, D.   270n29
Baltzly, D.   180n60
Bammel, C. P.   37n20
Barc, B.   32n1, 33n6, 35n13–n14, 36n18, 41n30
Barclay, J. M. G.   15n72
Barry, C.   89n35–n36, 91n45, 92n50
Barry, E.   261n54
Baudrillard, J.   231n26
Bauer, B.   286n132
Bauer, W.   6, 6n28
Bautch, K. C.   38n22
Beatrice, P. F.   37N20
Bebek, B.   169n6
Beck, E.   132n37
Becker, H.   15n72
BeDuhn, J. D.   9n46
Benko, S.   128n18, 137n51, 138, 138n59
Benson, E. F.   219, 219n13
Berger, P. L.   267n6
Bergermann, M.   156n55
Bethge, H-G.   115n84, 134n42–n43
Betz, H. D.   155n48
Beyschlag, K.   158n62
Blackwood, A.   219, 219n13
Blavatsky, H. P.   24, 183n75, 258–259

Bloom, H.   21n90, 22n92
Bock, D. L.   5, 5n24–n25
Böhlig, A.   104n1, 106, 106n15, 107n25, 133n38, 134n41
Borg, M. J.   292n162
Borgeaud, P.   210n1
Borret, M.   41n33, 42n36
Bos, A. P.   37n20
Bosky, B.   220n15
Boulluec, A. L.   3n2, 163n81
Bousset, W.   117, 118n101
Bovon, F.   191n7
Braden, G.   241n46
Brakke, D.   32n1, 282n109
Brankaer, J.   89n35
Brashler, J.   116n88, 117n95
Brock, S. P.   195n18
Broek, R. V. D.   116n94, 125n4, 130n28, 137n50–n52, 138n59–n50, 150n6
Brown, D.   292n162
Buckley, J. J.   138n55–n57
Buell, D. K.   72, 72n71
Burfeind, P. M.   22n92
Burns, D. M.   32n1, 72, 72n73–n74, 75, 75n83–n84, 89n35, 125, 127n14, 128n20, 149n3, 282n109
Bury, R. G.   41n29, 44n44
Bussieres, M-P.   104n3
Butler, E.   175n33, 176n40

Cahana, J.   44n45, 100n71
Cameron, A.   3n2
Campbell, C.   12, 12n60, 21n90
Campbell, J.   271n36, 281n102
Carlin, N.   266n2
Caruana, L.   267, 269, 277, 277n81, n83–n84, 278, 278n85–n86, n89, 279, 279n90, n92–n93, n95, 280, 280n96–n97, n99–n100, 281, 281n102–n104, n106, 282, 282n107, n110, n112–n113, 283, 283n114–n118, 289–291, 292n162
Casey, R. P.   55n11
Castaneda, C.   178n52
Cerrato, J. A.   158n60
Chabot, J-B.   193n11

## INDEX OF MODERN AUTHORS

Chadwick, H.   41n33, 42n36, 126, 126n7
Cherniss, H.   152n22–n23
Churton, T.   292n162
Clark, E. A.   37n20
Clarke, E. C.   171n18
Clarke, E. J.   15n72
Clinard, M. B.   15n72
Clivaz, C.   190n3
Collatz, C-F.   44n44, 156n55
Combès, J.   182n74
Corrigan, K.   53n4, 55n10, 58n18, 62n31, 65n44
Cox, R. S.   301n9
Crouzel, H.   37n20
Crum, W. E.   39n25, 42n35
Cruz, G.   220n15
Cumont, F.   133n38
Curra, J.   15n72
Cusack, C.   230n23

Dahl, N. A.   19n89, 32n4
Davidsen, M. A.   230n21
Davies, C.   15n72
De Lacy, P. H.   152n22–n23
Debord, G.   241, 241n47
Dechow, J. F.   37n20
DeConick, A. D.   2, 3n2, 7n34, n37, 8n38, 11n58, 12n60–n61, 15n70–n71, 18n82, 19n88, 35n12, 37n20, 44n43, 52, 52n1, 110n56, 111, 111n64, 112n74, 118n101, 138n59, 149n5, 190, 191n5, 197, 197n23, 206n41, 211n3, 243n57
Denyer, N.   154n44
Denzey Lewis, N.   11n57, 134n44
Diels, H.   154n40
Dieterich, A.   272n48, 274n59, n62
Dillon, J. J.   40n28
Dillon, J. M.   5n21, 153n24, 170n9, 171n18, 174n27, n31–n32, 176n41–n42, 177n43–n45, n47–n48, 181n65–n67
Dirkse, P. A.   116n88, 117n95
Dodds, E. R.   174n32, 37n20
Dottin, G.   57n16
Douglas, M.   10n55
Doutreleau, L.   3n4–n5, 4n6–n8, 9n44, 17n74–n78, 18n79–n80, n82–n86, 40n28, 91n44, 127n16, 153n29
Drews, A.   286n132

Duvick, B.   176n40
Dunning, B. H.   72n73, 134n44

Eckersley, A.   215, 216n9
Edelstein, L.   152n19
Edwards, M. J.   53n6
Ehrman, B. D.   195n19
Einarson, B.   152n22–n23
Ellman, R.   183n75
Emerson, R. W.   169, 169n7
Emmel, S.   125n2
Endres, J. C.   38n22
Erikson, E. H.   268n13, 269n22,
Erikson, K. T.   15n72
Escolar, D.   205, 205n40
Estes, D.   299n3

Fallon, F. T.   106n22
Fauconnier, G.   12, 12n63
Festa, N.   172n21
Festugière, A-J.   57n16, 64n39, 105n11, 116, 116n89–n90, n92, n94, 117, 117n96, 118n101, 153n34
Finamore, J. F.   37n20, 153n24, 170n9, 171n18, 174n27, 177n47, 181n65
Fischer, C.   235n34, 243n56
Fitzgerald, F. S.   257, 257n25
Flannery-Dailey, F.   243n57
Foerster, W.   157n59
Forster, E. M.   219, 219n13
Fossum, J. E.   37n20, 46n49, 157n58, 159n69
Foster, P.   159, 159n19
Foucault, M.   6, 149, 149n1–n2, 154n43, 162, 162n80, 163, 163n82
Fox, M.   203n33, 205, 205n39
Franzese, R. J.   15n72
Fredriksen, P.   127n15
Freedman, D. N.   5, 5n22
Freke, T.   286, 286n132–n134, n136, 287, 287n143, n145, 289
Freud, S.   269n22, 270–271, 271n37–n38
Frickel, J.   158n65
Funk, W-P.   32n1, 33n6, 35n13–n14, 36n18, 41n30, 89n34, 95n58, 106, 106n17

Gandy, P.   286, 286n132–n136, 287, 287n143, n145
García Martínez, F.   142n78

Gärtner, B.  5n23
Gaskin, R.  170n10
Gero, S.  137n52
Giversen, S.  32n1
Goehring, J. E.  138n57
Good, D.  128n19
Goodrick-Clarke, C.  274n59
Goodrick-Clarke, N.  274n59
Grant, R. M.  5, 5n22, 19n89, 125n3
Graves, R.  243, 243n55
Gray, M.  225
Green, H. A.  20n89
Green, M. J. A.  226n5
Greenberg, D. F.  15n72
Grey, A.  228n15
Grypeou, E.  128n17, 129n24–n25, 136n47–n48, 137n52, 143n80
Gummere, R. M.  152n20

Haar, S.  157n58, 158n65, 159n69
Hadot, P.  58n19, n21
Hammond, H.  4–5
Hanegraaff, W. J.  12n59, 21n90, 116, 116n93–n94, 225, 228n14, 229n18, 230n24, 235n35, 241n46, 242n53, 244n58
Hannah, B.  275n71
Hannah, D. D.  190n3
Harkins, A. K.  38n22
Harnack, A. V.  5n20
Harrison, J. E.  218, 218n11
Harrison, J. R.  104n3
Hayduck, M.  170n11, 171n17–n18
Heintz, F.  157n58–n59
Heller, L.  259, 259n38
Henderson, J. B.  3n2
Henrichs, A.  57n16
Henry, P. 81n2,
Henry, W.  196–199, 199n28, 200, 200n29, 201–202, 204–206
Herrero de Jáuregui, M.  130n29, 132n37
Hershbell, J. P.  153n36, 171n18
Hilhorst, A.  105n9
Hill, C. E.  18n82
Hillman, J.  275n71
Hinkle, B. M.  271n35–n36
Hoeller, S. A.  274n61, 292n162
Hoff Kraemer, C.  225
Hofstadter, D.  243

Holl, K.  44n44, 136n49, 156n55
Homans, P.  266, 266n2–n5, 267n7–n10, 268, 268n11–n13, n15–n21, 269, 269n23–n25, n27, 270n32, n34, 271n38, n40–n41, 275n70–n71, 290, 290n158, 291n160, 292
Houston, S.  292n162
Hurston, Z. N.  299, 299n1–n2, n4, 300, 300n5–n6, 301, 301n10, 302, 302n11, 303, 303n13, 304, 304n14, 305, 305n15, 306, 306n16, 307, 307–308, 308n19–n21, 309n22, 310n23, 311, 311n24, 312, 312n25–n26, 313, 313n27–n28, 314
Huxley, A.  243

Iricinschi, E.  3n2, 127n15
Isenberg, W. W.  282n11

Jackson, H. M.  84n12, 133n38
Jacobus, d. v.  194n17
James, M. R.  195n19, 217, 219, 221n16–n17, 243n55,
James, W.  269n26, 290n159
Jaynes, J.  243, 243n55
Jenkins, J.  5, 6n26–n27, 189n1, 256n20
Jenkins, P.  5, 6n26–n27, 189n1, 256n20
Johnson, D. M.  155n47
Johnston, S. I.  210, 211n3
Jonas, H.  245, 279n92
Jones, J. W.  269n22
Jowett, B.  56n14, 58n21, 76n86
Jung, C. G.  24, 243, 243n55, 267, 269, 269n28, 270, 270n29–n33, 271, 271n35–39, n41, 272, 272n42–n50, 273, 273n51–n57, 274, 274n58–n65, 275, 275n66–n69, n71, 276, 276n72–n79, 277, 277n89, 281n102, 289–291

Kaestli, J-D.  190n3, 195n20
Kakar, S.  269n22
Kaler, M.  7n34, 22n93, 104n3, 106n14, n20, 107, 107n27–n28, n33, 108, 108n35–n38, 109n51, 110n55, n62, 111n63, n67, 112n68, n72, 115n81
Kaplan, C.  301n7, 203n12
Kasser, R.  35n12, 36n16, 107n26, 109n51
Kazantzakis, N.  279n91
Kehl, A.  195n20
Keizer, L.  292n162

Kellerman, J. A.   194n16
Keniston, K.   10n53
Kern, O.   73n77
Khoury, G.   226n6
Kidd, I. G.   152n17, n19, n22
King, K. L.   3n2, 4n17, 6, 6n31–n33, 32n1, 34n9, 35n14, 38n23, 41n30, 45n48, 46n50, 95n58, 249n1, 266, 266n1
King, S.   223
Kissling, R. C.   37n20
Klauck, H-J.   104n2, 106n22, 107n25, 109n48, 110n62, 112n68, 113n75, 157n59
Knust, J.   125n3–n4, 138n56, 142n77, n79
Kranz, W.   154n40
Krause, M.   106n22, 107, 107n24, 131n30–n31
Kripal, J.   197n22, 198n26, 205n38, 225, 225n1, n3–n4, 269n22, 286, 286n138
Kroymann, A.   17n74–n75, n77
Kugel, J. L.   142n77–n79

Labate, B. C.   229n17
LaHaye, T. F.   256n20
Lahe, J.   12n62
Lambden, S. N.   37n20
Lamberz, E.   61n27
Landau, B.   189, 189n2, 190n4, 191n8, 194n14, n16, 195n20, 200, 200n30, 201, 204n35
Langan, J.   222n18
Lasserre, F.   155n47
Laruelle, M.   258n30, 259n37
Layne, D.   175n33, 176n40
Layton, B.   5n19, 7, 7n36, 282n109, 32n1, 125n4, 134n42–n43, 151n9, 155n49–n50
Layton, R. A.   37n20
Le Boulluec, A.   163n81
Leadbeater, C. W.   243n54
Lehtipuu, O.   3n2, 4n13
Leinkauf, T.   116n85
Lem, S.   259n40
Létourneau, P.   153n27
Liddo, A. d.   225n2, 229n20
Litwa, M. D.   149, 150n7
Livingstone, R.   267n9
Llunggren, A.   260n49–n50, 262n56
Locke, S.   235n36
Logan, A. H. B.   32n1, 35n13, 282n109
Long, A. A.   152n14, n18, n23
Louchakova, O.   259n36

Lüdemann, G.   159n69
Lukianenko, S.   259, 259n39
Lupieri, E.   9n47
Luttikhuizen, G. P.   32n1, 34n10, 35n13–n14, 37n20, 38n23, 41n30, 151n12

MacDermot, V.   57n17, 89n33, 157n56–n57
Machen, A.   210, 212, 215, 215n7, 216–220, 221n16
MacRae, G. W.   72n70, 106, 106n13, 107n23, n25, 113n75, 115n81
Mahé, J-P.   136n45, 117n96–n98
Majercik, R.   62n31, 179n55–n56
Malina, B. J.   15n72
Malinine, M.   276n74
Mannherz, J.   258n28
Mansfeld, J.   45n46
Marcovich, M.   4n9, n11–n12, 17n75–n76, n78, 18n85–n86, 55n11, 130n27, 153n33, 158n61, n63–n64, 159n66–n68, n70, 160n71–n76, 161n77–n79
Marjanen, A.   150n6
Markschies, C.   4n18
Martin, T.   232n31
Mazur, Z.   53, 53n7, 54, 54n8, 59n23, 62, 62n31, 70, 70n65, 73, 73n81, 81, 83n10–n11, 87n29, 93n51, n53
McGuire, W.   271n39, 272n46, 273n54, 276n72
McNamara, M.   195n19
McWilliams, P.   15n72
Mead, G. R. S.   272n48, 274, 274n59
Meier, R. F.   15n72
Mendell, H.   116n85
Menzel, B.   258n31
Merki, H.   154n37
Merkur, D.   269n22
Milbank, J.   174, 174n29
Moore, A. J. H.   225, 225n4, 226–227, 227n7, n10–n11, 228, 228n12–n13, n16, 229, 229n17, 230, 230n25, 231, 232n31, 233–234, 240–242, 243n55, 244
Moore, J. E.   306n17
More, H.   4, 4n13
Morowitz, H.   243, 243n55
Murdock, W. R.   106, 106n13, 107, 107n23, n25, n27, 112n68, 113n75, 115n81
Musgrove, F.   10n52, n56

# INDEX OF MODERN AUTHORS

Mussies, G.   117n99
Myers, F. W. H.   240, 240n44

Narbonne, J-M.   52, 53n4, 81n3, 99n68
Narby, J.   229n17, 243n55
Nehamas, A.   163n82
Nelson, V.   212, 212n4, 249
Newman, J. M.   292n162
Neyrey, J. H.   15n72
Niese, B.   142n78
Nock, A. D.   5n20, 57n16, 64n39, 105n11, 116, 116n89–n90, n92, n94, 117, 118n101, 153n34
Nolan, C. E.   301n9

Obeyesekere, G.   269n22
Oldfather, W. A.   152n21
O'Neill, W.   179n57, n59
Oort, J. V.   133n38, 139n64
Opsomer, J.   172n23
Orbe, A.   108n38
Orlov, A. A.   150n8
Osborne, C.   158n65
Osho,   292n162
Owen, A.   238n38

Pagels, E.   6, 6n29–n30, 18n82, 291n161, 292n162
Painchaud, L.   104n3, 134n42, 136, 140, 140n67
Parrott, D. M.   151n10, 153n28, n31–n32, 55n11, 72n70, 116n88, 117n95
Parsons, T.   267, 267n8
Parsons, W. B.   266n2, 267n7, 268n14–n15, n17, n19, 269, 269n22, n25, n27, 270n32, 271n38, 279n95, 291n160
Partridge, C.   229n18, 285n131
Partridge, C. H.   229n18, 285n131
Pasi, M.   227n8
Pearson, B. A.   20n89, 36n18, 128n17, 136n48, 138n56, 153n25–n26, 156n51, n53–n54
Pépin, J.   155n48
Perrett, J. J.   301n9
Pétrement, S.   157n59
Pettipiece, T.   136, 136n46
Philips, J. T.   284, 288
Pietersen, L. K.   3n2, 15n72
Pistelli, H.   169n8

Pleše, Z.   32n1, n4, 34n10, 35n13, 41n30–n31, 195n19
Poirier, P-H.   136n45
Possamai, A.   230n22
Price, R. B.   219n14
Puech, H-C.   52n2, 53n6, 276n74
Pynchon, T.   257n23

Quandt, W.   57n16
Quispel, G.   276n74, 292n162

Ramelli, I. L. E.   128n20
Rasimus, T.   18n82, 32n1, 36n18, 37n21, 44n45, 46n49, 62n31, 125n4, 130n29, 132, 132n37, 136n48, 137n52, 138n56
Reed, A. Y.   190n3
Reinink, G. J.   192n9
Reuling, H.   37n20
Richards, F.   219n13
Riches, A.   174n29
Riedweg, C.   104n5
Rist, J. M.   152n18
Rizzuto, A-M.   269n22
Roberge, M.   127, 127n9, n14, 128n21, 129n25, 130, 130n26–n27, 131n30, 132n37, 141n71
Robert, L.   227n9
Roberts, K. A.   301n9
Roberts, J.   200, 201n31
Robinson, J.   279n92
Rodriguez, J. P.   302n8
Roig Lanzillota, L.   4n9, 4n12, 14n66, 104, 104, 104n6, 105n7, 107n30, 109n49, 128n20, 132n37, 149n4, 151n13, 152n14, 154n37, 189n1, 194, 195n15
Roof, W. C.   14n69, 21n90
Rosenstiehl, J-M.   106n14, n20, 107n33, 108, 108n35, n37–n38, 110n55, 111n67, 112n68, n72, 115n81
Rosenthal, B. G.   258n34, 259n35
Roszak, T.   9, 9n48–n49, 10, 10n50–n51, 257n22
Rousseau, A.   3n3–n5, 4n6–n8, 9n44, 17n74–n78, 18n79–n86, 19n87, 40n28, 90n44, 127n16, 153n29
Rowland, J.   215n7
Royalty, R. M.   3n2
Rudolph, K.   19n89, 106, 106n21, 125n4
Ruelle, C-E.   132n37

Sagnard, F.   91n44, 101n74
Saki   219, 219n13
Salaman, C.   245n59, 116n91, 117n97
Schur, E. M.   15n72
Schenke, H-M.   32n1, 104n1, 106, 106n16, 110n62, 127, 127n9, n13, 128n21, 130n29, 131n31, 141n71
Scher, A.   133n38–n40, 134n41
Schibli, H. S.   37n20
Schmidt, C.   57n17, 89n33, 157n56–n57
Schoedel, W. R.   110n56
Schwartz, M.   257, 257n27, 258n33, 260n45–n48
Schwyzer, H-R.   81n2
Scott, J. C.   46n50
Scott, W.   117n96, 118n101
Sedley, D.   152n14
Segal, A. F.   20n89, 32n4
Segal, R. A.   274n61, 276n74–n75
Sellars, S.   241n48
Sevrin, J-M.   282n109, 131, 131n30–n32, n36, 141, 141n73, 142n75
Shamdasani, S.   270n29, 272n45, 275n71
Shanon, B.   229n17
Shaw, G.   168
Sieber, J.   101n73
Silverstein, T.   105n9
Simonetti, M.   37n20
Singer, J.   292n162
Smail, D. L.   216, 216n9
Smith, A.   37n20
Smith, C. A.   12n62, 19n89
Smith, G. S.   3n2
Smith, J. Z.   37n20
Smith, M.   7n36
Smoley, R.   22n92
Solmsen, F.   104n5
Sorokin, v.   249–250, 250n2, n4, 251n5–n8, 253n9–n13, 254n14–n16, 255n17, 256n18–n19, 257, 257n26, 259–261, 261n51–n53, n55, 262, 262n57, 263
Stählin, O.   8n39–n40
Steel, C. G.   116n85, 172n23, 182n70–n72, n74
Still, T. D.   15n72
Strieber, W.   197–198, 198n26–n27, 199, 201–202
Stroumsa, G. A. G.   32n1, 136n45, 142n74–n75

Strugatsky, A.   260
Strugatsky, B.   260

Tardieu, M.   32n1, 37n21, 38n23, 39n26, 69n53, 89n35, 105n11, 126n8, 128n19, 134n44
Tarkovsky, A.   259, 259n41, 260n43
Thom, J. C.   152n21
Thomassen, E.   57n16, 67n47
Tigchelaar, E.   142n77
Tischendorf, C. V.   105n8
Toepel, A.   194n16
Tolle, E.   21, 21n91
Tomlinson, W. K.   301n9
Totkirch, K.   260n49–n50, 262n56
Touati, C.   190n3
Tracy, R.   215n7
Trevijano Etcheverría, R.   106n18, 107n28
Trexler, R.   189n2
Tröger, K-W.   104n1, 110n62, 116n94
Trouillard, J.   172, 172n24
Trungpa, C.   179, 179n58
Tullberg, O. F.   193n11
Turner, J. D.   18n82, 32n1, 52, 55n10, 56n15, 59n22, 65n40, 67n47, 68n53, 71n66, 83n11, 89n34–n36, 92n50, 130n29, 149n3, 282, 282n109–n110, 282, 282n109–n110, 299n3
Turner, M.   12, 12n63
Turner, R. B.   299n3

Ullmann-Margalit, E.   202n32
Unger, D. J.   40n28

Vallee, J.   205, 205n36–n37
Van Banning, J.   194n16
Van den Broek, R.   116n94, 125n4, 130n28, 137n50–n52, 138n59–n60, 150n6
Van der Horst, P. W.   192n10
Versluis, A.   21n90
Vielhauer, P.   106n22

Wagner, R.   243n57
Waldstein, M.   32n1, 33n5, 34n7, 36n15, 39n24, 42n35
Wallis-Budge, E. A.   105n10

Ward, M.   308, 308n18
Wehr, G.   270n29, n33
Westerink, L. G.   179n57, n59, 180n61–n62, 181n63, n66, 182n74, 183n75
Westhues, K.   10n52
Whittaker, J.   14n67–n68
Wilberding, J.   127n14
Williams, F.   44n44, 136n47, 136n47, n49, 139n62
Williams, J. H.   225
Williams, M. A.   8, 8n41–n42, 36n15, 36n17, 43n42, 45n47, 46n49, 125, 125n1, n4, 126n5–n6, 128n17, 136n48, 137n52, 138, 138n56, 139n61, 142n76, 159n69
Willis, J.   64n39
Wallis-Budge, W. E. A.   105n10
Wilson, R. A.   243, 243n55
Wilson, S. G.   20n89
Winslade, J. L.   225n2

Wire, A. C.   95n58
Wisse, F.   3n2, 32n1, 33n5, 34n7, 36n15, 39n24, 42n35, 126n8, 127, 127n9, n13, 128n21, 141n71
Witakowski, W.   193n12–n13
Witherington, B.   5n25
Worth, A.   216, 216n9
Wright, J. E.   104n4
Wucherpfennig, A.   108n38, 110n53

Yamauchi, E.   158n65, 19n89
Yarbro Collins, A.   105n11
Yamauchi, E.   19n89, 158n65
Yeats, W. B.   183, 183n75
Yinger, J. M.   7n35, 10n52–n55
Young, R. M.   257
Young, W. P.   256, 256n21

Zeldovich, A.   259n42
Zellentin, H. M.   3n2

# Index of Subjects

Abonoteichus  227
Abraham  40, 113, 142
Abraxas  274, 274n62
Acts of Thomas  193–195
Adam  35–39, 42–43, 75, 134–135, 139, 141–142, 192, 238, 256, 276, 287
Abel  37
Aeons  55n11, 63, 67n47, 71–73, 87–88, 90–92, 95, 101, 115, 172n23
  Aeonic copies  71, 73
  Aeonic antitypes  71, 73, 88
  Pleromatic aeons  63, 67n47
  Self-generated aeons  71n66, 71–73, 87–88, 92
Agency  62, 76, 83, 300, 302–303, 307, 314
  Human agency  300, 302–303, 307, 314
  Of angelic mediators  76
  Real generative  83
Afterlife  189, 274
Alan Moore  225–226, 230–231, 240
Allogenes  53, 55, 56n12, 59, 61–62, 65–66, 67n47, 82, 84, 87, 94, 94n57, 95, 98, 281
Amelius  53, 56, 56n14, 65, 65n43
Ammonius Saccas  53n6, 98
Ancient astronaut theory  190
Angels  3, 36–39, 41n32, 46n50, 75, 108, 112, 113n75, 117n97, 137, 157, 199, 211, 230
  Evil angel as the biblical creator  38
Angelification  149
Apocalypse of Paul, 104–107, 109–116, 118–119
Apocryphon of John  32–33, 35–38, 40–47, 129, 138, 195, 249, 282, 287–288
  Sophia  36, 41, 129, 138
  Demiurge  32n4, 39n26, 41, 43–47
Aristotle  37n20, 57n16, 115, 116n85, 119, 152, 170n9–n10
Aristotelian  40, 115, 119, 150, 161
  God in actuality  161
  God in potentiality  161
  Material cause of deification  150
Arthur Machen  210, 212, 215–221, 223, 223n20
Artifact  22, 25, 216
Asclepius  109, 226–229, 287
  Coptic  109
  Magical caduceus  229

Augustine of Hippo  23, 133n38, n40, 135, 139, 142n77
Autogenes  57–58, 65, 68, 91

Barbeloites  8, 90n44
Barbelo Aeon  56–59, 62, 65–66, 71–74, 83, 85, 88, 90
Baptism  59n22, 91, 143n81, 281–282, 282n109, 287–288, 302
Basilides  7–8, 10, 274, 276
Being  11, 14, 16–17, 19, 21–22, 24, 32, 36, 41n32, 43, 54–56, 58–63, 66–71, 74–75, 82–83, 86, 88, 98, 101, 106, 109, 116, 128–129, 133–134, 136, 139–142, 152–154, 159–161, 163, 170, 172n21, n23, 173, 174–180, 189, 192, 196–198, 201–202, 204–206, 232, 245, 249, 260, 262–263, 273n57, 280, 307
Biblical God  3, 8, 14, 16, 105, 118, 120
  As accursed god  41–42
  As the craftsman of this cosmos  41
  As the god of Moses  41
  Creator  36–39, 41–46
  Chaos and Darkness of  38
Body  4, 36, 36n15, 37, 37n20, 64n37, 69, 72, 74, 83, 93, 104, 109, 112, 117–118, 120, 125, 130, 138n55, 151, 157, 169, 171–174, 176–178, 180, 197, 203, 214, 220, 222n19, 244, 262, 273, 275, 281–289, 306, 308
  Collective body  261
  Out-of-body experience  104, 117
  Physical body  37n20, 72, 151, 177
  Psychic body  36, 36n15, 37n20
Borborite  125, 125n4, 135, 137, 137n52, 138, 138n55–n56, 139, 143, 144n82
Bridal Chamber  277, 282–283

Cain  37, 127, 143
Cainites  128, 128n17, 143
Carl Jung  24, 243, 267, 269–277, 281n102, 289–291
Carpocrates  7, 127
Carpocratians  8
Catharists  139

## INDEX OF SUBJECTS

Catholicism  3, 5, 277, 279–280, 300–305, 307, 312, 314
Celsus  32, 40–42, 44, 100,
Chakra  235, 287–288
Chaldean Oracles  179
Children of the Light  249, 251–257, 259, 262–263
Christian  4–9, 12, 14–16, 23, 25, 32, 35–36, 38, 40, 42–46, 72, 98–100, 111, 120, 125n4, 174, 181n66, 204, 211n3, 231, 302–303
Chronicle of Zuqnin  193, 193n11, 194
Clement of Alexandria  8, 8n39–n40, 55n11, 91n44, 101, 101n74, 132n37, 154n43, 163, 163n81
Cognitive
  Blending  13
  Hubris  93
  Transgression  81, 88, 90, 93
Colorbasus  7
Contemplative ascent  60–62, 65, 81–82, 87
Corpus Hermeticum  24, 64, 116, 244
Cosmogenesis  68, 169
Cosmos  14, 36n15, 40–41, 43, 54, 62, 68–70, 73, 77, 85n20, 87–88, 92, 105, 107, 114–116, 119, 127, 139n63, 142, 168–169, 172, 172n23, 173–174, 176, 177n47, 178, 179n56, 180, 180n60, 210–211, 244, 277, 282
Cosmology  7, 104–105, 115–116, 119, 130–131, 143, 199
  Apocalypse of Paul's system  116
  Aristotelian system  115
  Platonic system  115–116
  Sethian cosmology  131
  Tri-dynamic cosmology  143
Counterculture (-ral)  3, 7, 9–10, 12, 14–16, 19, 20–22, 32, 44–45, 76–77, 84, 100, 120, 190, 206, 225, 241, 243, 284, 299–301, 303–305, 314
  Apocalypse of Paul  120
  Counter-Memory  266–67
  Esotericism  241
  Gnostic  3–25
  Hermeneutical Innovation  76–77
  Identities  15
  Spirituality  20
  Movements  22
  Narrative of Christian origins  190
  New Orleans hoodoo  299–315
  Plotinus and Gnostics  100

Counterculturalism  77
Craftsman  41, 43–44, 44n44, 108n38
  *See* Demiurge
Cult  17, 132n37, 217, 255, 257
  Contemporary gnostic cult  255
  Cultic Milieu  12
  Greco-Egyptian cult  98
Cultural
  Alignment  303–305, 307
  Symbol  268, 280
Curse  38–39, 39n26, 41–42, 140, 312
  Of the biblical creator  42

Daemons  173, 175–176, 176n40, 178, 178n53, 181, 183
  Prohodos  174, 174n32, 175–177, 179, 182
Damascius  132n37, 172, 180, 180n62, 181, 181n63, n66, 182
Darkness  36n15, 37–38, 68–70, 109, 126, 128–129, 131, 133–134, 137, 143, 233–234, 273n57, 274
  Paraphrase of Shem  126–130
Death  17, 43, 95, 104, 116, 140–141, 143, 153, 157, 211, 220, 231, 233, 236–237, 239, 244, 254, 255, 270, 274, 280, 286–287, 289, 307, 311, 313–314
Deification  160, 162
  Self-deification of Gnostic  149–151, 157, 157n59, 159, 162–163
Deity  14, 14n67, 16, 36, 38, 46, 56, 81, 86n20, 87, 91, 94–95, 111, 114, 132n37, 136n47, 150–152, 156–157, 160–161, 216
  Creator deity (demiurge)  152
  Primal (unknown)  150, 150n7, 160
  Mediate deity  150–151, 156–157, 161
Delphic maxim  155, 155n45
Demiurge  32n4, 39n26, 41, 43–47, 56n14, 64, 70, 73n77, 86n20, 90–91, 105, 107 109, 111–112, 115, 119–120, 127–129, 136n48, 138, 143, 152, 163, 169–170, 172–174, 176–177, 179, 181, 183, 183n75, 244, 249, 252, 255
  As rebellious  43
  Cosmos as an image of an image  70
  Creator deity  152
  Demiurgic weaving  170
  Demiurgic creativity  181
  Generosity of demiurge  169
  Sorcerer  177
  *See* Craftsman

Demon Sex  125–126, 130, 140
Derdekeas  126, 128–130, 132, 132n37, 135, 141
Diatessaron  193
Dionysius  93, 179–180, 180n60, n62, 181, 181n66, 183, 183n75
Divine  19–20, 35–36, 43, 52, 54–57, 62, 64–65, 69, 75–77, 81, 87–88, 91, 93, 96–97, 100, 108, 110, 112–120, 126, 128, 132, 130n40, 135, 136n47, 138–139, 141, 143, 149–163, 168–177, 179–180, 198, 228, 234–235, 238, 240, 245, 249, 258, 260, 270, 280–283, 286, 286n138, 289, 291–292, 292n62, 299n4, 300, 302–303, 308, 314
Divinity  19, 21, 65, 111, 117, 136, 139, 149–153, 155–157, 159–162, 168, 171–173, 175–176, 179–180, 182–183, 225, 255, 279, 300
  Higher self  149–150, 153, 156–157, 237
  Innate  151–153, 162
  Inward divinity  149–151, 153
  Mediate divinity  150, 156
Dualism, Cartesian  229

Earth  3, 14, 36, 38, 71–74, 86, 88, 88n31, 108, 111–112, 114, 127–130, 132n37, 134–135, 156–157, 173, 203, 222n19, 236, 240, 244, 249, 251–252, 255, 257, 259, 263, 310
Ecstasy  15, 24, 25, 261, 287
Ecstatic vision  149
Emanation  55, 58–59, 63, 150, 171
  Plotinus's theory of  63
  Pleromatic aeons  63, 67n47
Enlightenment of the body  285, 286, 286n138
  Tantric  286
Epictetus  152, 152n21
Epigram  218, 221–222, 222n19
Epiphanius  4, 4n15–16, 32n3, 44, 125–126, 136, 136n45, n47, 137, 139, 143, 156
  Love-Feast  125–126, 137, 138n55, 139
  Myths of archon-seduction  136
  Nicolaitans  136, 136n48, 137, 137n52, 138n56, 139, 143
  Nicolaitan theology  138
Esoteric  6, 21, 115, 183n75, 218, 220, 225–226, 228, 228n14, 230, 241, 245, 250, 252, 258–260, 299, 303, 306–307, 312, 314
Esotericism  228, 228n14, 230, 241, 245
  Entheogenic Esotericism  228, 228n14

Eugnostos  55n11, 68n52, 106
Eve  35, 37–40, 42–43, 45, 238, 256
Evil  33n6, 36, 38, 43–44, 46, 72n70, 90, 108n38, 127, 140–141, 163, 171–172, 177n45, 211, 215, 217, 219–223, 262, 272–276, 283–284, 309, 313
Exile  72, 88–89, 89n35–n36, 90–92, 94–97, 101
  Inferior category  96
Existence  21, 36, 40–41, 54–55, 58, 128, 138, 150, 168–170, 172, 174–175, 182, 196, 202, 212, 221, 223, 234, 238, 276, 279, 283
First Principle  55n11, 60, 65, 82n8, 83, 90, 101, 134
  Self-reflexive thinking  55, 62
  The nature of ascent to  83
Frame  11, 13, 24, 32–35, 35n13, 39, 39n25, 44n45, 110n62, 151, 168, 217, 286, 288
  Johannine frame story  32–35, 35n13, 44n45
  Mental frame  13
  Story  35, 35n13, 39, 110n62

Genesis creation accounts  33, 35, 41, 46
Geradamas  72n72, 156
(The) Good  9–10, 16, 20, 23, 35n12, 44, 61n30, 62–63, 65, 70, 82, 82n8, 95n58, 101, 154, 172n23, 275–276, 308–309
  Substance and intellect  62
  Perfect living being  61n30, 62
Gnostic  3–4, 6–9, 11–25, 35, 38n23, 40, 44n45, 45, 47, 52–56, 68–70, 73–77, 81n3, 82–90, 93, 95, 97–98, 100, 104–106, 111, 115, 118–119, 125–128, 135–136, 138–139, 142–144, 149–151, 153–158, 161–163, 190, 199, 205–206, 210–211, 219–221, 223, 225, 229, 243–244, 249, 252, 255–258, 261, 263, 266–267, 270, 272, 274–281, 284, 286–288, 292, 299–300, 303–304, 314–315
  Visionary ascent  81, 84, 86–88, 89n36, 92, 95, 96, 100
Gnosis  3, 7, 13, 17, 35n12, 44n43, 45, 52, 72, 75n83, 89, 125–126, 215, 218–219, 225, 229, 235, 242–245, 279–280, 283, 286, 291, 299–301, 303, 306–307, 314–315
  *See* Knowledge

INDEX OF SUBJECTS

Gnosticism  4–8, 11–12, 12n62, 15, 18n82, 19, 19n89, 20, 22–24, 32n4, 35n12, 45, 46n49, 84n11, 125–126, 132, 136n48, 139, 150, 157n58, 190, 245, 266, 269, 282, 290–292, 314
  Counter memory of the Christian past  266
Gospel of the Egyptians  69, 141–142, 282
Gospel of Eve  156
Gospel of Philip  280, 282
Gospel of John  20, 23, 25, 34, 158
Gospel of Judas  111, 291, 291n161
Gospel of Luke  34
Gospel of Mark  34
Gospel of Matthew  34, 189, 193
Gospel of Judas  111, 291, 291n161
  Apostles as archons  111
  Passions  111
  Psychic realm  111
Gospel of Thomas  155
Gospel of Truth  156, 276, 276n74

Hairesis  3, 3n2
Helen  214–217, 220–221, 223, 275, 283
Hell  73, 210, 217, 223n20, 226, 275, 277
Heretic  3–4, 6–7, 15
Heresy  4–6, 6n31, 11, 20, 44, 158
Heresiologists  3–5, 7–8, 150, 157, 162
Hermes Trismegistus  237
Hermetic  9, 20, 25, 32n1, 116–118, 237, 217n10, 229, 231, 242–245
Hippolytus of Rome  4, 55n11, 130, 132n37, 157n58, 158, 158n60, 274, 274n64, 276n76–n77, n79, 277n80, 279, 279n92
Hoodoo  299–308, 311–312, 314–315
  Gnosis  299–305
  Human agency  300, 302–303, 307, 314,
  Materiality  303–304, 307, 314
  Ritual prescriptions  299–300, 303, 307–308, 314
  Rituals of Attraction  307–311
Hoodooist  299, 299n4, 303–306–308, 311–312

Ialdabaoth  36, 36n16, 37–39, 40n27, 41, 41n31–n32, 42–45, 249

Iamblichus  153n24, 168–178, 179n54, 181–182, 211
  *Commentary on the Sophist*  177
  *Commentary on the Timaeus*  176
  Daemons  175
  Divine Mind  152, 152n23, 153, 155, 169–170
  Dyad  171
  *On the Mysteries*  211
  Ochema  174
  Self-alienation  173
  Theurgic rites  168, 173, 181n64
*Ice Trilogy*  249, 256–257, 259–262
Imagination  69n53, 70, 229, 235, 240–242, 244–245, 262, 272, 272n46, 273
Incarnation  93, 162, 174, 261
Intellect (-ual)  9–10, 14, 20–21, 37, 54–58, 60–68, 69n55 81–84, 91, 94, 94n57, 99–101, 108, 113, 129–130, 132n37, 150–151, 153, 160–161, 206, 210, 218, 229–230, 236, 260
  Ascent above intellect  81, 81n3
  Divine intellect  56, 56n14, 57, 64–66, 81, 160
  Intellectual self-determination  83
  Three intellects  67–68
Invisible Spirit  55n11, 56, 56n12, n15, 57–59, 62, 66, 91, 94–95, 101, 287
  Invisible Spirit's Triple Power  58–59
Irenaeus  3–4, 5n23, 8, 16, 17n74–78, 18n79–n86, 19n87, 23, 32, 32n2, 38n21, 40, 40n27, 42, 44, 68n52, 69n55, 70n61, 90n44, 110, 127–128, 137n49, 138, 138n58, 141, 143, 153n29, 157n58, 279, 279n92, 283n119
  *Adversus Haereses*  138, 279

Johannine  32, 34, 35n13, 44n45
  Community  159
  Frame story  32–35
Jonathan Talat Philips  284–290
Justinians  8
Justin Martyr  4, 4n10, 7–9, 18n86, 37n20, 38n23, 87n25

Kalyptos 56, 56n15, 57, 27n16, 58, 58n18, 65, 68, 91
Knowledge
  Secret 197, 300, 303–304, 306, 314
  Self-Knowledge 149–150, 154, 154n42, n44, 156–157, 162–163
  *See* Gnosis

Laurence Caruana 267, 277–284
*Letter to Flora* 32
Life 8, 20, 36n15, 37n20, 81, 95, 117–118, 125n4, 132n37, 156, 168–170, 173, 176n40, 180–182, 189, 200, 203, 204, 205, 211, 214–215, 220, 223, 229, 236, 239, 241–242, 245, 249–250, 253, 255, 269, 273–274, 276, 278–280, 285, 287, 291, 299–300, 302, 307
  Afterlife 189, 274
  Alien life-form 205
  Divine life 173
  Noetic triad of Being, Life and Intellect 55, 58, 58n20–n21, 59–62, 64n38, 65, 66n47, 75n83
  Perfect life 156
  Seven good forces created by Life 140
Lord 17, 19, 55n11, 110n53, 112, 180, 282
  God of Hosts 36

Macrobius 64, 64n39, 73n77
Madness 214–215, 281
Magnetism 305–307, 309–310, 312, 314
  Form of esoteric knowledge 306
  Ritualized forms 314
Mandaeans 9
Mani 9, 25, 133, 136
Manichaeans/Manichaeism 132–136, 139, 143, 144n82
Marie Laveau 301, 307–308
Material
  Culture 300, 302, 304
  Materiality 69, 112, 174, 302–304, 307, 314
  Materialist Philosophy 229
  World 107, 108, 108n38, 170, 177, 236, 239, 249, 283
*Matrix*, the movie 243, 243n57, 244
Metaphor 62, 127, 131, 138, 151, 153, 160, 260–261
  Cognitive metaphors 151

Metaphysics 52, 54, 56, 62, 68, 75n83, 76, 115, 119, 168, 170–171, 174–175, 291
  Gnostic 54–56
  Gnostic transcendental 68
  Plotinian and Iamblichean 170–173
  Prophodos 175
  Sethian Platonizing Treatises 56–58
  Valentinian Tripartite Tractate 55–56, 62
Middle Platonic 56, 58n21, 95n58, 155n47
  Tripartite divine Intellect 56
Mind (νοῦς) 14, 14n67, 21, 37n20, 44n44, 57–59, 60n25, 62, 66–67, 96, 109, 131, 151–156, 160, 169–170, 177, 178n50, 239, 241–243, 245, 252, 272, 282–283, 306
Moses 25, 33–34, 36, 40–43, 44n45, 159n69, 299
Mystery (-ies) 39, 52, 131, 157, 192, 177, 182, 183n75, 203, 211, 217–218, 229, 234–235, 239, 282, 286, 286n132
Mystical
  Experience 190, 194, 268, 279, 279n95, 291
  Texts 190
Mysticism 196, 197n22, 217n10, 258, 262
  Apocalyptic mysticism of symbolists 258
  Psychological mysticism 291n160
  Ufology and Science 196, 197n22
Myth 32, 35–36, 38–40, 44n44, 45, 46n50, 52, 69n55, 86n20, 90, 93, 126, 130, 136–139, 142–143, 150, 152, 163, 180–181, 192, 231, 237, 243, 270–272, 276–277, 279, 286–287
  Archon-seduction 130–139
  Biblical demiurgical myths 136n48
  Egyptian mythology 196
  Gnostic myth 40, 90, 126, 136, 138, 143, 150
  Mythic path of Jesus's hero's journey 281
  Orphic myth 179, 180n60
  Promethea myth 231
  Sethian myth 35–40, 90
  Valentinian myth 90
Mythopoesis 39

Naassenes 8, 130n27, 153n33
Neoplatonism 168, 170, 172–174
  Iamblichean 173
  Neoplatonists 55, 72n74, 168, 183n75
  Theophany 168

## INDEX OF SUBJECTS

New Age   11–12, 12n59, 21–22, 24, 189–191, 195, 199, 204, 206, 242, 259, 262–263
   Modern New Agers   11, 21, 190
   New scripture   12, 25
   Religious thought   190, 206
   Western New Age   259
Nicolaitans   8, 136, 136n48, 137, 138n56, 139, 143
   Theology   138
Norea   153, 153n26, 135, 137
Numenius   56, 56n14, 159n69

Occult   211–212, 226–227, 233–234, 257–258
   Occultist   225–227, 234–237, 243n55
   Comics   226
Odes of Solomon   193
Ogdoad   107–108, 110, 110n61–n62, 111, 111n63, 112–116, 118, 134n42, 282
Ontogenesis   55, 64, 87, 90
Ophites   32n1, 42, 45, 68
   Ophians   8, 42
   Ophite-Sethians   42
   Ophite diagram   197
Origen   32, 37n20, 40–42, 44, 95n58, 100n72
Orphic   57n16, 73n77, 128n20, 130, 132, 132n37, 139, 179, 180n60, 183, 183n75, 215, 217n10

Pan   210, 210n1, 212–223
   The Great God Pan   210–223
Pantheism   245n58
Panentheism   245n58
Paraphrase of Seth   130–132, 136, 139, 143
Paraphrase of Shem   125–126, 128, 131–132, 136, 138–144
Paul   16, 18n82, 20, 23, 25, 34n9, 104–120, 158, 161, 195, 218n12, 287n145
Peter Homans   266–269
Philo of Alexandria   35, 72, 142n79, 159n69
Pistis Sophia   105n11, 126n6, 140, 157
Plato   14, 25, 40, 43–44, 46, 54, 56n13–n14, 58n21, 61n30, 67–68, 70n64, 73–76, 82n8, 84–88, 93, 95n58, 96–101, 152–155, 168–169, 170n9, 172n23, 175, 182n73
   Alcibiades   149, 154, 179
   Axiochus   153
   Charmides   154
   Daemons   175

Divine mind   152
Divine spirit in soul   153
Myth of creation   152
Numerical ratios   170
*Parmenides*   56, 61n27, 182
*Phaedrus*   86n20, 89, 89n36
Platonic cosmos   169
Platonic demiurge   44–46
Platonic metaphysical doctrines   75
Platonic school   75, 95n58, 172
Platonic thought   40, 44, 52
The Good   9–10, 61n30, 62, 70, 82, 82n8
Seeds of intellect   153
*Timaeus*   40–41, 43–44, 46, 67, 70, 115, 168, 170, 176, 180n60
Unmoved Mover   115
World Soul   169–170, 173
Platonism   5, 41–42, 45–46, 82n8, 83n10–n11, 87, 87n25, 96, 99, 154, 168, 170, 172–174, 176
   Assimilation to god   149, 154
   Divine kinship   154, 154n37
   Neoplatonists' ontogenesis   55
   Platonist   4, 41, 45–46, 83, 83n11, 86–87, 96–101, 132, 151, 154, 168–170, 171n12, 172, 172n23, 174–176, 179, 180n60, 181–183
   Theurgical Platonists   170, 172, 172n23
Platonizing Sethians   55–56, 58, 65, 68, 71n66, 82–85, 87–88, 91, 94–95, 97–98, 100–101
Pleroma   70, 90–91, 108–109, 111–112, 170, 274–275, 283, 289
Plotinus   17, 32, 40, 42–44, 52–58, 60–77, 81–88, 88n36, 90n43, 93n50, 95n59, 96–101, 170–174, 178, 182
   Aeonic Copies   71, 73
   *Against the Gnostics*   53, 81, 85
   Anti-gnostic critique   52, 83, 100
   Debate with the Gnostics   64–72
   *Enneads/Enneades*   84, 88, 170, 172
   Mystical union with principle   82
   On gnostic demiurge   70
   On gnostic portrayals of Sophia   68
   Plotinian Metaphysics   170–173
Plutarch   152, 152n22, 153n24, 154n43
Pneuma   14, 114, 130, 153, 287
   Stoic   153
Poimandres   116–118, 156n53

330                                    INDEX OF SUBJECTS

Porphyry   40, 42–43, 53, 61–62, 73, 75n85,
    81–82, 85, 98, 98n65, 99n69, 127n14,
    153n24, 171
  *Life of Plotinus*   53
Primordial Self   59–60
Proclus   56n14, 65n43, 73n77, 172, 176n40,
    179, 180n60
Prodicians   8
Promethea   225–245
Pseudepigraphy   39
  Pseudepigraphic revelation   99
  Pseudepigraphical narrativization   32
Pseudo-Zostrianos   85n20, 92–93, 93n52,
    95–97
Psychology   229, 229n18, 271, 274, 275n71,
    37n20, 168, 180, 183n75
Ptolemy (Valentinian)   7, 32, 44, 44n44
Protophanes   56–57, 57n16, 58, 65, 65n44,
    68, 91
Pythagorean   20, 168, 229
  Cosmos and harmonious structure   168

Reality   9, 21, 24, 52, 54, 62, 64, 76, 83, 126,
    172–174, 178, 181–182, 225, 229–234, 236,
    240, 242–243, 245, 249, 284, 288
Realm   14, 17, 22, 36n15, 38, 54, 57, 61, 64, 71,
    73–74, 83, 85, 85n20, 108–115, 117–120,
    163, 177n45, 178, 178n53, 211, 231, 233,
    236–237, 239, 249, 282, 289
  Celestial   109, 114, 119
  Earthly   109, 112, 114
  Divine   112, 115, 117, 119
  Intelligible   54, 57n16, 74, 83, 85, 85n20, 113
  Psychic   111–112, 119
Religious Experience   24, 198, 226, 290n159
Repentance   40, 69n53, 71, 73, 88–92, 95–97,
    101
Resurrection   156, 258, 270, 282
Revelatory Milieu   12, 24–25
Revelation of Adam   141–142
Revelation of the Magi   189–202, 204–206
Ritual   14, 18–19, 21, 96, 150–151, 181n64, 195,
    204, 228n14, 230, 238, 254, 261, 282n110,
    299–300, 303–314
  Baptismal rite   59n22
  Five Seals   282
  Sex-rite   283
  *See* Baptism

Sabaoth   36, 137, 140
  Sacred History   35, 277
Saklas   36, 44, 141
Saturnilus   7
Savior   33–35, 38n23, 39, 43, 44n45, 126, 141,
    151n10, 155–157, 180n62, 279, 283, 287
Schema   13, 88, 90, 90n44, 92n50, 93, 95n59,
    97
Scripture   3, 5, 7, 11–12, 12n62, 14, 16–20, 25,
    34n10, 35, 35n11, 36, 46, 72, 195, 206
  Jewish scriptures   12n62, 34n10
  Christian   5, 35
Seneca   152, 152n20, 195
Serpent   42, 131–132, 135, 197n25, 229, 235,
    238, 243n55, 273, 273n57, 275
  Cosmic   229, 243n55
Seth, Seed of   8, 43, 72
Sethians/Sethianism   8, 20, 32, 35–36,
    40–46, 58, 62, 84n11, 90n44, 93–96,
    98–101, 130, 130n29, 131–132
  As Christians   41–42
  As Ophians or Ophites   42, 45
  As philosophical heretics   42
  Counterculture   32, 44–45
  Demiurge   41, 45
  Elect   72, 74, 86n20, 87–88, 90, 101
  Myth   35–40, 44n44
  Nomenclature   71–72
  Opponents   33, 35
  Platonizing   62, 93–96, 98–101
  Self-generated Aeons   71–73, 92
  Theology   40
Sexuality   134, 139n63, 140, 142, 283, 292,
    292n162
Simon Magus/of Samaria   7, 136n47, 149, 151,
    157–159, 275
Simonians   136n47, 158–159
Sin   89n35–n36, 90–92, 92n50, 93–95, 109,
    142
Socrates   73, 152, 154
Sodomites   125, 127, 140–143
Sophia   36, 41, 68–70, 89n36, 90–94, 97–101,
    129, 138, 249, 258, 283–284
Soul   15, 17, 37n20, 41n31, 54, 57, 57n16,
    58n21, 61, 61n30, 64–65, 67–75, 81–82,
    86–87, 88–97, 100, 104, 110n62, 112–113,
    113n75, 117–120, 130, 138, 149, 151, 151n10,
    152, 152n23, 153–155, 157, 168–183, 197,

## INDEX OF SUBJECTS

211, 213–215, 241, 245, 249, 251, 272, 281–283, 309
   Ascent of the soul   64, 71–72, 104
   Contemplative ascent   60–62, 81–82, 87
   Elect   91, 93
   Immortal soul   89, 89n36, 96–97, 152
   Individual soul   86, 93–94
   Incarnated souls as members of Sophia   97
   Plotinian Soul   57, 171
   Repentant souls   92
   Self-generated soul   93
   Sethian elect   72, 74, 86n20, 87–88, 90, 101
   Transmigratory cycles   89
   World Soul   169–170, 173
Spirit   10, 14–15, 17, 33n6, 36–37, 43, 55n11, 56, 56n12, n15, 57–59, 62, 91, 94–95, 101n73, 107–108, 110n62, 113–114, 117n97, 118, 126, 128–129, 131, 132n37, 133, 133n39, 135, 137n49, 141, 143n81, 152–153, 159, 161, 170, 199, 210–211, 213, 218, 229, 239, 252, 284, 287–288, 299n4, 303, 309–314
Spirituality   11–12, 14–15, 17, 19–25, 172, 190, 228, 257, 284
   Gnostic spirituality   11–12
   Servant spirituality   19
Standing One   159n69
Stoic   40, 117n96, 128n20, 152–153
Supreme One/Priniciple   55–56, 59, 62, 64–66, 81–82, 87, 90, 94, 99
Symbolic loss   266, 266n2, 267–269, 271, 273, 277–279, 285, 290–291

Tarot   234–235
Teachings of Silvanus   153
Temple
   Jerusalem   32, 36, 39, 43
   Apollo at Delphi   154
Tertullian of Carthage   3n1, 4, 4n13–n14, 8, 17, 17n74–77, 18, 23, 91n44
Testament of Abraham   113
Testimony of Truth   155
Theodicy   273
Theodore bar Konai   133, 133n38, 139
Theurgist   174, 176, 176n46, 211
The Great Declaration   157–162

*The Red Book*   269–270, 272–276
Theodotus   101
Theogony   55, 76, 128, 132n37, 281–282
Titans   17, 179–180, 180n60, 181, 183
Transgressions   7, 9, 15, 15n70, 17–18, 20–21, 53, 54, 68, 70, 72, 74, 76, 81, 88, 90, 93
   Aesthetic   54
   Cognitive   81, 88–96
   Cultural   72–76
   Gnostic   15n70, 20
   Hermeneutics   52, 68
Transcendence/Transcendent   7–9, 11, 13–14, 19, 21, 24–25, 35n12, 36, 36n15, 40, 43–44, 54, 56, 56n14, 58n21, 59n22, 60n25, 64–66, 68, 76, 81, 82n8, 83, 86n20, 87, 90–95, 99, 116, 199, 206, 212, 235, 249, 252, 260, 262, 276
   Deity   14, 81, 87
   God   7–8, 11, 13–14, 19, 36, 36n15, 40, 43
   Intellect   82, 82n8, 84
   World   64
Transformation   118, 151, 154, 163, 196–197, 201–202, 235, 240, 242, 254, 260, 279, 282, 286
   Of consciousness   151
Triad   55, 58–59, 62, 62n31, 65, 67n48, 174, 174n32,
   Being-Life-Mind   55, 62
Trinity   270, 277, 302
Tripartite Tractate   55–56, 62–64, 66–67, 279
Triple Powered One   56n12, 59–60, 61n27
Truth   10–12, 20, 22, 24, 36n15, 43, 67, 74, 75n84, 90, 90n36, 91, 99, 108n38, 140, 149, 155, 159, 206, 220, 244, 276
   Immutable   90

Ufology   189, 196
Unknowable One   56, 59–61, 66
   Father   91

Valentinus   7, 10
Valentinians   8, 19,32, 55–56, 68, 69n55, 90, 90n44, 101, 107, 110, 156, 282–283, 287n145
   Pneumatikoi   287n145
   Ptolemy   32, 44
   Tripartite Tractate   55–56, 62–64, 66–67, 279

Vitality   58–59, 62, 65, 65n40, 66, 67n48, 94n57
Vladimir Sorokin   249
   Collective body   261
   Cosmism   258
   Ice Trilogy   249, 256–257, 259–262
   Russian science fiction   259–260

Watchers   38, 38n22–n23
Wisdom   20, 34n10, 62, 63n35, 68–69, 93n52, 98, 137, 151, 155, 155n45, 238, 249, 258
   Chokmah   237–238
   Primal   68
   Wisdom's transgressive descent   68
Womb   126–127, 127n15, 128, 130–131, 131n35, 132n37, 135, 137, 137n49, 139, 141, 143, 244
   Cainite   128
   Womb   143
   Paraphrase of Shem   126–130

Worship   8–9, 14, 17, 19–20, 34n9, 36, 38, 40, 42, 45–46, 108n38, 132n37, 139, 177n46, 257, 302
   Of a foolish apostate   45
   Supreme God   14, 17
   YHWH   8

YHWH   3, 8, 13, 17–19, 36, 249
   *See* Biblical God

Zeus   132n37, 180, 181n66, 183n75
Zora Neale Hurston   299–301, 303–307, 311–314
Zostrianian   89, 96–97, 101
Zostrianos   53, 55, 66, 67n47, 69, 71, 73, 82, 84, 85n20, 87–89, 91–98, 281
   Cyclical metempsychosis   93
   Platonizing Sethian treatise   55
   Pseudo-   85n20, 92–93, 93n52, 95–97